Tall in the Face
of
Adversity

S J Briggs

ArrowGate

Published by Arrow Gate Publishing Ltd 2020

13 12 11 10 9 8 7 6 5 4

Copyright © S J Briggs 2020

A CIP catalogue record for this book is available from the British Library.

ISBN 978-1-913142-15-5
eBook 978-1-913142-16-2

Arrow Gate Publishing 85, Great Portland Street, London W1W 7LT
Visit www.arrowgatepublishing.com to read more about our books and to buy them. You will also find articles, author interviews, writing tips and news of any author events, and you can sign up for our e-newsletters so that you're always first to read about our new releases.

Dedication

To Mum and Dad
Thanks for giving me life and doing your best for us all.
Alan
For giving me my first break in the building industry.
My ex-wife Jackie
Thank you for the 24 beautiful years we spent together.
7th Parachute Regiment RHA
My Brothers in Arms, I salute you all.
Rebecca MET Police
For obtaining a long overdue criminal conviction.
The Veterans Association London
For saving me from a life on the streets.
All my friend's past and present
For helping me to become the person I am today

Author's Note

I wrote my memoirs over eight years as a tribute to people I have known and I want to highlight that child abuse is still sadly very prevalent today. I hope that it reaches those who have been affected by these terrible crimes, and give them hope that they can stand tall, just as I have. I have changed and removed certain references and names (other than those who gave me permissions) to protect (as they say) the innocent and guilty, including myself. All the incidents are true, and it was difficult to decide what to leave out.

– STEVE BRIGGS, 2020

Legal Disclaimer

Contents

Chapter One

Early Years

Well, where do I start? Although this is my autobiography, it is difficult to come up with the right words to describe my early years. I cannot use 'once upon a time' as this is no fairy tale. However, it does have a happy ending, of at least the future for me is now looking rosy it seems. So once again, where do I start? I know let's start at the beginning.

I was born on February 14th, 1966. The youngest of five siblings, my parents are Peter and Myrtle Briggs AKA 'Joyce' (sorry mum for using your real name at the start) I was born in Blackpool, on route to West London, while my father, was on embarkation leave from the British army. My sibling's names are

Peter (eldest brother) Theresa (eldest sister) David (middle brother) and Tina (middle sister). My father was a first-class military musician, with the Royal Lancashire Fusiliers and was also a member of the Royal Regiment of fusiliers, but more on that later on in the book.

My early childhood was somewhat of a blur. As the youngest, my early memories were moving around with the army. I remember living in a place called Frekelton, and Sutton Coldfield, which are based in the Midlands. I recalled living in Hong Kong, then a British colony.

One of my memories of Hong Kong was my brothers and sisters taking me out to the park. I was only about three at the time. It was a hot and somewhat humid day. It was no place to be when you are bright blonde and could be seen by people smugglers.

This particular day, apart from being hot and humid, will always stay in my memory, the sheer reason? My brothers and sisters left me, and I was lost miles from anywhere with no food or water, and in temperatures exceeding 100 degrees.

I remembered, walking along, crying my eyes out, making the dehydration worse. However, my fate was short-lived, because when my brothers and sisters returned home, there was a full-scale alert, and the Hong Kong Police picked me up and returned me to my grateful but panicked parents.

Although I'd been in danger, my fear was short-lived, as I was given copious amounts of ice cream, and soft drinks as a reward, and to regain my hydration levels. I wished I could say the same for my supposed babysitters because my parents scolded for their absent mindlessness. Every time I look back at this incident, I thank my lucky stars that I am still here today, at the time as I remembered, it was very traumatic, for someone so young.

My siblings would have you think that their version of events was an accurate indication of what happened, on that particular day 43 years ago. Although I am sure that they hadn't done it on purpose, later events would indicate that my recollection is the only correct version of events, of which will become clear later on.

After my frightening experience, life went on as usual but was about to change. My father's tour of Hong Kong was about to come to an end, and we were about to return home.

It's funny how some memories are lost with time. However, I distinctively remember the flight home to the U.K., the cabin air pressure gave me constant pain in my ears, and I was screaming, much to the displeasure of hundreds or burly squaddies of my father's regiment.

I remembered my mother cradling me in her arms, trying to comfort and to stifle my screams.

We came into land, and the pain stopped, and so did my painful experience. Our new life and adventure were about to start. It was only later on that I found out, my father at his request had 'retired' from the armed service, and we were settling in the U.K. for good.

The army resettled us at an end of terrace house in Northolt West London, and the address was 68 Bengarth road. The front of the house has a small triangle patch of grass. A problematic family had occupied the house before the council evicted them. When my father opened the door for the first time, we all walked in to explore our new home.

In the hallway, there were eight panes of frosted glass, which illuminated the entire corridor, stairs and upper landing. As we explored, the next-door neighbour's curious kids stood in front of the glass and were shouting. My mother was shocked to hear such language from them, as according to her, she said that we were so well behaved, and spoke politely, well compared to them, I suppose we were.

In the small bedroom, the walls were covered in graffiti, hanging from the ceiling was what can only be described as a noose. Scary stuff when you are three years old. The back garden was like a jungle, with piles of ash piling up by the back door, obviously the easiest way to dispose of them by the previous family. Although a little shabby, with a bit of effort, it was soon turned into a home, with a coal fire at the centre which fascinated us.

We settled in well with our new surroundings and soon became good friends with other kids. According to my mother we soon forgot that we used to speak 'the Queens English' as she put it, as was our association with the other kids; and soon started to drop our usual way of speaking, and adopt the language of the street, much to mum's annoyance. It was only a short time that we were accepted as part of the new neighbourhood, and quickly made friends with the others. We would play the usual type of kid's games associated with childhood.

Games like hopscotch, British bulldog, a game where one person would stand in the middle while the others would start from an imaginary line and try and outrun the single opponent and avoid being captured, if caught then they had to be the one in the middle. Skipping, knockdown ginger I.E knock on someone's door and run away, and hide and watch them come and open it, to find no one there.

We also played ball games, like rounder's, cricket, and football with about 20 per side, totally ignoring the sign that said, 'No ball games.' At the weekends we would all go over the fields and play cricket with our fathers, who liked to join in and teach some valuable lessons in the art of ball control. We used to play for hours on end, and of course, it always seemed sunny.

These were treasured moments, as the entire neighbourhood would be involved in weekend pursuits in one form or another. One of our favourites was picking blackberries. Every family from our end of the street would walk the short distance to where the blackberry bushes grew in abundance, and gather the bountiful harvest, rich in the ripe blackberries, and place them in any container they could carry.

Of course, as kids, we helped and eat more than we would place in the containers, and would be covered in sticky purple juice, but it was an excellent time for all and brought the community together. Sadly, however, I cannot say the same today.

When the harvest was safely gathered in, we would all return home, happy in the knowledge that we had all contributed, to a job well done. When all the fruit had been washed thoroughly, our mothers used to make vast quantities of jam, or better still freshly made apple and blackberry pies, which we ate with evaporated milk, as the cream was a rare treat in those days as I recall.

Once my father had cultivated the back garden, he grew vegetables, and none of us was short of fresh vegetables in our street. Although on occasions one of us would be sent packing down to the local greengrocer, for 5 pounds of potatoes, but only until our own produce was ready to harvest.

Sunday dinner was a big affair in our house as it was for the whole street, while us kids were sent outside to play, either in the garden, or to the park, or anywhere where we could amuse ourselves, and stay out of our mum's way while she was cooking. It would consist of a roast joint or chicken, roast potatoes, carrots, cauliflower, and my least favourite cabbage, or greens, and of course Yorkshire pudding, and lashings of gravy.

However, we aren't keen on greens or cabbage. Some of us had to remain at the table until we had eaten every morsel. Even if that meant eating it cold, I still shudder today at the thought of eating cabbage or greens, and now never partake in their consumption.

Although at the time, I thought my parents were cruel, and making us eat things like these, I am now glad they did, as it reminds me of how, in those days, food was something never to turn your nose up to, it was precious. Bearing in mind what our parents had to eat during the war years.

We grew up on food like stew and dumplings, pies, suet puddings like spotted dick, jam roly-poly pudding, and foods, which were high in fat. These foods were given as we were hungry, and cholesterol, was unheard of, or if it was, it made no impact on our lives. Believe me, when you are hungry, you would push cholesterol to the furthest portions of your minds, including mine, which you will read about later on.

Coming from the size of a family like mine, money was tight. Like the rest of the families on the road, we were poor working class. However, it seemed that life was so simple back then. The triangle corner of Bengarth Road, the part where we lived was as follows. Number 66 lived in by a Mrs Fortune, a frail old lady in her mid-seventies.

Us at number 68. Number 70 contained the Coshams, who like us had five kids, four boys and one girl. Number 72 was the Sanderson's, who had one grown-up daughter, and twin girls, as I recalled their names being Julie and Jane. Next to them at number 74, the Saunders, with two boys. Then came number 76, the Wards, Mrs Ward was a single parent with three boys and three girls. They were poor; unfortunately, two of the girls and one of the boys were profoundly deaf.

Finally, it was the Comer's at number 78. They had two boys, and this family were despised, Mr Comer, who was a miserable old sod.

On the opposite side of the road was a set of old people homes; these were maisonettes. As kids, we would tease some of the occupants, more on this later on. In one of the ground floor lived a younger man, who was forever fixing up old cars. His name escapes me, but he was a lovely chap and kept to himself. All in all, apart from the Comers, it was a safe and secure place to live.

As dad had always been a professional soldier, he found it hard to settle into civilian life. He tried his hand at many jobs, but still fell afoul of the management or as he liked to call them, and being a cockney, 'fucking jumped up college wankers, what do they know.' As usual, it would end up in him getting sacked, or resigning, and once again out of work.

His joblessness always put my mum under pressure, as she still had mouths to feed, and they would end up having a blazing row. In many ways, I cannot blame her for getting annoyed with him, for putting her in a position, when money was always tight.

Although I could see my dad's side as well, as I also get upset with people in 'so-called authority,' especially those who are graduates, don't get me wrong, I am all for education. However, it seems to me that some, not all who are university educated, have no common sense, and are ill-equipped in dealing with people correctly. Some, in my opinion, have their head stuck up their arses and think they are better than the rest of us, just look at all the politicians, and I am sure some of you will agree with me.

Anyway, dad was in and out of work always, and the pressure on my mum was immense. She had to go back to work to help with the household finances.

I remembered the day she would have to go to work, as I was lying in her bed, and she had to explain to me, which I found confusing. Not surprising, as I was only four. Although times were tough when I was growing up, it was a happy one. One of the best things I liked doing was 'helping' mum with the washing.

She had an old twin tub washing machine, on one side was the washer, and on the other a spin dryer, which was the source of amusement, as mum allowed me to sit on it when it was spinning. Which also helped to stop the machine from dancing across the kitchen floor, and out of the back door.

On wash days the kitchen was full of steam, great in the winter, but hell in the summer, even if the door was open! She would first sort out the washing into specific piles of whites, coloureds, woollens, cotton etc. The machine would then be dragged out and filled with water from the kitchen tap using a rubber hose, which was pushed on, and ill-fitting, allowing water to spurt out, mum simply rectified it by wrapping a floor cloth around it.

When the drum was full, mum would turn it on to heat up. When it was ready, she poured the powder in, along with the first load, the lid was then closed, and the washer started. After the first load was clean, Mum would lift it out with the wooden tongs, and place it inside the spinner, with me as usual placed on top.

When all the washing had been done, mum hung out the clothes to dry, she drained the machine and put away. Then it would be the time for lunch, followed by 'watch with mother,' for those who don't know a compilation of children's T.V.

I used to love this time of day, watching shows like 'Bill and Ben the flowerpot men', 'Andy Pandy', 'The Herbs', 'Hectors House', and my other favourites, 'Camberwick Green', 'Trumpton', 'Chigley', not forgetting 'The Clangers!' When the shows had finished, mum and I would have a nap, and she would lie on the floor in front of the fire, with me stretched out on the sofa.

These were special days for me, and were some of my best, as like most boys at that age, mum was not only mum but also our best friend. At about 3 pm, we would go and fetch my other brothers and sisters from school, I was either placed in a push-chair, and mum would walk to the school, pushing me all the way. Not like nowadays, where the school runs would involve a 4 x 4s jamming up the roads. I suppose that was the way it was then, as, unlike today, where there are more dangers.

As I said earlier, it was now my turn to go to school. I re-membered the day as if it were yesterday. The day started like any other, my other brothers and sisters had already gone to schools, and my dad was at work. Mum had been very quiet, as was I after they had all gone, and she seemed saddened. I was feeling the same, but nothing prepared me for what was to fol-low.

As usual, she placed me in the pram, and we set off for the journey to my new school. As I remembered, it was a crisp au-tumn morning, and mum pushed me down Bengarth Road, and we stopped at the Church Road crossing. When it was safe, we crossed over, and down another road, through an alleyway.

Once through the alley, we turned left and walked around the fenced path, which was the perimeter of the park. We arrived at the school. I got out of my pram and clung to my mum's leg, such was the fear of never seeing her again, and not knowing why! I looked up at mum, and she looked down on me and smiled. I could see the tears in her eyes, and she could see mine.

She knelt and kissed me before cuddling me close for reassurance. It mattered not, as I could not stop the tears from falling.

Mum opened the door, and with me still in floods of tears, we entered the school for the first time in my life. I continued to cry while we walked through the hall and onto the classroom. At that point, my teacher came out to greet us. She led us into the cloakroom, which was filled with hooks and benches, other kids' coats hanging up, apart from one, which was to be mine.

Mum gripped my hand tightly, before picking me up, to calm me down. She kept telling 'that I would be alright, and she would see me later,' but I was inconsolable. The teacher showed us where my hook was, and on it was a picture of some drums. Mum stood me on the bench and still crying; I tried hard to keep hold of her hand. My teacher held onto me and reassured my mum who kissed me for what I thought was to be for the last time. She was now in floods of tears herself, where she turned and walked out of the door.

As I recalled, it was several moments before I calmed down enough to meet my new classmates. I needn't have worried, as I soon settled in, and was playing with the others, and had now forgotten the earlier incident. I had no sooner been there, that it was time to go home again, and there at the door was mum with the other mothers. As soon as we had finished, we were allowed to leave. I ran up and flung my arms around her, but this time, it was through joy and not sadness, which had engulfed both of us that morning. I just couldn't wait to tell her about my day, which had been fantastic and fun-packed. That day, I didn't get in the pram, I walked hand in hand with mum, as I was now at 'big boy's school.'

Chapter Two

Special Days

After my first day at Gifford school, I couldn't wait to go back again to see my new friends. Although it was only a nursery school, it was my first step into the educational system. Every morning after mum had dropped me off; I would hang my coat up on my hook, and rush into the classroom, to get going, my fears had now vanished, and I loved every moment of being there.

The activities were, of course, fun-filled, consisting of finger painting, gluing on pasta, to make pictures, storytelling, and music lessons. Of course, there was playtime, which was the most fun, as my new friend and I would run around, and be boisterous. One day, we were both playing in the Wendy house and found some real fairy cakes painted with poster paint, in an assortment of colours. However, that didn't stop us from eating them, and once you got through the taste of the paint, they were delicious.

We were on our second cake, when the teachers realised what had happened, and stopped us for fear of poisoning. My friend and I were most disgruntled at the time, as we were enjoying our little picnic but I suppose during that time, the teachers were doing the right thing by stopping us. In those days, paint contained lead. To be honest, we were feeling somewhat sick, although I'm not sure if that was from the paint or overeating. As it happens, we were, and a rainbow of vomit, cascaded out from our little mouths.

All I can say is that this was a valuable lesson to not only my friend and myself, but for the school authorities, as they never made any more, painted ones. We were none the worse for it. Incidentally, my best friend at nursery school was Paul.

Our favourite game was acting out a role made famous from a robot in an SCI-FI T.V show, called 'Lost in Space'. I never forgot how we used to walk around saying its lines 'crush, kill, destroy,' in a robotic voice. Whenever I saw repeats of the show, it made me chuckled at those immortalised words. Looking back now, I suppose we thought it was the best show on T.V at the time. But we all believe that when we were at that age.

I would have to say that I did love nursery, as when I was at home, I was a different kid. I was somewhat shy and quiet, probably as I was the youngest, and my siblings teased me endlessly. David, my middle brother, was a right bastard. My parents saw him as the 'black sheep' of the family. He would often beat me, and my middle sister Tina, and would pride himself for doing so.

Although I think it was his way of trying to gain attention from my parents. My eldest brother Peter would go on occasions exact revenge on David, for what he had done, and my eldest sister Theresa would fight him off also. However, we would have to wait until our parents got home, and they would be disciplined. David would get a good hiding from my dad or mum, or both.

It wouldn't be polite not to mention my family, or not to tell you anything about them. So here it is. Peter, my eldest brother, was the firstborn, spoiled rotten. As a kid, he was great at sports more so athletics. When I was about four, my dad and mum argued, and my dad left. Upon his return, he had with a West Highland white puppy dog, which we called Mungo.

When I was about nine, Peter took Mungo and me out. Unbeknown to me, Peter had stolen a javelin from school, as he was training.

During this training, Peter asked me to run with the dog, as we did so he threw the spear, and it impaled me through my leg! And not to arouse suspicion, he devised a plan, which was that he would go home first, and tell mum and dad that I was behind him with the dog. I was to come back then crying and tell them that I had been walking the dog, and I fell onto a round piece of glass.

Even though I was in pain, and crying my eyes out, I agreed, so off he went, leaving me with the dog, crying and nursing a bleeding leg. When I got home and knocked on the door, Peter opened it and tried to look shocked. Mum and dad questioned me, and of course, I lied, told them the story that Peter had come up with but, it backfired, and my dad extracted the truth. Peter,

for his sins, was punished, and I got one for lying! So, I was doubly upset.

Many are the times where we would be rounded up as a
family, to watch him race. Mum would make some sandwiches
and a couple of flasks of soup to take with us where he was running. It was often cold countryside cross-country events, where
he would compete for the school or athletic club. Peter was a
schoolboy champion, as were the rest of the competitors. On one
race meeting, he was up against a runner called Steve Ovett. Yes,
the same Steve Ovett that was the Olympic 800-meter gold med-
alist in Moscow in 1980. I believe the government has awarded
him an OBE.

The race was over a 4-mile distance, with over 100 competitors. My brother was as fit as a butcher's dog, and still is to a
point. It was to be three laps of the course, and Peter was leading
the field by at least half a mile by the second lap. However, in the
end, he came in 10th. Not bad, you would think? But it annoyed
my dad, who asked him 'why he had come in 10th?' and 'all you
had to do was to keep running.' My brother's response was, and
to his detriment was, 'yeah but dad, its Steve Ovett, he is a schoolboy international.' He got a thick ear for that remark, and quite
rightly so, as my dad was right, as Steve Ovett, was nowhere to
be seen after the second lap, but who went on to win the race.

Although this was a setback, in Peter's mind, he would be a
better runner, if he had a new set of spikes, and pestered my
mum and dad for weeks for a set of spikes, which had been en-
dorsed by another long-distance runner, and Peter's idol name
David Bedford.

For weeks, my parents argued the toss over these spike shoes, as they were around £50 at the time, and made from kangaroo skin—a vastly sum in those days. In the end, they relented, and paid out for them, after promises from my brother to look after them. My dad warned him that 'you better had boy, or you'll be feeling them across your backside.'

As always, my dad was true to his word, and gave Peter a thrashing with the spikes, after finding them covered in mud. He had spike holes in his backside for weeks after that. However, my brother's achievements spoke for themselves, as he held 20 plus school and district records for athletics, which he still held even when I went to High school.

Theresa, my eldest sister, was also good at athletics. Although not in the same calibre as Peter, this was due to her smoking habits, whereas Peter never smoked, although he did try it, and was caught by dad, who locked him in his room, until he had smoked a packet of cigars.

A bit draconian, but it cured him; as a result, he was petrified of smoking after that. We all threatened him with 'the dreaded ash,' where we would chase him around with a full ashtray, much to our amusement.

As I said, Theresa was good at running, but due to her habit, she would stop halfway around the cross-country course, and have a cigarette. Smoking would affect her standing in the race, but she would still come in at around 15th. A great position from about 100 or so competitors even if it was nicotine-based.

David was very bright, and not bad at sports, but I never saw him compete. Tina was obsessed with gymnastics, and she was enthralled by seeing Nadia Comaneci, the Romanian gymnast, who scored a perfect 10 in the 1976 Montreal Olympics. As a result, she was allowed to go to a gymnastics class. She was also great at netball, and I would accompany her to matches, as did my dad.

What about me? Well, I was pretty good at football and played as a goalkeeper. Alas, none of my parents came to watch me play, and so my interest dwindled. I was also good at sprinting 100 meters mostly, but again, no one watched me compete. But enough of that for now, that's for later on in the book.

It was now December and with Christmas fast approaching, decorations were the order of the day. At school, we were all busy in making paper chains, and snowflakes, made from white paper, folded several times, and where we would cut out shapes when unfolded, the pattern would be the same. It was also time for my first nativity play.

Although I wasn't an active member of the cast, myself along with the other members who did not make it, were given the task to make our own 'snowballs.' These makeshift snowballs were small rubber balls, wrapped up in a cotton wall. OK, so I wasn't playing Joseph, but mum made me feel special when she came to see me, which was nice.

At home, my parents brought down the decorations from their annual migration from the attic, and we would all help to put them up in the lounge. Decorations in those days were made from crepe paper and twisted across the lounge ceiling. Also, decorative paper lanterns would be unfolded and hung up, as well as paper chains and balloons.

The tree was like others in the street, artificial. It would be many years before we had a real one, was put in pride of place next to the coal fire. We decorated it in baubles, lights and paper streamers. If we were lucky spray, my parents used spray snow and sometimes-brightly foil-covered chocolate decorations.

Of course, no tree would be complete without a fairy, and she would watch over us throughout the festive season. The time to switch on the lights was the best part, to me, it was magical. To see they're sparkling glint would bring a warm glow inside me, the memory of which remains with me to this day.

The weeks leading up to Christmas were exciting for me as a kid. I say weeks as it was just that, not months as it appears today. The shops were adorned with Christmas decorations and had Christmas gifts proudly on display.

Most of these shops were small independents. The butchers would display the turkeys, and other festive goodies from behind mock-ups of old leaded windows made with black sticky tape. This was finished off with a touch of artificial snow, to add to the authenticity.

Everywhere was buzzing with activity and excitement. The bigger stores would have Grotto's, where we could visit Father Christmas. It was the highlight of my year, as I would meet the man, who would be delivering my presents on Christmas Eve. The other thing was that everyone who visited him would be given a pre-Christmas gift and it would be a plastic toy made from Taiwan. Every day I would open up another door from my advent calendar, counting down the days only added to the excitement.

Christmas Eve was unique, not only because of the sights and smells associated with the big day but also because we would all go and select pillowcases and put them downstairs ready for the arrival of Father Christmas. Before going to bed, we would, of course, leave a mince pie, a glass of sherry for the arrival of the big man, and not forgetting a carrot for his reindeer.

After we had carried out the pre-Christmas routine, we would kiss our parent's goodnight before going to bed. Finally, the big day arrived, like all kids we were up before sunrise, about 4 am. Amidst a flurry of excitement, we would wake mum and dad up, raced downstairs, to see if Father Christmas came. Our empty pillowcases had now been filled to the brim, with presents.

The joy on our faces was immeasurable. We would all remove our presents from our makeshift sacks and start to play with them. Few of our gifts may not be wrapped, but to me, that was OK, saves time, when you want to get on and play.

One of the best gifts I got as a kid, was a two-story garage, complete with a miniature Michelin man illuminated sign. I loved that toy and played with it for hours. While we were playing mum would be preparing dinner, while dad would be in the bathroom, having a wash and shave, mum had hers. It would then be our turn to get washed and dressed, and we would take turns to be next in the bathroom. In our house, you had to be quick, before all the hot water had gone.

After washing, we would go back downstairs to resume playing. All of us would check out and compare each other's gifts, while mum would slave away in the kitchen, while dad would be relaxing in his armchair watching T.V.

Several hours later, mum would ask us to take our presents upstairs so that she could set the table for dinner. It was a great feeling seeing the table laid out, as it wasn't used that often, most of the time we would eat from our laps.

Before mum served dinner, we all had to watch the Queen's speech, although mum enjoyed it, for me, I couldn't wait for it to be over. Afterwards, mum would come out of the kitchen loaded with plates full of Christmas dinner, and we would all pull crackers, and put on our hats.

Christmases were a magical moment that I will never forget, and I thank my mum and dad, for making them unique.

I looked back on those times, and now realised the sacrifices they both made for us kids. Although as a kid, we all took it for granted, it was something we should all remember, as those times for me at least are few and far between, and doesn't last forever.

After dinner, it was our turn to wash the dishes and allow mum and dad to relax. Being the youngest, I hated the thought of this, I would throw a tantrum, by pretending that I had 'broken my legs.' It was a plan that often worked, much to the dismay of my brothers and sisters, and was a standing joke for many years.

Boxing day was a relaxing day, we would be playing with our toys, dad, as usual, was asleep in his chair, and mum was carving up the turkey carcass, and gammon joint, which we would eat cold with pickles.

Sometimes, she would cook a pork joint to accompany the piled high meat leftover from Christmas. After Boxing Day, mum and dad would be back at work. At the time dad, as I re-called, was a postman, whereas mum, worked for the home help. I'm sure for them; it was a more relaxing time, after the exhaus-tive efforts over the previous two days festivities. It was up to my elder brother Peter, and elder sister Theresa to look after us.

It was a welcome relief to go out after being cooped up for two days. We went and knocked the other kids and exchanged stories about Christmas. I went over to see my mate, Andy Ward. I asked him about Christmas, and what Father Christmas had bought him. Unfortunately, they never celebrated Christmas, as they were Jehovah's witnesses. It wasn't until many years later that they had their first real Christmas after Mrs Ward found a new man in her life. It seems that she only joined the religion when her husband left. After hearing that Andy hadn't got any presents that made me feel bad, so we played with mine, and I shared some of my leftover sweets.

The rest of the week remained the same, and before I knew it, it was New Year's Eve. I remembered thinking that it would be like Christmas and that we would be in line for more presents! Still, I can be forgiven, as I was only five. New Year came and went, and with it, a new decade.

We were now in 1972. After the Christmas and New Year break, it was time to go back to school. A New Year, a new term, and Infants school with some new adventures lay ahead. As mum had increased her hours at work, it was up to my eldest sis-ter Theresa to take me to school along with Tina. My eldest brother Peter was at high school, and so was Theresa, but she walked with us every day to school before getting off herself. David, my middle brother, was also at school, but it wasn't Gifford, and the name of his school escapes me.

Back in school was a way for me to escape from family life, although I loved my family, it wasn't always pleasant.

After about a year, I moved up into Gifford Infants; this was different from the nursery, as it was here that the real learning started.

I soon made friends, and my best friends were Sukanta, Jatinder, and Afzal. My mum never understood why I was friends with 'people like that,' and it was a long time after, that I understood what she meant. In a nutshell, it was because they were Asian! And no mum wasn't a racist. Anyway, we were inseparable and were all very close.

At playtimes, we all used to straddle one of the benches and act out scenes from another T.V show that was doing the rounds at that time. The show in question was 'Voyage to the bottom of the sea.' For those of you who don't know what it was, I shall tell you. It was about a super submarine, and its many ventures deep under the ocean. I think they made a more modern version, later on, called 'Sea quest DSV starring Roy Schieder', who played Chief Brody of the Jaws films.

In the show, the submarine would come across some kind of sea monster, that would violently rock the boat from side to side. We would hold onto each other and mimic the scenes. Each one of us would also act as a Captain and give orders. It was a great game! Or so we thought. The playground was massive, in one part; it had huge tree stumps, which were placed there as stepping-stones.

Also, at one end was a brick wall, which we would hide our 'treasure' that we had found—bits of shiny paper, lolly sticks etc. We would dig out some of the crumbling mortar and pushed them as far inside as we could. In the winter the walled area would freeze, making a high slide. We would each take a turn in squatting down, while two of the others would take hold of a hand each and drag the other one squatting down.

Our other favourite game was Cowboys and Indians. Again, we would chase each other around, either firing invisible guns or if we were lucky cap guns, which made a loud cracking noise when they were fired. Of course, we all had horses, well not quite, we would just piggyback one another. Nether the less rain, wind or shine, we had great fun. In class, we were taught new skills, like maths, English, as well as reading.

One day our teacher was telling us nursery rhymes, one in particular stuck in my mind, and I shouted out in protest, 'what are little girls and boys made of?' And it goes like this. 'What are little girls made of? Sugar, and spice and all things nice, that's what little girls are made of? What are little boys made of? Slugs and snails and puppy dog's tails, that's what little boys are made of.'

As soon as the teacher had finished that last sentence, I blurted out the words 'No we are not!' I don't know why I said it, but I felt most indignant, and I still feel that it was a revolting rhyme to teach kids, in their informative years. Some may argue that it was only rhyming, but not to me.

Anyway, that little outburst earned me a smacked backside and humiliating time of standing in the corner. There were many more days like that. Nevertheless, the days and weeks flew by, and we were learning more and more as each day past. However, maths was a strain on me. No matter how hard I tried; I found it challenging to pick up. I don't know why this should be, as I was certainly not thick, it was just like numbers don't engage in my brain, as it does in some people. It was like a form of dyslexia, only in numbers and not words. But I got by with the arithmetic that I knew, so I was happy enough.

February 14th, 1972, it was my 6th birthday, and mum and dad had bought me my first ever bike. It was called a chipper, and it was yellow. The bike was made by Raleigh, who had launched a series of new bikes, starting from the chipper, then onto a tomahawk, and their best creation a chopper! It had the gear lever in the middle of the crossbar and was the number one bestseller back in the seventies and the number one bike if you were anyone, and whose parents could afford it.

It was a birthday like no other, and I had my new bike, complete with stabilisers and bell. I was also chosen to be a magician's apprentice at the local youth club, and I would also have a birthday party! Mum pulled out all the stops at the party. I had all my friends around, and there was Andy Ward, his sister Leslie, Stephen Masters, or 'Dumbo' as we called him on account of his sticky-out ears, he later had an operation to pin them back, Joanne Martin who was a tomboy, and her brother Stephen

As you would expect, like all kid's parties, it was chaos. Mum and some of the other parents, had made sandwiches, cakes, jelly and ice-cream, sausage rolls, and of course no party would be complete without a birthday cake, and mine was chocolate, with five candles on top. We washed it all down with fizzy pop or squash.

We all had a great time, and when it was finished, and the others went home, along with their goody bags, I was allowed out on my bike and raced around the triangle patch outside our house. My ride was cut short; however, as it started to rain, also, I had noticed that my rear tyre was going flat.

When I bought the bike inside, we noticed that there were two drawing pins stuck in the tyre. Much to my dad's dismay, as he had to fix it. The nails had been scattered by old grumpy guts Mr Comer at number 78, and when my dad found out, there was an almighty row, where Comer, not for the first time came off second best, as he was no contest for my dad, who towered over the little pipsqueak.

And that was the start of a feud, which would last for some time. It culminated in an almighty punch up at a later on. For weeks I zoomed around the triangle on my bike, so that I could get used to it. Dad took off the stabilisers. First one, and then the other, of course, I would fall off, but eventually managed to stay on, and so I would venture out further afield.

Around the corner was a park, it was a 10 minutes' walk. The park was called Lime Trees Park. There was a kind of a youth club building, where you could play inside, children's park, and a more extensive playground for bigger kids.

Although we loved going there, it wasn't without its faults. It wasn't due to the activities or playground features, but due to the other kids who came from the Lime trees housing estate. When they were about, there was always trouble.

The gangs from this estate were from the Hyland family, and one horrible kid in particular called Kevin, but also the Procter's, especially Robert. This entire family used to have the same speech impediment, where they would lisp after nearly every word—a little bit like the boxer Chris Eubanks. There was also another nasty family, although I'd forgotten their names. They were terrible people and the bain of my life, that was until high school, more on that later on.

In the park nearest the building, there was a particular ride that we were most fond of, it was a roundabout, in the shape of the planet Saturn, complete with rings, where four chairs were situated. On the top was a wheel which propelled us around at high speed, thus, making us feel dizzy.

The park had all one could ever wish for including slides, roundabouts, seesaws, climbing frames swings, and later on they added some adventure things like zip wires, and tyre swings etc. It was a great place to hang around.

Apart from the park, there was what we used to call the 'fields.' These fields were behind Compton Crescent, although technically they weren't fields, more like a heavily wooded area, with open space in-between.

We had several adventures growing up there, and it would be a place where we would make camps, or go 'bird nesting,' i.e. stealing bird's eggs, to make a collection. A practice that I am ashamed to be a part of now, but as kids, we found it exciting.

One spring evening, we were outside playing, when old Mr Comer came out to vent his anger at us which was a big mistake on his part. My dad came out, and as I said earlier, this was the day of the big punch up. Comer was a short man, with a big mouth, backed up by his gobby wife and two teenage sons. Seeing my dad having a go at Comer bought my mum out to try and diffuse the situation, and at 6 foot and 15 stone, my dad towered over Comer, who was five and a half feet tall.

I remembered Mrs Comer had said something to mum, and things escalated from there. All the neighbours were out watching the furore, as were all of us kids. There were shouts of 'hit him, Mr Briggs,' and 'go on dad.' Comer's boys had decided to stick their oar in, which intensified the furore.

At this point, my brother Peter got involved. As dad and Comer squared up to each other, dad had him in a headlock knocking the seven bells out of him. One of the boys smacked my dad, and the other called mum a 'bitch'. It was the final straw as Peter started fighting Mr Comer's boy. Peter at the time, was into Kung Fu and was a big fan of his idol Bruce Lee. As there was two against one, he started making Kung Fu moves. As one of the boys stepped in, Peter Kung Fu kicked him under his rib cage and winded him.

While holding his chest we all heard him say 'just going to get my D.M's on mum.' D.M's was short for Doc Martin boots, or bovver boots, as they were known back then. Peter continued fighting with the other son, when all of a sudden, about 20 of Comers son's friends came racing around the corner. It was apparent that Comer's son rang up his mates before putting his boots on!

Peter was outnumbered, and the only solution was to get on his toes and run. Of course, being as fit as he was, he gave them all the runaround, to our amusement. All we could see was him running chased by Comer's mates. After that, the local 'Bobby' I.E Police officer, came along and broke it all up. The fight was one of my fondest and funniest memories of that time.

Although no charges were bought, as it was in those days, and peace was quickly resumed. As a result of that, we found out that Comer and his family were moved out by the council, and moved to another area. It seems that the backlash was due to several complaints to the council, from the other neighbours, fed up with Comer's attitude. So, all's well that ends well, I supposed.

Shortly after the Comers had moved out, a new family moved in, and peace we now had peace in the neighbourhood. We could now play outside to our heart's content, without listening to old Comer moaning ever again.

Due to the hardships at that time, mum had found a different job with more money. She was now working for the Lyons cakes factory and often worked long hours to boost the family finances. Dad once again had quit his job as a postman, probably after a row with the management. However, they gave him his dues, and he found another job, with a company called 'Renaddress.' Part of his job was in the evening, and he had to fold thousands of envelopes, and leaflets, and distribute them during the day.

A lot of the time, we were roped in to help, which I thought was fun. It seemed life was getting better all the time. Also, dad had joined a Territorial Army unit, and I supposed it was a way for him to let off steam, and to satisfy his thirst for military life.

Spring was now in full bloom, and with it came Easter. At school, I was learning about Easter and the traditions surrounding it. We were also making our own Easter nests, complete with miniature chocolate eggs. However, my friend and I had annoyed the teacher by not coming back to the classroom when he instructed. As a result, and with tears in our eyes, we had to stand at the front of the class, while specifically chosen kids were allowed to come up, and take out one egg each, from my friend's nest and mine.

We both thought his form of punishment, was extreme but was the sign of the times in those days, and besides, it taught us a valuable lesson in discipline, and it only left us three eggs each. Still, I needn't have worried, as chocolate eggs were abundant for me when I got home. Easter was as good as Christmas in our house.

Well, I think so at least, as on Easter Sunday we would get dressed in our most elegant clothes and have a day out in one of the Royal Parks. Mum would pack a picnic, and we had a great time together. Talking about Sundays, on occasions, we had to go to Sunday school, as my sister Theresa had got involved with the Salvation Army.

Apart from learning about Jesus, it wasn't that bad, as most of the time, we would just draw or do colouring, mainly pictures around religion. Still, it gave mum and dad some respite! Also, as Theresa was involved with the Salvation Army, mum had given her a tambourine, draped with ribbons, and at that time, as I was close with her, I would stand and watch her perform.

At least once a month, we would all be packed up, and head off to Acton to visit my Aunt and Uncle, and my cousins. Also, my Nan (dad's mum) who lived with them. I loved going over to their place, as my Aunt Barbara always spoiled me, as she used to say, 'I was her favourite,' which made me feel special. Aunt Barbara was my dad's sister.

They lived in an old block of flats, on the ground floor near Acton high street. These were built around the time of King George and were freezing.

I don't remember much about my Nan, apart from seeing her sitting in her chair in dark clothing, with a beard, which tickled me when I kissed her! To be honest, I was a bit frightened of my Nan, I don't know why, as she was a lovely lady, but to me, she was imposing.

Anyway, I later found out that she was, in fact, a lady! What I meant by this, was that before meeting my Granddad, she had been married to a wealthy trader and that they gave birth to a daughter whom they had named Barbara. Her previous name and title were Lady Flood.

Nan had been born and bought up from a middle-class family in Edinburgh. She had met my Granddad when he arrived at their house looking for work.

He was a labourer and worked on the railways helping build the railway between London and Scotland and would be responsible for laying the sleepers ready for the tracks to be laid.

Grandad was as strong as an ox and built like a brick shithouse. To make more money, he started offering himself out as an odd job man, and they fell in love and eloped. You could say the original Lady Chatterley.

When we were at my Aunt and Uncles, the kitchen table would be bought out and piled high with food. As kids, we eat first, and when we had finished, it was the turn of the grown-ups. My dad and Uncle would sit either end, and at the word go, they would 'pick their noses', and dab their fingers on all the food which was at arm's length.

As kids, we found it hilarious, but our mum's and Nan thought it was somewhat disgusting, but still had a chuckle themselves.

My Uncle Ralph was a practical joker, and when my Nan needed to go to the loo, he and my dad, would carry her, pull down her knickers and just plonk her down, before leaving the toilet, and closing the door.

When she finished, Nan would shout out for them to get her out, but being a practical joker, my Uncle would just leave the poor old dear there and have a laugh at her expense, so would my dad. It was when she feigned having a heart attack before they relented and helped her out. Nan must have had at least 100 heart attacks to my knowledge.

When she was dying of a heart attack Uncle Ralph, as always saw the funny side and told her "look for years you had heart attacks, so now you're having a real one, you should have died by now." I did hear that my Nan loved him for saying that and died happily.

There was a time I visited and had a nasty fall. My sister Tina and myself were playing outside on the grounds. We sometimes climb walls amongst other things, and I fell headfirst and landed on my chin, giving my first ever case of stitches, and leaving me with a permanent scar. Suffice to say that apart from that, our monthly visits were always fun-filled, and a joy to behold. Oh, before I leave this chapter, I must mention the names of my cousins, who were Karen, Clive, and Caroline.

We also loved visiting our maternal grandmother. She lived in Lydden near Dover in a tiny two-bedroom stone flint cottage and was one of five cottages, which were owned by James Robertson Justice, the actor. The small house had a backroom with kitchen, and a front parlour, and was a tight squeeze.

Mum often told us that it was a cosy home when she was growing up as she was from a big family. My mum's brothers and sisters' names were Clive, Pauline, Douglas, Wendy and Sheila, so eight in total including Nan and grandad. Nan was a great old lady, always dressed in a pink housecoat, and she always wore a hair net.

She was a fantastic cook, and always used the same bone handle knife, which she'd sharpened often that the middle is worn. The kitchen was a type of gazebo style add on. The original kitchen had been part of the backroom and originally had a coal-burning range. The gazebo had a leaning glass roof and was an ideal place for letting the light in of which Nan hung flower baskets, which had spider plants in them. Off to the right was a small bathroom, which was also a later add on which had a washbasin, toilet and small bath.

The original toilet was outside, and Nan used it as storage for garden tools. At the rear of the cottage was the beautiful hilled garden, which was a riot of colour, and housed the vegetable garden. Of course, both Nan and grandad were keen gardeners, and had 'green fingers.'

Although the secret to the garden was grandad's 'special' fertiliser, which consisted of well-rotted human waste, in other words, it contained faeces. Behind the garden was a small road that led to a 'hill' owned by the ministry of defence. We always played for hours, climbing to the top of the hill then rolling down due to the steepness.

The woods were a great place to explore, dotted with huge craters leftover from WW2 caused by either 'doodlebugs' (flying bombs) which had prematurely crashed on their way to London, or by German pilots shot down by the RAF, the British royal airforce.

On occasions, our aunty Wendy and Uncle Bill would come over from Deal a few miles from Nan's house with our cousins Lizzy, Lorraine (Babs), Will, Sharon and Christine. As I remembered, Nan and grandad owned a beautiful old English sheepdog named Peter. We all loved Peter as he had a brilliant temperament, who would allow us younger kids to ride on his back.

Occasionally, we would go to visit our Aunty Pauline and Uncle Bill, and our other cousins Annette, and Kevin, and head off to the beach at Dover, or further afield at Ramsgate. When we sat around the coal fire, our Grandad would often fall asleep, with a cigarette in his mouth, and the hot ash would fall onto his shirts and burn small holes, much to Nan's annoyance. We would shout at him to 'wake up' where he would reply that he was merely 'resting his eyes.'

One Christmas, my parents had asked us to spend Christmas with Nan and Grandad. It was like yesterday, we were allowed to sit in the parlour, where Grandad had built up a roaring fire, and we all laid down to watch its flames and to hear the crackles and spits. As I recalled, I had been given a chocolate toolset, of which I shared with my siblings. I can say that it felt like a magical time as we were all happy!

The following Christmas, we visited our Auntie Irene and Uncle George (Dad's eldest brother) who lived In Lancaster near Preston. They had a 3-bedroom house which was also full of our Cousins, and their names were, Irene, Sue, Marie, Pauline and Trisha. Also, Uncle Ralph and auntie Barbara were there with Karen, Clive, and Caroline.

The house was jam-packed and boisterous with a cacophony of voices, and it was noisy. On Christmas, all of us gathered into the living room. You could imagine the scene, with a house full of kids and adults alike. There was standing room only in the living room, as it contained all the adult and kids' decorations and a vast number of presents.

My parents gave me a battery-operated car which had a hook-like instrument at the front, and when it reached an obstacle, it would stop and then turn around using the hook device. I also had gifts such as clothes, colouring books, and my first set of toiletries, and one was called 'soap on a rope'. After the gifts presentations, my brothers and sisters took them upstairs and put them in the rooms we all shared.

The rooms had double beds, and we were topping and tailing in the beds. It was a welcome distraction at night as the rooms were cold with condensation on the walls and the bedsheets. After washing and dressing, we walked downstairs, where the adults were having a well-earned rest after opening their presents, and also enjoying a Christmas drink.

While waiting for the Christmas dinner, we all gathered around and were playing board games with each other. Finally, they served dinner. It was a traditional Christmas dinner, and the kids, myself included, settled to eat. The adults sat on whatever piece of furniture they could find and ate theirs. Although the house was cramped, we all had a fantastic time and was something that I shall remember with fondness.

A few days later, we packed up and went our separate ways. On the journey home, we were all in a jubilant mood and reflected on our time with our extended family. Again, all too soon, Christmas had passed, a new year was about to begin.

It was now 1973, and the start of a new school year. As usual, we walked to school, and with a little bit of pocket money that we had, we stopped at the corner shop to buy sweets. When at school, I wasted no time in telling my friends how good my Christmas holiday was, they, in turn, did the same, and we compared presents that we'd received.

Chapter Three

Latchkey Kids

Like most kids growing up in the seventies, people viewed us as 'latchkey kids.' What that meant was that we looked after ourselves when our parents were at work. I can't speak for the rest of the neighbourhood, but in our house, we had a key on a piece of string attached to the front door which we accessed via the letterbox.

We pulled the string through and let ourselves into the house. Not very security conscious I know, but unlike today it was much safer back then. In fact, in those days, we could leave our doors open, and walk into each other's houses, without living in fear of someone breaking into our home, besides, none of us had much worth stealing in those days.

Being the oldest, the burden of responsibility fell onto Peter's shoulders. A task of which he resented, as he felt it was an annoying burden, and not one done to the best of his ability. Usually, he would get up before us, creeping downstairs and make his breakfast, skimming the cream off the milk! He would always deny this, of course, and there would be an argument between him and Theresa.

He would also deliberately burn the toast, knowing full well that we wouldn't eat it, and end up eating it himself. Bloody selfish even back then. And to be honest, he still is to a point. Anyway, after breakfast, he would go to school, leaving Theresa to take us to school. As usual, we would take the same route to school. Sometimes if we had a few pence, we would stop at the sweet shop near the school, and pick up at least dozen-penny sweets, before getting into school,

On one occasion, my sister Tina left me to go to the sweet shop, I carefully selected the sweets, and the shop keeper placed it into two separate bags. Unbeknown to me I was running late, of course, Tina knew this, which was the reason she allowed me to go alone, the shopkeeper informed me that I was now late for school, so I packed the sweets in my duffel bag, and ran off to school.

I got into the cloakroom, and removed my coat, as I did so, the deputy headmistress appeared from behind me, which made me jump out of my skin, causing me to drop my bag. I heard the sound of breaking glass from my thermos flask, and panic set in, what should I do? I opened the bag and pulled out the flask, and other contents, which included my packed lunch, and of course the sweets. But by now they were somewhat soggy from the contents of the flask. I was now the proud owner of a smashed thermos, soggy sandwiches, and half-melted sweets.

I was also in trouble for being late and had ten merit points removed from my 'house.' In a nutshell, this was proving to be a bad day, I had no lunch, a broken flask, of which I was sure I would get it in the neck from my parents. An irate class due to the lost points, but worst of all a pissed off sister, of whom I had to give all the remaining sweets which were still edible. So, no sweets either! Thank God mum and dad understood about the flask. Well at least mum did, dad thought I was a 'moron' as usual. However, that was more to do with Tina's influence in stirring up the situation, and she was good like that.

Life continued like that for me, at least I had some good friends of which to rely on, but at school, I was struggling to grasp math, although I was getting good at the other subjects, math was not my strong point, and I fell behind. Due to my poor knowledge of the subject, the other kids teased me, which was bad enough, but to suffer the indignity of my siblings was even worse.

On the upside, strange as it seems, words such as moron, thick, useless and I would only become a dustman was well and truly part of my vocabulary.

Being the youngest, I was always the butt of my brothers and sister's jokes, as it was difficult for me, to express myself. As a coping mechanism, I would bang my head on the floor, or hold my breath, in a vain and infantile attempt to make them stop. This plan didn't work and only succeeded in aggravating the torment, of which I was receiving.

Due to the constant piss-taking and banging my head on the floor, I started to suffer from migraine headaches. I also started to stutter when I spoke, and became sickly, due to stress. All of this, and I was only 6! In the end, the only way I could eradicate the constant bombardment was to stop speaking and crawl into a 'nutshell,' for self-protection. I am sure there are others out there that feel the same.

As a result of my shyness and overall quiet nature, I became an easy target for the school bullies, and they beat me up regularly, despite my sister Tina's attempts to diffuse the situation. Looking back now, I am grateful for her support, without Tina and her best friend Shirley Matthew's, I am sure it would have been much worse.

The problem with being bullied, at the time of when I was growing up in the seventies, was that people often overlooked it. And right now, schools are still filled with bullies, even though the school authorities should deal with such practices.

For me, the bullies changed my persona. The more I was bullied, the deeper I went into myself. I was a nervous wreck and hated confrontation. As I grew, I started to fight back. I remembered on one occasion when I got home after being bullied. After seeing me battered and bruised, he turned around and told me, that if I didn't fight back, he would give me something to cry about.

The next day at school, the bullies started again. Recalling dad's words from the previous evening, I fought back. One of the bullies started on me, and I swung around and punched him in the face bloodying his nose. Seeing his face full of blood and crying, made me feel good. However, that was a big mistake on my part, and it only escalated in his friends pouncing on me and giving me a good hiding.

When I got home dad was waiting there, seeing me bloodied and bruised, he sat me down and asked what happened, at first I was concerned that he would give me something to cry about, but after hearing my version of events, he smiled shook my hand, cuddled me and told me that that was the only language that bullies understood.

Encouraged by his words and actions, my next day at school was to be a happy one. Even though the bullying never stopped, I always fought my own battles, sometimes I won, and sometimes I lost, but regardless of the outcome, I still stood my ground.

Eventually, due to all the bullying, the stress of home life, the school kind of became my battleground. I started to become a nuisance and would disrupt the class. I had also unconsciously become a bully myself, and often began to pick on one boy in particular named Peter Blandon.

Peter, like me, was going through some bad times at home. Yet I thought it would be fun to tease and hit him, to the point of making him cry, something I was not proud of. It was when I went to high school and was reunited with Peter, that I apologised, and we became friends.

Back at school, my behaviour was getting worse, and the teachers always punished me, where I would have to stand in the corner. As a result of spending so much time in the corner, my schoolwork suffered, which added to my stress levels, as I found it challenging to catch up. However, it wasn't all that bad, as we had a new teacher at the school. An Australian named Mr Okenew. I found him to be more understanding as a teacher, and for a time, life became more bearable.

Due to the bullying and my estranged home life, things worsened, so did my behaviour, and with it, my wrath on Peter Blandon escalated. One day, in particular, we were being shown how to make an artwork using flour and salt. Although Peter and I worked together as a team, things just didn't work out the way Mt Okenew planned. I started well; however, as Peter's artwork progressed, mine was not. So, in my frustration, I went back to my old ways and decided to smash Peter's project. As a result, Peter burst into tears. However, to my dismay, Mr Okenew saw when I did it, and he decided to make an example of me, by spoiling my work.

Upon his actions, I began to cry. You can imagine the scene! Peter and I sat at our ruined projects, crying our eyes out. Due to our uncontrollable tearful tantrums, Mr Okenew furnished us with our new nicknames, which were blabbermouth Blandon, and blabbermouth Briggsy! From then on, whenever Peter and I started to cry, either by my actions, or a combination of another influence, Mr Okenew, would shout out 'shut up blabbermouth Blandon and Briggsy'. I can tell you; it would stop us in our tracks.

Later on, at high school where we both met again, we reminded each other of our earlier times, and just for fun, this time, and we would sign off with blabbermouth! I have to say that Mr Okenew was a great teacher, he seemed to understand me, more so than other teachers, my only regret, was that I never had the nerve to confide in him, as to what I was going through.

As a kid and being the youngest, I was petrified to speak out and inform my peers. Being bullied at school and home increased my fears, and I became more withdrawn. As a safeguard, I would only speak when someone spoke to me! Although dad had always told me, to tell him the truth, I very often never said a word to him. And all this even though I knew he would back me up.

Looking back, I wished I had been there for my mum and dad more often than I ever did. As I said earlier, due to my life being as it was my frustrations grew worse, and the only way I could get attention, was with tantrums, most of the time, I remained silent.

On the rare occasion that I would talk, I would stutter uncontrollably.

Even now I find it difficult to cope in certain circumstances and being whom I am, I held onto memories and tend to remember them very often, which causes me immense pain, despite all the comforting words that people give.

I tried all sorts to get unpleasant thoughts out of my head, and sometimes I succeed if only for a short while. Due to the bullying, the school authorities moved me from Gifford to my new school, which was nearer home. The school name was Northolt CFM. The school was at the Target roundabout in Northolt, at the top end of the Church road near the A40 duel carriageway. The good thing is that I would now be going to school with my best friend Andy, who also lived on my road.

The main school was an old Georgian building, with several prefabricated classrooms dotted around the grounds. On the first day, the headmistress greeted me, and I was handed to my new form teacher, although their names escaped me.

In the mornings before lessons, someone would ring the handbell, and we would start the day in assembly and sing hymns. The headmistress would do a reading, and after that, we would all go to our respected classes. The school was somewhat different to Gifford, and I had to rely on my friend Andy to show me the ropes.

Due to my insecurities, when it came to math I suffered, as the math teacher was a loud, obnoxious man, who delighted in inflicting physical punishment to us kids, should we step out of line. His name was Mr Griffith.

As I was unable to understand numbers, I would cheat and look over my classmate's work. On one such occasion, Mr Griffith caught me, grabbed hold of my hand and slapped me hard six times with a ruler! Thank God for that kind of treatment doesn't occur now.

Anyway, my hand was swollen and sore, very painful bruises across my hand, and with tears streaming down my face, I tried to continue with my lesson but failed miserably. Again, this added to my stress levels.

Many years later, I discovered that my inability to do math was not one of laziness, but it was a condition similar to dyslexia which affects 2-3% of the population! For those of you who are curious, the medical term for this condition is dyscalculia. The upside of the condition is that sufferers such as me, have a higher I.Q. than others, and seem to excel in other subjects. My I.Q. is 146. Not bad at all.

With my ever-increasing stress, I learned a different way of coping. I became boisterous and disruptive in the classroom, which was to the amusement of my classmates but bought me into conflict with the teachers. I didn't mean to become the class clown and seen as a bad influence, and it was just a way of me coping and dealing with stress.

When I did not have a math lesson, I excelled at other subjects, English, History, Geography and art, and I learned to fight properly. I believe it was also born of frustration, from both my home life and at school. Being the new kid, some of my classmates seemed to take to me; others looked and treated me as if I was stupid. I wasn't sure it was because I was the class clown. I believed it was because our personalities clashed.

One kid called Stuart Helier came from a middle-class background, and being an only child was spoilt rotten, and his parents saw him as a perfect boy. Not only that, the teachers saw him as being the blue-eyed boy, and he waltzed around the school as if he owned the place. He was always at hand to put his oar in and stir up trouble for me and others, and then stand there with his angelic look and the halo above his head.

His favourite trick was to slag off everyone, including myself behind our backs. He also delighted in telling his friends that he was the toughest kid in the school, and he could beat up anyone. And that was a big mistake on his part as one occasion, Andy and I were sitting on one of the roofs partially covered by overgrown trees, which resembled a covered walkway.

It was a scorching hot day, and Stuart was walking underneath the covered area with another nasty spoilt kid Andrew Warren. Unfortunately for them, they failed to see Andy and me, and as usual, Simon was slagging me off. With Warren agreeing to his every word. At one point, I heard him say that he could 'beat me up.'

I had heard enough, and I jumped down from my vantage point and squared up to him. Being arrogant, he claimed that he wasn't saying anything and denied everything, even though both myself and Andy heard him. He looked at me as if I was dirt and proclaimed that I was a 'dirty poor scumbag!

Well, that was the final straw, and I punched him in the face bloodying his nose. He tried to fight back, but he also broke his thumb, as he would curl his fingers around it, and as he hit me, anyone closer could hear it break. Andrew Warren, being the school weasel ran off to alert the teachers.

By the time they had appeared, Helier was crying and screaming blue murder, again the teachers took his side despite my protests and Andy's testimony. Due to this, my parents were summoned to the school, as were Helier's. I needn't have worried though, as Helier's father, who was a stuck-up bank manager, tried to disrespect my dad in the head's office. Another big mistake, as my dad knocked him out cold! Good old dad, thankfully no charges were bought, and it was dealt with amicably in the end.

My life at Northolt CFM was an up and down affair. On the good days, I excelled at certain things, and I often acted in small classroom plays seen by the whole school at assembly. The reason was and still is, that I am very good at accents, and would often come out with a different one at rehearsal, which inevitably led me to act as the lead role.

One role I was particularly good at was to play St George. The play was a big affair, as it would be shown at the school fete. The big day arrived, and I was nervous before the play; however, my anxiety passed one of the teachers announced that Henry Cooper, was not only going to open the fete but would be staying to watch.

Those of us who know, Henry Cooper was the number one British heavyweight boxer, who had knocked down Cassius clay, or those who now know him as, Mohammed Ali! I was now no longer nervous, I was excited, and gave the performance of my life, and even got a mention in the local rag, and better still Henry shook my hand for excellent performance and gave me a signed photo.

At the age of eight, my life was a series of ups and downs, mainly downs I may hasten to add. Homelife was a constant struggle, as dad was on his umpteenth job, and mum was working full time for Lyon's bakery. As the youngest, life was becoming a strain.

My eldest brother Peter was now working full time, and then he would be out boozing heavily, then he ended up having jaundice. His girlfriend, Lorraine's family, bought him a fruit hamper, and in pride of place was the biggest bar of Cadbury milk chocolate.

As Peter was bright yellow because of jaundice and very ill, he would lie on the sofa, and I would cradle his head on my lap.

However, the brotherly love didn't go as far as him sharing his chocolate. Unperturbed by my attempts to be offered any, I managed to steal it, and eat it at my leisure.

I denied all knowledge, and my middle brother David was suspected of the chocolate theft. David got a good beating from Peter, better that than from my dad beating me for stealing the chocolate. In my unique way, I tried to make it all better, by offering to go down the shop for Peter to buy him another one if he gave me the money.

To my surprise he did and also allowed me to keep the change for some sweets of my own, so my guilt was very short-lived, and Peter never suspected me, and I never divulged the truth until many years later as an adult. My only regret was allowing my brother David to take the blame and get a good beating for me.

However, at the time, I felt nothing for him, as he had a mean streak, and would beat my sister and me at every opportunity, so I supposed I thought it was poetic justice. Although as an adult, I hoped he could accept my apology. Family life was changing fast, and as it did so, the memories changed. Peter had now had his friend living in his room as a lodger.

His name was Jimmy, and they had been school friends and were now workmates and drinking partners. Peter had now passed his driving test and had bought his first car a Renault, and he remained faithful to the Renault make all his life.

One evening, Peter and Jimmy were at home, in the room that they shared. When mum came home, she spoke to Peter in a way that he thought was disrespectful, and they both had words. When dad came back, mum told him that Peter had been argumentative and rude to her. Peter was adamant that it wasn't the case, and asked Jimmy who said, 'she did say that to me in a stroppy indignant way.'

Mum was angry, and she nagged my dad to give a beating, as Peter squared up to dad, they exchange blows, of which Peter was worse off. The confrontation was the final straw for Peter, and he packed his bags with Jimmy, and they walked out. After they had left, mum and dad had a terrible argument. It transpired that Peter moved in with his girlfriend, Lorraine. It would be some considerable before I saw him again.

Theresa now had a Saturday job working at Wimpy in Ealing West London. Sometimes mum would take me and my sister Tina there as a special treat, after shopping. Of course, as Theresa worked there, and she was having a 'fling' with the owner, we never had to pay. Back in those days, the Wimpy was a rare treat, as this was the only burger franchise that was around, as McDonald was to come many years later. The only other places to eat were either fancy restaurants or greasy spoon cafes.

David was now at Drayton Manor grammar school, which was costly, but my parents thought it would be better for him, although their generosity and understanding toward him were short-lived.

He was also working at weekends doing a paper round for Alderton's one of the newsagents in the Northolt area. On one occasion, David asked if I wanted to come and help him doing his paper round.

I was surprised at his request, as he enjoyed beating me and my sister Tina up. However, on this particular day, I saw the love he had for me as his little brother. I remembered running down the road with him, as we ran, David kept shouting out that we're going to run like the wind. I have to say that I enjoyed his company. I was proud to call him my brother.

While at Drayton Manor, there was a school play called 'Moses' and David had been chosen to play the title role. Tina and I went to watch the school play with my parents. And it was a musical—David sang beautifully throughout the play.

However, after his performance, David was a little bit upset, as the band we're playing too loudly, and he felt that they were drowning out his voice. He needn't have worried, as his performance was flawless, and he was mentioned in the local newspaper.

Tina was with her friends, especially her best friend Debbie O'Brien, so apart from seeing my friends when they were in, I was pretty much left alone, and had to amuse myself, and make new friends with our dog Mungo. Although Tina spent a lot of time with Debbie O'Brien, she also had other friends.

She too like David had acting aspirations, and she acted in a play as Mrs. bumble in the school production of 'Oliver'. Again, mum took me, and dad came along. I will never forget dad's face when he saw Tina perform, as he had tears streaming down his face, and you could see that he was proud of her achievement.

The performance, just like David's, was excellent. Again, the school and the production appeared in the local newspaper. There was even a congratulatory letter written by Lionel Bart, the writer of the original film and play 'Oliver'. Getting back to my brother David, he was bright, but due to being the third born, he had resentments, and his behaviour in the home grew worse.

As I mentioned earlier, my brother Peter had left after an argument with my parents, and was now living with his girlfriend Lorraine, and her family. Due to this his protection for Tina, and me and to a lesser extent, Theresa was no longer there. Peter's absence became David's cue to increase his bad behaviour towards us, knowing that he wouldn't get a beating from Peter.

When he became unruly and beat up Tina and me, Theresa would do her best to come to our aid, most of which were unsuccessful. The only option she had, was to tell mum and dad, David would get a good hiding from dad, and the next day, David would take it out on us kids, it was a never-ending vicious circle.

As kids, we had our little annoying traits. One favourite was we would all sit on the sofa and cross our arms and pretend to watch the T.V with mum and dad. Not unusual, you would think, but not for us. When we thought mum and dad were not looking, and still sat with folded arms, we would pinch each other, and try to get the other to cry out and grab the attention of mum and dad.

This prank would continue until either mum or dad would get angry or shout at us to pack it in! However, being immature, we would stay and being the youngest, I would cry out the loudest, which would gain a clip around the ear from dad mostly.

Sometimes it would get worse, and David would get the belting, as it appeared that he was the main culprit. Another annoying habit that we participated in was pretending that one of us would have fleas, and we would 'blow' them away after being touched by the family member. Again, this was more often than not David.

On one occasion we sat around the dining table for Sunday dinner. Dad was having a pint before dinner, and mum was in the kitchen. It was at this time that we thought it would be fun to partake in taunting David with blowing his fleas away. During his protests, mum who had heard us all and ran into the dining room, brandishing a carving knife, screaming and shouting.

She took out her stress and annoyance on the person closest to her, which just happened to be Theresa. In her rage, she lashed out with the knife and hacked my sister along her arms. We were petrified, as we had never witnessed this type of spontaneous violent outburst from mum before.

With blood pouring out of her wounds, Theresa wrapped them, at the same time dad appeared and hit the roof at mum. After their argument, dad rushed Theresa to the A&E, leaving myself Tina, and David scared to death trying to eat, which as mum was still in a mood, we did so in silence!

When dad and Theresa arrived home from the hospital, Mum and dad had a blazing row, while we were upstairs cowering in our rooms. We heard the screaming and shouting downstairs between mum and dad. We also heard ornaments being broken, and we try to go to sleep with the noise of violence ringing in our ears.

The next morning, we got up for breakfast, and we went downstairs. I could see that mum had received a black eye from dad. None of us dared to speak to mum and asked what happened, and besides, we've all heard it the previous evening. These outbursts which affected mum was later explained as PMS and wasn't the last time we witnessed it.

Although David was a pain in the backside, some of the thrashings he got weren't always warranted. Many are the times that I heard and witnessed him beaten black and blue. Firstly, by mum, and when dad arrived back home, she would rant and rave at him telling dad how bad he had been, so poor David got another good hiding, and all this before there was a buy one get one free. Joking aside, I generally felt sorry for him on occasions, and cried with him, as at the end of it all, he is my brother, and I love him!

I looked back now and remembered when we shared a bedroom. David would invent stories. These were a form of horror story based loosely on the Frankenstein genre. Unlike the Frankenstein monster, ours he named Stedad! Which was a combination of both of our names.

His stories were great, and it made me feel closer to him like I had never experienced before, and deep down, I knew he felt the same way as me. In many ways, David was my hero. On several occasions, I had to rely on him to help me out with the bullying of which he never thought about his safety.

I remembered one day my best friend Andy jumped on me, he had my head in an arm lock and was strangling me, as I couldn't breathe, was getting weaker even though I was fighting hard for my life, if it hadn't been for David's intervention, could have been in a far worse situation.

David had seen Andy Ward on top of me and had dragged him off, which allowed me to compose myself and gained the upper hand against Andy, for which I beat up quite severely. Although now I am ashamed of those times, and for what I did to Andy, I am grateful that David was there on many occasions.

With the number of beatings, he got, he started to rebel, which made matters worse for him. One time he had been lying on his bed reading, I was downstairs reading a comic, and Tina was around Debbie O'Brien's house. However, Theresa was at home and with her friend Ruth and was also upstairs.

An argument ensued between David and Theresa, and all I caught was 'I'm going to tell mum when she gets in.' When mum arrived home from work, Theresa wasted no time in speaking with her. It transpires that Theresa claimed to have seen David 'playing with himself!' The accusation incensed mum, not that she needed any encouragement, and she beat David black and blue.

Again when dad arrived home, she told him, and before he could get his coat off, or get a cup of tea, he went upstairs, and with David still sobbing, he beat him again, with mum standing by his side goading him to hit him again, and again. It was a terrifying day, and I just wanted it to end.

To hear the poor boy, scream in pain was heart-breaking. The next day, I saw the full extent of David's good hiding from the night before. As you can imagine, he was somewhat subdued. I think he felt sorry for himself and rightly so. I felt sorry for him too, and I made him a cup of tea and some toast to try and cheer him up.

He seemed pleased with this, and we started to talk, and he started to cry as well. I found this challenging to deal with, and the only thing I could think of doing was to cuddle him and tell him that I was sorry. After he had composed himself, I went back downstairs, and I left him in our bedroom reading a book.

After a while, Tina had arrived home after spending the night at her friend Debbie O'Brien's. As she got home, Theresa told Tina everything and Tina decided to wind him up about it. It was the final straw for him, so he hit her, and despite his apology and pleas, Tina ran out of the door shouting as she went that she would tell mum!

David looked petrified and ran upstairs crying, and I just sat down, pretending that nothing happened. I knew I should have done something at that point, but I just didn't know how to deal with the problems and thought to myself that if I pretended not to hear or see, then I couldn't comment or denied that I've ever heard or saw anything.

A few moments later, David called my name, as I entered the hallway, I witnessed David collapsed and fell down the stairs. He had taken an overdose! Not knowing what to do, I panicked, and ran next door and explained to Mrs Cosham what had happened, and she rang an ambulance.

To everyone's relief, the doctors saved him. However, this incident was the last one, which my parents could cope with, and they decided that David was too unruly, and they placed him in a children's home. He was 12, and I knew that family life would never be the same, as its fabric had been torn apart!

Chapter Four

The Summer of 76

After David had been placed in the children's home, life it seemed to stand still for me. I became almost a recluse in my bedroom that I once shared with my brother. Although though I went out with my friends, I still longed to have my family around me.

My sister Theresa had now become the girlfriend of Dave Shine. He was a strange bloke very annoying as I remembered, but my parents liked him, and he was around our place more often than his own. His family was worse than mine; it seemed. In other words, he was from a broken home, his parents were alcoholics, and they neglected him. As a result, he would be allowed to eat with us, and my mum became a surrogate to him.

Tina was now doing gymnastics, and spent most of her time with her friends, although on occasions when she was at home, we would play in the garden on our swing. I cherished those days as we had such a good laugh. The best bit was when dad came home, and he would have a bag of 'chewing nuts'. These were chocolate-covered toffee balls, and we shared them out, although I'm sure she didn't share them equally, nevertheless they were still enjoyable. Mostly, I would amuse myself in my room, which wasn't bad as mum and dad had bought me a second-hand train set, which I played with for hours.

The school was just the same, although by now, they had moved to a brand-new site, just a stone's throw from my house. However, even being a brand-new school, my frustrations grew, and my behaviour continued. It was mum's birthday; I was sulking and refused to do any work until I was allowed to make her a birthday cake and a card.

The school agreed on the proviso that I would do my work later. I was allowed to go to the attached nursery and make a cake in the nursery kitchen, and make a card, however, after I finished, I went back on my promise and still acted up. In many ways, I was a spoilt brat, but I think it was my way of gaining attention from my parents. And although I'm not proud of the way that I did it, as a 10-year-old kid, I just didn't understand.

It was now 1976, and this was the year that the summer would hit record temperatures. The school was arranging a PGL adventure holiday to Wales. I remembered begging my parents to let me go even the cost to them was £75.00, a lot of money in those days. Finally, my parents relented, as they saw it as a way for me to experience different activities, and hopefully help me to get out of my wayward ways.

The holiday was magical, the camp was great, and we enjoyed activities, which included pony trekking, canoeing, sailing, rock climbing etc.

The camp had a large log cabin type of canteen, medical bay, and the tents were massive and comfortable, but my god, it was hot!

Although I had a fabulous time with my friends, when I returned, I still refused to co-operate and was always in trouble. I felt sorry for my mum and dad, as they had spent a lot of time, money, and effort to try and help me. In the end, the only way they got me to behave was to tell me that they would put me into care just like my brother David!

It was a scary thought, especially after we had visited him a couple of times at the home, so in the end, I calmed down, and knuckled down and got on with my education, much to the relief of my parents.

At school, I made some new friends, which were a calming influence on me. Of course, some of the old faces were still there, that I despised Andrew Warren for instance. However, Stuart Helier had moved with his parents to Surrey, so at least I didn't have to put up with his crap.

Although Andy Ward and I were still friends, I also met Tony Cornish a colossus of a lad, and a fantastic artist. There was Andy Packman, another great bloke, and my mental mate Paul

Murphy. Another good friend was Darren Bender and his sister Jean who I fancied like crazy, as she was stunning.

All of these new faces were a year older than me, but we hit it off instantaneously. Tony, as I said, was fantastic at art, and his speciality was drawings of Tarzan a T.V serial played by Ron Ely, which was popular at the time. These were so lifelike; it was like looking at a photo of the actor. It was with Tony's guidance that my art was refined, and I became very good at it, although I do say so myself.

My specialities were drawings of the Marvel comic superhero characters. I spent hours copying my favourites and had them plastered all over my room.

Other friends included Reggie Taylor, David Pervez, and Derek Edwards, Ray and Ron Cooper, although I say these were friends, they were more like acquaintances.

One day I was around Reggie Taylor's house, and he asked if I wanted to go and see a strip show, I asked him who would do the stripping, and he said it was going to be a cousin of his. I thought about the idea and agreed to go with him, and others Reggie had asked along. Reggie explained that for me to watch a strip show, it was going to cost me 5 pence. At that time, I didn't have any money on me, so I ran all the way home, and asked my dad if I could have 5p of which to buy a comic. Dad gave me over 10 pence, so I rushed around Reggie's house; we made our way to where the strip show was going to be.

I handed him over 5p and settled down in the scout hall, which was chosen as the venue. Suddenly Reggie's cousin appeared, and she slowly started to remove her clothes provocatively. When fully naked, she stretched out on an old sofa that was at the scout Hall and was performing acts which I never believed existed. Although shocked at first, I have to say that not only myself but all of us have become somewhat aroused with her performance.

After the show had ended, we went our separate ways, and I went to the sweet shop, to spend the other 5p on sweets. I took a long way back home which started around the back of Walford high school's grounds and took me around the top end of the fields and then onto Compton Crescent, into Bengarth Road and then home. Back at home, I went upstairs to my bedroom, to eat my sweets and to think about the earlier events.

Out of all these friends, Andy Packman was the one I gelled with the most. I would often stay at his house at weekends, and we would stay up on Saturday night to watch all the popular T.V shows at the time finishing off with our favourite Hammer house of horror.

Andy was an only child, and his mum was a great bubbly woman, who although wasn't married she did have a part-time boyfriend. But most of the time, she and Andy lived alone. I liked going around there, as Andy had a pet hamster called Snowy. I was engrossed in this animal, and asked mum if I could have one, to my surprise she let me, and I got one of my own which I named Honey, and I loved her.

My home life seemed to improve as well, and the good times had resurfaced. I think it was because it was less crowded without Peter and David, but most of all, Dad had kept down his job, albeit a new job at a company called Kramer. Although it was still a struggle, money was coming in, and for the first time, my parents were able to buy some new things, all on the 'knock' of course.

Nowadays, credit is more readily available, and everyone seems to be doing it. But back then, it was a lot different.

I have to say that I'm getting ahead of myself here. I forgot to mention that when the school was at its old site on the Church road, I went on another school trip to France. The reason was that one of our teachers was French and had arranged a cultural visit with her childhood school. It was so we could not only learn a new language but get aquatinted with our new French pen friends.

Andy Packman, Stuart Helier and me shared a room. However, it wasn't bad, and Stuart and I had a kind of a truce. It was the first time we had ever been and found it strange that we had, what we thought was two toilets in the room. Of course, we didn't know that one was a bidet.

I very nearly didn't make it to France, as a few days before I had two accidents. The first was I stubbed my big toe, which swelled up so bad that it had to be drilled through the nail, to release the blood. I never forget that this was over Easter, and as soon as the Doctor pierced the nail, I threw up. However, as I had stuffed myself with chocolate eggs, it was like a chocolate fountain.

The second accident was more self-inflicted. I was trying to remove the hard outer shell of a golf ball with a bread knife. I aimed to get to the elastic wrapping, and the small inner fluid-filled ball, presumably designed to allow for a better flight when the ball had been struck. Why I do not know, I had just seen it from Stephen Ward and thought it was a good thing at the time.

Due to the immense pressure of the elastic, the ball exploded, and the inner ball burst open and sprayed ammonia into my eyes! For a week, I had to have eye drops administered, and my eyes were covered with bandages. Thank God, they were removed one day before the French trip, so happy days!

On one of the nights we were at the hotel, Andy was out of the room, so Stuart and I thought it would be funny to put Andy's teddy bear named Rupert on the window ledge. When he returned to the room, Andy wasn't happy, he had an almighty tantrum, as Rupert was not under his blanket. While Stuart and I were pissing ourselves laughing, Andy was getting more and more frantic, while searching the room.

As he did so, the French sky changed, and a storm erupted, and it pissed down, it was then that Andy caught sight of his beloved Rupert on the ledge getting soaked! By now, he was crying his eyes out while Stuart and I were in pain from all the laughing. Andy opened the window with such force that it almost broke.

Rescuing Rupert, he was like a mother cradling her newborn. We couldn't believe how anyone could get so attached to a tiny stuffed bear. It was sometime later that he explained that it was sentimental, as it was from his Gran, who died two days after he was born, so sorry Andy.

Apart from that night, the trip went off without any further incident. We were given an insight into French history and culture. As we were staying in Normandy, we visited the D-day landing beaches. It was an exciting time for me, as I loved history, and explored the original concrete machine-gun bunkers. My favourite part was visiting the Bayeux Tapestry. In the museum, which holds it, we had handsets, which gave a running commentary on its history.

As fascinated as I was, the commentary was in French! It was when we were leaving that I found out that I had picked up the wrong colour handset, which was blue, and should have picked up the red one! Anyway, it was still a sight to behold and thoroughly recommended viewing.

The next day we were to meet our pen friends in their school. Mine was a boy called Francois. None of us could understand each other's language, so it was hard going. A football match was arranged, and as confident as we were, we were thrashed 10-0.

After the match, we were each allowed to go to our pen friends home for 1 hour. Francois took me to see his family, who owned an orchard. They were a lovely family, but being French, they liked a drink, even the kids were encouraged to partake. So, when in Rome, I did.

They gave me a glass of the strongest Cider, hand-pressed by Francois father. As I have never drunk any booze before, and to the amusement of my host's, I was pissed after one glass. After being returned to the hotel, I went to my room and was sick as a dog! And I wanted to go home. The week flew by, and it was time to leave. It had been a great experience and one that I would once again replicate later on in life!

After the France trip, the elation soon passed back into sadness. I still craved attention from my parents, as everything I tried to do to gain attention was swept away. I would show dad my artwork, but he was always too busy to notice, and mum was always working. I felt alone and helpless, as I had no one to confide in, my behaviour got worse, and as a result, school life suffered.

Due to my frustrations, I started to write poetry. I suppose it was like keeping a diary, and at least I could share my feelings, even if no one would read them.

My interest in stories grew, and it was increased when one of my favourite authors was invited to talk to the school about his latest book. The author in question was Roald Dahl!

As I recalled, he was very tall, and it was his calming and encouraging words, that my love of literature grew. However, even though I was writing some great stories, I still struggled at math, and the pressure became intense, as did my embarrassment.

The worse thing was the taunts by the other kids, and so too, my sister Tina, and David when he would be allowed to come and visit from the home. A direct result, this only added to my frustrations, and the more I struggled, the more it increased, and I would shy away and hide in my room.

My mum and my eldest sister Theresa could see my pain and tried everything they could to help me get over the math problem.

They had bought vinyl records, which consisted of the times tables. They had thought that they would help. These records were red, and I would play them, but it just didn't sink in. In the end, I gave up, as I was so ashamed that I couldn't grasp it.

By now, my stress and anxiety levels increased, and the only way I could cope was to lash out at anyone who got in my way or scolded me for being 'thick'. Due to my behaviour, my parents were desperate to get to the bottom of it. They spoke to me asking me questions, why I felt the way I did? My only and best answer was 'I dunno'. Frustrated with my lack of response and not opening up to them, it was suggested that I would go and see a child psychologist.

The day arrived when I was to see the 'special doctor' as mum and dad explained to me, and I was left alone with him. He asked several probing questions and asked to perform a set of tasks, which I found easy. It was only when he gave me math questions that I struggled to cope and failed miserably.

It was deemed that I was extremely bright in normal activities, and I had a higher than average IQ. However, due to my math solving problems, I was diagnosed as being an imbecile! I have never understood that diagnosis, after all, how can I have a high IQ, and be an imbecile? It was many years later, and as an adult that doctors diagnosed me as having a numeric form of dyslexia. Its medical term is dyscalculia and is more common than was first thought.

Thank god for advances in medical science.

Even though I had been 'diagnosed,' my behaviour was also put down to eyesight problems. And the inability to read the blackboard. Due to this, I went to the opticians to get my first pair of NHS specs. The eyeglasses only added to my behaviour, as people called me four eyes, as well as thick, and moron. No wonder I was messed up, and it was far from the truth.

The answer to my parent's prayers came in the form of a T.V programme. This documentary showed a 'special school,' which allowed pupils to learn at their own pace, and good behaviour rewarded. I remembered mum asking me if I would like to go to a 'special school.' As I had also seen the programme, I said 'yes.' With that in mind, my parents went to see the school headmistress and discussed if they knew of any schools within the London Borough of Ealing. With inquiries made and an agreement with the headmistress and other members of staff, they unanimously agreed that it would help me.

It was now late September 1976 and was the start of a new term. I had been given time off school and was going on a 'day out' to visit my new school. The school was Cavendish, and its location was in Drayton Manor area of Ealing. As we entered the road to where the school was, I noticed that there was another school, on the same street. To my relief, the first school we came to be a nursery, and Cavendish was the other school. Dad parked the car, and we all walked through the entrance.

What struck me was how small it was. As we stood in the entrance hall, the headmistress greeted us. Her name was Mrs Colley, and she was a warm, kindly person with a vibrant smile and made my parents and myself very comfortable. We all went into her office, and she spoke in length about the aim of the school. The school had arranged for another pupil to show me around the school while the adults discussed my case further.

I was taken out by and shown around by Martin, a tall, slightly overweight, long blond-haired kid. We seemed to hit it off straight away, as he told me I looked like Suzi Quattro, a well-known glam rock artist at the time. Although he could talk as his hair was longer than mine!

Martin introduced me to Barta, the school nurse. Barta was great, she was around 58, and was only a few years away from retiring. I asked Martin should we call her Miss. He just laughed and said, 'No, mate, we ain't gotta do that here'.

At first, I was shocked at his comments, but I knew that I would fit in. Martin was a great tour guide. We went to see the rest of the teachers. First was Sholto, next came Ron, then Wendy. Next was Ren's, the carpentry teacher, and Ren's was his nickname, his full name was John Reynolds. Afterwards, I met Richard and Mark Bolton, or Bolton as he was to be called. Finally, there was Paula, the arts and craft teacher. When Martin had introduced me to the staff, he showed me around the school, which, due to its size, took a minute.

I immediately liked the place and hoped mum and dad was as impressed as I was, after meeting Colley. When I returned to her office, I went to sit by them, and they explained that I would be starting the following Monday. It was at this point that I knew that I would be part of a school programme, which would cater to my needs. For me, Monday couldn't come quick enough, and I was so excited when it arrived. It was a new school and a fresh start to the beginning of my new life.

Chapter Five

Cavendish

I remembered my first day at Cavendish like it was yesterday. Due to the distance from where I lived, we were picked up by school minibus. That was a first for me, as I had always walked to school. The minibus arrived at 8.00 am, and Margaret, who was the chaperone, greeted me.

Our driver was Tony, and both of them were amazing and looked after our welfare. I was the first pupil on the bus, and we made several other stops to pick up others, these would be my companions not only at school but also as travelling partners.

As I arrived at Cavendish, I felt a little nervous, but excitement at the same time. Colley, who along with Martin, showed me to my classroom, once again greeted me. I was introduced to Richard and Bolton, who were to be my form tutors. After being introduced to them and the rest of my classmates, we set to work.

Describing my form tutors, Richard was tall slightly a gangly man, with long blonde hair sported a pair of NHS thick-rimmed glasses. He had a strange way to him, and although I didn't know it at the time, he was to be part of my life in ways, I could never imagine, but would soon become apparent and disgusting in its manner.

Bolton was very different from Richard, and it was slightly shorter with a thick mop of short light brown curly hair, he also sported a moustache I was very physical in appearance. To me, Bolton was a much more genuine man than Richard.

To my horror, the first lesson was maths! My heart sank, and I felt sick. However, my concerns were short-lived, as I realised that I was not alone, and I was helped by Richard and Bolton and was put at ease, as the atmosphere was laid backed and relaxed.

The best part was the lesson was only 15 minutes, and for the first time, there was no pressure on me to be as good as the rest. We were allowed to talk, and eat sweets, something which was never heard of while I was at Northolt CFM. Also, we were allowed to call the teachers by their first or last name. If anyone of us wanted, we would talk at any time, and I heard some kids swearing, and thought they would be in trouble. I waited to hear either Richard or Bolton chastise them, but no, they didn't bat an eyelid.

At first, it was a shock, but that soon passed, and I was joining in with the rest of them. There wasn't even any more learning to do, the maths was all the teachers taught us, and the rest of our time was that we were encouraged to concentrate on a project of our own choice. They also explained that when complete it, we would be getting a project prize, which would be any toy, or model we wanted.

I couldn't believe it; it was like I had died and gone to heaven. After our 'lessons,' we had a break and went to play outside. As I was new, Martin was by my side, introducing me to the other pupils, and he showed me the rest of the school and its facilities.

Behind the school was the playing fields, surrounded by a wooded area, and in-between was an old wooden structure, which we called the 'fort!' Although the field wasn't as big as some, it was big enough to hold football matches and sports day. After the break, we went inside, and on to our next 'lesson,' which was art. Paula was the teacher, and she was like the rest of the staff, very friendly and understanding of our needs, as all of us pupils, had some kind of behavioural problems, and learning difficulties.

I loved art at Cavendish; we used real clay and were encouraged to be as artistic as we liked. Paula was particularly adept at the potter's wheel and showed me how to use it to great effect not only that she was a fantastic artist in her own right.

For the first time, I felt like someone was listening to me. But all too often, the lesson finished too soon. After packing away the art materials, we headed off to lunch. I loved eating school dinners at Cavendish, and I know it may sound unrealistic compared to school meals I had at my previous schools.

However, as Cavendish comprised of only 16 pupils and eight staff, the meals were incredible, as the cooks weren't under pressure.

I would go as far as to say that it was like eating a home-cooked meal that your mum would prepare. The only difference was the desserts were always special, before going to Cavendish, I had only seen a chocolate éclair in a baker's shop, let alone ate one.

The best thing was there was always seconds of dinner and dessert, and hardly any food was left on the plate, especially when we had desserts as we could only dream about, and if it's anything to go by, my first real day at Cavendish was a real tonic. I felt alive again.

When I got home, I was buzzing with excitement and chatted for hours with my parents. I must have bored them to tears and my sisters. But I didn't care. It was as if I had been reborn again and given a second chance at life. In many ways, it must have been a relief to mum and dad, as they could breathe easier knowing that I was happy and contented at last.

The next day was just like the first, being such a small school, we were a very close-knit family. Everybody knew each other, and I made friends very quickly. My best friend at Cavendish was Chris, he was a passionate football supporter, and his love was West Ham.

Incidentally, mine is Queens Park Rangers, and at the time, they were an exceptional team. Chris and I had a special bond and were forever out on the playing field, honing our skills on the footie pitch. I liked to play in goal, as my hero at the time was

Phil Parkes, the Q.P.R goalkeeper, and I had dreamed that one day, I would be like him.

Chris, on the other hand, was an outfield player and likened himself to Trevor Brooking, who was West Ham's star player. I have to say that Chris was a very talented player. We would play in all weathers and would come in soaked to the skin and covered from head to foot in thick mud. It didn't matter, as we would head off to the toilets and wash off the mud. Most of it would, of course, be left all over the floor sinks and even down the hallways.

After washing and getting changed, we would give Barta our muddy kit, and she would stick them in the washing machine, while the caretaker would be cleaning up our mess. I would never be allowed to get away with it at my previous schools. Don't get me wrong; Cavendish wasn't without its discipline or rules.

The only difference was that we had a student's council, which were referred to as justices.

These justices were not only voted for by us kids, but they were also presided over by the chief judge, who was also one of us kids. Although Colley would sit in when there was a call for it, the ultimate decision was left to the justices, under her expert guidance.

Although I had many friends, due to all of us having different behavioural and emotional problems, it wasn't without fault or its fair share of grievances. One such occasion, I was sitting in the play car and was approached another kid called Chris, or pissy Chrissy as he was called. I had minded my own business, and he started calling me names, and pulling me about, as he thought that I had muscled in, and pushed him out of the car.

Chrissy accusation was far from the truth, I snapped, and I hit him, and we fought, with Chrissy coming off worse. After the fight was broken up, I started to walk to the canteen for lunch, when suddenly; Martin grabbed me from behind. 'I revenge for hurting Chrissy,' he muttered.

Being a large frame, he pinned me to the ground, and I had to use all my strength to wrestle free, from his clutches. And this infuriated Martin, who was crying his eyes out, due to rage, not fear! As he came at me again, Ali, another huge kid, restrained him. I looked at Ali, who shouted for me to run, and I did, straight to the canteen to get lunch.

I heard Martin screaming and shouting, and by now he was being restrained and calmed by Bolton. Although Martin was a kid, due to his immense strength and rage, he managed to escape Bolton's clutches, and he flew at me, while I was sitting down and eating. Fortunately for me, Bolton and now Richard managed to grab him before did any real damage.

The next day in assembly, I thanked Martin for not killing me and awarded him 30 points. I also awarded Ali 30 points for helping me; of course, I thanked Richard and Bolton, for their intervention. The student with the most points at the end of the year was awarded a special gift.

It was fast approaching my first Christmas at Cavendish. It was a magical time, as we were all involved in making decorations and decorating the tree in the entrance hall. By now, I had grown in confidence, thanks to the understanding and support of the staff.

Due to them, I had been allowed to pay back my parents and family by proving my worth. Although we didn't have lessons as such, I had improved in maths, which I never had before, which was due to the excellent staff encouragement and understanding of kids with special needs. It was almost like a bond that never existed with the teachers I had before.

With my newfound freedom and growing confidence, I had excelled in art and carpentry. So much so, that I had made dad a fantastic tool chest and other handmade gifts for the rest of my family for the upcoming Christmas. I had also drawn a picture of the headmistress Colley for her office, and several others for the staff room.

Colley had informed me that a visitor had remarked that I had a talent and even offered to buy the picture hanging in her office for £15.00, a vast sun back then.

Thankfully Colley loved it so much, that she declined the tempting offer.

Although I was happy, there were still things that I missed at home. The main one was my brother David. Mum and dad told us that he would be coming home for Christmas, which didn't go down to well with my sisters; however, I wanted to see him.

Three weeks before the big event, we were all watching the T.V; it was dark and freezing. Just as we had settled down to watch a film, there was constant knocking at the door. As I opened it, to my surprise, it was my brother David, and he was just standing there freezing his arse off. He smiled and walked past me. As he walked into the lounge, my parents almost fell off their chairs in shock.

As David stood there, he broke down and cried his eyes out. When I saw this, my heart sank, as I felt so sorry for him. He went to sit down and still sobbing, and he explained that he had a fight with another boy and had run away from the children's home. In his haste to leave, he had no shoes or coat and was barefooted.

He had run 20 miles and was in a terrible state! I remembered him begging my parents to allow him to come home for good. But apart from them allowing him to stay for a night, they contacted the home the same night, and they returned him the next day.

Although he was their son, and in desperate need of their love, they couldn't show it toward him, which saddened me, as seeing him like this wanting a cuddle and some affection from mum and dad made me feel for him, and I cried also.

As David stayed in my room at night, we talked, and although I was younger than him by a few years, I told him that no matter what, he was still my brother and I love him. As I recalled, we both cried and hugged each other.

The next morning as my dad drove him away, he turned and smiled at me before waving. He looked dejected and alone, I felt his pain, I also wondered when I would ever see him again, and I hoped that it would have been soon

At Cavendish, it was now the end of the winter term, and our last day before the Christmas break was fantastic. We were all given presents from the staff members, and they had laid on a Christmas party for us all. I felt so special and didn't want to go for the break, as I would miss my friends and the teachers. However, I felt proud that I had presents of my own to give to my family, and couldn't wait to place them under the tree, so reluctantly I left to go home.

As the big day arrived, we were all around the tree, and my family loved the gifts I made for them. I remember ed my dad opening the present that I had made for him. It was a toolbox that he'd always wanted, and it had taken me two months to make.

Dad smiled at his gift, after he had opened all his other presents, and saw that they were new tools of which he had requested. That was another magical family Christmas as all the family was there. Even my eldest brother Peter showed his face, so a great end to my year, with a New Year to come, and a new term just around the corner.

It was now 1977, and the new term arrived, which was a relief for me, as although Christmas and New year was great, I couldn't wait to start school again! That was an unusual feeling for me, as I had always hated school, but Cavendish was different, it was fun to learn, the staff were great, and so were my new friends.

The first day back at school was just as fun as it was before the Christmas break. Unfortunately, there were a few changes, which I couldn't understand, and only found out the reason later on in life. The first change was that my best mate Chris had left along with his mum Wendy, who was one of the teachers and was a very wonderful person, who through her personal experiences with Chris made her the ideal candidate, for kids with special needs.

The other change was that I had been moved out of Richard and Bolton's classroom, and moved into a smaller one with four others, and was now run by Bolton only. Again, I understood why, later on, which will become clear later on in the book. The new changes didn't matter, as Bolton was a first-class teacher, as all of the staff were.

Under Bolton's supervision and guidance, I flourished, and my schoolwork improved significantly. Everyone liked me, and my name was put forward to become a justice. I was elated when I was chosen, and became a firm member of the judges when we met for 'trials.'

The ultimate accolade was after a short while; I became the chief justice and proved my worth on numerous occasions. The worst-case that I had to preside and give sentence on was when Ali kicked Chrissy in between his legs, with such force, that Chris ended up in the hospital. The justices and I had to call a 'court,' at short notice; such was the seriousness of the case. The sentence was overwhelmingly agreed to, which was to exclude Ali for three months. We fell short about expelling him for good after the evidence proved that it was Chrissy had provoked Ali and smashed up his bike.

As I have said, I was never short of friends at Cavendish. Well let's face it, with such a small school, it was hard not to. Apart from my old football mate Chris, Martin had now left. Martin had a violent temper more so than the rest of us kids, and it was deemed that he needed more one to one care.

If my memory serves me right, here are the rest of the cast; Eric, Ali, Warren, Chrissy, Edgar, Trudy (a tomboy) Rosemary, Mike, Alan (a talented musician) Ronald, Tony, Brian, Martin, and my good mate Chris, and myself.

With Wendy now left, Pauline, another lovely lady, replaced her. I used to visit Pauline in the library whenever I could, she was not only very understanding she was very good looking, and I must admit, I did have a crush on her.

As I was a keen footballer, Bolton thought it would be good to build a team.

Bolton was at the time a health fanatic, and part of his duties was to take sports.

Now as I have said the playing field was tiny, in fact, it was only the size of a five-a-side pitch. Even the goals were for five-aside. Even so, he got all us boys playing and also encouraged the girls.

In the end, he picked the best team which consisted of me in goal, Ali, Edgar in defence, with Warren and Chrissy in mid-field and attack. The rest were the substitutes.

Bolton had arranged a match with another special needs school just a short walk away from Cavendish.

We started well, but then they scored an easy goal, and with that, I went to pieces, and couldn't save myself, let alone a ball. I was having a nightmare of a game, and they were 5-1 up by half time.

Warren, who although a friend, was always wanting to be the centre of attention, took over the role of goalkeeper, and due to my frustration, I stormed off and cried my eyes out.

It was Barta who calmed me down. It didn't matter that Warren took over my place, as he conceded a further eight goals, and we lost 13-1.

Anyway, the following week, we were to play them again at their ground. We had been practising all week and knew we could win. So armed with our game plan, we walked the short distance to their school and prepared to battle once again.

Bolton kept the same team, as the week before, only this time, we were fantastic. I played a blinder and saved two penalties. Warren was also on top form as he scored six goals, Ali had a brace, Chrissy scored 1, and Edgar slotted home 4. And all that before half time!

The second half wasn't as frantic as the first, and Bolton made several substitutions. Ali made way for Ronald, Chrissy was swapped with Mike and Edgar allowed Tony to come on. Only Warren and I stayed on, by the time the game ended, our new subs had scored another eight between them, final score 21-0. A momentous match and revenge and honour had been satisfied. Triumphantly we walked back to Cavendish, and celebrated, with a special lunch, and instead of the usual water, a vast range of fizzy pop was awaiting us. So, all's well, that end's well.

Cavendish seemed to bring out the best in me, and as such, my home life improved significantly. I enjoyed being at home, and my confidence grew, and I felt that I could hold a conversation with my parents more easily. Also, as I was at a different school to my mate Andy ward, we had more to talk about, and our friendship grew.

Andy and I would go out at every opportunity and stayed out as long as we could. As we had some playing field nearby, we would often go and explore and make camps. One camp we made was all wood, which we had found, but alas, it was without a roof. However, that small problem was solved as dad had bought a large piece of plywood, which would be ideal.

The problem was that he had purchased it for another project. That didn't stop Andy and me from using it in our plans, so we 'acquired' it. Obviously, with such a large piece of timber, it was bound to be noticed that it had disappeared from the front garden.

When dad arrived home, he went mad and questioned me as to where it was. I just stared blankly at him and said I didn't know, as I had been down the park all day. Dad knew I was lying, but couldn't prove that I had taken it, although he did notice that some of his tools had gone missing, so I didn't get away with it for too long, and boy did I felt his full wrath! The only good thing that came out of this was me, and Andy had a great camp and used it every day.

Back at Cavendish, after 'lessons,' the rest of the day was our own. We all had bikes, which we had either bought with us or had made from scratch with the skilful help from Ren's. My friend Eric had the best bike, which he made in the workshop.

It was a red 5-speed racer, and it was beautiful. When Eric first brought it in, it was a complete wreck. However, after he had lavished hours of love and care on it, the bike was a marvel to behold. All of us loved nothing more than riding these bikes in the playground or having timed races around the building.

At other times, we would build ramps and see how far we could jump. At first, it was just jumping the furthest, then Ali suggested that we skipped over people. A great idea we thought, so without a care in the world, we would all take turns in jumping over the most kids in one attempt. Our exploits didn't go unnoticed, and we regularly had a captive audience from the builders on the site opposite.

Warren turned out to be a champion, and he lapped up the accolade for weeks after, which got tiresome after a while. As I explained earlier, there was a wooden structure called the fort I loved playing in this, as it was two-storey, with many exciting nooks and crannies.

Due to its age there always had to be a teacher around. It was just as a precaution when we played on it. Warren Ali, Eric, and I decided to play pirates and were chasing each other around the fort. I climbed up onto the upper storey and was 'swashbuckling,' when suddenly I slipped and hurt myself, much to the amusement of my fellow pirates who ran off, leaving me crying and in pain.

Richard, who had been outside, came to my aid and comforted me.

However, I was soon shocked back into reality, as he rubbed his hand over my genitals. I knew it wasn't right, but I thought it could have been a mistake.

However, this mistake as I saw it was anything but, as he has done it again only this time, he put his hand in between my legs, and he rubbed my genitals again. His actions made me feel sick, and I knew then that I had to escape his clutches.

I managed to get away from him, and ran off to see Barta, although I never told her what happened, and kept it a secret up until now. In fact, at the time of writing these other things have since come to light, of which I shall divulge later. However, I have to warn you all that it is not pleasant. And something that I haven't disclosed until I decided to write this book.

Chapter Six

Summer Camp

With the school summer holidays on their way, Cavendish like all schools in the borough was organising a school trip. It was an exciting prospect when it was announced. However, as I had been on two previously school trips at Northolt, I didn't rate my chances of going as like most family's money was tight.

The trip was in Wales, and it was another camping trip. I was given a parental consent letter and was nervous at handing it to my parents. As they read the letter, they had no problem in giving permission. It appeared that the total cost was £15.00 for two weeks.

Now I'm not sure if they were OK with the price, or if it was to get rid of me for the two weeks. Whatever their reasons, I was going and couldn't wait for it to arrive. Almost all the other kids' parents had agreed, apart from a couple, who had already arranged their family breaks.

The day arrived, and two minibuses were waiting for us. The staff, who had driver's licences, were to take it in turns to drive with the other members of staff were making their way to the site.

All of us were excited at the thought of camping and couldn't wait to set off. Richard was our driver for the first part of the journey, and Bolton was the co-driver.

As we set off, we started to sing, and the bus was alive with excited kids. Packed lunches were handed to us before we left, so we were well stocked with goodies, and swapped things that we didn't like. After several hours, we arrived at the camp, which was in a beautiful part of the Welsh countryside.

Several tents large and small had been pitched, and we all sat around before being told what the itinerary was to be. Some of the tents were for single occupancy, and as I was given one for myself. I was excited, as it meant that I could go and rest by myself whenever I wanted.

The first day was amazing, it was scorching hot, and the site was near a lake, naturally, as kids, we were to get stuck in and go swimming. None of us needed much encouragement as we dived in. Richard and Bolton soon joined us in the pool and were frolicking around in the water.

Although I was adept at swimming, Richard decided that he would make a beeline for me. He grabbed hold of me and suggested that I lay flat with him supporting my weight with his hands. He explained that it was to show me how to swim better.

At that time, I had forgotten about his indiscretion in the fort earlier in the year, so I trusted him implicitly, besides Bolton was nearby, so I felt safe.

After only a few minutes, I felt his hand slid down my body, and he slid his hands into my swimming trunks and touched my privates again. I struggled and managed to get away and out of the water.

I was so traumatised that I couldn't say anything, and just dried myself off and returned to my tent and sobbed.

My other friends knew nothing of what happened, and I could hear them laughing and joking, which brought me back to my senses. I wiped my eyes and pulled myself together and went back to join them.

Before I dived in, I saw Richard on the other side of the lake, seemingly oblivious of his actions!

At first, I was as nervous as hell, but that soon subsided, when Ali and Warren shouted for me to join them. After a few hours, we were called back to the site, for evening dinner. I had forgotten about the earlier incident and sat with my friends waiting for Barta and Colley to finish cooking.

Meanwhile, Bolton and Richard were pouring out drinks, I was relieved when Bolton poured mine out, and after tucking into dinner, I went to sit next to Paula and her husband, who had come to join us.

As we all sat together as a group around the campfire, the camp supervisor and owner sat with us and told us a ghost story about a drummer boy, that had died in a nearby field, and if we listened carefully, we could hear him playing his drum!

When dusk fell, we went to our tents to snuggle in for the night. As I slid inside my warm sleeping bag, I heard, it was Bolton and Richard coming around to ensure we were safe. I prayed that it wasn't going to be Richard. I pretended to be asleep when they came to my tent.

Bolton was seeing to Ali and Warren, who were sharing a tent, so it was left to Richard to check on me. He crawled inside and sat beside me. With my eyes shut tight, I could feel him come closer to my face. I could now feel his breath against my cheek, and my heart was pounding.

The more I wanted him to stop, the more he was trying to force his hand in between my legs. I kept moving to stop him from trying to touch me, I wanted to shout out, but the fear gripped me, and I felt paralysed and then able to do so.

By now, he had put his hand in my bag, and tried to touch me again. I was praying for him to stop, and at that point, it seemed my prayer had was as someone called his Richard's name, and he disappeared! As soon as he had gone, I closed the tent zip and placed my bag against the entrance.

After Richard had left, I felt safer. I climbed back into my sleeping bag and started to cry, must have been crying for some time, and cried myself to sleep. I fell into a deep sleep, but my dreams were laced with images of Richard, and I had a terrible nightmare.

I awoke with sounds of nature calling to me. It was another beautiful sunny day; I could hear the others, so I got up and washed before dressing. We had breakfast, and Richard winked at me. I desperately wanted to say something to Colley and the other teachers, but I just couldn't say a word, for fear that they wouldn't believe me, so I just smiled at him before I went with my friends to the lake.

Like the day before we had a great time swimming and messing around, there was a funny moment, when Ali dived in and got stuck in the mud. Although he had been frightened, he soon saw the funny side of it.

After lunch, the teachers had arranged for us to take a trip to the local village. Richard was the designated driver and was eating an apple and a drink. Ali, who was always impatient, kept shouting from the minibus for him to hurry up. Due to the constant berating instigated by Ali, Richard lost his temper and threw his drink and apple away.

For some reason, I felt sorry for him and asked Barta to keep another apple and drink aside for his return. When we were safely inside the minibus Richard, and the camp owner took us to the village. Now this village name was famous in Wales, as it's the longest name in the UK. It's called Llanfairpwllgwyngyllgo-gerychwyrndrobwllllantysiliogogogoch. The place is in Anglesey, and the name is difficult enough to pronounce when sober, try saying it after a few drinks! Those of us who went had a great time and decided to pronounce the name but ended up in fits of laughter.

After a few hours, it was time to go back to the camp. Warren decided that it was a good time to act up and was a pain in the neck. As the camp master was driving, he decided to make an example of Warren and stopped the bus. He spoke to Warren in an attempt to calm him down.

That just agitated Warren even more, so the camp master took him off the bus and left him there. Don't worry, after he dropped us all back at the camp; he did go back. By this time, Warren had learned his lesson and had calmed down. He never uttered another word for the rest of the night, so it was a peaceful night for all.

The camp was a fantastic place, but soon the break came to an end. Although it was a sad occasion, I still had another four weeks of summer to go. Most of the time Andy and I made the most of it and made more camps, although we did spend our other time at Walford High School's swimming pool, which would become my school later on.

The pool was always busy and was popular with every kid in the neighbourhood and beyond. Some days, it was so busy that it was almost standing room only! Nevertheless, it was a great source of amusement. As money was tight, pocket money was in short supply.

For me to have my own money, I looked at ways to find a weekend job. At first, I tried my hand at a paper round with Andy. The papers we delivered were from a local press; usually, they would be free if picked up from the shop. However, there was a small if they were delivered. The upshot of this was, we not only get make tips; we would also work it so we could skim some off the newsagent's charge!

Okay, it wasn't a fortune, but it kept us in sweets, and our favourite brand was 'Merrie Maid' chocolate-covered toffee's. I decided that I wasn't making enough money, so I asked at the Express dairy for a Saturday job. In those days, it was down to the milkmen to choose a Saturday boy/girl, and the money would come from their own pockets.

On my first time of trying, Tony, a great bloke and such a laugh took me on, but my god did he work me well, and I thoroughly earned the £5.00 he paid me. Most weekends I would make about £10.00 with tips, not bad money for an 11-year-old. Our delivery area was in Greenford the next town from where I lived in Northolt.

Part of the round was a road called Barbican. I remembered the first house, as the bill was always £1.74 and a half. The owner would always give me £1.75, and his passing comment would always be 'keep the half' Bloody tight sod he was, even at Christmas.

Some parts of it were in blocks of 3 storey flats. Tony would do the ground floor flats, and I would do the second and third floors and as I got to the top of one block and knocked on the door for payment. Richard, my teacher from Cavendish, opened it!

I was shocked, as I had no idea that he had lived there. At first, I didn't know what to do, but he handed me the money for the milk, and as I turned to go, he gave me a tip of 75 pence. Wow, I thought, and my opinion of him changed, perhaps he had felt guilty for his action at the summer camp? I thanked him, and I resumed the rest of the round.

Back at school, Richard came to speak to me, and asked how long I had been working on the milk round, and would I be there the following week. I told him that I had just started, and I would be staying, as Tony liked my personality. He seemed pleased for me and hoped to see me again the following weekend. I didn't think there was anything in it, so I thanked him, and carried on with what I was doing.

The weekend arrived at last, and again, I was out with Tony on the round. We followed the same route, and as usual ended up in Barbican where Mr 'keep the half' was as generous as ever, with his miserly tip, even Scrooge paid better than he did. Still, my big pay-day was just around the corner, or so I hoped. As I got to Richard's flat, the door opened before I knocked at it.

Standing there to my surprise wasn't Richard, but a portly slightly balding man grinning from ear to ear. He introduced himself as Peter, and that Richard had told him all about me. He seemed nice, and I made no connection, as to why he was there, or even how he knew Richard.

Again, he paid the milk bill as Richard had done the previous week, but he too gave me 75 pence, so I was happy. Due to the amount of money I was earning my sister Tina wanted a bit of the action, so reluctantly, I allowed her to come with me the following week.

So not only did I have her yacking away in my ear trying to impress Tony, but also, I had had to share my wages and tips! Thank God that she only came out once, as she found her own Saturday job working at the hairdresser's in the local shops on the Church Road 5 minutes from where we lived.

Each week I was there come rain or shine delivering the milk, and Peter and now Richard become good friends. It was almost my birthday, and Richard and Peter had invited me to their home for a birthday treat. I had asked my parents, and as they had met Richard at parents evening at Cavendish, they agreed.

The day of my birthday arrived, and Peter came over to pick me up. He had a white Renault 12 TL, which I found fascinating, as the only vehicle that I had been used to being in was my dad's yellow Minivan, which was the pits. Many were the time that Tina and myself would crouch in the back on a Friday night to watch my dad play in a band who used to meet in Paddington station. Compared to Peter's, it wasn't the best, and the good thing was that I sat in the front.

On the journey to their home, Peter told me that Richard had to go out, and it was only going to be the two of us. He explained that he trained social workers and was responsible for helping special needs children. As I walked through the front door for the first time, the smell oozing out of the room was terrific. Peter had cooked BBQ chicken. It was a first for me, as I had never eaten BBQ food before.

As we sat down, Peter lit a cigarette, and we sat there talking. I asked him what it was like to smoke, as although my parents smoked, I never tried it.

To my astonishment, he handed me the cigarette, and I puffed away. He also offered me a can of beer, which I declined. After a short while, Peter gave me a present, which turned out to be a model kit of a jumbo jet. He had even bought the paints and glue.

As we sat there talking, he would ask me strange questions about my home life. Being naïve, I openly answered them. Well, I had no reason why I shouldn't have. At the end of the evening,

Peter drove me back home. He was invited in for coffee of which my sister Theresa made, and he sat there talking to my parents, while I read my comic.

After he had left, my mum and dad talked to me, and told me that I wasn't allowed to see him anymore as he was 'queer' I never understood what they meant at the time, but what happened, later on, made me realise what they were on about, and it was something that I have kept hidden for over 30 years.

Chapter Seven

Moving On

Despite my parent's advice of not getting involved, I decided that I would ignore their advice, and when I explained the problem to Richard, he suggested that I take his and Peter's number, and ring them by reversing the charges. At first, I was worried that mum and dad would find out, so I left it for a while. After a few weeks, I plucked up the courage to do so. I used a phone box near the parade of shops at the target roundabout on the Church road.

After I got through, I spoke to Peter, who came to pick me up and drove me to his flat. I explained the situation as regards to my parent's advice. At that point, Peter laughed, and explained that he and Richard knew people in Government, Peter referred then as auntie Virginia and Uncle Leon, and they would be able to 'help me'.

It was only later on in life that I became aware that he was talking about MPs who were part of the government cabinet at that time. After hearing these words, I started to relax and had a great time with him at his house. After several hours Peter dropped me off again at the target roundabout and said that I could ring anytime should I require help.

Before getting out of his car, Peter gave me £5.00 'pocket money!' And this was a large amount of money in those days, and it was the start of a new friendship. I walked home with a pocket full of cash and armed with my excuses, I smugly walked indoors and lied to my parents as to where I had been, and never informed them about the money.

The school authorities decided that due to our age, Edgar, and myself were to be transferred to a mainstream school to catch up with schooling. It was because we were now twelve and would be entering our high schools after the summer break.

At first, I felt extreme sadness, as I would be leaving Cavendish and my good friends, however, it was required, as we had lost so much time 'enjoying' ourselves while being pupils at Cavendish. The school chosen was just a stone's throw from Cavendish, and we would still be picked up, so we had the best of both worlds, as we would even see our friends daily.

Drayton middle school was an old building of about 150 years or so, and it reminded me of my time at Northolt CFM before the new school was built. It had a walled playground and compared to Cavendish there were at least 100 pupils and staff.

TALL IN THE FACE OF ADVERSITY

My first day was somewhat daunting when I was introduced to my new schoolmates.

I needn't had worried as I settled in well, and my new schoolmates welcomed me into their environment. Due to the amount of schoolwork that we missed out on, we had to work hard to catch up with the other pupils. Edgar struggled as unbeknown to myself; he could hardly read or write. However, I flourished and settled in well, whereas Edgar had to have extra tuition.

However, it wasn't too long before my old destructive ways would reappear and show its ugly head.

The reason for this change was I came into a new environment that I was not used to, and the change in routine affected me. Cavendish was a school of about 20 pupils, and going to a larger school meant I was thrust into a new world.

I also had some enemies, who for some reason, didn't like me coming into the school at such a late stage and had decided to try and bully me. However, from what I had learned previously, I wouldn't allow them to do so, and with my temper, I would beat them black and blue, much to the dismay of the school.

The school authorities wanted to transfer me back to Cavendish. However, a resolution was reached, and I had a social worker assigned to me who helped me through my destructive ways.

After the intervention, I started to knuckle down and get back on track with my learning. I later became popular with the girls, and as we were all starting puberty, we would 'experiment' with each other, and would often disappear and 'snog' each other while touching each other's genitals.

All too soon, the fun was coming to an end, and it was quickly approaching the summer break, and soon we would all be going our separate ways. It was a month before the break, and the school had decided to do a sponsored walk. As I was still in touch with the teachers at Cavendish, I persuaded them all to sponsor me. After the walk, I returned to collect my sponsor money from my Cavendish contacts.

I arrived at the back of the staff room and was greeted by Bolton, who congratulated me, and paid his money. He also paid Mrs Colley and Richards money. However, the temptation of having the money turned me into a monster, and I became greedy, and returned the next day, to get the cash from Colley, Richard, and Bolton.

At first, I was nervous and hid out of the way until Bolton and Colley had left for the day. I walked to the back door of the staff room, where Richard greeted me. To my surprise, Bolton hadn't told him that I had been the previous day and collected the money, so I got paid again. (I have to say that I felt guilty that I had done it and went back sometime later to repay the money).

After Richard paid me, he offered me a lift home, so I accepted. However, as it was a roasting hot day, he first suggested that I went back to his flat for a cooling drink. Even though I was apprehensive due to what he had done, he seemed different, so I had no reason not to trust him.

When we got in, I sat down while Richard went to get the drinks as I was drinking and stuffing myself with the goodies that he provided. As I did so, he started to rub my head and back of my neck. I froze in terror and felt sick at his touch.

However, my survival instincts kicked in, and I stopped him in his tracks, by telling him that my mum and dad would be coming home soon. That snapped him into reality, and Richard agreed to drop me off, when I returned home, I rushed upstairs and threw up, such was my fear. Mum being worried asked what had happened, but as usual, I lied and told her that it was something I ate, and I was feeling poorly.

I must have been a good liar, as mum believed me, and I went to my room, where I silently cried myself to sleep.

The next day I was subdued and was moody, as I got to school, I just wanted to be left alone. However, another pupil from Drayton Manor high school picked on me, as I walked the short distance through the park after being dropped off at Cavendish.

Even at the age of twelve, I was tall for my age, and would always stand up for myself, so naturally, I retaliated and knocked him to the ground. I started to knock seven bells out of him until his mates jumped in and helped him. I must say I got a good kicking from them, but by God, I got as many of them before they got me.

After they had gone, I was left battered and bruised, I walked to school, and was seen by the school nurse, who cleaned me up before I went to see the head and explain what had happened. The police were called, and I told them what happened in the park. However, nothing came from their investigation, as the other boys were too scared to speak, as they were also were embarrassed with getting a good hiding from a primary school kid, so great result all round.

It was the last week at Drayton Primary, and it was a party atmosphere. As we were classed as the seniors, an end of term disco was arranged for the last day. All of us were allowed to decorate the school hall, and we busied ourselves with making the decorations and food ready for the evening's entertainment. We all turned up in our finest clothes and danced to the music of the time.

I remembered that one of the girls fancied me, so we ended up having a bit of a fling behind the school stage. Okay so it wasn't full sex, more like sticky fumbling, but for a twelve-year-old, it was exciting all the same. The disco finished at 9 pm sharp, and before we parted our separate ways, we exchanged phone numbers. Though I lost contact with them all but remembered the short time, I had known them all with great fondness.

It was now the summer holiday, and not much to do apart from living my last summer as a kid, for coming up was my enrolment into high school. I spent a lot of my time with Andy and boy did we make the most of it. Day after day, we would explore the 'woods' near to where we lived.

Andy and I, and our other friends would make camps, go bird nesting, but best of all was spending hours at our future high school open-air swimming pool. However, I still had time to go and visit Peter at his flat. I had told him about Andy, and he suggested that I bring him along, so I did.

Peter would come and pick us up usually at the weekends and take us both out to various places. On occasions, we would take it in turns to drive his car. And I mean drive, as Peter would typically take us to remote areas or parks and allow us to take full control of his vehicle.

Initially, like most new drivers, we meander all over the road or track. But after several lessons, we mastered the controls and were soon driving like professionals. When we got bored, Peter would take over, and Andy and I used to sit on the door edge and hold onto the roof straps with our feet firmly on the seats while Peter was left driving faster and faster at our command. It was like a drug to us, with our top half hanging out of the window laughing like hyenas.

Most adults would frown on this type of behaviour, but with Peter, there was nothing but praise for our actions and was actively encouraged. We wanted for nothing, if we wanted something, we just asked, and he gave us. Sometimes, Richard was around, but mostly it was only Peter.

It was if we were one big happy family, but with the bonus that he showed us with money every time we went to see them. I can honestly say that summer 1978 was the best summer I had ever experienced, but all too soon, it was over, and my new grown-up life was about to start at Walford.

The last weekend before the start of a new term, mum took me out to the school outfitters to buy my new school uniform. I had a black blazer, black trousers, white shirts, and a black pull-over with the school crest on the breast, which was also on the blazer breast pocket, black shoes, and a black-tie with a red and gold diagonal pattern. I was now fully fitted out in my new school ensemble, including PE kit and on Monday morning, I would be starting my first day at Walford!

As it was the last weekend, as soon as I got home from shopping with mum, I hung up my new clothes and went to call on Andy. The first thing we did was to ring up Peter, and he collected both of us. Both Andy and I wanted to go to Chessington zoo (now called Chessington world of adventures).

Peter, as usual, would be happy to oblige us, and with Richard making up the fourth, we headed off. A few hours later, we arrived, and couldn't wait to go in. It was a scorcher of a day, and after seeing the animals, the men bought us the biggest ice creams you have ever seen.

We both stood near the Giraffe enclosure and started to tuck into our ice creams, while Peter and Richard stood back to take photos. As we were posing, all of a sudden, a huge blue tongue ripped the ice creams out of our hands; it seemed the giraffe needed cooling down!

Neither of us complained though, as it was quite funny seeing a giraffe eating our ice creams. And besides, there was always plenty more goodies to be had. For those of us who remember, Chessington at that time had a funfair, so we headed off to enjoy ourselves on the rides, and amusement stands.

Like all great adventures, it all finished too soon, and we had to make our way home. We were dropped off at Lime Trees Park, with a pocket each full of cash, and a head full of great happy memories.

Chapter Eight

Walford

My first day at Walford was still fresh in my memory as if it were yesterday. It was a chilly start to the morning, and mum was at home having a day off. She had asked me to go to her car, as she had a parcel that she left in it. As I handed her the package, she smiled and gave it back to me.

Confused, I asked what it was, mum kept smiling and told me to open it. To my surprise, it was a beautiful set of Parker pens, including my first fountain pen, along with ruler compass, protractors, and pencils, all in a beautiful case. With tears in my eyes, I hugged mum before putting on my blazer, placing the new gift in my inside pocket.

Mum was as proud as punch and cuddled me before I set off for my first day at my new school. As she waved me off, Andy met me, and we both walked the short distance down to the school. It felt strange walking through the enormous blue gates that we had walked past many times. But now we were entering them on our way to the school complex.

The driveway up to the school building seemed to go on forever. However, that could have been down to our nerves and mixed emotions. As we got to the main entrance, we were all ushered into the main hall. We felt so small against the background of the school, and the older kids were watching us, which added to our apprehension.

At the front of the hall was a stage, and we all sat down, waiting for the head to address us and welcome us to the school. The head was a Mr Yeager, a tall thin man, and the deputy Mr Clarke, and the heads of year Mr Pegram a Mrs Tew accompanied him. Mr Yeager explained what we were to expect, and what the school rules were.

He then passed on the 'baton' to Mr Clarke, who placed us in our houses, and the heads of year read out our names to which form teacher we were to be assigned. To my dismay, Andy and I would be in different forms and would only see each other at break times.

My form teacher was a Mrs Walker, who was one of the home economics teachers, and our form was 2WK. As I joined my new classmates, I felt nervous, as none of us had ever met each other. I'm sure my new comrades felt equally the same. When we were all assembled, we followed our new form teacher to our form room, which was in the home economics block.

Mrs Walker explained that in the future, we would line-up, wait for her to lead us to the class. She also said we would have to sit down at our desks as she called our names from the register. Afterwards, we had to fill in our timetables, as to what and where our lessons would be held. After a while, we all started to get to know each other, and our nerves seemed to dissipate.

I found myself sitting next to an Asian lad named Ajay. It just so happened that I had gone to school with his brother Naresh, while at Northolt CFM.

As Mrs Walker read out the register, she called out an unusual name, or so I thought at the time.

The name was Isaac, at first, we all sniggered, much to the annoyance to Mrs Walker, as she calmed the situation, I turned and smiled at Isaac, and we hit it

off. After that initial somewhat timid first introduction, Isaac and I became good friends and were inseparable. I was closer to him than I was my own brother's. Isaac was an only child and lived in Greenford about a 30-minute bus ride away. His parents were Northern Irish, and his dad was a strict disciplinarian, and his mum was a lovely cuddly woman.

At break time, I met up with Andy again, and we talked about our first morning. He was with some new friends, and I introduced him to Isaac before the bell rang again and we returned to our classrooms. As I lived right behind the house, I went home for school dinners.

At lunch, I went home, and mum had made some sandwiches. I talked about my morning and must have bored mum to tears, as I babbled on without taking a breath it seemed. After lunch, I returned to school and went to the sports hall to be given the times for P.E and games.

All of us sat down on the rows of wooden benches facing the P.E masters. In turn, our names were called, and we were assigned our dates. When it came to my turn, the head of P.E asked if I was related to Peter, as I was, he told me to go and check a roll of honour stuck to the wall and count how many school records Peter had achieved.

I stood in awe and counted the numerous records my brother had recorded, in all, I counted 14 records for school and county, although I was told there were more than that, and that I had to live up to his career. These records were still not beaten by the time I left school, and I am proud to be his brother, although we don't see eye to eye even now.

The remainder of the day was made up of going to different areas of the school and getting used to where we would be going to be taught. Before the end of the school day, we returned to our form classes to be sure that we had everything we needed to know for our first real day at school.

When I got home, my head was buzzing with the day's events. Just like at lunchtime, I babbled on about my day, and couldn't wait for the next day, after meeting new friends. After telling mum all about my day, I changed out of my uniform and went over to Andy's house, and we talked about the day's events while walking to the woods near our homes.

We had an hour before we had to go home for our evening tea, and we didn't waste a moment of it. As dusk fell, we went back and said our goodbyes before going in. Mum was still cooking, and I sat and watched some T.V. After a few moments, dad arrived, not only did our dog Mungo alert us to his arrival, but dad always seemed to have his unique way of letting us know he was home.

I'll explain his daily ritual upon returning home. In our kitchen, we had a wall-mounted can opener, which dad had put up at head height. He used to walk through the 'backdoor' and walk straight into the opener cracking his head. Stumbling back, he would shout obscenities, which was funny enough. However, as he stumbled, he would bang into work surface with such force, that the five salvers stored on the top of the wall unit, would slide off, and each one would drop on his head one by one followed by more obscenities. By this time, all of us were pissing ourselves laughing.

Although dad didn't see the funny side, he would pick up the salvers, and place them in the same position as they were before they fell. It was if he was setting himself for the same punishment the following day, and he never failed to disappoint us all.

He would enter the living room holding his hankie on the part of his head, which had been cut, and still muttering, would sit down, and remove his shoes. As he did so, Mungo would come up to greet him, and dad would always say to him 'go away dog, drop dead, die!' Again, it was a source of amusement to us all. I just like to point out, that dad loved Mungo, although he would never admit to it.

The next day at school, we started our first real day of learning. The first lesson of the day was science. None of us had ever been in a science lab before, and we were intrigued by all the equipment that we would be using. The classroom was unlike the others that we had been into, as we were sitting on high stools with long benches instead of individual desks.

Attached to the benches were gas taps, which would become a source of amusement later on in my school life. As I was at a stage of puberty, I was starting to get interested in girls. So much so, that I decided to sit next to one of the girls named Lisa. I have to say she was gorgeous, and her friend Susan was beautiful too.

As the lesson started, I sat closer to her and began to flirt with her, but as hard as I tried, I could never win her over, so after several attempts gave up. The day seemed to go quickly, and I spent most of my time with my new friend Isaac. I also made friends with Colin Brennan and his mate Dave.

My other new friends were Ajay, Roland, and Tony Barton. Throughout the week, I attended different classes and to various lessons which included Music, Maths, English, Art, metalwork, woodwork, geography, home economics, French, and PE

The first week ended, and as excited as we were, we had to talk to anyone who would listen. Andy's first port of call and mine was to ring up Peter and go and see him. As usual, he would pick us up at our regular preferred place. This time we took Andy's younger brother Philip. Peter didn't mind, he liked that, and all three of us went to his house.

When we arrived, Richard was also waiting, and they suggested by then that we should go out shopping at the toyshop. With all of us piled into the car, we headed off to the toyshop. As Andy and Philip were Jehovah witnesses, they never celebrated Christmas or birthdays and coupled with the fact that they were from a one-parent family, money was not easy to come by.

As we entered the store, their eyes lit up. To say they were kids in a sweet shop would be an understatement, and the excitement was overwhelming. All of us looked at every toy, some we could only dream about, as the prices were way beyond what our parents could ever afford. However, with Peter and Richard, money was no object.

I picked out a radio-controlled truck, while Andy picked out a kite, with Philip opting for a simple clockwork toy. We couldn't wait to play with our new toys, and we all headed off to Horsenden hill where Andy used his kite for the first time.

As he got his kite airborne, I opened my truck and drove it around. Philip wanted to play with his gift at home, so I allowed him to drive my new truck.

After several hours, we had our fill of playing with each other's toys, so we packed them away. Before we returned to Peter's car, we were all treated to ice creams, so all in all, we had been spoiled. Peter, who was a keen photographer, had bought his camera, and we posed for photos which either Peter or then Richard would take.

We thought these were innocent pictures, but looking back, I now know these were to the sexual gratification of Peter and Richard, as we were in a clinch with either of them.

We didn't realise it back then, but today it's commonly known as grooming. After a rewarding day and for me to explain why I had been given an expensive gift, Peter bought some cigarettes and suggested that I tell my parents that a friend's dad worked in a cigarette factory and that my new truck was an unwanted toy.

After arriving at home, I handed the cigarettes to mum and dad and lied about where I had been, and why I had a new toy. I explained to parents what Peter told me to say, to my surprise, the plan worked, and nothing more was said about it. The other lie was not aimed at me, but to Philip.

As he was profoundly deaf, Andy explained to him not to say anything about Peter and Richard, as it was a secret, and he agreed. My life was like that at that time, and my secret was safe. Also, even though I had introduced Andy and Phil to Peter and Richard, they asked if I knew more boys they could befriend.

As I was a now good friend with Isaac, I asked him at my next opportunity if he would like to meet them. Without hesitation, Isaac agreed, and it was arranged for the next available weekend. Mondays were a good day for me, as in the evening, I would meet up with Isaac, and we would go to the 'spaceship,' which was a juvenile disco in Greenford, so-called due to its unique shape.

The spaceship was a great place to go for us kids, as it allowed us to let off steam. Okay, it wasn't a nightclub, but for now, it was a meeting place to meet girls. On my first outing with Isaac, we hit it off with two beautiful girls named Tracy and Sarah. I went off with Tracy and kissed her senseless. Isaac was also doing well with his new 'bird'.

Back at school, I was settling in well and was making new friends. However, my class clown act would always rear its ugly head, and I was constantly in trouble. I had also now started to smoke more compared to the occasional cigarette. I had begun pinching my dad's tobacco, of which he never knew, and I never told him, sorry, dad.

Once again, the weekend arrived, and as usual, it was time to make my call to Peter. This time Isaac came with me, and Peter and Richard made him feel as welcome as they had made me. As per usual, they asked us if we wanted anything in the way of gifts.

As Isaac had introduced me to the sport of fishing, we both opted for fishing equipment. Peter took both of us to the best fishing tackle shop in Greenford named Tooks. Isaac opted for a new rod, which was bright yellow, whereas I needed a fishing box seat. As I recall the rod and seat were well over £150.00, an extreme amount of money back then, but Peter didn't bat an eyelid.

Of course, being given such expensive gifts meant that both of us would have to lie to our parents as to where we had got them. I told mine that Isaac's parents had bought me my box seat, and Isaac did the reverse, again neither of our parents found out the truth.

As Isaac and my friendship blossomed, Andy took a back seat, as he had other friends of which to hang around with, one of them was Kevin Hyland, and his mates from the Lime trees estate, of which were all bullies. Due to his association with them, I decided to keep my distance and hung around with him when they weren't around.

With Andy not in the picture, Isaac and I were inseparable, and he became my new best friend. It was like we were brothers instead of friends, and we had great fun and had no shortage of girlfriends.

I always visit Peter and Richard with Isaac in tow. As we were growing up and more sexually in tune, we would speak to Peter about girls and our feelings and wanted to see what it would be like to have sex. Peter and Richard didn't seem fazed by our questions about sex and suggested that we watched some films that they had at their flat.

It had been arranged that they would set up a film day at their flat. When we arrived, we saw they had set up a cine-projector in the lounge. Richard had to go out, and myself, Isaac and Peter sat down to what we both thought to be girls on film.

Peter turned on the projector, and the film started. To our surprise, it was a porno film!

However, this wasn't girls, and it was boys! As we sat back and watched the movie with boys of different ages performing varying sexual acts with each other. We felt a little apprehensive but watched it all the same.

Peter seemed to relish watching the films, but Isaac and I were disappointed, as we wanted to see naked girls. Both of us asked if he could get movies with girls and boys having sex. Peter smiled and agreed, as his friend Charles could get some from Sweden where he lived and worked.

It didn't take long for porn films to arrive, but before we saw the movie, we came to see Peter who put on another film involving boys. Again, we didn't complain, as we thought what the heck, as soon we would be watching girls having sex. As usual, Peter seemed very excited about watching the boys in the film, and we could see that he appeared to be aroused. Isaac and I didn't feel anything and thought it was a good laugh.

It was now our time to watch our film. As Peter changed the reels, we could hardly contain our excitement and started to get aroused ourselves with the anticipation of what we were going to see. The film was terrific. For the first time, we were watching naked women and men having sex. We had never seen the nude female form before, and both of us had erections, which didn't' go unnoticed by Peter.

At that time, we didn't realise his true sordid intentions, and he asked if we wanted to see more films like that. In our naivety, we agreed, which would later be our downfall. From then on, we were in Peter's clutches. I am sure it would haunt every one of us who visited Peter and his friends forever.

As I have already said, Richard was my schoolteacher and Peter was a social worker, and also trained social workers. He also used to write and organised many social events. On top of that, Peter was also part of the PIE! It was an undercover secret organisation, of which he was a founding member. Let me explain PIE stands for Paedophile Information exchange, and they campaigned for the government to abolish the age of consent, thereby legalising sex between adults and children. In other words, permission to have underage sex with children as young as four. Virginia Bottomley and Leon Brittan, who were the two leading ministers for Margaret Thatcher's government.

However, at that time, neither my friends nor myself knew about at the time we were frequenting with them. To be honest, we never even heard of paedophiles. The following weekend

Isaac couldn't make it, so Andy and myself met up and went to visit Peter. Richard was also there, and so watched more porno films and some other boys.

Peter, being liberal-minded, had bought beer and cigarettes, and we all sat down to watch the new films which their friend Charles had supplied from Sweden. All of us had a can of beer and started to watch the movie. I never liked the taste of beer, and Peter added a drop of lemonade to mine, which took away the feeling. As we settled down, some of the boys left, which left Andy and me alone with the adults.

After drinking about half of my shandy, I felt sick and sleepy and went for a lie down in Peter's bed. A short while later I awoke to see Richard their masturbating in front of my face. I was shocked to see this and called out. Richard put his penis away and left the room, and I called out again.

Andy then walked in and looked as white as a sheet, and we both decided that we had enough and demanded to go home, and Peter duly agreed. Neither of us spoke of that day and sat silently throughout the journey. We never even talked about it when we walked home after they dropped us off.

For a while, we kept our distance from Peter and Richard. However, the thought of losing money and gifts became too strong, and we soon got involved again. As I was keeping my distance from Peter and Richard, I concentrated on different ways to entertain myself. At school, I had made many friends, including Ajay. A few years back, I had been at school with his brother Naresh and knew him quite well. I would go to his house, which was a top flat overlooking the Church Road.

Ajay came from a reasonably large family and consisted of his eldest sister Sneh (once Miss India) Rakesh his elder brother and as I have said, Naresh. One of our favourite games was that we would stretch a length of fishing line at chest height across the lamppost and attached to a tree opposite his home, and watch, as unsuspecting persons would get caught up in it much to our amusement.

On occasions, we would tie the line to an empty milk bottle and leave it on the wall. Again, the first person to walk into the trap would drag the container off the wall, and it would smash to the ground, making them jump. One night, again, we baited our trap and peered out of the window from the top floor bedroom.

To my horror my eldest sister Theresa and her then-fiancée Alvin who was walking along to the Church to have their wedding bands read, sprung the trap, this time, the bottle flew off the wall and hit Alvin in the leg. Thank God it never broke, and they weren't injured.

After that, we decided it was too dangerous to carry out the fishing line trap, so we thought up another novel way of laughing at the unsuspecting public. Rakesh being the eldest come up with the best idea yet, and his tremendous but simple plan was to superglue a 50 pence piece to the pavement, and it was flawless. Again, we all convened to the bedroom and waited for our first victim. We didn't have to wait long, much to our amusement; a guy tried prising the coin off the deck. Eventually, he gave up and walked off red-faced. Over the next few weeks, we laughed at all the folks who fell for our prank.

Finally, someone came along, and was so desperate for the coin, that they had bought out a hammer and chisel to prise it off! With the amount of time I spent with Ajay, I got to know his eldest brother Rakesh.

Rakesh was 15 and was in his final year at Walford, and he was an above-average student. I only knew his best friend as 'killer Khan'.

They suggested that I come out with them at the weekend to do some 'shopping.' Being as naïve as I was, I agreed, so we headed off to Uxbridge which had a huge shopping centre.

When we arrived, we walked to the Marks and Spencer department store. They asked me to stay outside and keep watch. After a few moments, Rakesh and Khan walked out and pulled two cardigans from out of their jackets.

They removed the price tags and did some bogus damage to them. They explained to me what I had to do to get refunds on the items, of which I would receive a share. At first, I was scared, but the draw of making money was too much to ignore, as was the thought of getting caught. As I walked over to the refunds desk, my heart was pounding.

I nervously stood in the queue and waited my turn to be called. It was now my turn, and I pulled out the cardigans from the plastic bag that Rakesh had given me and explained to the assistant that mum had bought the items, and they were faulty.

The checkout operator asked for a receipt, but as I did not have one, I explained that mum had lost it. However, to my surprise, the assistant just handed me a full refund of £30.00! All I had to do was sign my name on her refund book and walk out.

Once outside we shared the money, and with £10.00 each decided to go on a spending spree.

I couldn't believe how easy it was and asked if we could do it again the following weekend, and they agreed. Over the next few months, we had refined our way of obtaining goods, and took shoplifting to another level, as each time we were given refunds without question. We even wrote letters claiming to be our parents just in case, and it was foolproof.

With each success, our confidence grew and grew. It was always the same; we would head to one of the towns, find a store, steal and obtain a refund. I would just like to say that I never actually took the goods, I was the lookout, and would go and get the refund.

Some of the items like toys we would keep for ourselves, some we would sell at school, but whatever way we played it, we would always have money from our ill-gotten gains. On top of that, I would still be visiting Peter and Richard, with Isaac, Andy, or one of the others, and get some money off them, so you could say, I was quid's in!

However, our shoplifting spree was about to come to an end. As we had grown in confidence, we felt we were untouchable, and our next spree would be our last. Rakesh and Khan suggested that we go to Heathrow airport and try our hand in the shops.

After playing around the terminal 3-building arcade, we went to one of the many shops. As usual, I remained outside, while Rakesh and Khan went inside. A few moments later they returned with Rakesh holding a Monopoly set. I thought that they were stupid, as we wouldn't get much money, but the game was for Rakesh personal use. We walked to Hatton Cross tube station and boarded the train home.

Inside the carriage, Rakesh unwrapped the set, and in front of the other passengers started to jump on the box, in an attempt to make it look old. I thought it was funny to watch the two of them jumping up and down on a Monopoly set and didn't think anything of it.

At our stop, we got off to changing stations, as we went through the revolving door, Rakesh bashed his knee, and the contents of the set flew out of his hands and scattered everywhere!

As we picked up the contents, a car pulled up, and two men called us over to ask for directions to terminal 3. As we walked over and started to speak, we were grabbed from behind and pinned against the wall. It turned out that one of the train passengers had contacted the Police, and plain-clothes officers had nicked us.

All of us were separated, and searched, as we were underage, we weren't handcuffed.

The police led us into the back of a waiting Police car, where the search continued. I was wearing a snorkel parka coat, and for those, whoever wore or owned them, would know that these types of jackets had many small nooks and crannies and were ideal for hiding anything, or so I thought.

As the officer was searching me, he found several tightly rolled up one-pound notes tucked into the small pencil-sized pockets on the left upper arm. In all, I had five pounds concealed in these pockets, to be honest, I had completely forgotten about these notes, I had placed in there for a rainy day.

With the search concluded, the officers drove us to Hatton Cross Police station. Rakesh and Khan were already in the custody suite and were waiting for their parents to turn up. Then came my turn, I was shaking like a leaf, at the thought of them telling my parents, as I knew that my dad would kill me.

I cooperated with the officers, and to be fair; they treated me with respect and understanding, which calmed me a little. I was given a cup of tea and waited for my parents to turn up. As I started to drink my tea, I saw my dad walk in, and I shit myself, as he looked annoyed. I sat in the room with him, to wait for the officers to come and speak to him.

Before they returned, dad told me to wait until I got home. He didn't have to say anymore, as I knew that meant that I would suffer a severe belting. Soon the officer returned, and they explained the charges to me, and I gave a statement. Before leaving, they told my dad not to be so hard on me when I got home, as this would make me a better person. However, I knew that his words would fell on deaf ears.

When we got back into the cold night air, I saw my eldest sister Theresa and her fiancé Alvin standing outside, who had come up with dad for support. I can tell you that I was never so relieved to see them standing there, at least my ordeal with dad wouldn't be so bad.

Dad stormed off ahead to go and get the car, while Theresa and Alvin stood by me for support, as by now I was crying my eyes out at the thought of getting thrashed by dad when I got home. Alvin assured me that I would be alright, while Theresa put her arm around me to calm me down. Dad turned into the car park in his yellow minivan, and Alvin sat in the front, with myself and Theresa sat in the back.

It wasn't long that dad gave me a triad of abuse. I forget how many times I was called a 'fucking moron,' and that he wished I were dead! I knew then that I was in big trouble when I got in.

We all arrived home; I walked in first followed by Alvin and Theresa, with dad bringing up the rear. Before I could say anything in my defence, dad flew into a rage and started to beat the living daylights out of me.

Thank God Alvin was there, as he shouted at dad to calm down, and managed to pull him off me. I was crying from his blows and was shaking with fear, I looked at him, and his face was bright red with rage with tears of his own.

Alvin loosened his grip on dad, and he lunged at me again and bloodied my nose, Alvin pulled him away, and dad looked at me. I could now see that he was fearful about what he had done and went to sit down.

With tears streaming down my cheeks and blood pouring from my nose dad slightly calmed started to talk to me, while Theresa helped to stop the bleeding and wash away my tears. In his defence, I knew that dad had done it for my own good, and he cried as he hated hurting us kids, but his temper was something that he could never control.

It is a trait that all of us share. Thankfully as adults, that ugly side is rarely seen these days. After what seemed like hours of verbal abuse from dad, mum came home from work and helped calm the situation. As I sat battered and bruised, my parents asked why I had done it.

Choking back the tears and flanked by Theresa and Alvin, I found it hard to talk, as my stutter reappeared which added to my distress. At first, all I could do was shrug my shoulders and repeat 'I dunno.' This infuriated dad even more, and he shouted at me again, calling me a 'fucking moron.'

Mum decided to take control and told dad to back down, and Alvin took him out to the pub, leaving me alone with mum and Theresa. I opened up and told them that Rakesh and Khan had cajoled me, and as they were bigger and older, just didn't know how to say no to them.

However, deep down, I knew that my behaviour was down to my experiences with Peter and Richard, but I would never admit to it. Besides, at that time, I truly believed that both Peter and Richard were the only ones who really listened. Mum sighed when I told her and decided that she would come to school with me to explain the situation. Before I went to bed, and still tearful, I cuddled mum and apologised for what I had done.

The next morning, I awoke full of dread. Dad had gone to work, and mum had taken the morning off to come into school to explain the situation. As I got ready, I felt sick to my stomach, as well as nursing my bruises I got from dad the night before including a black eye.

It felt like I was doing the long walk to school the kind of steps associated with a condemned man. Neither mum nor I said more than two words as we walked, and I held my head in shame.

As we got to the main entrance, I noticed both Rakesh and Khan flanked by their parents heading to the headmaster's office. It was so quiet, you could hear a pin drop, as we waited to go in. It was deemed necessary that we all go in individually.

Rakesh and his parents were first after him, Khan went in, and then mum and me. As we got in the head's study, we sat down. The head, Mr Yeager, was a very tall man, and very calm, also there was his deputy Mr Clarke. As the adults spoke, I sat bowing my head.

However, I did pick up some of the conversations. Rakesh and Khan admitted they had been shoplifting for over a year. They had also disclosed to the Police about the involvement of other boys from school. The boys were to be questioned too.

After the meeting with the school, mum left, and I went to my form class. My form teacher had been told about my misdemeanour and talked to me privately. She had also spoken to Ajay who was Rakesh younger brother and even my form mate.

For the first hour of school, I kept silent about what had happened; however, that was soon forgotten at break time, when I broke my silence. I needn't have worried, as my school mates revered my antics, and they treated me with respect. Everybody wanted to hear all about it, despite the school's puerile attempts to keep it quiet.

Over the next few weeks, I was only allowed to associate with Isaac or Andy and was closely monitored at home by dad. I soon found ways to stay out of his way as not to infuriate him. Obviously, after being arrested and charged, I was petrified and went to see Peter and Richard, who seemed to understand.

On one of the occasions, I met Charles, who was responsible for porn films and was moving back to the UK. After telling them what had happened, they calmed my nerves by giving me beer and cigarettes.

Charles put on one of the porn films that he had bought over, which involved two women and one man. I found it very erotic, and I started to get an erection, which didn't go unnoticed. Now relaxed from the beer, Peter and Richard took out their penises and started to masturbate.

Due to the amount of booze I consumed, I didn't think anything of it, and they persuaded me to do the same to myself. At first, I was reluctant to do so, however, due to the erotic nature of the film, and the fact that they gave me £5.00 each I did. As I was young, I climaxed very quickly, which the other three men enjoyed.

Peter then suggested that I masturbate them, and as I did so, Charles started to grab me in a way I didn't like, so I pushed his hand away. And that seemed to infuriate him, and he shouted at me telling me that I was allowing the others to do so. And his anger snapped me back into reality, and to my horror, I realised my mistake and felt sick at the thought of what had happened. I made my excuses, and despite their protests, I left and went home crying my eyes out.

Before I got home, I composed myself, I said hello to my family, and made excuses that I was feeling sick before I retired upstairs to my room. Again, I never spoke to anyone about what had happened, and I was ashamed at myself. After that incident, I kept myself at arm's length, and stayed away from Peter and

Richard, and instead concentrated on my childhood. With what had happened, my childhood I had already ruined, only I didn't know that at the time.

Chapter Nine

Court

After my ordeal, I concentrated on knuckling down at school and kept out of trouble. I made myself scarce at home by staying in my room. However, it seemed that I was being taunted about shoplifting, as everywhere I went, I was reminded of it. It didn't matter what I watched or read there would always be something associated with thieving.

Even my favourite programme, Grange Hill, had some episodes about shoplifting, and it felt like my misdemeanours were haunting me. A month had passed since my arrest, and I had calmed down, although that was short-lived as soon as the post arrived when one of the letters was a summons for me to attend Uxbridge juvenile court.

The day that it arrived, and dad saw it, he blew his top, and I felt his full wrath of verbal and physical abuse. Thank God mum was there and diffused the situation, as it could have got much worse.

When dad had calmed down, mum sat me down to explain that the court date was set for the following Friday and that I wasn't to worry and just to tell the truth when I was in front of the judge.

Being the person, I was, I couldn't help but worry, and the days seemed to drag on adding to my anticipation. By the time the court day arrived, I was a nervous wreck.

It had been suggested that we travelled with the other boys whom Rakesh and Khan had cajoled into their little scam.

The other boys lived a few streets away in Hindhead gardens and were as scared as I was! Mum and dad spoke to their parents, and they all agreed that we weren't bad lads and it was all Rakesh and Khan who had set us up.

On the way to court, I spoke to the boys, and we told jokes to each other to lighten the mood. Outside the court, we all felt physically sick and couldn't wait for it to be all over. Walking inside the court building, we were greeted by the clerk of court, who pulled all our parents away to talk to them.

I overheard him tell mum and dad that he did not doubt that, as I was so honest, that the experience would make me into a better person and would cure me of my misdemeanours. He also explained that Rakesh and Khan was the type to carry on and follow down the path of crime.

His words to my parents, rang true, as I found out many years later, that Rakesh and Khan, had been involved in a high-profile deception, and had been sent to prison for ten years each.

Rakesh and Khan only served a fraction of their sentence, but they were always in and out of trouble with the authorities. They were caught again for another crime, and they got a more substantial sentence of 15 years in prison. Looking back now as an adult, I could see that the Clerk of court, was correct, at the time that we were in the court after he had spoken to our parents. So, I suppose, that's what people say, that karma comes back to haunt you in the end.

After his talk, he came over to usher us into the courtroom for the first time, where we sat down and waited for the judge to appear. As he did so, we all stood up until he sat down before indicating to us to sit. I noticed that Rakesh and Khan were nowhere to be seen, and it had emerged that they would be tried separately as they were undoubtedly the ringleaders.

When the judge was ready, he asked me to stand up. I was petrified, and to my surprise, he called me over to his bench and reassured me. He was a relaxed man who seemed to understand the situation. He went through the charges and a list of stolen items, which I pleaded guilty or not guilty, depending on the charges I faced.

It had been suggested that Rakesh and Khan were like juvenile criminal masterminds, and at least three-quarters of the items did not relate to my co-defendants, or myself. I learned later on that their fate had already been decided.

Although we were mostly not guilty, as we had been accomplices, the court gave us a token sentence. The judge was very understanding, with our plight, and all of our sentences reflected our minor crimes and our previous good characters.

I was given a £15.00 fine, and 24 hours in an attendance centre, which seemed like a prison sentence to me before they explained that attendance meant 2 hours every second weekend, where we would be taught physical education, and arts and crafts. That sounded great to me. However, the attendance centre was based in Slough, a good hour from where we lived, which meant mum or dad would have to drive me there.

After the sentence, it was if a weight had lifted off my shoulders. I knew then that I would have to prove myself to my parents and the school. Back at school, I concentrated on my schoolwork and kept myself out of trouble.

Homelife seemed to improve and even going to attendance sentence changed my outlook in life, and never got involved in any crimes, a trait of which I have honoured throughout my life.

In the late seventies, for those of you who are of a certain age, two memorable things were being talked about, and the first was a fantastic piece of T.V viewing, a series, called 'Roots'. It was a true award-winning story written by an American author Alex Haley.

Alex was an Afro-American, who had traced his family tree to its early beginnings back to slavery days, and his first ancestor Kunta Kinte was sold into slavery. Each week my family and myself were gripped by the series and never missed an episode.

Of course, this was a huge talking point at school, and being a multi-racial school, it caused some problems with different racial factions, and tensions grew high. One day, Isaac and I were talking about the show, and some black pupils overheard our conversation and misrepresented what we said.

One of the black pupils claimed that I called him, 'chicken George', who was one of the characters in the series 'Roots', which I disputed. However, the black pupils didn't believe me. And soon, Isaac and I were surrounded, and one of them punched Isaac in the face.

I can assure you all, we have never been racially abusive to anybody, and detest those who do. Due to being smacked, Isaac lashed out and caught the first kid breaking his nose. From that point, arms were flying everywhere, and we were fighting for our lives.

At the height of the melee, a group of onlookers had gathered around to view the seemingly one-sided fight. Even with the noise of the crowd, I could hear my sister Tina shouting out my name and getting frantic. With no teachers around to stop it, we were heading for a right beating, that was until some of Tina's friends pulled us out and broke it up.

Battered and bruised, we walked to the toilets to clean ourselves up, and the crowd dispersed, and the furore died down. Suffice to say we were careful with what we said in future, and never mentioned Roots again, well never in school time.

The fight brought Isaac and me closer as friends than ever before. We were like brothers and spent all our spare time together.

Both of us were popular with the girls and were never short of girlfriends everywhere we frequented, and were surrounded by a group of would-be partners and being pubescent, our hormones were always raging, and both of us had our fair share of sexual exploits.

The second, and probably the biggest story that became headline news, at that period, was that of the 'Yorkshire Ripper' Peter Sutcliff. Due to the Rippers action of mass-murdering prostitutes, the whole of North of England was on high alert, and the communities were terrified at his actions. His killing activities gripped the nation and were never far from the news. With each new victim, the fear worsened, as the investigating team, through mistakes and false leads seemed unaware of whom they were looking for and appeared to be nowhere near in catching him. However, years later, he was caught, much to the relief of a grateful nation.

After my scrape with the law, and having completed my attendance in full, I concentrated my efforts on other things. With Isaac and I as close as we were, we not only shared girls we shared hobbies. Isaac had got me into fishing, and both of us would spend a lot of our time sitting on the banks of the Grand Union canal, or at another popular site at Ruislip lido.

The lido was a vast lake which had been modernised and made into a family resort with swimming areas. On one side with sand, the other grass, with ice cream parlours cafes, a medical centre, a boating lake, and for those more adventurous, water-skiing—not forgetting the fishing area of course. As we were novices at the sport, we never caught anything, but we had such a laugh, whenever we were together, much to the annoyance of the more serious fishermen.

I spent so much time with Isaac that we would often stay at each other's houses. The first time Isaac stayed at mine, he wore Dr Martin boots, which were the fashion at the time. However, they were no match for my dog Mungo, who would always attack him, and bite his ankles.

Being me, I thought this was a source of amusement and would laugh my head off. Isaac was petrified, and jumped up on the chair, with me still laughing, I had to explain that it wasn't him, it was the boots, as Mungo had been kicked by one of the kids in the road, who would wear them, so hated anyone who did.

After he took them off, the dog was fine, but Isaac was still dubious, and never wore them again around my house. Soon after Isaacs' run-in with my dog, I came home from school and found mum crying. I also noticed that Mungo's dog bowl had been put in the bin.

It was then that mum told me she had taken the day off work, to take Mungo to the vets as had been feeling poorly for some time. It suddenly dawned on me, that Mungo had been put to sleep, which was the reason mum was so upset. Of course, this upset the rest of the family, no more so than my dad, when he arrived home from work.

My family loved Isaac, and as a result of my association with him, my home life improved significantly, as they knew that I would always be with him, or so they thought. The reason for this was that we were still going around to see Peter, but due to being with Isaac, they always assumed that I was with him, and likewise his parents thought that he was with me.

God only knows what would have happened to us if either parent had found out the truth. Although both of us would go and visit Peter, our association with him was decreasing, as we were always busy doing other things. We only go around when we were short of money or cigarettes, which were always plentiful.

The best part of going with Isaac was that I felt safer, when Richard was around, who much to my relief was very infrequent. The other reasons we didn't visit was that we were well and truly into girls at that time. On one occasion, we were sitting at a bus stop in Greenford, where Isaac called over two girls he knew, who came over to join us.

One of the girls was called Amanda, and I fell for her, as she was stunning. At first, I was a little bit shy, but I soon got in my stride and chatted her up.

After half an hour, we were 'going out,' and wasted no time in 'snogging' each other.

I spent a lot of time with Amanda or Mandy, as she preferred to be called, and I fell head over heels in love with her. Thinking back now, I supposed she was my first love. She was a marvellous and amazing artist and a lovely person, as soon as I got home after seeing her, I would ring her up, and we would talk for hours although we had been with each other all day.

We had been going out for about three months, OK, so it wasn't that long, but at that age, it was a lifetime. However, my life was about to be turned upside down. One day at school, Isaac came up to me and handed me a letter. As I read it, I was devastated, as it was a Dear John from Amanda.

I can tell you that it felt that my heart had been ripped out, and as stupid as it seemed, love can happen at any age. Many people called it puppy love, but to me, it was as real as anything.

To add insult to injury, dad on his way home from work, stepped out in front of the bus and got knocked over less than 20 feet from the pedestrian crossing. Thank God, one of the passengers from the same bus came to his aid and due to his intervention, saved dad's life.

Due to his accident dad was in the hospital for months, he had several life-threatening injuries, and had to be kept in a medically induced coma. It was a terrible time for the whole family. Mum would visit dad every day after work, with my sister Theresa and Alvin, while myself and Tina would stay at home.

As mum was the only breadwinner, money was tight, and she struggled to pay the bills, and that was with Theresa and Alvin contributing. Several weeks later, dad had come out of the coma, and his memories were slowly returning.

I remembered when I was on school holiday, dad rang up from his hospital bed and asked for his 'fags, cheque book, rent book, and lighter'. As I looked through his coat pockets, I found several copper disks and three gold looking ingots. When mum came home, I showed her what I had discovered, as Alvin and Theresa were there, they took a look.

Alvin looked at the ingots and explained that they were real gold and that he had some 'contacts' that could sell them for her. Due to the amount of debt, she agreed, and Alvin got £400.00, which was a fortune in those days and mum could finally breathe a sigh of relief.

In the meantime, dad was getting stronger; he had suffered a severely broken leg, broken spine, bad lacerations to his face, and several broken ribs. However, mum never asked him where he got the gold. Although it was explained that as dad had worked at an electronics company called Kramer, and him being the storeroom supervisor, had access to the gold that used in making the electronic components, and so decided to 'borrow' some.

Several months later, and with dad on the mend, I was allowed to go and visit him. Mum picked me up after she had finished work, and we both went to the hospital.

Seeing dad for the first time in almost four months was a revelation to me. It was as if all the naughty things I had put them through were erased from his memory. It was very emotional for me, as dad cuddled me, and I could feel the love he had for me, and the love I had for him grew. As we were leaving, dad looked at me and told me to 'be good,' and winked at me as he said it.

Dad remained in the hospital for a further three weeks, and all of us were pleased to welcome him home. The only problem was that dad had a plaster cast up to the top of his thigh and was on crutches, so this would pose a problem in time.

A few weeks later dad had arrived home, Isaac brought along a letter from Amanda, asking for me to go back with her. However, I had already been told that another girl had interests in me, so I checked her out before making my decision.

The new girl was called Sue, and we hit it off instantaneously. Being a hormone raged adolescent, the first thing I noticed was her huge boobs. As a result, I decided to turn down Amanda and concentrate my attention on Sue. She lived near the Lime trees estate in one of three houses, which were owned by the police. Her dad Bob was a mounted police officer based in

Hammersmith. Her mum Barbara worked in a nearby garage she also had a younger sister called Sandy.

For weeks I would walk her home but never went inside, as she wanted to break the news to her parents, that she was in a relationship. At first, I thought this was strange, but after a while, I understood her reason. Sue told me that Barbara wanted to see me. I was very nervous at this thought, but I needn't have worried, as Barbara was fantastic.

Sue's mum made me feel at home; she was a wonderful woman, and she took to me straight away. Due to Bob being in the police, it would be weeks until I met him. I remembered the first time I met her dad. Sue and I were inside the shed, which they made into a summerhouse, we were supposed to be painting the inside, but were heavy petting instead.

Sandy was supposed to be outside playing with her friend and also on lookout duty. However, she failed to notice that Bob and her mum had decided to walk around the back entrance. At the last second, she shouted out 'hello daddy' which was just enough time to allow Sue and me to adjust our clothes and pretend too hard at painting.

Suddenly, the door opened, and Bob was standing there and wanted to know what was going on. Our excuses fell on deaf ears, and Sue's dad told me to leave. As I went to collect my bike, I heard Bob and Barbara arguing. Sue looked worried and tried to get me away from the area. As she did so, Bob opened the patio doors and growled at me to 'take a rain check!'

I got on my bike, and rode like the clappers, and didn't stop until I got home. The next day at school, Sue told me that her parents had an almighty row, and the conclusion was that her dad wanted to see me that same evening for tea.

Throughout the day, Sue tried to reassure me. However, it made no difference what she said, as I had been in trouble with the police, and never trusted them since my court appearance.

When school finished, I slowly walked home, and reluctantly got ready for my tea around Sue's house. In no hurry setting off to walk to her house.

My heart was beating so fast and hard, and I thought it would burst right out of my chest. Every step became an effort, and I felt sick to my stomach.

After what seemed to be hours of walking, I reached Sue's house. I was shaking like a leaf, and the sweat was pouring off me such was my anxiety. As I knocked on the door, I was secretly hoping that no one would be at home, no such luck for me, and the door opened, and standing there was Bob. To my surprise, he was smiling and gave me a warm welcome.

As I entered the house, my fears dissipated, and I was put at ease, by the relaxed atmosphere. As I sat there in the living room, Bob offered me a cigarette. I was apprehensive at first, but I took one and was shaking so much that I had trouble lighting it. After a few puffs, my nerves disappeared, and I felt at ease.

When Bob spoke to me, he wasn't the scary monster I had visions of before I had arrived, he was laid back, and put me at ease. After a while, he also offered me a beer, and we talked intensively about the topics of the day. As a police officer, I asked him if they would ever catch the Yorkshire ripper. He looked at me and smiled before replying that he didn't know.

We next started to talk about my background. I told Bob where I lived, and that my Dad had a severe accident a few months previous. He looked curiously at this and asked where Dad's accident had occurred. Upon telling him, his face changed to one of shock. It appeared that he had been on the same bus as Dad, and had witnessed the accident, and was the first to help, and had saved Dad's life.

After this, I was welcomed into the family as it were and spent most of my time at Sue's as I could. As a teenager, I had raging hormones and would try and take the petting further with Sue. After a while, she would let me touch her intimately. She wrote about it in her diary, but referred to the sessions as 'nookie bear', to cover up in case her diary fell into the wrong hands. She chose these words, after seeing a celebrity ventriloquist Roger Decourcey, and his dummy which he had named Nookie the bear, and it worked a treat.

Even though myself and Sue were very close, it never came between Isaac and me, or our friendship. If anything, it made us closer, and although it was wrong, as teenage boys, we would still chase the girls, or 'birds' as we referred to them in those days.

As we progressed at school, we had to make choices of what subjects we wanted to study for our fourth year at school while preparing to do our mock and final exams. English and Maths were, of course, compulsory. My final choices were Technology, History, Human Biology, and Geography. At

Walford depending on your intelligence you would either be placed as an O'Level, or C.S.E (now commonly known as G.C.S.E)

I was in the O'Level category, which surprised me, and Isaac was in C.S.E doing the same subjects. I just want to point out that Isaac was in no means stupid, he just didn't do well in previous exams, so the teachers at the time thought it was in his best interest to do C.S.Es.

As close as we were, Isaac and I were placed in different classes because we were in different exam categories and only met up in break times. Consequently, we both started to branch out and meet new friends.

Isaac spent a lot of his time with some of the school bullies. Sadly, we drifted apart, which resulted in some animosity between us. Over time, this grew and came to a head when we clashed in one lesson and came to blows, which continued at the local park.

Not contented with trading punches, Isaac ripped a branch off one of the young saplings and started to whip me with it. However annoyed at this, I somehow pulled the tree out by its roots and beat him with it. Our friends who had been watching intervened as the fight was becoming out of hand. After, we made an uneasy pact, and we both knew that our close friendship was now at an end, although we continued to associate, it was never the same.

Due to the fight, I decided to give Isaac a rest for a while and look for alternative ways to amuse myself and keep myself out of trouble. Another friend of mine called Peter asked if I was interested, in working at the butcher's in nearby Greenford, As a Saturday boy. Of course, I jumped at the chance, and he took me the following Saturday, to meet the boss, who gave me a job straight away and it was down to my friend Peter, who showed me the ropes in my new position.

Finally, the day arrived when we were leaving Walford, our school uniform such as it was, was to be used as a notebook with all of us leavers signing our names and leaving messages, just as previous leavers had done so over the years. It was also the day that space shuttle 'Columbia' was televised. As I had an interest in space travel, I asked my woodwork teacher, which I hadn't any interest, if I could watch it instead of staying in the woodworking class sitting at the back with the 'so-called wasters'. Unfortunately, Mr Hand refused. However, I ignored this and went anyway.

Upon my return, I was taken to the Deputy's head and immediately expelled on my last day. With nothing more to add, I went home and chilled out in the garden in the sunshine. About an hour later, there was a knock at the door. Opening the door, and to my surprise, the rest of my mates stood there soaking wet.

It transpired that they all felt aggrieved from me being expelled, and all jumped into the school pool. And they, in turn, were dismissed, so they joined me at home. Although we had been expelled, as it was our last day at school, we were still allowed to return to do our exams a couple of weeks later.

It was my 16th birthday, and as usual, I went to work at my position as a Saturday boy at J hunt butchers. As it was my birthday, Chris, the manager and the other butchers kept finding more and more ingenious ways, to ridicule me, in a jovial a lighthearted way. After work, they took me to the local pub and bought me a few drinks.

Although I was happy with this, I had to cut it short, as I had arranged to go to Sue's house, Sue also told me that her parents Bob and Barbara, were going to take myself, Sue and Sandy out for dinner. When I got to Sue's house, I had a bath and changed into some fresh clothes which had been collected from my home earlier in the day.

As I came downstairs, the telephone rang, and Bob answered it. After the conversation had finished, Bob explained to Maine, that my mum and dad who will meet Maine at the restaurant and they had forgotten to switch off the iron. I had to go home before meeting up with them to switch it off.

Arriving home, I opened the door into a dark house, as I went into the living room to switch on the light, there was a big surprise, which came as a shock. Unbeknownst to me, my parents had arranged with Sue, her parents, and the rest of my friends for a surprise 16th birthday party for me. I must admit that it was a total surprise for me, I was not something that I was expecting, but I thanked my parents for doing so, as the night was fantastic.

After the party, I now had a few weeks before I went to work full time at J hunts, and I took full advantage. Two days after my birthday party, my friend Sean came around to see me, and he said that Peter and Richard wanted to see me and that I should go with him to see them.

I was reluctant to do so, but after thinking, I decided to go as long as Sean would back me up, as I had decided to confront Peter and Richard and ask them outright, about the abuse that I suffered from them. Sean agreed to this, so we both went off to see them. When we arrived, Sean knocked on the door, and Peter opened it. He invited us in, and we sat down.

Sean and Peter were having a conversation, and I sat there in silence. I noticed that Richard wasn't in the flat so I decided to ask Peter where he was. Peter looked at me with a smile on his face and told me that Richard, had gone to see his family and wouldn't be around for a few days.

I was disappointed. I decided to confront Peter as I felt that I had the upper hand with Sean being there. I asked Peter the reason he and Richard had abused me, and other boys from our past. He laughed at this and asked me about any proof of abuse. I looked at Sean at this point, and to my horror, Sean blankly stared at me, not saying a word. I tried to encourage Sean to help me out, but he just bowed his head and said nothing.

Although I was alone in this, I still pursued Peter about the abuse that I had suffered, and again Peter just laughed and denied any knowledge of abuse, and dared me to go to the police. I wasn't going to let him off lightly and continued with my questioning, which incensed Peter to a point where he asked us both to leave.

He slammed the door behind Sean and me and went to sit down in the stairwell, and I had it out with Sean, as to why he wouldn't say anything. Sean stared at me, blankly and couldn't help. I was disgusted with this attitude and started to get angry with him, at that point, the door to Peter's flat opened again, as he told both of us to 'fuck off'.

Once outside, I was still criticising Sean, and I asked him again if he would come to the police, and tell them what has happened to myself and other boys. Sean looked at me with tears in his eyes and said that he couldn't. I knew then that I was alone, and without back up from Sean, the chances of the police believing me were non-existent.

Armed with that information, I decided to keep it a secret, and I never told anybody, not even my parents would know nor the rest of my family, until many years later as an adult. It was a decision that I have regretted almost all my adult life and a decision that would haunt me for most of my life.

Chapter Ten

Work

My first job was working at J Hunt butchers' shop in Greenford, where I worked as a Saturday boy. I started two weeks after I had left school. The manager, Chris, had been replaced by Simon, a typical early 1980s bloke, with a stupid stereotypical porn star moustache.

He was a nasty loud-mouthed man.

I was given menial butchery jobs, which included cleaning out chickens, preparing the offal, on top of cleaning up after the other butchers, running errands, and making tea. Sometimes, I would be sent out to other butcher shops in the town to Dewhurst's just around the corner, for a 'long weight,' or a 'skyhook'.

Not as stupid as they thought I was, I would play the game, and go off for a period, and have a smoke instead. Of course, when I got back to the shop, I told them that they didn't have the 'skyhooks,' or 'long weights.' making them believe I had gone, much to the amusement of the others, including Simon, who would call me a 'moron,' or his favourite of 'thick twat!'

As I was a trainee, I would also have to take in the meat deliveries, such as sides of beef, whole lambs, pigs etc., and put them either in the chiller, or the freezer. After a week, I was deemed fit to learn more butchery skills, which included jointing up the sides of beef, de-boning.

I can tell you; butchery is tough hard work, the typical day started at 6 am, and finished at 6 pm, with a 30-minute break, and was fast-paced and none stop. I also had to serve customers, of course. Wednesday was early closing, which was the norm back in the day and closed all day on Sunday, and all for a princely sum of £15.00 a week!

Not a day went by when I wasn't verbally abused by the butchers, goaded by Simon, which was acceptable in those days, but me being me, would take it all in my stride. I had been working at J Hunts for about three months; when I snapped and had enough. The day was busy, I'd been tasked in cutting cheese into portions, before wrapping it and pricing it up. However, no one had explained to me that I needed to 'tare' the clingfilm, before packing and pricing the portions of cheese, so, therefore, they were priced wrong.

After I finished, I had to take in delivery of beef and hang it in the chiller. As I was doing so, Simon rushed in, slamming the door behind him, and started ranting at me for being a 'fucking useless moron!' All the while, I was holding a side of beef trying to hang it up, but he kept on shouting right in my face. It transpired that the man in charge of weights and measures had carried out a spot check, and had noticed, that the cheese had been incorrectly weighed and priced, and in Simon's reckoning it was all my fault, because I was, as he put it, 'a fucking thick moron, made by thick moronic parents!'

I was so incensed by this and saw my chance for retribution and revenge. After he'd finished ranting, as he bent down to pick up a box of chickens, I dropped the side of beef, that I had been holding throughout his tirade on him, I almost flew out of the door of the chiller, and walked into the shop opened the till, and took out the money I was due.

Taking off my white coat and threw it at the rest of the arseholes, who by now could hear Simon's pitiful cries. Before storming out, my passing gift was telling them all to 'fuck off,' before leaving.

Due to my rage, I decided to walk rather than get the bus home, as I felt that it would help me to calm down.

I arrived home, my mood had stabilised, and triumphant at my mornings' work.

To my surprise Mum was at home on her day off and was shocked a seeing me home early, I explained what had happened, and although disappointed she understood my predicament.

She was concerned about what Dad would say when he found out. She told me to stay put, and she disappeared for what seemed an eternity. After a while, she returned and told me to go and speak to 'Alan.'

Alan lived down the road and was a respectable old school local builder. He was a master craftsman, and was well known and liked by everyone. He'd built up his business from an early age and was successful to the point that he'd put his two kids through University, where they had both qualified as doctors.

I knocked at the door, and Alan appeared, inviting me in. We sat down with a cup of tea, and he explained that he was offering me an apprenticeship as a trainee builder. Although Alan was well-liked, and he also had a fearsome reputation, who spoke his mind, and told you how it was going to be. Put simply, he would take no shit, and woe betides anyone, who failed to do what Alan asked of them. Bearing all this in mind, I accepted his offer and started the next morning.

Working for Alan was an experience; he was a tough boss, and would physically clip me round the ear if I made mistakes, firm but fair, and a great laugh. He taught me everything about the building industry, including making and splicing in architraves and original features, as some of his best clients, were patrons of stately homes, and the work had to be of the finest quality. Compared to the butchery trade.

I acquired the skills very quickly; of course, it was all down to Alan's guidance. I passed my apprenticeship and City and Guilds qualifications. I respected Alan, and he was proud of me, which boosted my morale no end, I was also earing good money £100 a week in my hand, a far cry from the pitiful £15.00 a week I was on at J Hunts.

With the extra money, I could buy my first scooter as I was a mod, and all my friends had theirs. Dad wasn't keen on me getting one, but Mum was OK with it. Mum came with me to Suttons Scooters, based near Ealing. She stood as guarantor much to Dad's annoyance, although they argued about it later.

My first scooter was a Vespa 50 special in red. Dad came with me to pick it up, and after a while of driving around in a private car park, he left me alone, after a while, I felt confident in driving home. Although nervous, I was proud to have my independence on the road. I stopped off at a local car shop and purchased a set of multi-coloured handlebar tassels, just like my friends had on theirs.

I got home and wasted no time in calling Isaac, and Sean, to come and look. Soon afterwards, they arrived on their scooters, which they bought a few weeks before I did. Isaac's was blue, and Sean's was white. We set off for a ride, I led, followed by Sean, with Isaac bringing up the rear, so red, white and blue, the colours of the Union flag, which was the adopted flag of the mods. We rode for a while. We stopped briefly to speak to some girls who had called out as we were driving.

These girls were also mods, or modettes as they preferred to be called. All of them were wearing miniskirts, stockings, Fred Perry shirts and parka's, and were made up, which was the norm in those days. None of us wasted no time, in 'getting off,' with them, which was part of being a mod back in the day. After we had our 'fun' with them, we went off, not before taking their phone numbers. Of course, we all bragged about our escapades at the pub later.

With our freedom due to having our own transport, we were treated like 'ace faces' amongst the MoD community, and we also didn't fear anybody, as we teamed up with other friends and joined a scooter club named St George the Elite. All of us would meet up every day after our work, and drive out somewhere, involving booze and girls.

On occasions, it would result in a fight with other factions, ending up with us getting drunk and getting our 'leg over.' Back in the day, we wouldn't let our social life interfere with our working life, and regardless of what time we would get home, we would still get up and do a hard day's work!

After a night out, Alan would just shake his head and smile, followed by 'you look like shit again boy'.

However, I never let him down, and always gave 110% while working, as I was happy at work, and enjoyed my job.

I'm sure my attitude was the contributing factor in Alan, giving me the business for a mere £150 for the tools and client base when he decided to retire.

Something that I can't thank him for enough, and one that changed my whole outlook in life.

After Alan had retired, I continued to build the business and had a fantastic client base. However, my social life was getting out of control, as I was getting into things that could have jeopardised my whole future.

It all started when Isaac had been knocked off his scooter by some 'rockers' in their car. Isaac was left with some serious head injuries, including a shattered eye socket, and was in a medically induced coma, for three weeks. While he was in the hospital recovering, the rest of the boys and I had found out who was responsible and planned revenge.

The scumbag was Perry Wise, who lived a few streets away from my friends and me. Wise had a gang, who would attack anyone, regardless of who they were, and were well known to the Police. In those days, we policed the streets, and deemed it necessary, to teach Wise and his scummy pals a lesson they would remember for a long time.

Wise owned a 1950s classic car associated with the Rock and Roll movement and was his pride and joy. Armed with several hammers, crowbars, and cutdown scaffold poles, we set off to administer justice for Isaac.

Parked outside his house, we set about the car and caused thousands of pounds worth of damage, and this made a hell of a noise, which alerted Wise and his mates, who were in his garage. They rushed out, but we were hiding by this time. We later ambushed them around the corner, much to their surprise. They had no chance and were given a beating of their lives.

I just want to point out, that we didn't use the hammers that we had, this was using our fists, and looking back, I am ashamed of that, but at the time, we were young, stupid, and felt it was necessary. There were only one of Wise's mates that never got the same treatment, as he was on holiday, although he got swift retribution upon his return. After this incident, we never had problems from the rockers or any other faction that was around at the period.

Due to the situations that we were getting into, it was only a matter of time before we got into real trouble with the authorities. Although looking back, we weren't the tearaways that were so prevalent these days. However, it was enough to put the fear into my parents, and even though I never allowed it to affect my business, dad was concerned.

One evening before I went out, dad asked for a man to man chat. As we sat down, he explained that he and Mum were concerned and suggested that I join the Army. Of course, I was dead set against that idea, but when dad explained that I could lose all that I had worked for, I told him I'd think about it. Dad, not wanting to push it, suggested that I join the Territorial Army, and as he put it, 'just see how it goes,' as I could leave at any time. With his words still ringing in my ears, I said my farewells and left to go out with my mates.

We'd been invited to a party arranged at the last minute by one of our friends whose parents had gone on a holiday. Looking back, it probably wasn't one of their best ideas, leaving home in the hands of their teenage son.

We wasted no time, in hitting the booze, and spliffs that had been bandied about and eyeing up the talent that had been invited. As you can imagine, it was heaving, and being Mods, we just got on with and became somewhat boisterous, especially when someone played The Who's track, 'My generation,' which was kind of a mod anthem at that time.

It wasn't long for the party to turn into a drug and alcohol-induced sex orgy, and every inch of the house was used for such purposes. As usual, Isaac and I had the pick of the modettes and chose two girls, that we knew had been after us.

As we were getting into it, so to speak, there was a loud knock at the door, at first, we thought it was the Police, but on second sight, it was around 10 'smoothies.' They also wanted a piece of the action. It was a big mistake on their part as we out-numbered them 2-1 with more of our mates on their way.

Annoyed at this interruption, not only for them being rock-ers but also for them halting us in our tracks for getting our 'end away,' we rushed down the stairs, just as they were barging their way through the door. I had picked up a pool cue that I had found, and rushed downstairs, as more of them burst in,

I hit one of them around the head, this escalated in a full-blown punch up, with claret being sprayed all over the house.

The rockers, realising they had made a colossal mistake, as our other mates had now turned up, which effectively sur-rounded them, and their escape routes.

Bloodied and bruised bodies were everywhere, the girls were screaming, which of course alerted the somewhat annoyed neighbours who had by now called the Police.

When we heard sirens, there was a mass exodus as revellers disappeared.

However, Isaac and I and few of our friends remained pre-tending we were innocent victims.

And to our surprise, the Police believed us. Suffice to say, that was the end of the party, the clean-up was now the priority.

As no one wanted to press charges, the Police simply handed out a verbal warning and left us to pick up the pieces. Luckily, and to our surprise, there was nothing damaged, and my mates' parents never got wise to the escapade, even though it was brown trousers time for a few days after they arrived back home, as we were sure the neighbours would mention it, but they never did.

My life at that time revolved around a never-ending toil of socialising, I never shirked my work commitments, and completed my client's jobs on time, and to a high specification. However, although I always finished my contracts, I noticed that work was slowly drying up. It was the norm in the building industry, as it has its up and downs, and is affected by various factors, such as inflation, and hits the smaller and individual building contractors more so than the big guns.

Over the next few months, I was barely scraping by with money, due to work drying up. It was then that Dad made another suggestion of me joining the army, or at the least the TA. However, still not convinced by this, I sought alternative employment.

It was Mum who suggested that I go and see the Manager of the local Waitrose store in Hayes, of whom she knew, as she worked for the John Lewis Partnership. He was one of her previous managers who transferred to Waitrose from John Lewis, of who are part of the same company.

Mum insisted on going with me to see the manager at Waitrose, of which I relished her company as one, she could introduce me to the manager, and two, she could be my taxi for the day. Arriving at the store, we asked a member of staff if she could get the manager, as we were there to see him.

A short while later, the manager appeared and greeted mum like they were long lost friends. He then shook my hand and introduced himself to me as Michael Meehan. Mr Meehan showed mum and me to his office, where we sat down. I explained my situation, he then turned around and told me that he didn't have any vacancies at his store, but a newer one that was going at the branch in Chiswick. As he was on the phone ringing up the branch manager at Chiswick, the deputy manager walked in and offered myself and mum some coffee, of which we accepted.

After Mr Meehan had finished on the phone, he explained that the branch manager of Chiswick, was eager to see me, and he had arranged for me to go the next day to speak to him. I was happy with this answer and shook him by the hand before myself and mum, left the store accompanied by him. After mum and I had left, I decided to treat mum for breakfast before we went home.

The next morning, I awoke early, showered before getting ready for my first interview. I put my best suit on before leaving to catch the train for Chiswick.

I arrived at the store at 8 am although my appointment was not until 8:45. I decided to come early rather than late, before entering, calming my nerves with a coffee and a cigarette. I managed to get the attention of one of the members of staff, explaining, I had an appointment with the branch manager. I followed them through the store and upstairs to his office, where they knocked the door, where a large, rather portly man came out, he shook my hand and introduced himself to me as Mr Portsmouth.

After sitting down, he asked several questions which I answered openly and honestly. The last questions that he asked me were whether I would be hard working, which I replied yes. At the end of the interview, he'd offered me a position as a fruit and vegetable assistant and start on the following Monday, which allowed me four days rest recuperation before becoming an employee.

I went home and was in a jubilant mood after my interview. I walked upstairs and got changed out of my suit into something more comfortable. I told my mum and dad how the meeting went, they were pleased for me, as a thank you to both of them, I offered to take them out for dinner in the evening at a local restaurant.

We were just leaving for the restaurant in the evening when we had a phone call. It was from Alan's wife who informed us that Alan, had suffered a fatal heart attack. Although we still went to the restaurant, the celebration that should have been was tinged with sadness due to Alan's passing.

The next morning, I went to see Alan's widow and the rest of her family, to offer my condolences. Bringing along a large bouquet and was invited in, remembering the good times we had with Alan.

After sharing reminiscences, with them, I took my leave and went home.

Later in the day, I sold the tools and the van, as I had no longer need of them due to my new job. I managed to get £500 off the buyer, but was still faced with sadness at Alan's passing, and felt that I needed to do more, for him and his family. The only thing that I could offer was to give them the £500, to help them pay for this great man's funeral. At first, they refused, but I insisted. as without Alan's guidance, I wouldn't have been the person that I was and become.

All too soon, the weekend was over, and it was Monday already. Although the last four days have been sad, I had to put that well and truly behind me and had to focus on my new position at Waitrose. Again, I left early to catch the train to Chiswick, which would give me plenty of time, to allay my fears before starting my new position. Just like the day of the interview, the store was locked. Although I explained, I was there to start my new job in a fruit and veg department.

I was shown through the store, and upstairs and into the canteen. I sat down and waited for someone to show me who I was to report too.

While waiting, another member of staff came in, ordering a coffee. Sitting down on the same table that I was at, and he introduced himself as Manoj. As we were talking, it was clear, we both had a lot of things in common. Starting to talk about football, as both myself, and Manoj, supported the same football team, which is Queens Park Rangers.

We were engrossed in conversation when another new start came into the canteen and sat down beside us. Both of us introduced ourselves to the new staff who told us his name was Neil. We'd been speaking for a while when another member of the team came into the canteen to talk to myself and Neil.

He was a smartly dressed gentleman with a thin moustache, and his name was Mr Mackay. He explained, the store was just finishing off a stock take, and would soon be introduced, to our department managers. As he said that, our department heads appeared. Neil was going to be working in the produce department, headed by Ron Barker, and mine was Jeff.

After introductions, we were both led away to our different departments, and they explained our duties to us. My duties were to ensure, the fruit and veg were full at all times. The other part of my responsibility was to put away the delivery in the upstairs warehouse. Jeff handed me over a full-length Brown coat and a small razor type blade.

The department was relatively small and only had just been relocated from the original position, after the store refurbishment. As Jeff was showing me around, the rest of the fruit and veg staff arrived. These were three elderly ladies, and their names were Ivy, Lily and Indira. There was also another member of staff called James, of who I would be meeting later, as he was on holiday.

I picked up my duties fast, and I relished working in the department, although an easy job to do, it was somewhat tiring, with all the heavy lifting work that was part and parcel of the position. My first week seemed to fly by, and I was making friends.

The following week, I met James, he was the assistant fruit and veg department manager, and later found out from Jeff, that the only reason why James was promoted, was due to the number of years that he had worked at the store.

However, Jeff explained that James was somewhat lazy in his attitude and work, and he was hoping to find a replacement to take over the role as his assistant manager. At that time, I had no idea, that I was to be his choice, and that he trusted me implicitly with the tasks that James wasn't quite able to do.

I'd been at Waitrose for one month and had made many friends and was well-liked by everyone, including the management. These included Manoj, Andy, Matt, Mike, and Tim. Although these were my closest friends, I was still friends with the other members of staff but were not as close as I was with these guys.

As Waitrose was a part of the John Lewis Partnership, as employees, we were also partners of the business, and as shareholders, we would benefit from the yearly bonus after the profits. Every year it was announced the percentage of how much we would be receiving, as partners.

One year, the management agreed that the yearly bonus was set at 22%. With this huge bonus, I thought that it would be a good idea to go on holiday abroad. I asked all of my friends if they wanted to come with me. It was only Andy who was able to commit, as the rest had other plans.

After speaking, we decided to book a club 18-30 holiday to Corfu. We booked the holiday for mid-August, so we had three months to prepare ourselves, and to ensure that we had everything associated with our holiday, including passports.

The day of our holiday arrived, I was to go and meet Andy at his house, and Alvin, my brother in law, kindly offered to drop me off. Although I was nearly 3 hours early, he invited into his home, where we had a few beers, and we both read the riot act from his mum and dad, on how we needed to behave while abroad. My parents had already read the act to me before I left home.

It was now time for us to leave to catch our train directly into Gatwick Airport. Neither of us had ever been abroad before, and I felt it quite daunting as to what we had to do at the airport.

Nervously we walked up to our check-in desk and handed over our luggage.

Once free of luggage, we decided to check out the airport facilities, I made a beeline for the duty-free, where I purchased 200 cigarettes. After this, we ended up in the airport bar to quench our thirst how to start our holiday off in earnest with a few cooling beers.

While we were drinking our beers, our flight information was called, and we made our way down to the departure gates. We boarded the bus that would take us off to our waiting aircraft, which was operated by the carrier Dan air. The plane was a Trident which had the engines at the back nearest the tail.

As I was a smoker, I asked Andy if it would be OK if we could sit at the rear seats, as that was where the smoking section was. Andy agreed to this, so we went to sit down. While we were strapping ourselves in, I noticed, the emergency door seal was being held into place by Sellotape. Both of us thought that this wasn't a good sign, which only led to our anxiety levels. It also didn't help, that the seats were being held down by bolts which hadn't been screwed down, as a result, the seat wrote backwards and forwards.

Although this made us nervous, our nerves made way, when two beautiful blonde girls joined us, who both sported the largest breasts we had ever seen, and who was wearing, the shortest miniskirts imaginable, inquired if they could join us. As we were raging with hormones, how could we refuse such an offer?

The girls sat directly in front, and ours faced towards the front of the aircraft. The aircraft engines fired into life, as they did so, then we could now smell the distinct odour of aviation fluid. We'd made acquaintances with Tracy and Michelle, strapped ourselves in, and awaited taxiing onto the runway.

As soon as the aircraft turned, the pilot powered up, and we hurtled at speed along the runway for take-off. As soon as we were airborne, we sat back to relax at a chat up Tracy and Michelle.

A few moments later, the pilot extinguished the non-smoking light, and I lit a cigarette, offering them to the girls which they took, all of us got to know each other very well.

They explained, they were staying in the resort of Ipsos. Ours was Dassia and was the next resort down from where they would be staying. We agreed that we would meet up after a few days over there. As we continued our conversation, the air stewardess came along with our inflight meals. It consisted of 2 small ham filled finger rolls, a Kit Kat chocolate bar, a piece of fruit and a cup of coffee or tea. Although this was not a substantial meal, as we were full of beer, it was a welcome sight.

After four hours of flying, we were making a final approach to Corfu airport. As this was an evening flight, our estimated arrival was going to be 10 PM, and as I looked out of the window, I saw the airport runway in sight.

The pilot was now on his final approach to the airport, and the wheels hit the tarmac. However, the aircraft bounced violently, and the pilot took off again because the pilot had overrun the runway. He turned around to attempt another landing. Although I wasn't a nervous person, I must admit that my heart jumped out of my chest at that point.

On his second attempt, we landed safely much to the relief of myself and the fellow passengers. Once the aircraft had come to a complete standstill, the aircrew opened the doors, and we exited the plane. I would never forget the smell that engulfed my nostrils, although not unpleasant, it was a smell that I wasn't used to. Again, we boarded the bus taking us to the arrival's hall, clearing customs and picked up our luggage.

As soon as we left the airport, we made our way to our transport, that would take us to our hotel, the Amelia was the last hotel at the end of the line. Having arrived at the hotel, we booked in, so that we could go and freshen up, and hit the night-life that Dassia had to offer.

There was a pizzeria near the hotel, and a small supermarket directly opposite. There was also a car and bike hire. We decided to check out the small supermarket. After buying our booze, we returned to the hotel to drop it off, before venturing back out again, to the bar opposite the hotel, named the grasshopper.

As soon as we ventured inside, headed straight to the bar and started drinking. The venue was heaving with holidaymakers, mostly from our age group. It seemed most of the patrons, were gorgeous women. After a few cocktails and beer, we made a beeline for two good looking girls that was sitting at the back of the dance floor. We introduced ourselves and asked if we could join them.

The girl that I was most interested in had long black shiny hair, was very tall and slim and very good looking. She introduced herself as Fiona and came from Glasgow. She was there with her sister Karen. Throughout the evening, we got to know each other very well. After a while, I started to get off with Fiona, and Andy did the same with her sister.

We asked them back to our hotel for more drinks, as they were staying at the same place, we both thought we'd get our leg over on our first night. However, once back at the hotel, Fiona was interested, her sister Karen, who was a lot older than her, turned matriarch and spoiled our evening. Andy and I decided to go back to our room and drown our sorrows.

The next morning, we both awoke with terrible hangovers. I had to crawl on my hands and knees to the bathroom. I decided the only way that I could wake up and feel more refreshed was it take a nice refreshing shower.   As the warm water hit my head, it woke me up, I climbed out of the shower and getting ready to face the day. I sat on the balcony and waited for Andy to have his shower before we both set off to the bar, for a much-needed coffee, and await the reps for our welcome talk.

The bar was located outside near the swimming pool, when we arrived, we bumped into Fiona and her sister Karen. I offered to buy them coffee. I spoke to Karen, who apologised to me about the previous evening. As we were talking, I was looking around the pool area and noticed the swimming pool was covered in a what can only be described as an oil slick. I pointed this out to her, and she told me that the pool had been like that for three days. A short while later the reps turned up, we made our way over and sat in the shade of the gazebo.

There were two reps, a male and a female. The man in a Hawaiian shirt, green skin-tight shorts and trainers, he also sported a tight long curly head perm. In short, he reminded me of a late 1970s porn star. The woman was more business-like in her appearance, wearing a smart blue skirt, white blouse, wearing sensible flat shoes. Before they started to talk, the barman came around with a tray of drinks.

These drinks were of the local brew called ouzo. We were each handed a glass and told not to drink it until the end of the meeting. During the meeting, they explained the history of Corfu and about the Greek people in general. They told us about the attractions around the area, and the best places to go and visit to eat in.

The holiday company, provided many excursions, deciding to book the tour that we liked the look of, and what we could afford, as they hadn't explained, trips were extra, when we purchased the holiday. When they had finished, they raised their glasses, telling us it was a custom, to shout yamass before downing the glass. Neither of us had drunk ouzo before, and had no idea, after drinking, if we followed up with water, the alcoholic effects would hit us hard.

After the meeting, we ventured out to look for a breakfast place. After a short walk, we went to a taverna called Zorbas. We sat down, the waiter bought over our menus, asking if we wanted something to drink, while choosing what to have to eat. We both chose large Coke's with ice.

Looking at the menu, we could see that most of the dishes had photographs so we could see what we are buying. I chose a light breakfast of tomato and onion salad, which came with bread and chips. Andy, on the other hand, decided on a 'full English breakfast'.

When my breakfast arrived, it looked as described, although I cannot say that Andy's breakfast. His plate consisted, a fried egg, dripping in cooking oil, the sausage, was more like a saveloy, the bacon had more hairs on it, then we had on our entire bodies, the so-called baked beans, were dried up and uninviting.

Looking at his plate and mine, and Andy said he wished he had ordered the same as me. However, as we were both ravenous by this time, Andy ate his without complaint, compared to what Andy had, mine was delicious.

After breakfast, we walked along the road, where we came across a small shop selling souvenirs. As the temperature was roasting, thought it would be a good idea, to purchase a hat, to protect our heads from the immense heat. Afterwards, we continued to walk towards the beach, walking on the sand, could feel the heat burning through our shoes.

We walked in between the parasols and sunbeds, checking if we could find two free ones so we could sit down. As soon as we had done so, were approached by a member of staff who took our payment. Due to the sun beating down on us, we applied sun lotion, to protect ourselves.

However, we both realised we had to do each other's back, which made us feel uneasy being men. We'd been lying under the sun for about 2 hours; when I suggested, we should have a drink. We sat at a table, looking out to the beach and ordered two large beers. Sitting there, chatting about the holiday, and what our plans were.

Andy suggested, after our beer, we go and hire a pedalo. We were taking turns to peddle and stopped off to go swimming. We could only achieve this if one of us stayed on board. After we had our fill, we returned to the beach and laid down on our beds, spent a good few hours sunbathing again.

After 3 hours, we went to the local pizzeria, which was next to the hotel. The pizzeria was owned by Yiannis, found a table which overlooked the beach, waiting for some service. Our waitress's name was Jill, and she was working the summer season before going back to University to finish her degree.

She was a great girl from Lancashire, and somewhat talkative, and would be the person to go-to for any gossip, how to find where the best places to go to in the evening. After eating, went back to the hotel, to chill out for a few hours on the balcony and have a few beers, getting ready to go out once more. After showering, went to the hotel bar, for a few cocktails.

After several cocktails, then back to the grasshopper bar opposite the hotel. Just like the previous evening, the place was packed and challenging to get served at the bar. After a while, of being cramped in, we left to go and see, if we could find another bar,

Walking up the road, we came across The Scots bar and ventured inside. As the name suggests, the bar was owned by a married Scottish couple, John, and Amanda. We were made most welcome, and had a great night, as they had a live band which went on until the early hours of the morning.

We staggered home to the hotel, once inside our room, we continued our drinking session and finished off the beer and started on the wine. However, we realised we didn't have a corkscrew, so we had to improvise. The only thing I could find was a coat hanger and used it, to push the cork inside the bottle. The wine was hideous in flavour, although that didn't stop us, from downing the entire bottle.

The next morning, we were rudely awoken by the male 18-30 rep. In our drunken stupor, we'd forgotten to lock our door. Seeing it as an opportunity, he'd let himself in and thought it would be funny, to wake us up, blowing a whistle close to our ears.

Not amused by this, I told him 'fuck off,' and he replied that it was the day of the excursion and we'd forgotten.

We had an hour to get ready and enjoy the beach party, including barbecue. Still hungover we climbed aboard the coach and sat at the front. The coach was full, and the occupants started to sing about our hotel.

Although not quite in the mood, we joined in regardless. As we drove along, we came to a stop, where we had to wait for a Shepherd and his sheep to cross the road. Due to my intoxicated state, I was getting slightly annoyed and shouted out for him to move his backside.

That didn't go down well with the rep, and he told me to shut up, which pissed me off. As soon as we arrived at the beach, I told him in no uncertain terms that if he spoke to me again like that, I would shove a broom up his arse. That seemed to do the trick, as he never talked to me again.

The beach party was just like we had imagined, full of scantily clad women booze and barbecue. After topping up our alcohol levels, Andy and I started to feel more human again. The party was now in full swing, which included beach games where two nonrelated couples would have to run into the sea, and exchange swimming costumes.

The funniest pairing was of a tall blonde girl, wearing the skimpiest bikini, I have ever seen. She'd been paired up with, a huge blackfella who hung like a donkey. It was the funniest thing, either of us had ever witnessed, as this man, was trying to squeeze his incredible hose, into a bikini bottom no bigger than a beer coaster.

Of course, we'd also have a good look at the naked women, while they were exchanging costumes.

After all fun and games; we went to have a fill at the barbecue, where we piled our plates up to the brink. As darkness fell, it was time to head back to the hotel.

By the time we'd arrived it was 1 am, although we could continue drinking at the grasshopper, we decided to have an early night.

The next morning, we awoke at around 11 o'clock, With the worst hangovers, from our day at the barbecue and beach party. Andy dragged himself to the bathroom and could hear him being sick, this was a source of amusement for me, and I chuckled to myself each time I heard him.

Eventually, I could hear him getting into the shower, so got out of bed, and went onto the balcony for some fresh air. After what seemed like an eternity, he reappeared and got himself ready to go out. I went in after him, to freshen up myself and get rid of my pounding head.

After showering, got dressed and went out onto the balcony, where Andy was resting. We decided to venture out for breakfast. Before leaving, we covered ourselves with sun lotion and ensured we wore our hats.

The time was now midday, and the sun was at its highest in the sky, the temperatures were well into the 40 degrees mark.

Due to the amount of alcohol, we'd consumed over the last few days, we started to sweat profusely, stopping at the local shop, and bought two large bottles of water. As we were walking along, we were drinking the water, as if we hadn't drunk water before in our lives.

We decided to go back to The Scots bar for breakfast. Due to the extreme heat, we sat outside under the covered veranda, which had a nice cooling sea breeze. John, the co-owner, greeted us at the entrance and handed us a menu. Unlike Zorba's list, we could see a lot of English dishes, we were more used to seeing, and both ordered gangsters pasty's chips and salad, two bottles of water, and two large glasses of Coke, with copious amounts of ice.

While waiting for our food, we knocked back the water and started on the Coke. We could feel our hydration levels increasing and felt more human again. When our food arrived, we ate like two people who'd been on a starvation diet.

With our bellies full, we sat back and continued to rehydrate ourselves, and talked about the previous day's entertainment, and couldn't help but laugh out loud, and were in fits of giggles, which didn't go unnoticed by John and Amanda. As they were not busy at that time, they took a break and came to join us. The 4 of us had a fantastic conversation, and we made a new set of friends.

As John and Amanda went back to their business, we decided to explore the area and continued to walk further along the road. We found another car and motorbike hire place, and thought it would be a great idea, to hire a pair of mopeds When we were handed over our mopeds, we could see they weren't as well looked after, as you would find in the UK.

However, this didn't deter us from going on an adventure. As I had experience in driving a scooter, I felt more comfortable driving it, more so than Andy.

Even though I'd ridden in the UK but Greece, they drive on the opposite side of the road, neither of us had any experience of that.

How we survived on those roads, I will never understand. The ride was petrifying, not only had we had to contend with driving on the opposite side of the way, we'd to contend with the Greek drivers, who, and to be fair to are crazy.

It was after we returned to the hotel, and spoke to other holidaymakers, we found out, Greece had one of the highest mortality rates on the road than the rest of Europe.

After our brush with death on the Greek roads, we had to find a less dangerous activity, to keep ourselves amused, throughout our holiday. Most of our time we spent on the beach, walking along the coast road, and seeing what we could find, to keep ourselves out of trouble.

One day, as we were walking along, we bumped into an English lad who we met, serving drinks at the grasshopper nightclub. He was on his way, to the next town of Ipsos, we pooled resources, and got a taxi, rather than walking.

When we arrived, the lad went his separate way, and we went to found a good pub to have a drink. We walked a few metres and came across a bar called Manolis. As we made our way inside, we bumped into the two girls, and we'd met on the aircraft Tracy and Michelle.

We went straight over today, they got up and embraced us as if we had known them for years. We ordered drinks, and sat down with Tracy and Michelle, for a great afternoon, with them drinking, which culminated in an invitation back to their room. Suffice to say, without going into too much detail, was one of the best days, of our entire holiday.

The next morning, we awoke still in their room in the same bed. We said our goodbyes and found a taxi back to Dassia, and our hotel, we freshened up and spent a lazy day on the local beach. In the evening, we made our way back to Ipsos, where we'd promised to meet Tracy and Michelle, at the local nightclub called Zeus.

As we entered, we headed off to the bar, where we were to meet, Tracy and Michelle, only to find, they'd already got off, with two other blokes.

We were somewhat pissed off and went to another nightclub to enjoy the rest of our evening.

We didn't have far to go, when we found another club, named Greco's as soon as we went in, decided to drown our sorrows, and headed straight to the bar, where we ordered the largest drink, that was on offer. It was named the fishbowl.

These drinks were the most massive cocktails we ever had. We had two of these each, mixed with other spirits and beer. After a short while, we both needed to go outside, for some fresh air. As the humid air hit us, we could fill the effects of alcohol, and our heads were spinning. We felt our legs buckling underneath us, and thought the best idea, was to go back to Dassia and get ourselves into bed.

Inside our hotel room, we were in a terrible state, from all the alcohol, both of us were sick, and collapsed on our beds and fell into a deep drunken stupor. When morning arrived, still fully clothed from the night before, and felt like shit.

After several hours, we made ourselves presentable and went to the shop to buy some provisions as we are far too sick, and the temperature, was too hot, for us to venture out, no further than our balcony.

Back in our room, we sat on our balcony and read our English newspapers, and rehydrate ourselves, stuffing our faces with biscuits, crisps and cakes. As the day progressed, feeling more human again. After a while, we opted to stay local and go to the local pizzeria next door to the hotel.

When we got there, they were having a film night and was showing Rambo. We ordered a pizza each but stayed off the beer and drunk soft drinks instead. While watching the film, I started to feel unwell, I felt cold and shivery, even though the evening temperature was 20 degrees.

I told Andy that I was going to return to the hotel and go to bed. Andy was okay with this, and I left him to it and returned to the hotel room and climbed into bed. In the early hours of the morning, I woke up just as Andy was returning from his night out. He had been drinking and told me that he had been over to the grasshopper after he had finished watching the film. However, I was feeling that bad that I just ignored him and fell back to sleep.

Over the next few days, we both continued with our alcohol filled path of destruction, so much so, that we didn't realise how much we were spending. We were now in our second week, and it was only then that we decided to count our money and found that we had spent more than we first imagined.

Both of us had 800 drachmas each, and after counting our money, we were down to our last 100 drachmas. As we had five days left of our holiday, we knew that this wasn't going to be enough to carry us until we got home. We sat down on the balcony and tried to come up with a solution.

After a while, we had decided to buy some groceries, to minimalise the amount that we were spending. However, it didn't matter how hard we tried to cut back; our money quickly diminished. The only other solution that was available to us, to try and steal from the small supermarket that was in the area.

We had limited success in this area, as both of us felt very guilty for one thing, we also didn't have the nerve to do so, and when we did, we only managed to nick one packet of bourbon biscuits and a litre bottle of water. Due to having hardly any food, our holiday was becoming a nightmare.

We became irritable as we're living in each other's pockets, which grated on our nerves. We annoyed each other, to a point where we both sat on the balcony, Andy was reading a newspaper which was a week old, and adding to my frustrations and boredom, I thought it would be a good idea to set fire to it, while he was reading.

Once Andy realised his newspaper was on fire, threw it at me and rushed into the bedroom, closing the patio doors behind him. I tried to batter away from the paper, and rushed in a room, not realising the patio doors were closed. I bounced off the glass, and by now, my T-shirt was alight! I patted out the flames, and extinguished the rest of the burning newspaper, before it spread, and caught the building and the surrounding areas alight.

Throughout this, I saw Andy in the bedroom, laughing. I attempted to open the patio door, but he had locked it. I was battering on the door for him to unlock, and he just continued laughing at me, this started to make me feel angry, and I was going to lose my temper. He kept saying he would unlock the door after I had calmed down.

After a short while, I had calmed down, and Andy unlocked the doors. He had a grin like the Cheshire cat, and after I had thought about it, I saw the funny side, and as I'd started the fire in the first place, put it down to karma. We both sat down, and had a good laugh, at the mess that we had put ourselves in.

We then tried to come up with a different solution to our self-made predicament. We later came up with a plan to take money from shrines dotted along the road, placed by families of loved ones who had died in a car or motorcycle accidents.

We'd been told by the reps, that the shrines contain an effigy, of either Virgin Mary, or Jesus, or another religious saint. They also included a small glass of wine, bread, and some coins, which were there, to nourish any weary travellers, and that in return, they would replenish the items that were taken, when they were next in a vicinity.

With our new plan, we decided the next day we would put it in motion. We arose early the following day, our breakfast consisted of two biscuits and a glass of water each. After our meagre breakfast, we left the hotel, on our quest to seek out the shrines and to commandeer their contents.

The first shrine we came too, we opened up, and as expected was full of a picture of an effigy, the bread, wine, and a few coins. The food and wine were unpalatable, so we pocketed the change, a moved on to try and find the next one. We could only imagine what it must have looked like from any passers-by, especially the local residents.

After walking the length and breadth of the road, we found a shady area to sit down, so we can count out, and share the money that we had taken. We noticed some steps to sit on, which was shaded by some olive trees, and found we'd managed to find 20 drachmas, with what we had left, from our original money, it came to 45 drachmas.

We worked out if we were careful, we could live for three days that we had left, on the money that we had in our possession. We both agreed that we felt wholly ashamed of our actions but felt that it was necessary for us to live, and vowed to return the money if we should ever return to Greece.

As we were sitting there, contemplating the errors of our ways, we could hear a loud voice behind us. Looking around, we could see a nun walking down the stairs we sat on, she was wagging her finger, and shouting at us in Greek.

As neither of us could speak Greek, we assumed, that she had seen us take the money out of the shrines and was telling us off for doing so. We thought it would be a good idea at that time, to run off and go back to our hotel room. The last few days of our holiday were non-descript, we just couldn't wait for the departure date, and counted the hours down until it arrived.

Departure day arrived, both of us couldn't have been more relieved that we were going home after our disastrous nightmare of a holiday. Although we did admit our reckless attitude and naïve outlook, was a direct result of us being in the position that we had put ourselves in.

Arriving at the airport, we dropped off our bags at the check-in gate, and used our last ten drachmas, for two well-deserved pints of beer. Finally, our flight was announced, and we all but sprinted to the departure gates, to board the aircraft with haste. As we climbed the stairs to the plane, we just chose the nearest seats and sat down.

We were exhausted, hungry, and just wanted to get home as soon as possible. As the aircraft took off, we gave out a sigh of relief, as we were leaving and knew we were home would bound. When the inflight meals came around, as it was a morning flight, we were served breakfast, an omelette that resembled a chamois leather, overcooked sausage, dry overcooked bacon, mushrooms that looked like they had been left over from a disastrous cooking program, and baked beans that had seen better days. However, as we hadn't eaten any solid food for the last three days, it looked like a gourmet chef had cooked it, and we demolished it with great gusto.

After we had demolished our breakfast, we noticed that the person sitting in the aisle seat had fallen asleep, and not touched their breakfast. We took this as an opportunity and shared his breakfast and placed an empty container in front of him. As we were drinking our coffee, he awoke from his slumber, looked at his empty container, and said "I must have been hungry", before falling back into a deep sleep again.

With our bellies now full, we settled down and enjoyed a nice sleep ourselves for the remainder of the flight. We were awoken by the steward, who announce that we were coming into land at Gatwick, and could we fasten our seat belts ready for landing.

When touchdown arrived, we couldn't wait to vacate the aircraft, as soon as the doors opened, we were the first standing there wanting to get out. Back at the terminal building, we got through customs picked up our bags, and rushed to the station to board our train back to Chiswick. Our ordeal was now at an end. When we arrived at Chiswick station, Andy rang up his dad to pick him up, and I rang up my brother-in-law Alvin to do the same.

When Alvin arrived, he informed me, there was a surprise for me when I got home. He didn't divulge what the surprise was, but explained, I would be pleasantly surprised. I opened the front door, and dropped my bags into the hallway, and went into the front room.

To my astonishment, the surprise that Alvin had told me about, was standing there to greet me. I couldn't believe my eyes, as the surprise was my middle brother David. I hadn't seen him or been in touch with him for around five years! I couldn't help, but put my arms around him, I give him a brotherly hug, and he did the same.

Excited at seeing David, we both sat down and talked about where he had been for the last five years. It transpired that he'd been working on a kibbutz in Israel. But he had decided to return home, and build a relationship with my mum and dad, and the rest of the family.

After several hours, I had to take my leave of him to have a long soak in the bath and to get my washing on. As I was in the bathroom, David knocked on the door as he had bought me a cup of tea. He then left me so that I could enjoy my bath in peace. After I'd finished, and had changed into some fresh clothes, I went back downstairs to continue our conversation.

At that point, mum and dad arrived home, and we all talked as a family once more. It was agreed, David could stay, until he got himself back on his feet again. As Theresa and Alvin were living back at home, the only space that he could be offered was in the room, which was once our coal, shed which was near the kitchen.

Although small, it would make an ideal cosy bedroom for him. We got the spare single bed downstairs and put it in the room for him, and he made his bed before offering to cook hour dinner. I can say that I was pleased to see him, and hoped that he would remain at home for some considerable time.

After a week Theresa and Alvin, moved out, as they'd been offered a council property on the Woodend estate located at the top end of Northolt. With the extra room, I was allowed to have the large spare bedroom which had a double bed. It was a welcome change, as I had been sleeping in the box room for what seemed like forever.

The only obstacle that now remained was that my middle sister Tina would be relegated to the box room.

When she arrived home from work, she protested to mum and dad, but her protests fell on deaf ears which were a surprise to me, as she was always daddy's blue-eyed girl.

For me, it was great to have David back again in my life, as I missed out on so much time with him, while he was at the children's home.

We grew closer, reminiscing about some of the adventures we had shared in the past. And even regaled his stories, of our character stedad.

David settled in well back at home and even managed to find employment, all be it via an employment agency. After three weeks of him being home again, we gained another house guest, which was my cousin Will, who'd been invited up, at the request of my auntie, as he was struggling to find work in Deal.

That meant that he had to share my bedroom, although he too had to sleep in a single bed. As David had found employment with the agency, he suggested, Will came with him, to sign up with the agency himself, and he too found work via them and was working with David in a warehouse.

Life it seemed at that time, was a happy one for me, although the happiness would not last very long. What seemed at first, the idyllic lifestyle that I had long hoped for, was about to be shattered after six weeks. One evening, myself dad my cousin we're sitting down to our evening meal when my mum came home and was in a foul mood. Dad asked her what was wrong, and she drew her daggers out and was gunning for David.

As David wasn't at home as he was still at work, my dad asked her what her problem was. She explained that she inadvertently, found a book in his room, of which the reading material wasn't what she wanted in her house. As the row started to get heated, David arrived home and walked into the living room, only to be confronted by my mum, who was screaming and shouting at him. My cousin and I felt somewhat uneasy at the situation that was unfolding in front of our very eyes. As mum was screaming at David because of the book, she could only describe, as being that of the occult.

My dad was trying to calm the situation, but mum would have none of it, so David decided to go into his room, to fetch the book, that she had taken a dislike to. When he emerged, he showed her the book, and it was a copy of, I Claudius. Mum didn't seem to care, that this book was only a classic novel, had been made into a successful TV show.

David was distraught and was crying and pleading with her, this upset me, and I could feel my heartbreak for my brother. It was then that I stood up and shouted at mum to leave him alone. However, she was adamant, that he was in the wrong, and wouldn't listen to any appeals at all.

I also got upset at this, and the way Mum was treating him, and I stormed out of the front room into the street. I started to cry through sadness and also through annoyance. My cousin Will joined me, and he sat next to me on the wall, where he offered me a cigarette.

As we lit our cigarettes, we were joined by dad, who sat on the other side of me and placed his arm around me in comfort. I never forgot the words that he said, which were 'there is no shame in a man crying, son.'

After a while, we went back inside, whereby this time, David had got into his room, and we heard him crying, which was heart-breaking to hear. Mum was adamant that she didn't want him in the house anymore. Dad looked at her, and they started to argue, this made myself and my cousin feel more uneasy, so we went upstairs into our bedroom.

We could hear the argument and tried to blank it out by playing a game of chess. After several hours it stopped, and the house fell silent once more. A short while after the argument, David packed his bags and left. Two days after he had left, my cousin also went back home, because he missed his own family, but also because of what had happened.

The situation tore me apart, as once again, I had missed out on building a relationship with David. Due to David and my cousin moving out, Tina saw it as her opportunity, to once again wrap dad around her little finger, and I was relegated once again into the small box room.

With all the upheaval, I once again resorted to my destructive ways. I saw this was my only way of coping with the situations. Once again, I started drinking and tried to burn the candle at both ends, while keeping down my job at Waitrose.

Back at work, I tried to keep myself busy and threw myself into my work, to try and forget the situation that I was facing. I met a new friend who had just started called Dale. He was into the heavy metal music scene, was obsessed with the group Status Quo.

On Saturday, Dale told me that he had been invited to a party, which had been arranged, by one of the other members of staff named Maureen and was going to be held at her friend's house. I asked him who else had been invited from work, and the guests were to include big Geoff as we called him, Maureen of course, and my other friend Mike Baxter.

As I hadn't been invited, I thought that I should go and ask Maureen if I could tag along with Mike and Dale. Maureen was quite happy for me to come along, and she asked us to bring a bottle or whatever type of drink that we would be having. I also went to see Mike, and he relished the idea of me being at the party as whenever we had been together in a social environment, we would have a great laugh.

The day of the party arrived, and I met up with Mike at the pub which was near where the party was to be. We had a couple of pints, I was having a great time, and we're waiting for Dale to show up, as he knew the address.

After having a few more drinks at the pub, we made our way to the party. Knocking at the door, Maureen greeted us, and we followed her upstairs to meet the other party guests and our other friends. As we entered the living room, we realised that the party only consisted of 12 other people.

We asked Maureen where our other work friend were or when they would be arriving. She told us that they had other plans. It was quite easy to see the reason, as without being rude, Maureen wasn't precisely the best-looking woman we had ever seen, although she had a heart of gold.

She was also head over heels in love with big Geoff. Let me explain the reason why we called him big Geoff, was that he hung like a donkey in the trouser department.

As we were there and had bought drinks, although the party wasn't all we had imagined it to be, we decided to stay and make the most of it.

We kept ourselves in our unique click, me and Mike, had bought two packs of beer each, while Dale had bought with him what was known as, a party seven. As I was looking around the room, I noticed a beautiful woman, sitting talking to the host of the party, and couldn't take my eyes off of her.

Mike, as usual, being a practical joker told me I had no chance with her, so I asked him to put his money where his mouth was, I bet him £20 that I would end up with her before the end of the evening.

Mike being cocky, took me up on my bet and we shook hands on the deal. I didn't want to look too eager, so I kept on giving her sideways glances, and I notice that she was doing the same to me. After I plucked up enough, I decided to take my chance and go and sit and talk with her.

The host had gone to speak to Maureen, so I was alone without any interruption. She told me that her name was Sarah and that she was good friends with the host called Liz. Sarah was very attractive. She had long blonde hair, very slim and with a lovely face and warm smile.

The more we talked, the more I was attracted to her, and I could see by her body language that she liked me also.

Every so often, I would look over to Mike, who would smile at me, and discreetly rub my fingers together to indicate that I was going to win the bet.

As the party progressed, we were all mingling together. I was speaking to other guests with my arm around Sarah. I looked over to where Mike was sitting, and I stared at him, and he nodded in my direction and acknowledged the fact that he now owed me £20.

Sarah was now in deep conversation with Maureen, Liz, and big Geoff. I whispered in her ear that I was going to speak to Mike for a short while. She turned smiled and kissed me on the lips and winked at me, and gently stroked my hand and told me to hurry back.

I smugly walked over to Mike and sat down. He raised his glass in my honour, and said 'Briggo, I take my hat off to you me old mucker'.

Mike wanted to hear all about her, and we had a great conversation on my prowess in pulling Sarah.

We looked over to where Dale had been sitting, and he was cradling was party seven can, and he had also knocked back a bottle of vodka he brought with him. With his can now emptied he thought it was a good idea to headbutt it, much to our amusement.

We'd noticed that he hadn't hit it square on his forehead and had hit his nose instead, giving him a nosebleed. While Mike and I were in hysterics, as were the party guests, the host took Dale into the kitchen to stop his nose bleed. And that was my opportunity to talk to Sarah once more. I sat on the chair next to her. As I did so, Sarah got up and came to sit on my lap. I knew then that she was mine, and we became boyfriend and girlfriend.

The party continued until the early hours of the morning. It was suggested by the host Liz, that we may as well all crash out wherever we were. Liz had a 10-year-old daughter called Katie, who was lying on the sofa, and Sarah was lying beside her. I chose a chair closed to the couch and sat down to get closer to Sarah and get comfortable to try and get some sleep.

I removed my shoes and stretched out my legs. I rested them on the arm of the sofa where Katie and Sarah were, and Sarah kept stroking my thighs. I commented on how lucky she was to be lying down, to my surprise, she asked me to join her.

At first, I declined as I felt that it would be too cramped for all three of us to be on the sofa, but Katie got up and went to sit on her mum's lap leaving me and Sarah free reign of the sofa. All of us had a blanket, and someone turned the lights off so we could get some much-needed sleep.

However, sleep was far from mine and Sarah's minds, and we started to kiss passionately. The kissing was just the start of it, she wanted me to have sex with her, I thought it was a crazy idea at first, I couldn't imagine having sex with a room full of people, but I couldn't resist her temptations, and we had amazing sex on the sofa. The only downside was that we couldn't contain our passion, and I'm afraid to say that we may have been somewhat noisy.

The next morning, we all woke somewhat worse for wear, although I felt alive, after spending the most amazing night with Sarah. Liz and Maureen had made tea for everyone, and we all sat the drinking. Of course, Sarah and I knew that the rest had known that we had sex together.

However, that thought didn't even enter our heads, and neither of us felt any shame. After we had drunk our tea, Sarah said that she had to leave to go home to Brentford. Before leaving, I took hold of her telephone number and also managed to obtain another fantastic kiss from her.

On Monday morning, of course, all of my work colleagues wanted to know all about my escapade with Sarah. I told them the truth about what had happened, as usual, they were trying to wind me up about it. Sarah explained at the party that she was seeing another man called Lester, who worked as a driver's mate for her mother's pride. The funny thing is, this was the same Lester, who delivered the bread for Waitrose. All I could do when I saw him was smile, knowing that I had sex with his girlfriend and that I had stolen her away from him.

Looking back, I did feel guilty about that, but at the time, I thought that he was OK. I met up with Sarah every day, and she told me about her family in Brentford. She had an older brother who was married and had two children. Her dad was 76, and her mum was 66. Sarah told me there was a 25-year age gap between her brother and her because her mother fell pregnant with Sarah at a later age.

We spent so much time together that I was burning the candle at both ends. I would typically come home at 2 a.m. and get up at 6 o'clock to start my work at Waitrose. Even though we were spending each moment together, I still would find time to associate with my other friends. I don't know if it was because of my age, or because I seemed to have an abundance of energy, but I never felt tired or irritable.

However, after about three months of dating, cracks started to appear with our relationship. Sarah was going on holiday with her family to Spain and failed to tell me, right up to two days before she was going to fly out. As it was near Christmas, she would be away for the Christmas period, and I was distraught that she never told me.

We argued for most of the two days we spent together before she went on holiday. While she was away, I met up with my friend Isaac and some of my other friends, and went to Shepherds Bush located in west London, to a Mod all-nighter held at the Bush nightclub situated on the Shepherds Bush roundabout. As soon as we arrived at the venue, we started to knock back the drinks, to a frenzied level.

When it was my round, I went to the bar on the other side of the dance floor. The only direct route to the bar was across the dance floor as there was no other way of gaining access to it, as a result with people walking back and forward to the bar, the dance floor was slippy due to people spilling their drinks on the way back to where they were sitting.

As I returned with the drinks, I slipped on the dance floor and as I fell forward one of the glasses that I was holding punctured my right wrist, which started to spurt with blood.

Isaac saw that I was injured, and he and some other friends helped me to my feet and took me over to where the bouncers were standing and asked if they could call an ambulance.

The bouncers just shrugged their shoulders and left me to it. Isaac acted and came with me in a taxi to Hammersmith hospital, where the accident and emergency registrar took care of me.

After examining my wrist, I was sent off for an X-Ray, to see if there were any glass still embedded in the injury. As the X-Ray was all clear, the doctor stitched up the wound and placed a bandage on it, and he discharged me later.

Isaac took me home and explained everything to my mum and dad, who thought I had been in a fight and were concerned about me Isaac reassured them, that I hadn't, and that injury was due to the fall on the dance floor. Mum and dad, we're OK about it, and Isaac left and went home.

Back at work, I was struggling to lift anything due to my hand, not seeming to work correctly. The pain was unbearable, and I had a severe weakness in my right hand.

I continued to work like this and thought that it would just take a while for the injury to heal, however, when Sarah arrived back home from her holiday with her family, she nagged me to go to the hospital.

Reluctantly I agreed to her pleas, and we went off to Mount Vernon hospital, where they took a new X-Ray, which confirmed that's my tendons in my wrist, had been almost severed entirely through, and was the reason why my hand wasn't working correctly.

Due to the severity of the injury, I was instantly admitted, for an emergency operation on my wrist. It was left up to Sarah to contact my mum and dad and explain the situation. They prepped me up for the surgery that was about to take place, and the next thing I remembered was waking up in the early hours of the morning in absolute agony.

After being given some powerful painkillers, I felt much relief and was allowed to go and sit in the patient lounge, where they gave me a cup of tea and some toast. I then waited for my mum to come and pick me up and take me home.

Mum arrived and was chaperoned by my elder brother Peter, they helped me to the car and as I was sitting in the back, both Peter and my mum, were giving me the third degree, and I felt like the inquisition was questioning me. Now back at home, their questions didn't stop, and I was bombarded from both sides.

My brother Peter felt that it was appropriate, as he had just qualified as a fireman. I soon grew tired with their constant questioning and told them both to go 'fuck off' and leave me alone.

I went up into my room where I could get away from their unjustifiable ranting and raving. I laid on my bed to relax, I heard footsteps coming up the stairs, there was a knock on my bedroom door, it was Peter coming to say goodbye, and he wished me well. I looked up at him and just nodded my head in agreement.

A short while after he had left, the anaesthetic in my system kicked in, and I fell into a deep sleep. I woke up several hours later, by someone knocking on my bedroom door, it was my dad who came to speak to me. He told me that he and mum were concerned as to what had happened, and again talked about me joining the army or TA, at least when I was fit to do so.

I told him that I had no interest in joining either of them, as I had a job at Waitrose, and that I was hoping to go back to become self-employed in the building trade again. Once again, dad nodded and didn't push me into making a rash decision. As he was leaving to go back downstairs, there was a knock on the door it was Sarah, dad and Sarah exchanged pleasantries, and he went downstairs so we could be alone.

I sat up on the bed, and Sarah cuddled me, before handing me a present that she had bought over from Spain, which was a bottle of blue labelled Smirnoff. She was also concerned and asked me how it happened, so I told her the full story, Sarah had her version as to why it had happened, and even suggested that I had tried to take my own life.

I laughed at the suggestion and told her that she was paranoid, as I would never dream about doing such a thing. She spent several hours with me before she headed home back to Brentford.

As I would be off work for five weeks, I started to go into steadily declining depression. It was exacerbated by the amount of alcohol I was consuming because of the pain. I drank to take my mind off it. On top of the alcohol, I was also taking painkillers for the pain, which also added to my depression.

With Sarah living in Brentford and I was living in Northolt, we would only see each other three times a week, compared to the amount of time that we spent together before she went to Spain, and then the fall. Everything also had a profound effect on my mental state, and the only way that I could cope was to drink more.

It was like a never-ending circle for me at that time, and the only person that I could confine with was Sarah, but due to myself destructive nature, we would generally argue, resulting in her walking out and going home. Throughout it all, I could see no other way to get myself out of the depression, and I would often drink myself into oblivion, to block out what was happening.

Finally, I was able to get back to work after I had been declared fit by my GP, and it was like a breath of fresh air! Upon my return, I was asked to go and see Mr Portsmouth, he sat me down, and ask if there is anything that he could do for me, I thought long and hard, and after a while, I couldn't tell him what he wanted to know, so I only answered 'no'.

As neither of us, had anything further to add, I left to continue with my duties. My time away from work, at the fact that my drinking and depression was a real problem, and that myself and Sarah were arguing, we both decided that it was time to finish our relationship. Although it was an amicable agreement between us, my work colleagues had other ideas on this and decided to disrespect Sarah at every opportunity, despite my protests against them doing so.

On one occasion, Maureen had overheard them and went off to go and tell Sarah they said. Later that evening, a call came over the tannoy system, for me to go outside, as there was someone was waiting for me.

As I had finished for the day, Mike, who had also finished suggested that we went for a drink at the local pub, and he would go with me to see who was outside. Once outside, I could see Sarah, who was accompanied by her brother, and his friend. Sarah started talking and told me Maureen had told her, that I was responsible for slagging her off.

I was shocked at hearing this news, as I had never said a word against her, as it was the others, who had done so.

Her brother decided to take the law into his own hands, and took a swing at me, as he did so, I ducked out of the way, and he punched Mike in the face instead.

Annoyed at this, I retaliated and head-butted him, and the two of us started exchanging blows in the street.

I was getting the upper hand on him until his friend started to rain blows down on me, so it was two against one until Mike, who had been nursing his broken nose, joined the fight.

Eventually, other members of staff came out and split it up. Sarah, her brother and her friend were told to go away, or the police would be called, as they had seen it all, and would have prosecuted him for GBH.

After they had walked away, Mike and I went back into the store to clean we up and to compose ourselves. As Mr Portsmouth was still there, we went to see him and explained what had happened, although he had already been made aware of the situation and was happy to forget the whole incident had occurred.   After the fight with Sarah's brother, I started to settle down back into my work.

I knew that I needed an escape, as if I didn't, I would end up in a worse situation than I had found myself. After a lot of soul searching, and another talk with dad, I decided to take up his suggestion and join the TA.

Raw recruit

My next available day off, I went down to the local TA centre based in Horn Lane Acton. It was a Royal Engineer Regiment, and their primary role was to provide searchlights for main military events, such as trooping the colour, or illuminating training areas for night operations.

I didn't know at that time of signing on, that the military would be the turning point in my life. My first weekend with them, was in London as they were setting up for the Queen's official birthday, and was to be marked, with a military possession at Horse Guards Parade. I was in awe of the spectacle and was proud to be a part of it.

A few weeks later, was given a medical, issued my uniform, and sworn in by the senior officer. I was to be sent for two weeks training at Gibraltar barracks, which was the main Royal engineer training facility.

On the day I and three others from the TA centre were due to start our training at the barracks, our unit what also on a training course nearby. And we were ordered to wear our uniforms before they directed us to the main gate, where we were handed over to start our training.

We were shown into the waiting area and sat down amongst the rest of the recruit, who was wearing civilian clothing which made us feel out of place. We had waited for 30 minutes, before three corporals walked in, and sat at the desk in front of us. Shortly afterwards, a Sergeant walked in and accompanied by the regimental Sergeant major.

As each one of our names was called, we had to stand up and were assigned a training Corporal as our mentor. As the three of us were in uniform, we were singled out and asked he reason we were the only ones wearing it. I decided to explain but was shouted down by one of the corporal's named Meakings.

Unsure of what to do, I again tried to explain the reasons only this time, I was shouted down by the Sergeant who had walked up to me, and was standing only a few feet away, and was looking me squarely in the eyes. I made a big mistake, and looked directly at him, rather than looking above his head. This action brought severe implications, and I had to stand there, and get torn down strip. I realised that this was going to be my life in the military from now on.

We were split into sections and followed our assigned Corporal to the barrack block, and it would be our home for the next two weeks. We had to do everything ourselves. I was quite surprised when we arrived at the block, as I was expecting a dormitory type of living quarters.

However, we had separate accommodation with four men per billet. The rooms were typical military type surroundings and consisted of four metal frame single beds, four basic cupboards, one table including four chairs, and to finish it off we each head a small green rug placed beside our beds.

Our Corporal came into our room, and we stood to attention. He gave us an order to stand down and gather around him at the table. He was there to explain what was expected, and also to show us how to make a military bed block. The block consisted of three itchy blankets and two sheets.

These had to be made into a precise block. One of the blankets had to be folded perfectly to a compact size followed by one of the sheets also folded at the same size as the blanket, followed by blanket and sheet. It would then be wrapped in the third blankets to form the block, and would then be placed on our bed space, and our kit would be arranged in a specific order in the wardrobe.

After he had instructed us of how-to layout the bed block and our kit, he went off to instruct the rest of the billets under his charge. Three other men I was sharing the room with, were called Tony Cherry (lost him), Ian Beef (roast) and Alan McClennan (Jock).

Like my dad, I have been a professional soldier for nearly 30 years, he had schooled me in the military etiquette, and I was well prepared for the training regime that was to follow. I had also 'bulled' My boots, to a high glossy shine, and my uniform was with razor-sharp creases.

As we made acquaintances with each other, we worked together as a team to perfect the tasks that we had been given ready for the mornings first inspection parade.

Cherry was able to make each bed block identical, so that was his task every day. The roast had the job of highly polishing the floor, along with Jock who was given the task of finding and dusting every inch of the room, while mine was to 'bull' all of the boots. Pleased with our night's work, we settled down to sleep at around 1 am.

At 5 a.m. we were awoken by the screams and orders of the Corporal's arriving into the block rooms. We had ten minutes to carry out our ablutions and get dressed and ensure that our rooms were ready for inspection by them. We stood at the foot of the rugs and stood at ease, smartly coming to attention, when the three Corporals entered our room.

Through my peripheral vision, I saw Cherry, with Roast and Jock right in front of us. As this was our first room inspection, we stayed deathly silent standing to attention at all times.

The Corporals went to each bed space, as Roast had the task of room monitor, they started with his bed space first. What they did next was the cue for the remainder of us to start giggling. The Corporal was screaming and shouting a Roast, and they up-ended his bed, trashing everything in sight.

While this was going on, we were trying to stifle our giggling and took deep breaths to stop it from occurring. After berating Roast, they moved onto Jock. I noticed that he was trying not to smirk, but the Corporal saw through that, and they laid into him. Both me and Cherry had tears rolling down our cheeks, and no matter how hard we tried, we couldn't hold it in.

Giggling like hyenas, the Corporals turned their attention onto us. They were now standing nose to nose with us and were ripping into us. The scene was reminiscent from one that appeared in the feature film Life of Brian, by the Monty Python team.

Those of you who had seen the film can relate to the particular scene, where the Roman centurions are trying to stifle the giggling when Michael Palin who was acting like Pontius Pilate and kept referring to his friend 'Bigus Dickus'.

After our momentous bollocking, the Corporals left, and we now had the unenviable task of clearing up the mess they made because of our actions. And they made it even harder, as they had given everyone ten minutes to change into their PT kit, and get on parade. Once outside, all of us recruits had to go on a 5-mile run.

That was how life was to be in the armed forces. It was a constant barrage of discipline and hard work. Although I adapted to it well, others were not so fortunate. Over the next two weeks, we were put through our paces and learnt new skills such as map reading, skill at arms, which was weapons training.

Of course, as soldiers, we also had the relentless time of marching and various other military drill movements. All of us on the block, became good friends and we all learnt how to look after each other, and we became comrades which were what military life is all about. Although the regime seemed harsh, it wasn't too bad as we also had our fair share of quality relaxation time, or R and R as it is known.

One of the best things about being in the army in the barracks was the fantastic meals, where you could eat as much as you like, just as long as you cleared your plate. We had three square meals a day which may be to some people seemed excessive, but let me assure you, that you burn off the calories very quickly due to the extreme physical training that we had.

Our two weeks were at an end, and the final day was the passing out parade, which would be witnessed by friends and families. None one of my family was able to attend. However, that didn't deter me, from carrying out the tasks my superiors asked me to perform.

The Corporals, Sergeant and the Regimental Sergeant, set out my primary task, which was my ability to mimic a leading comedian called Russ Abbott, who as part of his repertoire, would take off a stereotypical type of Scotsman. It had been explained to me, by the NCO's, that the General, was retiring from military life, and as a parting gift, they wanted to give him a proper send-off.

At first, I was reluctant to do so, as I thought that I might be arrested and imprisoned for taking the rise out of such a distinguished officer. However, they reiterated that the rest of the officers at the camp were aware and loved the idea.

They gave me the fictitious name of Private Murphy. They had set up various short demonstrations, which was to be in front of the friends and families, the officers, including the General. My task was straightforward, I would act up in a non-military way in front of the General, I was then going to be dragged out, which was a simple and effective way of laughing at his expense.

The plan worked well, at each demonstration, I played Murphy the fool as a Corporal rushed me out. I went to the next event before the General arrived, and the rehearsal went as planned. My final task was that I was going to be presenting the General, an award at the final passing out parade.

Standing in the parade with the rest of my colleagues, I awaited my name to be called.

I was to be presented with a fictitious 'award', which was a smokescreen for the General. I nonchalantly marched in a non-military manner and went to accept my award given to me by the Generals second in command.

My drill movements where typically non-military, and I exaggerated the salute with resulted in me slapping my eye, much to the amusement of all those who were in with the joke. As soon as they presented my 'award', I then turned and stood to attention in front of the General, where I correctly saluted him explained my true identity, before handing him the award.

I then took one step backwards, saluted him again, and then marched off correctly back to my original place. When we were given the order to dismiss, the rest of my colleagues rushed off to be with their families. I, however, was asked to join the officers and the senior and junior NCO's in the officer's mess.

Inside, all the officers congratulated me for doing a great job. They later introduced me to the General, who warmly shook me by the hand, and praised my effort. He also mentioned that he enjoyed being the source of amusement. It had made his retirement, a most memorable one.

I was praised by the NCO's who insisted on buying me a rather large cognac, which I felt was a great honour. I was proud to be a part of it. It was time for me to leave the barracks and return home and was a place that I can say, holds a special place in my heart, as I have some fondest memories while being there.

After I returned home, I was feeling amazing, and it felt like I was turning over a new leaf. My time at the barracks seems to have re-ignited a fire that was burning inside me, I was fitter, healthier, and happier, which was something I haven't felt for in a long time.

Returning to work, I was a different person, and I threw myself into my work. Of course, I would still enjoy my time with my work friends; only now it would be in a more refined and relaxed attitude.

I was also religiously carrying out my duties with due diligence at the TA.

Only two things were missing that I could see, one was that I felt that the time was right, for a girl in my life, and the other, was that I missed being in the building trade, and I felt that I could now move forward and achieve my goals which I had set myself.

I'd managed to pick up new clients, who'd required my building services, and I would carry out their jobs in my spare time. You would be amazed at how much I could stretch time, which would allow me to carry out my work at Waitrose, the TA and my new clients.

My quest for finding a new girlfriend was about to become a reality sooner than I anticipated. I had been at the Chiswick branch for just over a year, I had made many friends in that time. However, the store was at a capacity where it couldn't expand anymore, and the company were looking to relocate premises or purchase some new land where they could build a new store.

The land they had earmarked as a possible site had been swiped from under their noses by Sainsbury's. The site itself was it a prime location behind the Waitrose store. That was the final death throes of Waitrose 106 branch Chiswick as the stored future had been determined.

I decided to apply for a position in a new store built in Harrow Weald. I passed the interview stage with flying colours and was offered a job in the warehouse of which I accepted. I would still be pinning my hopes, and I would find sufficient work, to go back to my first love in the construction industry.

Although I had gained some experience with working at the Chiswick branch, I had to undergo training at their store based in St Albans, as this store was the same size as the new store they'd just built. The company had provided taxis to pick us up while we were in the training phase, and it was through these taxi journeys, that I would go on to meet my future wife, Jackie.

I met some colourful characters at the St Albans store. I would meet with a new member of staff whom I would be working with named Lloyd. On the second day, it was then where I noticed Jackie, who was working in the patisserie section.

I took a shine to her, as she had long wavy light brown hair a beautiful smile a great figure and a cracking pair of boobs, and a beautiful backside. I noticed during lunch that she kept on looking over in my direction, we exchanged flirting smiles and met up after work, to await the taxis to take us home.

It seemed that fate was going to lend a hand, the taxi company made a mistake and had only sent one taxi for six people when they should have sent two.

I told them that I would wait for another one, but to my surprise, the taxi driver said that he was willing to take us all, as there wouldn't be another taxi for some considerable time.

It was here that I got to know Jackie better, as she sat on my lap for the journey, where we got on like a house on fire, and I took her phone number, and I decided to call her later on in the evening.

As it was a Friday night, we arranged to meet up in Harrow for our first date. It was a beautiful warm summer's evening, and I waited for Jackie at the bus stop.

When she arrived, my eyes almost popped out of my head, as she was wearing a figure-hugging grey pencil skirt, and a tight beautiful white blouse which showed off her voluptuous figure.

Jackie also wore black stilettos, and I noticed that she was wearing black stockings. I must admit, but she looked every inch a lady. We decided to go and have a drink and get to know each other, and afterwards, we went to have something to eat. We settled for a steak meal at the local Bernie Inn.

We got to know each other very well during the evening, and I offered to take her home, and she agreed. That was where I met her dad Nobby as he was known because their last name is Clarke. Jackie introduced me to him, and I noticed he was the spitting image of the comedian Eric Morecambe, of Morecambe and Wise fame.

I spent at least thirty minutes at Jackie's house, and while we were waiting for my taxi, we started to kiss passionately, which led to us having sex standing up lent against the wall in front of her house. Okay maybe it wasn't the most romantic, but it was as if we had known each other for years, but it was enjoyable all the same.

The next day I rang Jackie to arrange another meeting, and when we met up, I apologised for what had happened the previous evening on the balcony. Still, Jackie admitted that she had fancied sex and also needed it, just like I did. So, I suppose it was fine.

Jackie lived in Pinner, and she explained to me that her dad Nobby had a severe drinking problem, and he worked as a long-distance lorry driver, for a company called Boosey and Hawkes, a well-known musical instrument manufacturer. Her mum, Jan, worked as a care worker in the care home, which was in front of where they lived, and that she also had an elder brother called Alan, who lived in Leavesden hospital, as he was mentally disabled, the most pronounced being autistic.

I told her about my family, and also informed her, we were not very close and were somewhat dysfunctional. We had a great time together and went back to her place to listen to music in her bedroom, and as we were very attracted to each other, one thing led to another, and we had sex again.

Later on, we went back downstairs to meet her mum Jan, and her dad who by now was well and truly drunk. Jan was a lovely lady, and I liked her instantly. I fondly remembered Jan, as a quiet person with a wicked sense of humour and her passion was knitting.

Nobby, on the other hand, was different from either Jackie or Jan, as his only passion in life, was to go for a drink daily, even when he was working. He lived in his sleeper cab while travelling through the country. He would only be at home from Friday afternoons, where his first port of call was the Pinner club, where he spent most of his time.

When he came, there would be an alcohol-induced argument with Jan. Then he would sleep for a few hours, then came back downstairs again to sit in the living room with a litre bottle of vodka and twelve-packs of beer. It may seem that I am painting him in a bad light, but on occasions, he could be as pleasant as pie and do anything for you. The only day that he didn't drink to excess was on a Sunday where he would take Jan and Jackie to see his son Alan.

He would limit himself to only a few more drinks in the afternoon before preparing his bag and go to bed early, ready for his work the next morning.

My relationship with Jackie relationship blossomed, and we saw each other not only at work but in the evenings as well, I also introduced her to my family, but warned to keep my sister Tina at arm's length.

As Jackie has a kind heart, she forgot my advice and tried to get close to Tina, who would let her down later on in life. After a few hectic weeks, the Harrow Weald branch opened, it was twice the size of the old Chiswick branch that I had worked at, and had all the mod cons, that you could have wished for in a supermarket.

Although I enjoyed working there and met a load of new friends, I was starting to pick up some new clients, and therefore went back to do what I knew best, and that was home improvements. My business was going from strength to strength, and as I set my own working hours, I would see Jackie more often, as well as my friends and could devote more time to the TA.

Jackie had introduced me to Sally, who was her lifelong best friend and had known her since she was six years old. She decided to introduce us, and we met her at the pub for a drink. At first, I thought Sally was a nice girl, but all too soon, I realised that she wasn't as lovely, as Jackie had portrayed her to be.

It was after our third outing with Sally that her true colours reared their ugly head. Sally had far too much to drink, and she became violent with Jackie on our way home one evening. She was calling her all sort of names and even begun to disrespect me, and Jackie took offence. Sally didn't like that, and she started to punch Jackie.

I got in between them to break up the fight and Sally punched me, and also deliberately kicked me in-between the legs, which caused me extreme discomfort, and I instinctively hit her with such force, that she flew off of the pavement and into the road. Mortified with what I had done, I hated it because I didn't lash out in anger but in self-defence as an autonomous response after she kicked me in the balls.

Ashamed for my actions, and tears in my eyes I decided to walk away from Jackie ended our relationship there. As I moved away, I heard Sally screaming blue murder and obscenities after me, and Jackie screamed at her stop being such a nasty bitch and chased after me. Jackie said she needed both of us. I was inconsolable, as I would never hit a woman, I told Jackie this, but she just hugged me and pleaded with me not to go.

By this time, Sally had picked herself up and started to walk away. Jackie promised me that she would sort it out, and once again begged me to reconsider, and that she would call me the next day so we could talk about our future. The following day when I woke up, I still felt guilty about the previous night's event.

As promised, Jackie rang me up and explained that Sally was very sorry about the incident and claimed that she didn't remember doing it. Jackie mentioned that her parents are aware and they were in full agreement, that I had done the right thing, and would have done the same thing in my position.

After I had heard her words, I had changed my mind, and couldn't wait to see her again. We arranged for Jackie to come over to my house to visit, where we spent a great day and evening together, as we had the whole house to ourselves, where we talked about the incident, and that she needed me in her life.

I offered to apologise to Sally, but Jackie rejected my suggestion, as she thought it was Sally who needed to apologise to me. After our heart to heart, we both couldn't control our passions anymore, and we had more amazing sex in every room of the house, which lasted for several hours.

Several weeks had passed since the incident with Sally, and Jackie and I were closer than ever. My business was flourishing, but I could no longer sustain and devote my precious time with the TA. With a heavy heart, and after serving twenty-four memorable months with them, I resigned and handed back my kit.

As Jackie came with me, we decided to go and have breakfast to enjoy the rest of our day together. With the extra spare time that I now had on my hands, I could devote more time with Jackie and my friends, and to build my business up.

She got to know some of my friends from Waitrose Chiswick branch, and we were both invited to big Geoff and Maureen's wedding, held at Putney registrar office. Without sounding disrespectful, the wedding wasn't well planned. Maureen wasn't the most beautiful bride we'd ever seen; her nickname was four 'tits' as she had a habit of buying bras two sizes too small for her. Also, Geoff, wasn't the most hygienic of people and another one of his nicknames was 'Mr stinky', and both of them had some disgusting habits.

The day started badly and grew steadily worse. As they were walking into the registrar office, we all started to hum the Munster's theme tune. Okay you could say that we were disrespectful, but we knew them, and therefore thought that at the time it was funny. Not only that, but we could also see that both of them had left the price tags on their clothes.

It was another source of amusement to us all, which only aggravated the situation. After the couple exchanged the wedding vows and were now man and wife, we headed off to the reception party at Geoff's favourite drinking establishment, the Putney club.

When we didn't think anything else could get any worse, it transpired, that the landlord had forgotten to book the reception hall and all the tables and chairs were still stacked up against the wall. Of course, this proved an embarrassment to the wedding party instead, but all my ex-work colleagues and I from Chiswick thought it was hilarious.

Jackie wasn't privy to the laughter or ridicule, and she felt sorry for them both. Although embarrassing, I will say this, Geoff pulled out all of the stops, and within half an hour of arriving, managed to arrange a full buffet, and DJ, much to the surprise of us all. He had also put behind the bar £200, and we drank ourselves into a party atmosphere, so after a disastrous start, it ended up entertaining and was loved, and enjoyed, by everyone who attended.

At last, it seemed that my life had purpose and meaning in it again. Jackie and I were head over heels in love, I had some fantastic friends, and my business was booming. I now drank in moderation, and that was only when I was either with Jackie or with my friends.

I was delighted with my life and couldn't wish for anything else. We'd talked about moving in together for some considerable time but thought that we needed a little bit more stability behind us.

The year was now 1987, and Jackie and I had been together now for several years, as it was fast approaching my 21st birthday, I wanted to celebrate it uniquely with Jackie, so I bought her an engagement ring. On the morning of my birthday, Tina came into my bedroom and was singing Happy Birthday. It was a surprise that she was in such a jovial mood, as she was usually moody.

She handed over my birthday cards, and the present, which was a beautiful gold chain which mum and dad had bought for my 21st birthday. On top of that, I had the usual ceremonial key to the doors.

I got up after being handed my presents cards and gave Tina a hug and a kiss for her efforts, before getting a shower and getting dressed. I wasted no time in booking a table in the Bernie Inn steak house. After breakfast, I went to pick up the engagement ring, which I was to present to Jackie later that evening.

As evening arrived, I turned up at Jackie's house, to pick her up and take her to the restaurant. She looked stunning as usual, all the way to the restaurant my heart was pounding, my mouth was dry, and I was struggling to carry out a conversation with her, but she never suspected a thing.

We were shown our table and sat down and were handed the menus before ordering our drinks. As Jackie was studying her menu, it was the perfect opportunity to present the ring. I took the ring out of my pocket, placing it in front of her. It took a while for her to notice, as she was still picking out what she wanted to eat for dinner.

She put the menu down, and I sat there with a grin on my face which I couldn't hide. She smiled and didn't understand why I was so happy, and I tried to deflect her gaze down to the ring box, but she still wouldn't look down. The only thing I could do was tell her what was in front of her. She looked down and noticed the box. She looked at me and smiled. I then got on one knee in front of a packed restaurant and asked her to marry me.

To my relief, she accepted, the restaurant-goers had witnessed it and gave us a round of applause.

When the drinks arrived, I had arranged at the time of booking the table, for some champagne to be delivered as soon she accepted my proposal. Looking back, that was one of the happiest times of my life, although there have been many more since that time.

After our engagement, we told our parents, who were thrilled with our decision. We decided to move in together, and it was about to come real, as my mum and dad offered to allow us to live at their house and as we were now engaged.

We took up the offer, on the proviso that we also stayed occasionally at Jackie's mum and dad's house, as we didn't want them to think that we will not be grateful for their offer as well. It may have seemed that we were having the best of both worlds. However, that was far from the truth, as although it seemed idyllic, it didn't take long, for what was supposed to be a happy time for both of us to turn sour, due to my mum's actions.

Only a few days earlier, my sister, Tina had walked out and had moved in with my eldest sister Theresa, who was now living by herself and my nephew Lee, as she and her estranged husband Alvin, were going through a messy divorce. Jackie and I had been living in our parents' houses. But for some reasons, mum, whenever we returned from her parents' house, would be somewhat indignant, and not only to myself but even more so to Jackie, making it uncomfortable for being there.

Jackie found this an awkward position to live by and decided to go live at her mum and dads house, and I didn't blame her. The day that she left our home, my mum started an argument with me, so I went upstairs to pack my bags as well. My dad, as usual, tried to play the peacekeeper and came upstairs to speak to me.

As I went to open one of the drawers, the front of it fell off, which aggravated mum's already bad mood. Dad told her to go back downstairs to let him deal with it. He could see that I was physically upset, and as I repaired the drawer front, he gave me words of encouragement and told me, I would always be welcome back at any time. He also told me that he loved me unconditionally and would miss my company.

After I had packed, I gave him a huge hug and promised that I would return periodically to see both of them, after the dust had settled. I handed them back the front door key that I had. After saying goodbye, I could see dad had tears in his eyes, but mum was as cold-hearted as ever and showed no emotion. I shook dad's hand before running down the street after Jackie.

Looking back, I can say, leaving home was the best decision I ever made, although it saddened me to see dad so upset, I just couldn't live with mum anymore. The difference between living at my house and Jackie's was like night and day. Although Jan and Nobby lived different lives to what I was used to, however, they made me feel welcome.

I settled in well at Jackie's house and felt more at home there than I ever did at mine. I do admit that although I missed dad a whole lot more than I did my mum. It's not to say that I didn't love her, but unlike dad, she was always cold and callous in her actions towards us kids.

It was as if she had no heart or soul about her, but later on in life, she was always there for me and would do whatever she could to support me. As Jackie and I were now engaged, we were building up our bottom draw of household items that would give us a start when we had our own home.

Jackie was now working at the new Waitrose store in Northwood hills, and I was building up a large customer base with my business. We started up a joint bank account and would try to save as much money as we possibly could and build a nest egg for ourselves.

We still had quality time together, and we would go and visit her aunt and uncle, who would often have barbecues and parties. I got on well with all her aunts and uncles, and when her favourite aunt and uncle decided to move to Spain, they invited us out for a holiday.

They'd bought land and had a Villa built for them which had a swimming pool. We were unable to visit them at that time, but we did make plans to visit them later in the future. Only by the time that we did, due to Spanish regulations, they had to sell the Villa, and move to small apartments which were nearby in Alicante.

However, we were still welcome to visit them, and they had arranged for one of their friends who had a spare apartment, so we went on our first foreign holiday together, which we thoroughly enjoyed I was made welcome by everyone.

At that period, things were going well for both myself and Jackie, and we became closer with each passing day. The more I was with Jackie, the more I fell in love with her, and I felt a bond with her. She was not only my fiancé but my lover and also my best friend.

Our lives were heading in the right direction it seemed, although on occasions we would have a blazing row, but we never went to bed on an argument and always made up. As promised, I would always return home and spend quality time with mum dad, and when they were around, my two sisters and my nephew Lee, as well as my eldest brother Peter his wife Lynn, and his two kids Ben and Lucy.

As always, Jackie would always be by my side, and they accepted her as part of the family. We had some magical times, and enjoyed many memorable occasions together, as one big happy family. Of course, we would never exclude Nobby or Jan, and they would join us on occasions.

The only person missing in all of this was my brother David, of whom we lost contact with, and although the rest of the family never mentioned him, I thought about him almost every day. I even said this to my dad, and he admitted that he too wished that he could see him again.

My relationship with Jackie went from strength to strength, even her friend Sally admitted that we were good together as a couple. Neither of us could bear to be apart from one another, and if either of us were out with our friends, and the other stayed at home, then the other would never fail to ring up. My business was blossoming, and Jackie was doing well in her position at Waitrose, and even managed to rise through the ranks to assistant section manager of the patisserie section in another new store at Northwood Hills.

It seemed that our idyllic lifestyle would continue indefinitely. For years we were reaping the benefits of our hard work, but all good things come to an end.

Due to the industry I was in, just as night follows day, the work started to dry up, and I was struggling once more to acquire clients.

The choices I faced, were either to join the dole queue and sign-on or once again find alternative employment. I could not face being part of the unemployment set and once again searched for suitable jobs, even if it meant only for a short term, just until my business picked up again.

A few friends suggested that I try and apply for jobs on a building site. However, I just couldn't face working on a site, as with most building firms the only way they could cut costs, was to the cut quality of the materials.

As I had been trained to the highest standard, I couldn't lower my standards and use substandard materials. I applied for several jobs and even reapplied for a position at Waitrose or another supermarket. But my applications for these jobs proved to be fruitless.

It was now December 1989, And I was getting desperate for a job, and even more desperate for money, as I was spending the money that myself and Jackie had built up over the years. While searching the classified ads for jobs, I saw a job advertised for a company called APT controls, based in Hatch End. It was a week before Christmas that I received a letter to attend an interview. On the day of the interview, as usual, I smartly dressed in my suit. I was optimistic in my outlook for my upcoming interview.

A manager called Laurie Taylor conducted the interview, he had come from another company, and APT had acquired this company now based in Radlett under the trading name of Slavedor. This company had specialised in a manufacturer of electrical, mechanical garage door openers.

APT was the UK leaders in the design and manufacturer of car park barriers and pay and display machines and had purchased Slavedor to expand into the domestic market. Laurie explained to me that if they offered me the position, I would be part of a small team building the garage door openers. It was simple electromechanical engineering, but I thought that it would be suitable for my requirements, even in the short term.

I did well in the interview, and the next day Laurie phoned me and offered me the position.

I accepted his offer, and my start date was the 2nd of January 1990.

It was a new year, and a fresh start in my new job. I was shown to the department where I would be working alongside my colleagues, and I also met the team leader, a guy called Tony. He introduced me to the other two members of staff, Andrea, and also a new start, and Steve.

I was also introduced to Peter, who was in charge of the warehouse for Slavedor, and the technical engineer name Norris. I was placed to work with Steve, who was a tall lad and very friendly. We quickly established a rapport with each other, as we both supported Queens Park Rangers.

Our job was to prepare the motors used to power the garage door openers, which I found very easy to pick up. Tony and

Andrea were making the other parts for the machine, ready for them to be assembled as an entire unit.

During the day, myself and Steve had a great laugh together, and we couldn't help but to take the piss out of Tony, as he was not only a teenager, and some six years younger than myself and Steve, but he was also somewhat dim-witted and easy to wind up.

After we'd assembled the parts, we took our lunch break where Steve and I continued our bombardment of teasing Tony. We also talked about football, and I suggested that we both go and see Queens Park Rangers that night, they were playing at home against Cardiff City. Steve jumped at the chance. We decided that I would follow him home and have tea around his house before we set off for Loftus Road to watch our team.

After lunch, we resumed our work and started to assemble the operators. The work was somewhat monotonous. However, our days seemed to fly by, as we were relentless in tormenting Tony, who made it easy for us to make fun of him.

At last, the day was over, and I rang up Jackie to tell her that I was going to go and watch the football with my new friend, Steve and would be home later that evening. I followed Steve home, who had been given a lift by Peter in his van. Steve was in the back with Tony and was play fighting with him to wind him up a bit more, as I could see all of this going on, I couldn't help but fall around in fits of laughter.

We arrived at Steve's house, which was in Borehamwood, where he introduced me to his mum Annie, and his sister Lisa. Steve mum had made us both some sandwiches and a pot of tea.

After eating, we said our farewells and headed off to Loftus Road for the football.

Throughout the journey, we laughed and joked, as Steve had the same wicked sense of humour as I did. It was like looking at myself in the mirror, and you could say, he was my brother from another mother. At the stadium, we purchased our tickets and went to sit down in the Ellerslie Road Stand, which had a great view of the pitch but was near the Cardiff City fans away end.

As it was an evening match, there were very few Cardiff fans in attendance, and our home support was immeasurable, and as usual raucous in our songs and encouragement of our team. We didn't have long to wait for our first goal. As usual, the crowd erupted into a fury, and as football fans taunted the away fans which didn't go down too well.

We were overrunning Cardiff City on the pitch, and they had nothing to offer, and soon went down two-nil before half time. When a second half started, Cardiff scored very early on, but this was to be a consolation goal for them, as we beat them 4-1. Steve and I, along with the rest of the Queens Park Rangers fans were in jubilant mood and we're singing our heads off in praise of our team.

On the other hand, I wish I could say the same for the Cardiff City supporters, who had a long journey back to Wales and also had to suffer the indignity, of the relentless chanting as regards of their sexuality between them.

As we were both leaving, I decided to take the piss out of the Cardiff City fans nearest to us but in a Welsh accent, which didn't go down too well with one of them, who told me to 'leave it out boyo,' which I found a source of amusement, and continued with my barrage.

The next day at work, myself and Steve relived the match over and over again and planned our next soiree to go to the football again, which would be the upcoming Saturday, which was also being played at Leeds United's ground at Elland Road.

Saturday's match was just as entertaining as the midweek match we were playing. Leeds were a good team at that period, and who were formidable opponents, who made it tough for QPR to play against, and it was Leeds who broke the deadlock and scored first.

QPR was struggling to get out of first gear and was camped in their half defending like crazy, but to no avail, as just 60 seconds after their first, they struck again. Both myself and the rest of the fans were deadly silent.

However, our mood lifted when we scored, and the crowd got back behind the team again.

Just before half time, QPR had a break, and our star player Roy Wegerle scored an absolutely fantastic goal, after beating five opponents, and just before the half time whistle was blown. When the second half got underway, we were a different team from that in the first half so the half time team talk must have fired them up as they came out with all guns blazing.

However, our hearts sank, as Leeds were awarded a penalty! To everyone's amazement and relief, the ball hit the bar. With only five minutes left, Roy Wegerle wrapped up the points, and the crowd went crazy which almost blew the lid off the stadium.

I must admit that the game was one of the best matches I had seen played by one of the best teams that we have had. It was a superb result for QPR, to win away at Leeds was an achievement, as they were a magnificent side themselves. The journey back home was a great laugh and full of excitement.

Steve and I became the best friends, and he introduced me to his other friends Rob and Jay. Rob was a passionate Manchester United supporter, and Jay like Steve and me supported QPR.

Although Rob supported Man Utd, he would come along with Steve, Jay, and myself to Loftus Road to support the boys. Even though I had made some new friends, I'd always go back to my first love, of whom I adored, and that was Jackie. I would never allow anything to come between her and me.

My love for her was immense, and I thought it would be a good idea to introduce her to Steve, and they hit it off and became good friends themselves. We would go out for a drink together, and all three of us enjoyed each other's company, and Steve became part of my family. I was closer to him than my siblings.

Back at work myself and Steve we're like a tag team when it came to scolding and teasing Tony. You could argue that it was a form of bullying, and I suppose in a way it was. I would imagine, if it happened in today's society, then we would find ourselves in trouble and be deemed as anti-social.

However, it was a different life back then, and although I was not condoning our actions, Tony would do things, that would add fuel to the fire, so in a way, he was setting himself up for all of our jokes.

One such occasion, we had a delivery of blue end pieces for the garage door operators, and Tony was tasked with writing the word blue on each box so that the warehouse would recognise them from the original colouring. This was like a red rag to a bull for me and Steve, an opportunity not to be missed.

Tony had indeed correctly spelt the word blue. However, I jokingly told him that he had misspelt them and that the correct spelling was bloo! At first Tony didn't believe me, but as Steve was in with the joke, he backed me up and corrected Tony that my spelling was correct.

Although put out, Tony crossed out the correct spelling of blue, and instead rewrote the word bloo on each of the 250 boxes, that he'd rightly spelt in the first place. When Peter the Slavedor warehouse manager saw the boxes had been spelt wrong, he berated Tony calling him a 'complete and utter moron, much to mine and Steve amusement.

This form of entertainment as we called it made our days go much quicker, and we never tired from poking fun at Tony's expense, even the other employees from APT joined in with our banter.

Tony made it even worse for himself, when he had spoken to the management team, and claimed that they had called him an 'exceptional teenager'. I wished that those words were true; however, in Tony's case, they were unfounded.

After three months at APT, I handed in my notice. I had procured more clients and can confidently continue my business. I suggested to Steve that he came to work with me, as he had some experience as a labourer which he gained as his first job. Sadly, he declined as he wanted a steadier environment, and he needed the money to help support his mum.

I respected him for his decision, although I hoped one day that he would change his mind, and would work with me. Even though I had now left, it didn't stop my association with Steve, as I saw him more like a brother rather than a friend, and we spent a lot of time together watching football or socialising in the pub and having a fantastic laugh.

Sometimes it would be just Steve and me, and other times it would be with either Jackie of who he had a fantastic bond with, or with Rob and Jay. Once again, my business started to pick up, and I was back doing what I enjoyed most, which was renovating and doing general building work for specialized clients.

As my business picked up, and with the money, Jackie was earning, we decided to move in together in our own home. We found a one-bedroom flat in South Harrow, which was owned by a sport injuries chiropractor, who runs his business downstairs.

After viewing the flat with the agent, we agreed on terms and moved in a few days later. As it was furnished, we only had to bring our clothing and a few personal items. Although it was small for our needs, it was OK. The only downside was the rent which was £420 per calendar month.

At first, we could pay this amount. However, we soon realised that with the other bills and having to buy food and just general living expenses, we found it somewhat expensive and we were struggling to make ends meet. Unfortunately, we were only one month into hour 6-month contract agreement, and we were unable to terminate the contract early even though we explained our financial situation. Therefore, we had to remain within the property until six months had expired.

Within that time, we searched for a cheaper alternative and came across a more affordable, not as exclusive flat above a parade of shops right opposite Northwood hills station. The apartment was one bedroom and unfurnished, it was also noisy due to the relentless trains going past, but the rent was £120 cheaper than the flat that we were in at that time.

The other good thing was that it was only a stone's throw away from Waitrose Northwood hills, which would suit Jackie. Reluctantly we decided that it was the best solution and placed a deposit down and moved out of our old flat after giving notice within a week of signing the new agreement for the new place.

Jackie was upset at leaving our first flat and tried to blame herself, and I wouldn't hear of it. We decided after moving into our new place that we would look into buying our own house. We weren't able to purchase any properties in the Harrow and surrounding areas, as the prices were expensive and way above our price range. Also, neither of us knew anything about buying properties or even where we had to start.

Our saving grace was that my eldest sister Theresa had purchased houses before and had bought one with her new partner Steve in Dunstable. Also, my middle sister and her husband, Steve owned a nearby property Dunstable in a place called Houghton Regis.

We spoke to Theresa as regards our plans, and she was more than happy to assist us in buying our first home. She also introduced us to a financial advisor of home specialised in arranging 100% mortgages for first-time buyers without a deposit.

After looking around the Luton area, we saw a beautiful little end of terrace property on Amhurst road located on the Lewsey farm estate. We went to the scheduled viewing and fell in love with a property which was two bedrooms, a large lounge, and medium-sized kitchen, at the rear was a reasonably sized established garden, at the front was a large driveway capable of holding six vehicles.

As a qualified builder, I could see the full potential and visualised how I could improve it—initially built in 1955 and well-constructed, it was what you would expect from a property built around that decade.

The most immediate improvements that I could see was it required new double glazed windows, it still had the original metal frame Crittall style windows, which were the preferred windows at the time it was built.

After the viewing, we took advice as to how much to offer, as the asking price what's £48,000. The estate agent admitted that a member of his staff owned the property, which was an ex-council house. It was a slight problem, as that would be some conflicting interest, as he was not only acting on her behalf but as she was an employee, it meant that we might not be able to purchase the property.

We contacted our financial advisor, and he suggested that we offered £42,500, on the proviso, the estate agent didn't divulge this information to the solicitors acting on our behalf, or the mortgage provider.

After a nervous wait of two days, we had a phone call to inform us that they had accepted our offer. Jackie and I were over the moon and allowed ourselves a small celebration. We now had an anxious wait for the searches to be done for our mortgage application to go through.

Three weeks later, our prayers were answered, and it had all been accepted and that we were given a completion date. Armed with this new information, we tended our notice to terminate our contract at the flat we were renting.

We exchanged contracts, and we picked our keys up to our new home, and we arranged to hire a van so we could pack our belongings and move in. Jackie's dad came along to help us move, he also drove the van, with me following in my car.

It seemed a dream come true, especially after we'd emptied the van with our belongings and enjoyed our first cup of tea in our new home. The next morning, I started some of the jobs needed and begun the refurbishment of our house.

The previous owner had left several gardening tools in the sheds, one was a heavy-duty electric hedge trimmer, so my first task was to clear the garden, which due to being overgrown, was blocking out some of our natural light. The more I cut down, the more the garden seemed to grow in size.

I'd cleared so much overgrown foliage, that I noticed for the first time, houses were backing on to our property. As I was removing the rear of the garden, one of our neighbours in the properties behind us came up and introduced herself as Joan.

She was a sweet dear old lady and an amiable person, who was glad, at last, that our garden, which had been left to overgrow for so many years, would allow more light into her own beautifully kept garden. My next task in the garden was to hire a chainsaw, to cut back eight fully grown leylandii trees.

Now I might be a builder, but a lumberjack I certainly am not. Being the person that I am, I thought it would be easy to cut the trees down to floor level, especially as I had planned, to cut them down in short sections, around four feet each section.

Armed with my new toy of the chainsaw, I shinned up the first tree and tied a rope onto the first section, where Jackie and our neighbour, was going to pull down as soon as I had cut through it. At first, my plan was working successfully, encouraged by my successes on the other trees, I became too confident and cocksure of myself, and my last tree thought it would be more comfortable, to cut the section a lot larger.

However, as I cut through, Jackie and our neighbour couldn't hold the sheer size of the section and were struggling to hold it. I tried to get down to help them. The tree, instead of falling into our garden, had other ideas and fell into the property behind. Fortunately, the house behind was empty, and I jumped over the fence and manhandled the section back over into our garden.

We had been in our home for six months, and the renovations were taking shape. Also, Jackie had started a new job at Sainsbury's in Dunstable, and the commute to Northwood Hills every day was taking its toll. I found some new clients in and around Luton and Dunstable area, and work was picking up, and life couldn't be sweeter it would seem.

However, I had noticed a change in Jackie; she didn't appear to be usual herself and always seem to be lethargic. She was coming down with minor ailments, I came home one evening, and it appeared that she had been drinking, as she was slurring her speech, which was totally out of character.

I was concerned about her health, but she assured me that apart from feeling tired, she was OK. She promised, she'd make an appointment at the doctors and would rest more often. After the visit to the doctors, she told me that they had diagnosed her with a virus, which was believed, to be down to the stress of moving, and her new job, within a short space of time.

For her to minimalise any stress, I'd done my utmost to ensure she was often resting, to a point, where I was allowing her plenty of bed rest, and not allowing her to do any chores.

After three weeks of her doing very little, her health improved and she was back to her old cheerful self again, much to the relief of myself, and the rest of our families. Several months had elapsed from the time that she had been ill, and we soon forgot about it and continued with our daily lives.

My mum and dad even moved up to Dunstable to be nearer the family and their grandchildren. That was a pleasant time for all of us, as we could all get together a lot easier than we used too. As Jackie came from a small family, she enjoyed getting together, although, I wasn't as enthusiastic, simply because Tina and my personality often clashed. Although for the sake of her kids, we tolerated each other and even enjoyed ourselves.

Mum and dad have been in their new home for two months, and everything seemed to be going well. However, I had just completed a client's job and went home early. As I got through the front door, I noticed there was an answerphone message. As I retrieved the message, it was somewhat distraught news from my dad, asking me to ring him up as a matter of urgency.

I rang dad up, and he asked me to go around to his and mum's house, as Jackie was there, and I could tell from his voice, that there was something seriously wrong.

They lived a short distance away from where we lived, and I raced around there fearing the worst. Dad, who was on holiday from his work, opened the door and told me that Jackie was in the dining room. She had been sent home from work and had rung up my dad while I was at work, to go and pick her up.   As she was sitting there, her right arm was having involuntary spasms. She assured me that she wasn't in any pain, and it was only her arm that was causing her problems and had started while she was at work.

I suggested we go to the hospital for a check-up, but she said that she wanted to go home and just rest. Dad had made us both a cup of coffee, and her spasms became less frequent, so we sat back, and had a good chat with dad, before taking her home when there, she would rest with her feet up while I cooked our tea.

Eventually, the spasms stopped, and she was back to normal again as if nothing had happened. All she wanted was to have a nice hot bath and relax. I ran her a bath and suggested that I stay in the bathroom, just in case anything should happen, but she declined my offer, as she wanted a few moments alone by herself.

The next day it was as if nothing had happened, and she returned to work, and we had no further incident, again we just put it down to stress, and we forgot about it. After a while, our lives improved as everything was coming up smelling of roses. The renovations to home were in full swing, and I spared no expense in obtaining the best materials. As I had my own business, my accountant was very astute, and put down the materials for my projects at home, as tax-deductible.

Life couldn't get any better and felt that we were both blessed with what we had. The only thing missing in our lives were children, so we started to plan for our own family. After a few months of trying, Jackie was finding it difficult to conceive, even though we tried everything for her to fall pregnant.

We both underwent tests and found that both of us had minor problems. Although my sperm count was high, a lot of the sperm were non-swimmers, but that in itself wasn't the reason we found it difficult for her to fall pregnant.

Jackie's test results had indicated that she was suffering from a condition called endometriosis, which was affecting her ovaries. Still, they could be rectified and improved on, by her going on to the IVF program.

Jackie had been on IVF medication for three months, and she still found it difficult to conceive and was also having more heavier bleeds, during her monthly periods. But the passion of having children, grew ever stronger for us so she continued, in the hope that we would soon be blessed with a child.

As time passed, she started getting abdominal pains but put it down to constipation; however, this wasn't the case. What the

IVF doctor had failed to explain to us, was one of the side effects with the medication, that it increased the risk of the endometriosis increasing, and could cause, what was commonly known as chocolate cysts.

Her abdominal discomfort was getting worse, but she continued with the medication as prescribed. At that time, I was doing a job for one of my mum's good friends, where I had a phone call at their home, to say that Jackie had been rushed into hospital.

As they lived in north London near Highbury, I had a long journey ahead to be by her side.

By the time I had returned to Luton, it was 10 pm, and it was too late for me to visit her at the hospital. I rang up the ward and asked how she was doing, and they told me Jackie had been rushed to emergency surgery, as the cysts were on the verge of bursting, and without medical intervention, she would have died.

The next day I rushed to her side to be with her, as I entered the ward where she was recovering, the so-called IVF specialist was there, to tell her that the operation had been a success. He explained that it was the medication clomide, that had accelerated the endometriosis, and had caused the chocolate cysts, which was causing her the discomfort.

After hearing this news, I was livid, and I asked to speak to him alone. In his office, he tried to justify the IVF treatment of which he recommended, but I was having none of it, and ripped into him, as he had failed to notify us of the risks. I found him somewhat arrogant in his answers, and I lost my temper.

Fearing for his safety, he called his secretary to call security to escort me out.

I decided to make an official complaint based on the grounds of his medical negligence. After the investigation, the hospital trust discovered that he'd indeed failed to notify us of the dangers and he was severely reprimanded. Jackie spent two weeks in hospital before being allowed home to recover.

Her work had been notified and had been very helpful and understanding, and she need not worry, as her job would be safe and would be there when she returned. In the meantime, Jackie made a full recovery, and the hospital had upheld our complaint.

After Jackie's a close call, we decided to stop the IVF treatment and tried to conceive naturally, but it was to no avail. It was devastating news for both of us, but more so for Jackie, as she was desperate to have children, and I was powerless to help her and didn't know how to comfort her, everything I tried seems to irritate her.

Mum tried to intervene and offer advice, to both of us, but neither of us wanted to hear it. For the time being, we had to make do, with spending as much time as we could, with our nephews and nieces, but it was not the same as having our own kids. After a while, we resigned to the fact that we would never become parents and concentrated our efforts, on each other, which bought us closer together. Regardless of having my business and being immensely happy and deeply in love with Jackie, at the back of my mind, there was always something amiss. It would take me a further two years to realise what it was that I craved for.

Chapter Twelve

Honi Soit Qui Mal Y pense

The year now was 1992, and my business was booming. But I kept on having niggling doubts that something was missing in my life, but I could not work out what it was. I think that my sub-conscious mind was reliving part of my past, from 1990, which was watching news reports, about the Iraqi invasion of Kuwait. Iraqi tyrant and dictator Saddam Hussein had invaded Kuwait, which was seen by the western world, as an aggressive act of war.

Due to this unprecedented aggression against the small nation of Kuwait, The UK and USA and other countries prepared for a war with Iraq codenamed operation 'desert storm'. I cannot say for sure if this was one of the contributing factors of myself wanting to join the army, but I have to admit, that seeing the news report of the war, made me proud to be British.

The only other time that I felt like this, was when I was at school, and Britain sent over a task force, thousands of miles away to liberate The Falkland Islands, which had been invaded by the Argentinian armed forces. I remembered thinking back then, how exciting it would be to become a professional soldier and become a member of perhaps one of the finest military I have ever seen, the British Armed forces.

After a lot of thought and soul searching, I realised that it was the camaraderie that I experienced for the first time while I was serving as a TA soldier. I decided to go and speak, to the only person of whom would understand what I was feeling, and that was my dad.

I was coming from a military background, for many years as a professional soldier and first-class military musician. He knew exactly where I was coming from, we went to the local pub, and had a heart to heart about me joining, up as a full-time regular soldier.

Although he was very proud of me, for what I had achieved in my life, having my business, and finding alternative work when the building trade was at its slowest, he listened intently to my predicament. Still, he gave me encouragement to pursue my endeavours. I had done well and had settled down. I was still somewhat naive, and I would occasionally let my destructive past come back and haunt me. He explained that military life would bring the best out of me, and would turn me from boy to a man. I regaled at his stories that he used to tell me of when he was in the army, and that if he had not been in the military, he would have never seen, or visited some of the places he was posted to and worked as a soldier. He did suggest that I should think about it and would back me up with whatever decision I made.

After our man to man chat, I spent several days contemplating my future. I decided after our conversation, not to say anything to Jackie yet. Until I had agreed as to what I was going to do, I'd been working at a client's house for several days, and pass by an army recruitment office, while I would be out for my lunch.

I'd been thinking about my conversation with dad, and I couldn't get the thought out of my head. It was the second to last the day before I had completed work at my client's house. I walked along the street, as usual, to get my lunch, as I stood in front of the army recruitment office, it was like an unseen force that was pulling me in, so I took a deep breath and walked inside.

The recruitment Sergeant welcomed me, and he sat me down to take my particulars. As he was collecting the paperwork needed, I was looking around the office, and the various photographs of the different jobs, that I could expect if I decided to join up. Also, there was film playing which had multiple roles, and two stood out above the rest, which was the Royal artillery, and the Parachute regiments.

As the Sergeant came back with the paperwork, he asked me some questions as to what I wanted. I expressed interest in the artillery film as well as the Parachute regiment that I had just seen. He smiled as he explained that there was one regiment that may fit the bill, and that was the 7th Parachute regiment RHA, which took in both worlds.

I also explained that I had gained some military experience while serving in the TA. He was most intrigued by this, and I should have no problems in being enrolled due to this, he made a phone call to my previous TA unit.

After the call, we went through the paperwork, and after reading everything that was required, I signed on the dotted line. As soon as I had done so, I experienced several mixed emotions, which was excitement, concern, and apprehension. The recruitment officer explained that I would receive a letter from them after a few days.

On the way home, I was thinking of what I was going to say to Jackie, as I had not divulged my ideas, and had kept it a secret. I decided that honesty was the best policy and would tell her outright rather than beating about the bush and skirting around it. As I walked through the door, Jackie, as usual, was pleased to see me, and we shared a kiss. I decided that I would let Jackie tell me about her day, which would buy me some time, to find the courage to tell her what I had done.

Taking a deep breath, I came straight out with it and told her that I had signed up to join the army and that I would be notified in a few days. I could see in Jackie's face, that she was somewhat shocked and a little bit bemused. After allowing it to sink in, she took hold of my hands, and told me, that she would support any decision I made.

Looking deep into her eyes and could not only see the love she had for me but that she was also genuine in her answer. We both embraced and shared a passionate kiss, which leads to us making love, and we fell into a deep sleep, cradling each other.

I have to admit that every day, I grew more and more in love with Jackie, and knew that she felt the same for me. The only concern that I had was how the army would react as I had a mortgage, and would they allow me to commute, instead of living in the barracks. I spoke to dad about this concern, the only suggestion that he could come up with, was, to be honest with them, and talk to my commanding officer.

A few days after I had signed up, I received the letter, which included instructions, I would have to go through a stringent medical. If successful, then I would have to go through processing, which involved being sworn in, and completing other forms of paperwork.

On the day of my medical, I was as nervous as hell. I was called in by the medical officer, who conducted a physical examination as well as mentally, to ascertain my fitness to serve. I passed A1 fitness level, next, was the swearing of allegiance to Her Majesty the Queen, and completed the rest of the paperwork, before being inducted, and being enrolled officially. After completion, I was accepted as a member of 7th Parachute Regiment Royal Horse Artillery, and I was given one week to prepare, before receiving orders to report at the barracks.

I spent my time wisely in the last week that I was to be a civilian, and completed my final client's renovations and building works, and spending my entire free time with Jackie and both of our families, which tinged with happiness, and a lot of sadness.

But I knew that I was doing the right thing for myself. I spent my last day as a civilian solely with Jackie, as I wanted it to be unique for both of us, and something we can remember for a long time. Until I received permission to live off the barracks, I would be away from her, for the duration of my basic training. Arriving at the barracks was very daunting, as just like my time in the TA, I was ushered in, and had to wait with the other recruits, for our induction.

When they called me up, as I had previously been military service with the TA regiment, I didn't have to undergo the full induction process. I inquired if I could live away from the barracks, as I'd a mortgaged property. They explained, I would have to apply to the commanding officer, for special permission to do so, but while in the training phase, I'd have to remain in barracks.

Although I was slightly disappointed, I would make the most of living in barracks, and as I had already acquired some military experience from my time at the TA, I put my acquired knowledge to good use. I schooled the other recruits which became somewhat valuable, as, at our room inspections, we were well versed in military etiquette.

In the meantime, while in training, I petitioned the commanding officer, to allow me to live off base after I had completed the necessary training. I'd been at the barracks for four weeks when I was ordered to attend a meeting with the CO. I marched into his office and came to attention a few feet away from his desk.

As soon as I had done so, I saluted him and awaited his instructions. He had reviewed my request and was happy to allow me to live off the base. Although, I would be required to strictly adhere to be criteria, of ensuring I was on duty on time. Also, he expected, that whenever I travelled to and from the base, I had to do so incognito in civilian clothing. I would have to vary my route to and from the base, so I won't arouse suspicion or draw attention to myself.

He also explained that he'd received my service records from the TA unit, and had been highly commended, by the unit commanding officer. He seemed impressed with what I had achieved and was a marvellous officer, and one I was proud to serve under. After our meeting, I smartly saluted him, before doing an about-turn, and marching out of his office.

As soon as I could, I contacted Jackie on the phone, and she was ecstatic at the news, I'd relayed to her, and we couldn't wait to see each other again. After completing my basic training, I was allowed a week's rest leave, and the only thing I had on my mind, was going home to Jackie.

Walking through our front door, Jackie greeted me, but unknown to me; she'd arranged a homecoming party for me, which was a shock and surprise to me, it was nevertheless welcoming. After the great week, especially with Jackie I had to return to specialist parachute, and artillery training.

I was now part of the 7th Parachute Regiment Royal Artillery. The guns of which I was to be trained on were L118 105 mm light, these were excellent machines, and I enjoyed every minute of being part of the gun crew. Our gun number one was Sergeant Martin, who was an experienced soldier, having served in Operation Desert Storm. I fitted well into the squad and learnt every aspect of each job required to operate the gun. I passed the guns course quickly; I supposed it was the big kid in me that likes to play with toys.

I also had to undergo parachute training, which was the best bit, and although the first jump was scary, I couldn't wait to do the rest, and obtain my wings as I am a self-confessed adrenalin junkie.

For me, it seemed I had the best of both worlds, although I would be away from home for long periods, the thought of going home back to Jackie kept my spirits up, and I couldn't wait to see her at every opportunity. A year passed since I had joined the army and was doing well in my job.

I got on well with everybody I worked with and formed a close bond with all those concerned. Jackie was doing well at her job at Sainsbury's, and she too was enjoying her roles. My first time away with the army, was in Germany, and we were stationed there for an extended period. It would mean that I would be away from Jackie, on a 6-month tour.

Although I loved Germany, I would ring her every day, and we would write to each other regularly. One evening I rang her up and could hear that there was something wrong in her voice. I asked if she was OK, and she replied that she was, but I wasn't sure, as she was speaking, in what can only be described as slow-motion, and was slurring her speech. It was as if she had been drinking.   However, she explained that she was feeling fine and that she was just missing me.

Two days later, we were preparing to go out on exercise, when I was ordered, to go and see the camp adjutant, who told me, I had received an urgent phone call from the UK. I rang up home, and to my surprise, the phone was answered by mum, who told me that Jackie, had been taken to the hospital by her work colleagues, as she had started to have involuntary spasms in her left arm, and she was to have tests, including a lumbar puncture.

After the call, I explained the situation to my commanding officer, and they arranged for me to fly back home, to be by her side on compassionate grounds. Throughout the journey, all I thought about was Jackie. When I got to the hospital, she was in a terrible state. Her mum and dad were also around.

A short while later, the doctor appeared, and gave us the devastating news, that the test results indicated that Jackie, had been diagnosed with multiple sclerosis.

Neither of us had heard of this condition, but the doctor explained, that Jackie's nervous system the myelin, that protected the nerves was being eaten away, thus not allowing the information, to be passed down from her brain to the rest of her body.

The doctor was excellent, and explained it in layman's terms, as imagining a length of electrical wire, part of the plastic coating in sections had been cutaway, and therefore some information would be lost.

Although her condition was in the early stages, he told us there was no known cure.

Jackie's mum and dad comforted myself and Jackie, as they did so my parents arrived, and they too shared our sadness. After several hours, they all left and allowed me and Jackie to be alone together. By the time they left, Jackie had composed herself, sufficiently for us to talk.

I told her that I would resign from the army, but she would have none of it and made me promise not to do so. At first, I was reluctant not to do so but, in the end, I agreed, as she told me, that we could both work through it. The next day, I took her home and ensured that she did as little as possible, to aid her recovery.

Over the next few days, our parents visited, and my two sisters, who assured me that Jackie would be well looked after while I was in the army. After they left, we were alone again, we felt more at ease, knowing that she would be in safe hands, while I was on duty. After a week, Jackie was well enough, for me to go back to Germany, and someone from our families to be there, should she require it.

Upon my return, my commanding officer spoke to me, assuring me that they would support me, for as long as I needed it. Armed with that information from my commanding officer, I returned to active duty. Sainsbury's had also done the same for Jackie, and both of us couldn't thank them enough, and we would be forever grateful.

Over the next few weeks, things got back to normal, and Jackie had made a marvellous recovery and returned to work. I continued with my duties and concentrated my efforts, of being the best soldier I could, and before I knew it, two years had flown by, within a blink of an eye.

I would always give 100% and more in my role and strived to make myself the best of the best. My efforts hadn't gone unnoticed, my superior officers recommended me up for promotion, as a junior NCO.

After my promotion, my responsibilities increased. I now had the task of training the men under my command, a role which I thoroughly relished. Jackie was also promoted to team leader at Sainsbury's, and for the time being, her MS had gone into remission, and she would not have another attack, for many years. I excelled at soldiering, and I rose through the ranks very quickly. I'd been promoted again, after a year of my original promotion. As a result, I was the second in command of one of the guns. Due to my knowledge, I was again recommended to train as a Sergeant and would one day, take charge of my team.

My military career was taking shape, as was my relationship with Jackie. The hardest part was being away from her due to overseas tours. Although, I never let this get in my way or interfere in my duties. Whenever the tours finished, I couldn't wait to get back home, to be with her. My career tested our relationship to the maximum, and also, Jackie's MS took its toll on her. Sadly, due to several more attacks, Jackie felt that she was unable to continue in her role at Sainsbury's.

Jackie was well-liked at her workplace, and they offered her part-time hours. However, she felt that she wouldn't be able to give 100%, due to her condition, and Jackie didn't want to let her employers down or her work colleagues, she turned down their offer. However, Sainsbury's rather than just let her go, offered her medical retirement.

Jackie spoke to me about this, and I told her I would support her decision no matter what and would look after both of us, as she had always put me first before her own needs, and I felt that it was about time, for her to take it easy. Both of us knew that it would be tough going, but with the love and support, that we had for each other, we would make it work.

As Jackie had been medically retired, she would be entitled to a pension from Sainsbury's, so in the end, it worked out well for both of us. I made sure that Jackie had help and support while I was away on tours with the army. The arrangement we made, although testing, was for the best all-round, as we were able to work around our lifestyle.

The doctors placed Jackie on steroids, which would help her condition, but would never cure her. She would never let it get to her and would always look on the bright side of life, and strived in her recovery, and help others in theirs.   We'd discussed getting married, and we both felt that the time was right, for us to take the plunge into matrimony. We decided to get married on 24th August 1994, as this would also coincide, with a family holiday so that we would kill two birds with one stone. As neither of us had much money, it was to be a cheap and low-key affair but suited us to the ground.

Our wedding arrived, I had been given two weeks leave from the army, and because of lack of funds, everyone had rallied round to lend a hand. My mum paid for catering for us. It was beautifully set out, in a borrowed self-assembled gazebo, which was in our garden. The rest of the family, including Nobby and Jan, had paid for the booze, even my sister Tina, had paid for our niece Stephanie's bridesmaid dress, as did my sister in law Lynn had done so for our niece Lucy

Jackie would be driven to the registry office by my brother in law, Steve. However, this was just a ruse, as when he arrived at our home, as Jackie and her dad went outside, he drove off, and there right behind him, was a vintage Rolls Royce for the occasion, which I had pulled a few favours, to arrange for her special day.

Although it was a low budget affair, I tried to make it as magical as I could, and as the reception was at our home, we were limited to the number of guests, so we restricted these to our closest family and friends, and some of the neighbours.

I had invited some of my colleagues, and even my commanding officer whom I held in high esteem.

As I was a serving soldier, I decided against getting married in my ceremonial uniform, as I didn't want to draw attention to myself, as I wanted Jackie to be the centre of attention and the focal talking point.

She looked radiant in her wedding dress, and deserved her special day, as she'd always unselfishly put others, including myself first.

The next morning after our wedding, myself and my new wife Jackie, flew out from Luton airport and were travelling with my mum and dad, while my two sisters, Theresa and Tina and their families, would be flying out later that same day. We were all off to the island of Minorca, which we had initially planned as a family holiday; it was still our honeymoon.

Our hotel was run by a company called Sol holidays, German and Spanish guests predominantly frequented the hotel. So, their tastes were mainly catered for. However, there was also a large contingent of British holidaymakers, and we all mingled in with each other.

Finally, after my sister's and their families arrived, we all met up in the evening for dinner. After eating, we frequented downstairs, as the entertainment was about to start. It was had organised by the holiday reps and would include some party games, as Jackie and I were newlyweds, we were talked into joining in the fun.

We had a series of tasks to complete before the time allocated had run out. We were one of four couples chosen, which consisted of one Spanish couple and two German couples. The first task was us, men, had to form a figure of eight movements, in between our wives' legs—much to the amusement of the other holiday guests. Jackie and I were only pipped at the post, by one point by the Spanish couple, but it was all in good fun.

Secondly, we had to pretend that we were Tarzan and our wives were Jane, of whom we have just rescued. After carrying them around the stage in our arms, we had to carefully put them in their seat, followed by our best Tarzan call. I won hands down on this task.

We also had to run into the crowd, and acquire two things, one was a bra which was easy enough, but the other was a postage stamp. As soon as we were given the off, the three other men and I rushed into the crowd, to try and get the items required. The first one back to his seat with the items would be declared the winner.

I acquired the stamp from another British family, and the bra came from my mum! I rushed back to my seat, I was the first to finish, but as I went to sit down, I fell backwards off the chair, to the amusement of everyone. The British holidaymakers were well and truly rooting for me and were chanting my name for the next task.

The task, which I knew wasn't the best at doing, as it was to do disco dancing, and I have two left feet.

However, I made the most of it, and it was up to the crowd to decide.

As the music played on, Jackie and I danced our socks off, and were level on points, with a couple from East Germany.

After we finished, the rep asked who the best was, and although the crowd was rooting for us, we didn't win as the German and Spanish had chosen the couple from East Germany, and they were awarded a bottle of champagne, as their prize.

Even though we came second, we made good friends, from all the couples that participated, and the winner's shared the champagne, which ended a fantastic evening with all concerned. As I could speak German, I introduced myself and Jackie, to the West German couple Kurt and Dagmar, and we became good friends. They spoke excellent English much to Jackie's relief.

The next morning, we went down to the restaurant for breakfast, before meeting up with the reps for the usual welcome presentation, which included a talk from a kid's club's representatives, of whom were there, to give the parents a chance, of some respite away from their kids.

At first, my nephews and nieces, including my eldest nephew Lee were not keen on joining the kids club. However, to encourage them, I said that I would join, which, except for Lee, went down well with my other nephew and niece, Stephanie and Ross.

The kids club reps thought this was an excellent idea and joined in my deception and gave me a kid's club name of Barley Mow, who'd been a character in the children's program, called Bod. One of the reps, opted for the name Aunt Flo, also from the programme, the other, remained with her name. Like the kids, I was given a 'fun passport', a lifelong member of the kid's club badge, a kid's club T-shirt, the biggest they could find, was for a 6-year-old! However, I was determined to make it fit, and it looked like a boob tube. After my enrolment, I went back up to the pool area, to a round of applause by my family, and from the other British holidaymakers.

I thought that my moment of fun, to get my nephew and niece involved with the club would be an end to it and then I could enjoy my honeymoon and holiday without any distraction. However, due to my interaction with them, and the other kids, I didn't realise I'd made a rod for my own back.

We woke early, and we'd done, what every honeymooning couple would do, what was expected for them to do, before showering and going for breakfast. We had just walked into the dining room, when the British parents, kept shaking our hands, to congratulate us on our marriage, and to also thank me, for making the kids feel at ease, by joining the kids club.

After breakfast, we went down to the pool area to sunbathe, where we were joined by the rest of our family, who'd just finished their breakfast and been for a walk. We had been there for about one hour, when the reps came around, for the kid's club, announcing that it was time, for the kids to go and have fun.

I was relaxing, and a shadow appeared over me. To my surprise standing there, was the reps surrounded by all of the kids. It seemed that all of the kids wanted me to join them in a sandcastle competition. I looked at Jackie, who thought it was hilarious, as did the rest of my family.

Jackie was OK for me to join them, but before I did, I had to go back to our room, to pick up my children's passport, and put on the t-shirt they'd given me, as I had to be dressed, the same way as the kids. I also took the opportunity to pick up my Stetson hat, as it was going to be a blistering hot day.

Here was me on my honeymoon, holding the hands of my niece and nephew Stephanie and Ross, on our way to the beach, singing songs, and being encouraged by all the adults. At the beach, we all split up and given an area of which to build our sandcastles. Stephanie and Ross were paired with different partners, as I was their uncle, they would have an unfair advantage.

Neither of them was upset by this, as they were making new friends. I paired with another little lad, so we set about building, the best sandcastle imaginable.

Our castle had everything, including turrets, a drawbridge and even a moat filled with water!

When it was time for the judging, we all looked at the other castles, and the reps picked a winner, who was a little girl, who had built her sandcastle by herself, and consisted of one castle, made by a bucket and spade. That upset the little boy who I had with me, so for a joke, we stamped on it, which made her cry. I did feel guilty about doing it, and I did make amends to her, by buying her the biggest ice cream she could fit in her mouth.

After the competition, I returned to the pool area and to Jackie, who asked me how it went, and we both laughed afterwards. I had hoped, that would be the end of me, having to spend my honeymoon with all the kids, but how wrong I was, as every day after that, the British holidaymaker's kids, would come and knock on our door, and ask Jackie, if I could come out to play. Jackie didn't appear to mind, and I always made it up to her, after I had been out at the kid's club, and we would always spend our evenings, and night times together, and find our entertainment.

As the two weeks were up, we returned home, with a lifetime worth of memories, and something, that we would never forget. It was now back to reality, and I returned to assume my duties with the army. Once again, we were deployed, this time to Cyprus, as part of the UN mission, to patrol the buffer-zone between Cypriot and Turkish forces.

Cyprus was beautiful, and although we were there in a professional capacity, we still enjoyed the idyllic lifestyle, when we had rest days! On many occasions, we almost fell afoul of the Military Police, but always managed to stay one step ahead, much to our relief. As usual, I would write and ring up Jackie, at every opportunity.

Jackie would spend her time, and help other people living with multiple sclerosis, at the MS society in Bedford, as a volunteer. In her new role, she had made many new friends, all of which had the same condition, with varying degrees of severity. She also had taken courses in flower arranging, and arts and crafts, and would often be asked, to make bouquets for people, and also to produce wedding cards, and other occasion cards.

I was proud of her, as she was her unselfish self as usual, and my love for her due to her outlook grew more intense. With December just around the corner, we were preparing for Christmas. We'd invited over Nobby and Jan, as we had never had them over for Christmas before.

It was two weeks before the big day, and I got a phone call, it was Nobby, who explained that Jan had been diagnosed with terminal cancer. The news was devastating, as although Jan, had been in and out of the hospital for most of her life when Jackie was a child, we had no idea.

The worse thing about the call was that Jackie was out with some friends, and I had to find a way of telling her when she returned home. As soon as she walked through the door, I sat her down told her.

As you can imagine, she was overwrought, and I comforted her. The following week, Jan was undergoing some tests in the Middlesex hospital, and we went to visit her as I had a wicked sense of humour, which appealed to Jan. Before going, I had purchased two pig's ears and had attached them on one of Jackie's Alice bands.

I put them on, just before we saw her, and I looked like Mr Spock from Star Trek. I stood in front of her bed, and raised my hand in a Vulcan salute, and told her to 'live long and prosper', Jan loved this and was in fits of laughter.

Christmas Eve 1994 was a cold morning. I was getting ready to go to the barracks when the phone rang. It was Nobby, who told me that Jan, had been rushed into hospital the night before, and she was in the last moments of her life.

I rushed back upstairs and told Jackie, and she got dressed. I drove from Luton to Mount Vernon hospital, in what seemed like a matter of minutes, as everything was in a dream-like state. As we entered her side room, Jan had been hooked up to a morphine drip and was slipping in and out of consciousness, so we knew she hadn't long to live.

Jackie asked her dad, as to why he didn't notify us the night before, and he told her, that he only had the call, while he was at drinking men's club. The revelation disgusted us. He knew Jan had not been well but was his usual selfish self. Throughout the day, more members of the family arrived to pay their respect. Jackie's grandmother came, with her aunts and her uncle, to say their final farewell.

As the day progressed, Nobby said that he needed to go and have something to eat, as he claimed that he hadn't eaten for two days. He also said that he hadn't slept, so Jackie told him to go home, and we would call him, should anything happen. We both knew he would be going to get a drink, but Jackie didn't want him there, due to his selfishness.

When he'd gone, Jackie and I sat by the side of Jan's bed and held her hands. Her breathing was getting more and more shallow, and we knew it wouldn't be long before she passed away. Just before she drew her final breath, she opened her eyes and looked at Jackie and me, and smiled before passing.

We were devastated but had to break the news to the rest of the family. We composed ourselves so that we could do so, without too much grief in our voices. We tried to ring up Nobby at home, but there was no answer, so we rang the Pinner green working men's club, and behold he was there. I went to pick him up, and he stunk to high heaven with booze. Back at the hospital, he sat in the room, and promised Jan, that he would look after us, and himself. Of course, Jackie and I knew this was a lie. It was down to Jackie and me to arrange the funeral, but as Jan was an astute woman, she had prepaid for her funeral, so all we had to do, was inform the family of where it was to be taking place. The funeral itself was very emotional, as Jan had chosen the songs, 'it's a wonderful world' by Louis Armstrong to be played going in, and 'we'll meet again', by Vera Lynn going out.

After the funeral, we had the wake at Pinner green social club, which had been chosen by Nobby, much to our disapproval, but I must say that they did us proud. Although devastating, we tried to carry on with our lives, as best as we could. I was concerned, about how Jackie's health would cope with it, and likewise, she was concerned about me, but I knew that I would be OK, as I could immerse myself into my work.

As time went by, although never forgotten, it's got easier, and we continued to love and support each other, which would prove more important than we ever imagined, as our world was about to be shattered again.

It was September 1995. I was at the barracks when I got a call to say that my dad, had suffered a heart attack, while he was at his workplace. I rushed over to the hospital to see how he was. He was sitting up in bed and was laughing and joking with the nurses.

He said that he was OK and that he would bounce back, to his normal self in no time. After he came out of the hospital, mum persuaded him to take early retirement, which at first didn't go down well with him, but after being nagged by my mum and my sisters, he reluctantly agreed.

Relishing his newfound freedom, as he was able to see his grandchildren more regularly, but he started to get bored, so volunteered for a local charity shop, which he enjoyed. He also wanted to go and visit America, as he had always wanted to see the sights and wanted mostly to visit Las Vegas.

I remembered that my friend Steve had told his sister, that she'd had been on a tour of the USA, which was run by Greyhound bus tours.

I spoke to him about this, and he loved the idea. Dad and I went to the travel agent to see what they can come up with. They suggested a West coast tour of America, which took in many of the sites of which dad wanted to experience, which included two days and nights in Las Vegas. Dad's eyes lit up, and without hesitation, we booked the holiday.

It was now December, and fast approaching Christmas again, which was going to be a sad affair, for Jackie and me, due to coming up to the first anniversary of her mum's death, but we tried to make as enjoyable as possible. My eldest sister had arranged for my mum and dad to spend Christmas with her and her family at a Butlins' holiday camp. I had also arranged, a New Year's Eve party, for when they came back.

The day before they were going to leave, they came around with mum and dad to wish Jackie and me a Merry Christmas. As my dad was leaving, he winked at me and told us that he couldn't wait, to see us at the New Year's party.

We spent Christmas Day at my sister Tina's house, where we had a fantastic time, with her my brother in law, and our nephews and nieces. Boxing Day arrived, and we had planned a quiet time together and made our own Christmas Day for ourselves. I remembered it was a freezing winter, and I went to run a bath, as we planned to take it together.

As the water was running, there was a knock at the door, standing there was my brother in law Steve, who told us that we had to go with him to his house. He wouldn't tell us the reasons why, when we arrived, my sister was crying her eyes out and was devastated. She explained that dad had died, at first, I couldn't believe what I was hearing, but then her phone rang, it was our mum, who confirmed what she had told me.

We went around mum's house, to put on the heating, as they were travelling back from Butlins. None of us could believe the news, especially for Jackie and myself, who had buried her mum 11 months previous.

When we got to mum's house, we contacted our eldest brother Peter, to tell him the sad news. We were unable to contact David, as none of us had any address or phone number for which to do so.

As mum arrived with Theresa, Steve, Lee and Lisa, and was an emotional homecoming.

Shortly after they had arrived, Peter turned up, we were all shell shocked by the news, and couldn't believe that dad had gone. Over the next few days, my dad's body arrived back in Luton, as he had been at the mortuary in Colchester, where they had been staying in the Butlins campsite.

We were all asked, to go and see dad at the funeral parlour. We each took it in turns, to go and pay our respects to him, and every one of us found it difficult, especially the grandkids. Dad had put all his affairs in place before his passing, so it was just a question of attending the funeral.

Mum asked me, my brother Peter and my two brothers in law, the two Steve's, to be the pallbearers. I thought that this was a great honour to bestow for our dad, and thought it would be appropriate, as he had been in the military, for the majority of his life if I was to wear a ceremonial uniform, as a pallbearer. I asked my CO if I would be allowed to wear my uniform, and he didn't hesitate to grant permission.

The day of the funeral arrived, as promised, I dressed in my ceremonial uniform, which brought tears to my mum's eyes as it did so for the rest of my family, including my auntie's and uncles, who were there to pay their last respects. My uncle George was my dad's eldest brother, and he was shocked to see, just how I looked like my dad, as did my dad's sister Auntie Barbara.

We arrived at the crematorium in Luton, and we were given instructions by the funeral director, as to how we should carry his coffin. My two brother's in-laws were in front, and my brother Peter and myself at the rear. Mum had chosen the track 'my way' by Frank Sinatra, as the music going into the crematorium, as this was dad's favourite piece of music.

My brother Peter had written a beautiful eulogy for my dad, and he had to choke back his tears, as he was overcome with emotion, so I decided to go up and join him, I placed my arm around him, and he was able to continue. After the funeral had finished, the music that was playing, as we were leaving the crematorium, was one of dad's favourite military tracks performed for all fallen comrades, 'The last post', and it had been arranged, for a bugler a to play it.

It was a fitting tribute to dad, and one, that I will never forget. He was a brilliant man, fair but firm, and was my hero. In contrast, Jackie's mum Jan was a wonderful woman, and one of the kindest warmest human beings, I have ever met.

We held the wake at mum's house, and we remembered dad, the stories that he used to tell us all, about his life in the army, and what a wonderful dad he was to us all, and mixed in with the tears, was a house full of laughter.

My uncle George and Auntie Irene's daughter, our cousin Janet, was also there to pay her respects. However, she had always had a drinking problem, and as the day and evening went on, she was so drunk, that she caused issues, and said something detrimental to my mum, and they had a falling out. Much to the annoyance of my sister Tina, who lost her temper, and they fought, in the front garden. I managed to pull them apart, and my mum was screaming for my uncle George, to get out of her house, and take her with him.

He was mortified with Janet, as she had embarrassed him, and my Auntie Irene in front of our family, he slapped her hard, she had also disrespected my dad. My sister Theresa took my uncle George, and Auntie Irene, back to her house, and I took my cousin Janet, to mine and Jackie's house.

The next morning, I picked up my uncle, and aunty from my sister's house, and dropped then all off, at the train station.

My uncle George couldn't contain himself, as he felt guilty, and blamed himself. I wouldn't hear a bad word against him. Over the years, we all kept in contact with Uncle George and Auntie Irene, and we all became closer in the end.

After the dust had settled, we all continued with our busy lives, and over time, although we would always remember, dad and Jackie's mum Jan, we looked forward and would continue to do so.

I was thrilled, being in the military, and it showed. The years seemed to fly by, and it was if, we were a nonstop roller coaster, and I loved every minute of it. In 1999, the regiment was formed, into the 16 Air Assault Brigade, and been involved, in numerous overseas operations.

A year later, we were deployed overseas, this time to Sierra Leone, and in 2001, were involved in, Operation essential harvest in Macedonia. The regiment also sent several troops to Northern Ireland in 2001, who was at the forefront, of the holy cross riots in that year, while deployed, with the 1st Battalion the Royal Irish Regiment.

However, I wasn't involved in this, and instead, was one of two batteries deployed, to the Kabul area of Afghanistan, in early 2002. After I had returned to the UK, I was promoted to Sergeant, with my crew and gun. My gun crew were excellent soldiers and very experienced. We formed a close bond with each other, as did the rest of the gun crews and the regiment as a whole.

It was this bond and camaraderie, that can never be broken, and was only experienced, by servicemen and women, of all armed services. Civilians cannot understand the bonds that we have in the military, and even though we have tried to explain this, they can never fully understand. To me, my comrades in arms, are closer, then my siblings. And it is thanks to them that I am still here today.

19th of March 2003, this was the invasion of Iraq, and we were part, of a US lead coalition forces. Since 1991, the presidential tyrant Saddam Hussein, had continued to defy, the restrictions imposed on it, since the first Gulf war, operation desert storm. There were allegations that he had been stockpiling, weapons of mass destruction. Some of the weaponry, was chemical weapons, of which he had used, on his people.

Our role was to prevent Saddam Hussein and his forces, from using these weapons. We would also found, and also to destroy any legitimate military targets. On the afternoon of 19 March 2003, we fired the first shots of the Iraq war, by any coalition ground forces.

The next day, we crossed the border, in support of the US Marine expeditionary force. The regiment was instrumental in securing the strategic Rumalya oilfields and supporting the MEF, in their move north to Nasiriyah. We had been in conflict for several months and was taking ground rapidly, and we're achieving our objective.

We had been given a target and were awaiting orders, to destroy the target that had been verified. Suddenly, a column of Iraqi tanks homed into view travelling from East to West. As they were in the distance, and moving away from our positions, command told us to stand fast, and not to engage the enemy, as a tank can fire three rounds, compared to artillery guns, who could only fire two rounds, in quick succession.

Suddenly, the lead tank turned towards our positions, but we still didn't engage them, as we were still in a good position, and well camouflaged, and our hope, was that they would return to the column, and continue on their original path. However, to our horror, the rest of the tank's broke formation. They all headed towards our positions.

We continued to stand fast, and not engage them in a fire-fight, but they had other ideas, and they started to fire indiscriminately, in our general direction. They were getting closer by the second, and we're continually firing at us, and we were then ordered to return fire in our defence.

I could hear in my headset, that an airstrike had been ordered, but maintained my focus to the momentum. As all guns fired, I was requesting a reload of the weapon when I was blown off of my feet, and crumpled into a heap, after hitting my guns field spade. I was winded, dazed and confused as to what had happened, and I noticed that my hearing had gone.

I managed to get back on my feet again and looked around the devastating scene in disbelief. Some of my crew were severely wounded. My second in command was lying there, and his intestines were hanging out of the abdomen. I felt pain in my right hand, as I looked down, one of my fingers missing, and the wound was spurting arterial blood.

My first instinct was to the stem the bleeding, so I grabbed hold with my left hand, as I did so, I felt my finger was still there, and I pulled it upwards. I was still shocked and confused, and I could fill the adrenaline going through me. I started to hyper-ventilate and sweat profusely.

I then noticed that I had a 4-inch tank shell fragment, embedded in my right knee cap. All I could think of, that these were going to hurt the next day. My hearing was starting to return, albeit with severe ringing in my ears. Two medics rushed to my aid, and I sat down on a stretcher. With my hearing returning, I could now hear the blood-curling, agonising screams of my colleagues. After receiving some battlefield triage, we were removed and taken to a military hospital.

The next thing I remembered was waking up the next day, and surgeons had operated on my wounds. I sat myself up in bed, and went to swing my legs around, to get out of bed and walk, but was stopped by the medical officer, who sat me down, to explain the procedures they had done.

Apart from the wounds to my right hand and knee, surgeons stitched up several injuries on my face from shrapnel and the shell. It had sliced through my eyelid, my nose and my lip.

What I hadn't realised, was that after the initial blast, I was looking over my eyelid. I had also broken three ribs when I hit the field spade.

Wounds aside, all I could think of, was what happened to my boys. I later received information that had also had surgeries, and as soon as they were fit enough, they would be transported back to the UK, for further treatment and recovery.

I also heard that my boys had taken the full force of the shell burst and had shielded me from most of its devastation. I have carried the guilt and will do so for the remainder of my life. I also found out that the airstrike had destroyed and eliminated the enemy threat.

As I am not one to sit around and do nothing, I was determined to get back with the boys, and my regiment as soon as possible. Due to sheer tenacity, and bloody-mindedness, I began to walk after a few days, and exercise my right hand, to speed up the healing process.

All of this was against medical advice, but I could no longer sit there, while my colleagues we're still fighting. After two weeks, I felt fit enough to go back to active duty. By this time, the war was almost over. Coalition forces had defeated Saddam Hussein's forces, Saddam had fled and disappeared. I met up was the regiment, who were now in Baghdad, and had occupied Saddam Hussein Palace.

I was overjoyed at seeing my colleagues again but was also tinged with sadness, after news about other service personnel, who were either killed or in action.

The Palace was unlike anything I had ever seen before, no expense has been spared, on its decoration, and the amount of money spent on it was obscene. This evil twisted tyrant even had a gold-plated toilet. The rooms were richly decorated; all of us wondered how he came about so much wealth.

Our assumption was, he could just take whatever he wanted, and any person who opposed his regime would be terminated.

All of us could only imagine what it was like under his brutal regime. Now the war was over, Iraq's people could breathe a sigh of relief, and we were welcomed. After the years of oppressed rule, by Saddam Hussein. We witnessed jubilant scenes, as every statue, and the effigy of this despot, was being destroyed by his people, and we stood back and watched then do it, without interference.

As like all conflicts, with the victors come the spoils of war. What I meant by this was that anything that was not nailed down would be acquired and shared by everyone. In short, it was 'finders' keepers.' As we were now a part as a peacekeeping force, we were acquired to perform patrols, and to help the civilian population.

On one patrol, my squad and I came across a bank that has been shell damaged, so we went to investigate, and to secure the building, to prevent any looters. Although we turned a blind eye to anything untoward, as we felt it was justified, considering what the Iraqi people had endured. However, as the vault had been blown open, we couldn't resist, sharing some of the gold coins, and banknotes, which happened to be in our way.

After we had completed our job in Iraq, we were going to be going home, and made way for other peacekeeping forces, who would remain, to help rebuild the country, under a new government.

We heard later on that Saddam Hussein was recaptured, and after a trial, was hanged for his crimes. I, for one, am glad, that I was part of a force, to end this tyrant's barbaric regime. Upon returning home, we all had some much-needed rest and recuperation.

I couldn't wait to get home, to see my beloved Jackie, of whom I hadn't seen, for what seemed like an eternity. Although we wrote to each other and shared loving telephone calls, it wasn't the same. She had known that I had been wounded in action, which was somewhat, of a traumatic time for her.

My homecoming was an emotional event, and she had arranged for a small party in my honour. It was great seeing her again, as was seeing the rest of my family. Of course, everyone wanted to know what, it had been like, as they had only seen part of the conflict, on the TV, or read it in newspapers.

Although challenging to talk about the war with my family, I told them as much as they needed to know, as I found the memories too painful. My nephews and nieces were most intrigued, as their hero uncle as they put it, had returned.

I've never been happy, in being called a hero, as I never was, and I never claimed to be, as the true heroes to myself, were those who died in the service to their country. A lot of servicemen and women, if asked, would tell you the same thing.

There is not a day that goes by, without me thinking, of my comrades in arms. And usually ends up, with me in tears, and I will always remember them, for the rest of my life. Sometimes, I still wake up in a cold sweat, after reliving some of the horrors I witnessed, but I have learned to live with it.

In late 2003, the regiment moved from Aldershot to Colchester, and I joined the rest of 16 Air Assault Brigade. It was a welcome move, as the commute to and from the barracks, would be less of a strain, and would mean, I could spend more time with Jackie.

2006, saw the first of the regiment's, three tours of Afghanistan. The first of these, saw the regiment play a key role, in the break into Helmand province. This tour attracted much public attention and has often been described, as the most intense combat fighting, since the Korean War of the 1950s.

However, after I returned home, I decided that as Jackie's MS, was taking its toll on her, and had progressed to the next level. I spoke to her, and explained, that I would, after 16 years' service with the armed forces, would retire.

At first, Jackie was dead against the idea, but I was never really the same, after my injuries in Iraq, years previous, and had my fair share of tours, and felt, I'd nothing more to prove, and couldn't be taught anything more, than what I had already experienced.

Once I'd explained this to her, she agreed and would support me, with whatever I had decided. It was with a heavy heart, that I spoke to my commanding officer, and informed him of my decision. Although he would be disappointed, in losing an experienced senior NCO, he would fully understand my reasoning.

For me to transcend into civilian life, I received several thousands of pounds, to use in either training or whatever I required it for, so that I could go back, into the civilian population.

The week before I was going to retire, I had dined out in the sergeant's mess, which was a very emotional time, as I had spent 16 years with my colleagues, many I had come to know and admired greatly.

My official discharge date was November the 10th 2006. It hit me the hardest when I had to hand in my kit. I was now a civilian again, and I am not ashamed to say, I shed more than my fair share of tears, as I walked out of the barracks, for the last time. The army gave me an honourable discharge, which in itself is an honour. In total, including my service in the TA, I had served eighteen years, I'm proud to have served, in such an honourable profession, within the armed services.

Two years later, the regiment returned to Helmand. They were involved in heavy fighting, cumulating in the largescale operation to move a turbine from Kandahar, along with a heavily mined, and fiercely defended road, to the Kajaki dam. The regiments final deployment to Afghanistan saw the regiment's gun groups, and fire support teams, deploy to central Helmand Provence, to provide offensive support, to 16th Air Assault Brigade. Although I hadn't been part of these last two deployments, I sent my best wishes to the regiment, and to my Brothers in Arms, would all return home safely. As our regimental motto is 'Honi soit qui mal y pense', *May he be shamed who thinks badly of it.'*

Chapter Thirteen

Civvy Street

The transition from a professional soldier to civilian was not going to be an easy one. I'd made no illusions about the difficulties that lay ahead. In the year I was allowed to reinvent myself, I'd decided, to update my building qualifications, as the government had implemented changes to the building industry, which I felt were a good idea, as it would mostly weed out the cowboy builders.

Without resting on my laurels, I decided, to build up a client base, I would need a catchy name, and an even more catchy logo to entice potential new clients. I registered my new business, as Helpful Hands Property Services, and enlisted help from a good friend of mine, who was skilful in turning my logo idea, into a practical solution.

I'd taken inspiration, after seeing an advert for hand cream, and so explained, that I wanted a picture of a hand, and instead of fingers, would be replaced, with various building tools. I can honestly say that my logo designer understood completely, and come up with a fantastic logo, which I incorporated into my business stationery.

Wasting no time, in getting my name out there, and pounded the streets delivering my flyers, as well as posting them, in libraries and notice boards, and supermarkets, that allowed free advertising. I didn't have to wait long, before the phone rang, requiring me to come around, and give a free estimate.

My first job was a simple repair, to a water damaged bedroom ceiling. The client not only required a replacement to the roof but also enquired, if I could move the loft hatch, located at top floor landing, into a spare bedroom with, a set of stairs leading up to it.

After seeing the task in hand, I saw it was an opportunity to offer my best price for the work. I not only verbally told them a price, but I also posted them the quotation, and a few days later they contacted me and asked when I could start. As this was my first client, I started the very next day, and as promised, I completed the work on the time, specified in my original estimate. The client was impressed with my work, and paid me for my services, and took a business card, for any other repairs or renovations, that she may require in the future.

From that initial first job, the phone never stopped ringing, and Jackie was acting as my secretary, booking free appointments, as well as keeping my diary, for the work that I had lined up. I had so many bookings for work that I was fully booked up, for six months at any one time.

My clients all paid a deposit in lieu of the work, and I would give them two weeks' notice, before starting work on their jobs. It was a suitable arrangement for me, as it was not only building up my bank balance but meant that I could obtain a higher credit with my suppliers. All my clients were not only willing to wait for my services but were happy to do so; such was my reputation.

In a short space of time, I had gone from a fledgeling company to a thriving business. I had so much work that I had to employ subcontractors to assist me, and also had two other full-time builders as my employees. I was not only providing building services in Luton, as my reputation had extended to areas of London.

One client lived in the road called the Avenue, which was at the time, one of the most affluent areas of London, and this client was a wealthy Arab businessman. I went to his home and was in awe at the size of his property.

It was a beautiful mansion with immaculate grounds, and you could see the amount of wealth that he had.

As I arrived, the client met and showed me around the property, and what work he required for me to carry out. He had four wives, and each of them had their rooms with en-suite bathrooms. These bathrooms were as big as my entire house.

He explained that one of his wives, had grown bored of her bathroom and that she wished for it to be changed. When I looked at the bathroom, it was immaculately decorated, and no expense has been spared on the decoration. Everything was decked in beautiful Italian marble and granite.

Although I could see no fault in it, his wife didn't like the colour. She had set her heart on a different colour scheme entirely. I made a few suggestions myself, which he liked the sound of, and left it up to me to arrange it all.

I supplied him with an itemised quotation, of which he agreed to, and set a date to start work.

Due to the size of the project, I had my two experienced builders on-site, as well as other trade persons, who carried out the work to a high specification. We completed the work within the time frame specified and also came slightly under budget. My client was thrilled with and loved the quality of the workmanship.

Not only did he pay in full, but he also gave a generous cash bonus, of £500 each. He'd invited Jackie and me as guests at his dinner party, to celebrate his birthday, the following weekend. Accepting his offer, we were picked up, in his chauffeur-driven limousine. The party as you would expect was fantastic, and again money was no object when it came to catering and entertainment.

A few days after the party, I was at home when the phone rang, from a client who gave his name as simply Reg. I'd been recommended by his good friend, the Arab businessman, and inquired if I could come along to his home, to provide a quotation for work that he needed doing.

I went to the address provided, and again, was in awe at the beautiful home. I could tell that the client was somewhat wealthy, and assumed they were in business or were a wealthy private banker. I rang the bell and could hear footsteps in the hallway.

As the door opened, I was greeted by one of the most popular musicians in Britain.

I was gobsmacked, and stood there with my mouth open, not knowing what to do or say. When I spoke to him over the phone, I failed to recognise his voice. He looked relaxed and with a smile on his face, he asked jokingly,

'Are you coming in because you're letting the heating out?'

I apologised profusely and went inside. Upon entering his beautiful home, the hall and every room that I went into, were plush with fresh flowers. He showed me into the kitchen and asked if I would like a cup of tea, which he made himself. Although I would have expected a member of his staff to do so, he was very hands-on.

We spoke about the job, which was to revamp and remodel his bathroom, in the same style, that I had done at the Arab businessman's house.

We agreed on a price and a start date, and he suggested, that it would be a cash transaction, as he felt that the taxman, 'had enough money of his own'.

I'd never thought he would say that for being a celebrity superstar, but I have to say Reg is a down to earth individual, and unlike his diva image portrayed in the tabloid press. As usual, I would employ the same particular high standards that I had set in his job, and every job that I have ever done, which I believe is the reason I was so successful.

I completed the work as always, on schedule and budget. I cannot express how much in words, of how honoured I was, to have worked for such an amazing man as Elton John.

A few weeks later, I had an appointment for a job on the Euston Road in London. It was in an apartment block, which was very exclusive, and could only be afforded, by someone with extreme wealth.

As the door opened, I was greeted by the housekeeper. I walked through the huge oak panelled hallway, strewn on the walls, was various guitars, music awards, and also platinum, gold, and silver discs. Intrigued about the person who owned this home, I inquired with the housekeeper who owned it, and couldn't believe my ears, when she told me, that Eric Clapton owned it, and she referred to it, as his London pom deterrent.

She also explained that Eric was currently in the USA, but had heard good things about my work, from Elton John. I couldn't believe my luck that I had been recommended, by such a well-known superstar. A price was agreed, as usual, I carried out the work, to very high specifications and standards, as I've always done, for all my clients rich or poor. After completion, I was paid in cash, and also handed a sizeable tip.

As I had worked for two such influential superstars, it was now part of my portfolio, which opened a lot of doors for me, for some exclusive wealthy clientele. However, I never forgot where I come and started from, and treated all of my clients, regardless of their backgrounds, with the highest esteem, as I would always treat them, the way that I'd like to be treated, young, old, rich or poor.

Due to the business flourishing, I had so much money and was spending it, as if I had my orchard of money trees. On an average week, I would pay myself £4000, if a poor week £2000. With the financial freedom I'd gained, I would not only treat Jackie but would buy the best furniture that was available.

I handed out money, to friends and family whenever they needed a helping hand. I also purchased items, not necessarily as I needed them, but more so, I wanted them. One purchase I made, was of a top of the range BMW car, which I'd on approval, for a few weeks.

Although it had all gadgets and gizmos, you would expect from such a high-profile manufacturer, I hated it and returned it after four days. Instead, I purchased with cash, a brand-new, top of the range Ford Mondeo, which compared to the BMW, was classy, and it made the BMW, look like an amateur had built it.

Jackie and I enjoyed the wealth and spent a lot of time on expensive holidays. We wanted for nothing, but we still craved our children, and as Jackie was unable to conceive, we looked into adoption. We had everything that you could wish for a child, not only our own home, but financial stability, and a safe and secure loving environment.

Before we could adopt, we had to go through the usual assessment, with the adoption team. Even though we fitted the criteria, they turned us down. Their reasoning was solely based, on Jackie having multiple sclerosis, which we felt was somewhat unfair. Despite appealing against the decision, we were unsuccessful. It was a double body blow for us and scuppered any chances of having our children. We decided to turn our attention and ingratiate our immense love, on our nephews and nieces.

In particular, Jackie took a real shine, to my sister Tina's youngest daughter Nicole. She reasoned that she likened Nicole to herself when she was the same age. As she was medically retired, she had time on her hands, and it was arranged with Tina, for Jackie to look after Nicole, and pick her up from school. Jackie fell in love with her, as did I, but pre-warned Jackie, not to get so attached, as I knew that one day, Tina would pull the plug.

True to my words, Nicole's visits started to decline and eventually stopped. Jackie asked Tina the reason, and Tina, being the nasty little bitch that she was, claimed that it was Nicole's idea.

I came home one evening, to find Jackie in tears, and she told me, that she had pleaded with Tina, to allow her to see Nicole again, but had been subjected, to a foul mouth abuse from my sister. Seeing Jackie upset in this manner, annoyed me, so I took it upon myself, to deal with it directly. I rang Tina, and I let her have it with both barrels.

After our phone call, I comforted Jackie, as I was doing so, there was a knock on the door. As I opened it, there was Tina and my brother-in-law Steve standing there. They started an almighty row, which was only going to end one way.

As they continued their foul mouth abuse against Jackie and me, I lost my temper. Steve made the biggest mistake, as he tried to come at me and threw a punch, so I head-butted him. Tina, annoyed that I had hurt her husband, made an even bigger mistake, and tried the same, the only recourse, was I headbutted her also. As they were reeling from their injuries, I told them in no uncertain terms, to go fuck themselves, and they would no longer be welcome at our home.

After the incident, they shuffled off, like the two nasty little rats that they were, and I slammed the door behind me. I was enraged, and Jackie had to calm me down. I was not only annoyed with them, but with myself also.

I had always been there for my family, and given then money without question, anytime that they needed it, without asking for anything in return, not even asking them to pay it back.

Now, this may seem barbaric to some people, but if you had met my sister Tina, then you would understand, as she is the foulest mouthed, nasty racist person I have ever met, and I am somewhat ashamed of her.

Having that said, she helped me on many occasions, as a child. I do love her in my own unique way. Even now, If she asked for help, I would do so. That goes for any of my siblings, after all, blood is thicker than water, but on the same token, as the saying goes, 'you can choose your friends, but you can't choose your family'.

Later that evening, my eldest sister Theresa came around, to ask what had happened, as she saw herself, as the peacekeeper of the family, which was dad's role when he was alive. I told her the truth, and that I would do the same thing if anyone disrespected me, or Jackie ever again.

You see, although the army teaches you discipline, it also shows you, how to defend yourself, when you are about to be attacked, by an assailant. After hearing our version of the events, she suggested, that we make amends, and would act as the intermediary.

I only agreed to this meeting, when, and only when Tina had apologised first. After speaking, Theresa went home and put my terms to Tina, who agreed. The next day, we went around to Theresa house, and true to her word, and now both sporting black eyes, my sister Tina, and her husband Steve apologised to myself and Jackie. After our meeting, we put our differences aside and agreed on a truce.

After the incident with Tina, I started to have strange mental episodes. I would be furious, for the slightest little things, and when Jackie tried to intervene, I took my frustrations out on her and would start a convincing argument.

Since this was not in my nature, and the signs started showing, soon after I had retired from the army. I would also have terrifying nightmares imaginable. I would often wake up in a cold sweat. I started drinking heavily as a way of blocking out what was happening. It was like a never-ending circle, and the more I drank, the worse I became.

One evening, I started an argument with Jackie over a trivial matter, Jackie couldn't cope with my mood anymore, and she walked out into the kitchen and slammed the door. Here I was, sitting in the living room, still arguing with myself. Suddenly, I felt an almighty bang on my head, and collapsed on the floor, with blood pouring out of the wound.

I must have passed out momentarily, as when I came to, Jackie was kneeling over me, crying her eyes out, as she thought that she had killed me. She wrapped a towel around my head, to stem the bleeding, and drove to the accident and emergency department.

As nurses were assisting me in triage, we had to tell the truth, as the triage nurse had noticed imprinted on the back of my head, were the words 'lafet'. Of course, looking in a mirror, the words were 'tefal', which everyone should know is a well-known manufacturer of non-stick frying pans and saucepans. Looking back, although it could have been a lot worse, we had a great laugh at the time.

I knew then that I needed to seek professional help, as I didn't like the person that I had become, and was hurting the person I loved and admired the most, and that was Jackie. I promised her that I would book a doctor's appointment the next morning and take it from there.

At the GP surgery, I explained my symptoms to the doctor and told him what I was going through. The doctor then referred me to the psychiatric unit at the hospital. On the day of my evaluation, the psychiatrist, accompanied by a trainee greeted me, and they were recording the session for training purposes.

As the session got underway, I was explaining my symptoms, and throughout, it looked like he wasn't listening to what I was saying. I became somewhat perturbed by his methods, but I continued nonetheless, telling him everything that was happening to me, and I suggested that I may have been suffering from Combat Stress.

I had been talking for about half an hour, when suddenly, he stopped me in my tracks, what I heard next was a total shock, as he blatantly said, 'there was no such thing as Combat Stress, and you were merely 'pissed off'. Upon hearing these words, I snapped and flew at him with my hand around his throat, pushing him against the wall.

I screamed at him and asked, 'was this pissed off enough!' By this time, security had been called, and I was arrested and taken to Luton police station. I had now calmed down, and I rang my solicitor, who came to represent me at the interview.

My solicitor was outstanding and raised the question about the recording of the session, and that he required the footage of the consultation so that he could build a case before the police charged me. As the police had not yet recovered the footage, I was allowed out on bail on the understanding that I would come back the following day at 9 am.

The next morning, my solicitor met me outside the police station, and we went in together to see the duty Sergeant, to reconvene from the previous day. The police had acquired the original footage, and we sat down to view it, where they saw that the doctor had provoked the incident, by what he had said to me.

They had also acquired, a written statement from the doctor, and the trainee, which were both conflicting stories. After consulting with the police, they decided not to bring any charges against me, as the footage had verified my account, and so did the trainee's statement. As I had been exonerated, I was free to go, and my solicitor, under my instruction, started civil action against the hospital, and the doctor involved.

In the meantime, I had been referred to see a Combat Stress specialist in Bedford. As the specialist was a private practitioner, the sessions were somewhat expensive, but the Luton and

Dunstable hospital footed the bill, in an out of court settlement. I had several private sessions, and I was diagnosed as suffering from PTSD.

The sessions helped me immensely, and I am grateful for all the hard work and dedication from the team. Although even now, on rare occasions, I still suffer from flashbacks, only now I can cope with them.

After my counselling sessions, I decided that both myself and Jackie needed some quality time away from it all. Looking at the holiday brochures, we decided on a two-week break, on the Greek island of Crete.

We chose a beautiful hotel, called The Elpida based on the North East side of the island, in the village of Istron.

Jackie was excited at the prospect, and could hardly contain her excitement, and while I was at my work, she had told my mum, and her new partner Robin, as well as her best friend, Sally. When I arrived home, I found the house was full, as Jackie had invited mum and Robin around for dinner.

As Jackie had discussed where we were going and shown them the photographs from the brochure, they liked the look of it, and inquired if it would be possible for them, to join us?

I had no problem with going on holiday with them, and neither did Jackie.

We discussed the holiday further over dinner, and it was then, that mum explained, that she was being victimised by Tina, who had disliked mum's involvement with Robin after dad had passed away. This information was new to me, so I asked her to elaborate.

Tina had distanced herself from mum over the last few years and had stopped mum from seeing her grandkids. I asked if anyone knew about the situation between them, and mum explained that she had spoken to Theresa about the problems with Tina, and nothing had been done since then.

Annoyed at hearing this news, I told mum about the falling out with Tina and Steve, for the same thing. After dinner, I decided to call Theresa, and have it out with her, as to why I had not been privy to this information. Theresa explained that she kept it quiet from me, as she knew, that I would be upset, and aggravated.

Her words aggrieved me, and I made it clear to her that I was an adult, and not a child, and was more than capable of dealing with any situation. At the same time, I asked if there were any other secrets that I should know about, and they were too numerous to count. I wasn't happy with what Theresa told me, and I gave her a piece of my mind, then I organised a meeting at my house, with her and Tina for a family conference, before slamming down the phone on her.

I had given Theresa an hour for the meeting and at my house. Mum was anxious about it and suggested that Robin should head home, but I refused to let him leave, as I needed to sort everything out once and for all. When my Sisters arrived, I had calmed down. I wouldn't want the meeting to be a full-blown argument. We would sit down as adults, and discuss the problems.

It turned out that Tina, as usual, was the main protagonist, and disliked mum, for getting together with Robin after dad had died. I told her that dad had been gone for a while, and mum was old enough to make her own choices and mum's relationship none of her business.

Mum then spoke up, as the girls were getting upset and tearful. She explained and also told them that if dad walked through the front door right now, she would not be with Robin. I backed mum up on this point, but I also needed to know other problems that were also causing an issue.

Tina explained that she was also aggrieved, as to why mum, had not backed her up, for an incident between her, and my eldest brother Peter when she was a child. It was only then that I heard for the first time that Peter had abused Tina when she was six years old.

Shocked at hearing this news, and we waited for mum to answer. She tried to explain that she and dad had dealt with it, all those years ago. However, Tina was not convinced, and was getting more and more upset, and was crying her eyes out. I was annoyed, and appalled at this news, and intervened.

I suggested that I ring up Peter, and have it out with him, as in my opinion, he had overstepped the boundaries, of being the eldest, and was a paedophile. Tina would not allow me to do so, as she said, that she didn't want to ruin his life or affect his kids, and his wife, Lynn. I was gobsmacked at hearing this, and regardless of trying to persuade her differently, she wouldn't do it.

In the end, we settled everything and left Peter's despicable behaviour against my better judgement. Although when this admission came out, we did at least break the ice, and Tina agreed to allow mum to see her grandkids again. She even said that she would accept Robin in mum's life. And with that, we all decided to become closer as a family, and keep Peter away, and out of the picture. After the girls had gone home, me, Jackie, mum and Robin, continued to plan our holiday to Crete.

On the day of our departure, Jackie had to use her wheelchair because the MS had started to flare up again. We flew from Luton airport with Monarch, which was a late afternoon flight, and arrived at Iraklion airport Crete at 7:30 PM. During the trip, I inquired if I could sit in the cockpit, and was very fortunate to do so. Unfortunately, this practice stopped in the wake of the 9-11 attacks in America, so I was fortunate indeed.

Our accommodation was a further one hour drive. Arriving at the hotel, filled us all with dread, as it was built on a very steep hill. I looked at the mountain and wondered how I would pull Jackie up in her wheelchair, not to mention our luggage. It was then that I noticed a telephone, so we could ring the reception to announce that we had arrived.

A few moments later, a member of the hotel staff arrived in a battered old pickup truck. He loaded our baggage, and Jackie and mum were driven to the hotel reception, while Robin and I with two other guests walked. Finally, at the top, we were out of breath, which took a few moments to settle down before we could check ourselves into the hotel.

After checking in, we went to our allocated rooms and freshened ourselves. Mine and Jackie's room was on the ground floor, while mum and Robin's room was on the first floor. The room, although basic, was very comfortable, with a reasonably sized en suite bathroom, and a private balcony overlooking the sea. After freshening up and changing, we all met up in the hotel bar for a drink. Jackie and mum decided as it was our holiday, that they would indulge in cocktails.

Robin and I inquired if they had a very good brandy or cognac. The barman suggested that we tried the local brandy named Metaxa 3 star.

The drink was a very smooth brandy, and it starts from three and up to seven stars. He explained the unique flavour was due to the use of Cretan honey. We also decided to order two pizzas from the bar and have our first evening in the hotel.

The next morning when we got up, we noticed that the weather was cold, overcast with unexpected showers, as it was the height of the season in mid-August. As we had only packed summer clothes, none of us had any warmer items to wear.

After breakfast, we enquired at the reception where we could buy some warm weather clothing. The receptionist, Manolis, recommended one of the local shops in Istron village, which was a short walk from the hotel complex.

Walking down the hill was a challenge in itself as both Jackie and mum was struggling.

Jackie had insisted on leaving her wheelchair in the room, as she felt she would be able to walk, as her legs were a bit stiff due to her MS, just as long as she was able to take my arm. Mum also had trouble walking, but not because she had any kind of illness or disability, it was because she was somewhat overweight, and she asked Robin if she could hold on to his arm for stability.

Now it was OK for me, as I am well built and could support Jackie's weight easily. However, Robin can only be described as a wimp, with no muscle tone whatsoever, with spindly arms and legs. If you'd put a tall red pointy hat on his head, and a fishing pole in his hand, coupled with his rather scruffy beard, he could have quickly passed off as a gnome if he sat down on a toadstool!

Walking down to the village was somewhat comical, with mum and Robin struggling to bear her weight. Due to my sense of humour, I couldn't help but take the rise out of both of them. As we got to the bottom of the hill, both mum and Robin had, to sit down and catch their breath.

Upon seeing them puffing and panting on the wall, I couldn't help but fall into fits of laughter. Jackie at first thought I was cruel, but she couldn't help giggling herself after I had pointed out that we had walked down the hill, and not up to it. Being a practical joker as I am, mum and Robin saw the funny side of it when I demonstrated mimicking their behaviour.

We got to the shop, and asked if they had warm clothes we could buy from them, luckily for us; they had four pure wool fleeces in stock, which were a welcome addition to our wardrobe. As we put the fleece's on, we instantly noticed the change and decided to explore our surroundings and find a place where we could have a coffee.

We came across a quaint bar called 'Friends' and sat down. The owner, Manolis, greeted us warmly. He spoke perfect English and welcomed us before fetching our coffee. The place was bustling, as it was an internet café and had a mixture of Greek, and tourists as its patrons.

As we were sitting there, the sun started to burn off the dark clouds, and it became very hot. After paying, we decided to go and explore the village and surrounding areas. The village had two supermarkets, various tavernas, bars and small touristy type shops. As we were walking, we came across the beach and walked along the beach path, and saw a small Greek church. We ventured inside to take a look, and while we were there, we all lit a candle, in memory of my dad and Jackie's mum. After lighting the candles, we continued to walk around the beach area, before going back to our hotel and spending the afternoon around the pool.

While relaxing, Jackie and I took the opportunity to take in the beautiful area, as the hotel had marvellous views of Istron, and from our vantage point, we could see mountains, the ocean and the entire village. Jackie remarked on how beautiful the area was, and suggested that she would like to live there one day.

Throughout the holiday, Jackie's health improved, and it was as if her multiple sclerosis was non-existent. We assumed that this was due to the climate. Most days, we would go out ourselves and leave mum and Robin to do their own thing.

One evening, we decided to turn left going out of the hotel, to see what was further down that side. It was a beautiful warm evening, and we came across a place called the Istron taverna. It didn't appear that there were many tourists in the place eating, but after looking at the menu, we decided to take a look and try the food.

The owner introduced himself as Yiannis, and he was a joint owner, with his brother George, and his parents George and

Maria. It appeared that everyone in Greece and Crete is either named Manolis, Yiannis, George and Lefteris for a male, or if female, their names are limited to Mary or Maria.

Although there are a few other names, we found out that this was because of tradition and religion. As Greek Orthodox, their names bear reference to the Virgin Mary. We were made most welcome, and the food was excellent and was home-cooked, as Yiannis mum Maria, was the main chef. As we were eating, the place started to fill up with other holidaymakers.

As a result, they saw us as a good omen, and we were spoiled rotten by Yiannis and his family.

After our meal, we went for a romantic walk along the coast, before heading back to the hotel, where we joined mum and Robin, for a drink in the bar.

The next morning, we got up early, as we wanted to go and visit a few other places that had been recommended by Manolis, at the friend's bar. We decided to use public transport, as we were going to visit Knossos Palace, which was built by the ancient civilization, the Minoans.

While waiting for the bus, we started talking to a local Greek, who was well versed in English, and owned several ferries, that specialized in excursions other tourist attraction named Spinalonga. It was a small island, just off the coast of the mainland, and was home to the last leper colony in Europe.

He also recommended that we visit another place called Elounda used in the British TV programme, 'who pays the ferryman'. Although I had never seen it, mum remembered it very well, so we also decided to add that to our itinerary.

The palace Knossos was built by the Minoans of Crete. In 1900, the British archaeologist, Sir Arthur Evans, began digging at the site of Knossos, on the northeast coast of Crete. Within months, he had discovered what he named the "Palace of Minos" after the legendary king of Crete, whose labyrinth, was once believed to contain the half-man, half-bull creature known as the Minotaur. It is a fantastic place to visit, although due to its size and walking around, it was an exhausting day.

After a good night sleep, we woke up and ate a hearty breakfast, ready for our next adventure, which was to visit the island of Spinalonga.

We took a taxi to the ferry port in Aghios Nikolas and boarded the ship, ready for the short trip to the island. Throughout the journey, we had an English-speaking guide, and there were also other language guides; for the other Europeans that had come along. It was explained that the island of Spinalonga, was steeped in history, which was just up my street, as I love hearing and learning about it.

The island itself is located in the Gulf of Elounda in northeastern Crete, in an area called Lasithi, next to the town of Plaka. The island is further assigned, to the area of Kalydon. It is near the Spinalonga peninsula, ("large Spinalonga") which often confuses, as the same name is used for both.

The official Greek name, of the island today is Kalydon. Originally, Spinalonga was not an island. It was part of the island of Crete. During the Venetian occupation, the occupying forces carved out of the coast for defence purposes and built a fort there.

He also explained, that in 1578, the Venetians charged the engineer Genese Bressani to plan the island's fortifications. He created blockhouses that sat at the highest points of the northern and southern side of the island, as well as a fortification ring, along the coast, that closed out any hostile disembarkation. Proveditore generals, Di Candia, Luca Michiel, dug the foundation stone for the fortifications and built over the ruins of an Acropolis. Two inscriptions cited this event, one on the transom of the main gate to the castle, and the other, on the base of the rampart, at the north side of the castle.

In 1584, the Venetians, realising that the coastal fortifications were easy to conquer, by the enemies attacking from the nearby hills, decided to strengthen their defence, by constructing new fortifications at the top of the mountain. The Venetian firepower would thus have a bigger range, rendering Spinalonga an impregnable sea fortress, and one of the most important, in the Mediterranean basin.

In 1715, the Ottoman Turks captured Spinalonga, taking over the last remaining Venetian fortress, and removing the last trace of Venetian military presence, from the island of Crete.

At the end of the Ottoman occupation, the island together with the fort at Ierapetra was the refuge of many Ottoman families that feared Christian reprisals. After the revolution of 1866, other Ottoman families, came to the island, from all the regions of Mirabello.

During the Cretan revolt of 1878, only Spinalonga, and the fortress at Ierapetra, were not taken by the Christian Cretan insurgents. In 1881, the 1112 Ottomans formed their community, and later in 1903, the last Turks left the island. The island was subsequently used as a leper colony, from 1903 to 1957.   It is notable, for being one of the last, active leper colonies in Europe. The last inhabitant, a priest, left the island in 1962. This was to maintain, the religious tradition of the Greek Orthodox church, in which a buried person, has to be commemorated, at following intervals, of 40 days, six months, one year, three years and five years after their death.

There were two entrances to Spinalonga, and one was the 'lepers' entrance, a tunnel known as 'Dante's Gate'. The name was because the patients did not know what was going to happen to them once they arrived. However, once on the island, they received food, water, medical attention, and social security payments. Previously, such amenities had been unavailable to Crete's leprosy patients, as they mostly lived in the area's caves, away from civilization.

Due to the interest in Spinalonga, Victoria Hislop, wife of TVs 'Have I got news for you', Ian Hislop, wrote a best-selling novel, aptly named 'The Island', and was written in Crete, as they own a home there. Later on, the book was also dramatized on Greek TV.

Unfortunately, Jackie and mum, found it challenging to keep up, so decided to rest near the entrance, so didn't see the remainder of the interior, which I must say myself and Robin found it very moving.

Part of the tour also included a stopover to view the sunken city of Olous, which was just next to the town of Elounda. From the viewing balcony of the boat, you could see in the water, the buildings residential areas, where people used to live. As we were stopping off, at the same time, the crew prepared a barbecue on board, and we were able to go for a swim and explore this natural disaster site.

It was a fantastic adventure for all of us, and we took some excellent photographs of the day, including some of the sunken city, as I had a waterproof camera, and my snorkelling equipment with me and the memories would last a lifetime.

 Back at the hotel, we all went back to our rooms to freshen up, and we met again in the hotel bar and had a quick drink before we went out to eat at the Istron Taverna. As usual, we were welcomed by Yiannis and his family, who had a live band playing, the Greek instrument balalaika being the focal point.

Of course, the evening wouldn't be complete, without the obligatory Greek dancing, culminating in one of the most famous dances, 'Zorba the Greek'. After another fantastic day and night, we all returned to the hotel. Just as soon as it started, the holiday was almost over, and we had one last night to spend with our new Greek friends.

Mum and Robin had become very close with Yiannis and his family and decided to keep in touch when we all returned home. They made our last night memorable and even prepared a special meal for us before we left.

As with all holidays, the first few days after coming home was full of melancholy. However, we didn't have time to dwell on it, as it was business as usual. I started a new project for a client, and Jackie continued with her volunteer work at the MS Society in Bedford. After a while, we had settled back into the rat race, and it seemed that our holiday was a lifetime away.

The months flew by, unbeknown to us, mum and Robin, had been in constant correspondence with Yiannis, with a view of making a permanent move to Crete. They invited us round for dinner, where they broke the news to us, that the situation with Tina, has once again deteriorated, to such a point, where they could not live In England anymore.

They explained that Yiannis had a building project of his own, a property with fantastic views, and they could live there for as long as they wanted to, and it would be rent-free. I thought that there was something fishy about the proposal, so I dug deeper to extract what they were trying to conceal.

I found that since we returned home from Crete, they had several conversations with Yiannis who had asked them for £22,000 to complete the project to a high specification, for them to move in as soon as possible. Both Jackie and I were surprised because that was a massive amount of money to send over to someone they had only met on holiday.

I thought that they were crazy, to even think about it. But the news worsened, mum explained, that they had already sent £11,000 so that Yiannis could complete the next phase of the building work. We couldn't believe our ears and told them that the agreement might not be genuine.

Both of them reiterated that they trusted Yiannis and that their minds had been made up. I knew then that regardless of what I say, they would not change their minds. Several months later, they sent the remaining £11,000.

Eight months after they sent the money, mum called on the phone asking us to visit them. Jackie and I turned up to hear what they had to say. At first, we thought it was going to be bad news and that they had been ripped off for the money.

However, to our surprise, we were informed that Yiannis, had kept his promises, and mum initially would be going over by herself. At the same time, Robin would remain in England, to finalise the sale of their bungalow. They'd already arranged for an international moving specialist, to freight over their furniture, and mum would be going in a few days. Although shocked by the news, there was nothing more we could say.

Mum asked us to tell the girls until after they had left. That was something I couldn't do. Although there was friction between the girl's mum and Robin, they had a right to know what was going on. After speaking with mum and Robin, we went home to think long and hard about our next move, and how to break the news to my sisters.

Jackie and I had a restless night, as we struggled to come to terms with what we heard the night before. We came up with a plan on how we would break the news to my sisters.

I decided to go and see Theresa, but Jackie insisted she would tag along because as I was angry and upset. Tina had gone back on her promises of allowing mum to see the grandchildren and have regular contact. I told Theresa that mum was leaving the UK to live in Crete because Tina has broken her promises.

She too was upset, and it was then that she told us, that she had been keeping Tina at arm's length. She had come to that decision, after a falling out with Tina, who had been unkind to my nephew and her son Lee, who is mixed race, where Tina had called him a 'paki bastard!'

I was incensed, to hear what Tina had said to my nephew, and I was ready to go around her house and have it out with her, and her pathetic husband, Steve. If it wasn't for the intervention of Theresa, Jackie and Theresa's husband, Steve, then I am sure, I would have been in serious trouble. We arranged in private to go and see mum before she departed for Crete, and she and Theresa made amends.

We kept Tina out of the picture, but she found out and vented her anger on Theresa. When I heard this, I lost control and drove around to her house, and battered down her door with one kick. Thankfully, my nephews and nieces were at school, but I couldn't contain my anger any further and gave her and Steve a piece of my mind.

After that time, we had nothing more to do with her, and we stayed away, as did Theresa and her husband, Steve. Although we didn't have anything more to do with her, we still encouraged our nephews and nieces to remain in touch, which they did.

As time went by, Jackie and I became closer to Theresa and Steve and socialised with them regularly. We would get together at weekends, either at my house or at theirs and have cultural evenings with other friends, where I would cook either Indian or Chinese food, and had an enjoyable time. We were so close that we decided to go on holiday together. Our first holiday was a cheap holiday we found on Teletext in Limassol, Cyprus, which I knew well, as I had been stationed there while serving in the army.

The apartment block complex was very basic. As we entered our designated rooms, there was a strong smell of cat's urine, and we went to see the management, who bent over backwards to change our room's. We had a room next door to each other and would sit on the balconies, so we could talk to each other every morning, before venturing out.

As I was sitting there talking to Steve, we noticed, that the block opposite, had advertisements for 'private models.' We soon realised that we were in the heart of the red-light district of Limassol, and even though I'd been based there while in the army, I never knew that it existed.

One morning, Steve and I decided to sit around the pool and have a game of poker. Jackie and Theresa weren't interested, so they went out for a walk, and to go shopping. They had been gone for two hours, and when they returned, they were both out of breath, so we asked if they had been running. Steve and I were unable to contain our laughter when they explained that a car had pulled up, and the occupant had tried to accost them for sexual services.

As I have a wicked sense of humour, I suggested to Steve, that we could make money on this venture, and tried to persuade Jackie and Theresa to sell their bodies, and we would be their pimps. Of course, this was just harmless fun, of which they saw the funny side themselves, but as a precaution, we would always accompany them, even on short trips.

Facilities at the hotel complex, although basic, the staff were always there at a moment's notice and made all the guests very welcome. In the evening, the entertainment was first class.

On one such occasion, we had an evening with the other guests, and there were a variety of parlour games, where prizes could be one.

I was put up as the representative of our party, as one of the games was musical chairs. After all of the competitors were knocked out, there was only two of us left, me, and a 10-year-old girl. Both of us were eager to get the upper hand.

As we both circled the last remaining chair, the music stopped, we both rushed for the chair, but I couldn't believe it, when she pushed me over and won, much to the amusement of the other guests, and myself, and I couldn't get up off the floor for laughing so hard. All too soon, the holiday was over, but we started to plan our next adventure, as it had been filled with laughter from the time we arrived, to the time we left.

Back at home, my business was going from strength to strength. I employed another two builders, who were exceptional in their trade, and work ethics.

I looked after them, and their weekly wages were way above the market value. I was paying my employees for £2500 a week. All my supply accounts were paid off on time. We had two jobs on the go at any one time, where I would oversee both projects.

In my personal life, I'd spoken to mum, who was settling into her new home in Crete. Jackie was doing well, and her MS symptoms had slowed down, which allowed her to live a healthy life.

We planned to visit mum and booked a two-week break. We were pleasantly surprised when we saw her apartment and our concerns about Yiannis ripping her off dissipated. The apartment was two-bedroomed and had a beautiful kitchen and dining room area, a large lounge, and some fantastic views from the balcony.

It was apparent that the money mum and Robin had invested, had been used wisely, with no expense spared on the materials. We were shown around the island, which was more beautiful, then what we had seen, when we were on holiday with them. The two weeks flew by, and once again, we had an amazing holiday.

Returning home, we again continued to socialise with Theresa and Steve. We booked another breakaway in October, which was in Fuerteventura. Just like our previous holiday with them, the two weeks were filled with fun and laughter, and we couldn't wait to book our next holiday, which we planned for the following year. Our lives, at that point, couldn't be any better. However, that was about to change, and we would soon be affected by a devastating body blow.

It was now December 2007, we have had an amazing year so far, from our holidays to our booming business, life had been great. We were about to enjoy a Christmas break at a hotel in Bournemouth with mum and Robin. They had decided that they would spend Christmas in the UK. Two weeks before Christmas, we went to see Jackie's dad, and we spent some time with him.

Since Jan's passing, both of us had been ensuring that he was looking after himself. Nobby, Jackie's dad, received £45,000 from Jan's will. She also bequeathed £20,000 each to Jackie, and her brother Alan. However, because we are finally sound, we placed the money into an account. We had already found a care-home for Alan to help with his upkeep. We would use his inheritance for that.

When we arrived at Nobby's house, we were shocked to see how gaunt and ill he looked.

As usual, he had been drinking. Worried about his appearance, he allayed our fears that he had been taking good care of himself since Jan died.

He'd even made the point, that he had a fridge full of food, as were the kitchen cupboards. In the past, he had always exaggerated these claims, so as a precaution we checked. To our surprise, on this occasion, he was telling the truth and had even claimed that he had stopped drinking vodka, although he was still drinking beer.

While we were there, he asked Jackie if she could cut his hair with the clippers. As she did so, he looked like a Holocaust survivor, which concerned us both, but he again, assured us that he was doing well.

23rd of December 2007. We arrived at the hotel, which was right on the seafront of Bournemouth. It was somewhat exclusive, priced at £150 per person per night. With such an exclusive price, we assumed that the decor in the rooms would be as grandiose as the hotel reception area.

However, I have to say that I had been in better hotels, for a fraction of the price, as the carpet in our room, was somewhat threadbare, as was the furniture. The least I say about the hideous bathroom. We decided to make the best of it, and enjoy our Christmas break with mum and Robin, who had arrived the day before.

We'd agreed to meet them for dinner at the hotel. Men were required to wear a shirt, tie and a dinner jacket.

Jackie wore a beautiful white full-length gown, while I wore a tailor-made suit, from the exclusive tailors, the famous Savile row in London. We met up with mum and Robin in the hotel bar, and had a quick drink, before going into the hotel restaurant for dinner.

The dining room was very plush, and as you would expect, had several pieces of finest cutlery, and crystal wine glasses, with a centrepiece of fresh-cut flowers.

It was a silver service dining experience, and each guest, had their chair pushed into position by the serving staff.

Our meals were served by white-gloved staff, gently placing our vegetables, on our chosen main courses. For Jackie and me, we found this somewhat over the top, for a hotel in Bournemouth full of older people, as we realised that, we were the only two youngsters in the hotel.

After dinner, we returned to the hotel bar, where I could relax, and take off my tie and jacket.

As I went to sit down, mum was somewhat troubled, asking why I had removed my coat and my tie, and even suggested that I was embarrassing her. I told her to mind her own business, as, like her, we were paying the same money as them, and that I would not be trussed up like a turkey, to please anyone.

My comment didn't go down with mum, and we had a few brief words, culminating in us leaving her and Robin to their own devices. The next morning, we dressed smart but casually, and went downstairs for breakfast.

Mum and Robin were nowhere to be seen, and we chose a table and thought that we could finish our breakfast, before they both appeared, as I was still somewhat annoyed, from her comments the previous evening. Just as we had ordered breakfast, they appeared and asked I they could join us, which left us no choice but to agree.

To our surprise, mum apologised for her previous night outburst and asked for forgiveness. Looking her in her eyes, I told her straight, that I wasn't a little boy anymore, and I wouldn't be told what to do, by her or anyone. Mum ashamedly agreed, and we forgot all about it.

During the day, the hotel laid on several activities, which at first, we thought would be associated with the Christmas period. We were disappointed at the indoor bowling and ballroom dancing. Neither of us had any interest in any of the entertainment. There was also a card game of bridge, which we don't know how to play. And then there was Christmas bingo, where the bingo caller was dressed up as Father Christmas.

I have to admit that I have never been so bored in my entire life. As it was Christmas Eve, we always light a candle in memory of Jackie's mum. We took ourselves out of the hotel, into the brisk fresh winter sea air of Bournemouth, and found a church, so that we could say a small prayer, and light our candle.

After we had done so, we took a stroll along the promenade and spent several hours walking and talking, before returning to the hotel for lunch.

When we arrived in a dining room, mum and Robin we're sitting at a table and asked us to join them, of which we did. They then proceeded to tell us, about their morning's entertainment, and how they had won the carpet bowling competition, I couldn't contain my laughter, which was subduing my innermost boredom, in the end, I had to be blunt, and told them, that I was glad they had a lovely time, but I wasn't interested, which again upset mum as I had embarrassment to her again. We went back to our rooms after lunch, where Jackie telephoned her dad, while I relaxed to watch TV.

I overheard Jackie's conversation and her dad complaining that she was nagging him. As she was talking the line went quiet, and Jackie asked if her dad was okay, and he replied in the affirmative and mentioned that he was coming down with the flu and dropped the phone.

After the call, Jackie was a little upset and filled in the rest of the conversation, so I got a clearer picture. I told her that she shouldn't worry, as he was up to his old tricks, and had been drinking again. She tried to put it out of her mind and said she would call him back, to wish him a Merry Christmas the next day.

It was now afternoon tea, so we went to the dining room and sat down where mum and Robin located. I decided to have a Black Forest éclair, when it arrived it was massive. As always, I picked it up it started to eat it, as I did so, mum who had been leaning back on her chair, to speak to the person on the table behind, turned around sternly and said, 'Stephen use a fork, as that is somewhat embarrassing!'

That was the final straw, and I looked at her and told her to shut up. Mum then proceeded to talk to me, as if I was a child, so I stopped her in her tracks, and pointed out, that it was alright for her to lean back on her chair, and she thought I was embarrassing.

Jackie and I decided to finish eating and go to our room. She could see that I was annoyed and calmed me down. After the incident, I couldn't face going down for evening dinner, but Jackie, who had a calming influence, persuaded me to go. As we reached the reception area, we looked at the notice board, to see what the evening's entertainment was going to be.

After reading it, I felt that my life was over, as the entertainment was old-time wartime songs, followed by Christmas carols. Now, I was not opposed to having a good singalong, but this wasn't what I had in mind, as all I could imagine, was the old granny's sing along to Vera Lynn.

Jackie took my hand, and we laughed at the entertainment, before entering the dining room for Christmas Eve dinner. We were joined shortly by mum and Robin, and you could cut the atmosphere with a knife. None of us spoke very much over dinner, so I decided that I was going to have a good drink with my wife in the bar.

To be honest, neither of us couldn't care less, if mum and Robin joined us. As the entertainment started, I started to mellow out, as I was enjoying my favourite tipple, of Hennessy champagne cognac. Robin, in his wisdom, decided to try and match me, drink for drink, that didn't go down well with mum, and she started on him.

By this time, Jackie and I had enough, where we decided to go to our room, and enjoy our Christmas Eve night, with our form of entertainment. At 11:30 pm, there was a knock at our door. It was Robin, who had walked out of the bar, as mum had given him a mouth full of abuse, and like us, he had had enough. He stayed for an hour, before going back to his room, where Jackie and I joined him, to have it out with mum.

As we entered the room, mum was sitting on the bed crying and said that she felt like we were victimising her, so I put her straight, and told her, that it was her own doing, as she was making us feel inadequate and unable to enjoy the Christmas break. I don't know if mum saw it that way, but I had to tell her the truth, regardless if she was upset or not. Before leaving, Jackie and I gave her a kiss and cuddle.

As Christmas morning arrived, Jackie's first task, was to ring up her dad, and wish him a Merry Christmas. While she was talking to him, Jackie was somewhat concerned, as her dad told her that he was feeling very ill, with the He dropped the phone again, and by now, Jackie was worried, and when he reconnected, Jackie told him she would ring the ambulance, as he didn't sound very well. Nobby being his usual self, told her not to be stupid as he would be fine, and would be going back to bed again. Jackie insisted on calling the ambulance service.

While on the phone to the emergency services, she explained everything to the paramedics. An hour later, she received a call from one of the paramedics, who was outside her dad's house. He informed her that they had spoken to Nobby and he refused any form of treatment and told them to go away.

Jackie insisted that they knock on the door again, and she spoke to her dad, who confirmed that he was fine, and was somewhat anxious, that Jackie had contacted the ambulance. He refused medical care and told her that he would not go to the hospital, and was adamant that he was merely suffering from the flu.

After their conversation, I noticed Jackie was still worried, and I comforted her, telling her it would be okay. But to ease her mind, I suggested that we return home on Boxing Day, and cut our break short. After she had calmed down, we went to see mum and Robin and exchanged our Christmas gifts. Mum was a different person, as she and Robin had made amends, and the day itself was pleasant, and we had a good time. We explained our decision to return home because of Jackie's dad.

Boxing Day finally arrived, and we were eager to get home, so we ate a light breakfast, before loading the car and heading off. Jackie had tried to call her dad, but couldn't get a reply. I suggested that he may have been in bed and would therefore not answer the phone.

As we arrived home, Jackie was beside herself with worry. I wanted to go down immediately and told her to give me five minutes, but she insisted that she would go alone, Jackie believed that I would be annoyed with her dad, as he had let her down, on many occasions in the past. I agreed and asked her to call me as soon as she had any news, and would follow down later on.

An hour later, I received the call from Jackie. She was in floods of tears and could hardly speak. Without hesitation, I drove to Nobby's house and saw her standing outside, looking troubled. Inside the house were two policemen, and one of them came out to speak to me.

It appeared, that Jackie found the door unlocked, with the keys still in the lock, she had gone inside and called out to her dad, and as she started to walk up the stairs, she had noticed one of his ankles, and he was lying face down, on the landing floor. Fearing the worst, she knocked on one of his neighbour's door, and they went in to investigate, where they found his body and then they called the police. We were unable to enter the house until the coroner has removed his body.

After they had left, one of the police officers took me to one side, to explain that there was a mess in the bedroom, and suggested that I dispose of it, before Jackie saw it. I left Jackie in the living room to gather her thoughts and went up to the bedroom, wherein a small bin beside the bed, was the hideous sight of blood, and part of Nobby's stomach lining.

The smell was horrendous, and I tried not to gag, as I carried it downstairs to the toilet, disposing of it. After I had cleaned up, I disposed of the bin in a black bin liner and put it down the garbage chute. I rang up my mum and told her the sad news, and I would keep her informed, and to have a safe journey home to Crete.

To both our surprise, several hours later, mum and Robin turned up to the house as we're just about to leave. Jackie was in no mood, to accept them there, I made it abundantly clear to my mum, to leave her alone. It wasn't a personal thing, but mum didn't recognise that and thought that Jackie was rude. In the end, I told them to leave it alone and go home because Jackie was grieving. When they left, we decided to leave the house as it was, and return a few days later, to start the clearing up process.

When we returned, the electricity had been cut off, and the food inside the fridge had started to rot. As I emptied the fridge, I noticed that the contents, were four years out of date, as was the rest of the food in the cupboards.

However, we never knew, as whenever we had visited Noddy before his death, we had no reason to go and check. Throughout the house, we found 50 x 2-litre empty bottles of vodka, which he had hidden away.

The more we went through his belongings, we found paperwork that had not been dealt with, and that he had been in debt with his rent, and had not paid his gas and electricity bill, hence the reason they have been cut off.

He'd also not paid the telephone bill and had letters from debt collection agencies. All in all, we spoke to other people about him, who told us that when Jan had passed away, he had squandered the money that she had left him, purely on booze!

After several hours, Jackie had collected some personal belongings, to keep as mementoes, as nothing else in the house, was of any use. It would be down to the council, to discard of the items, before renovating and renting out to new tenants. Over the next few days, we contacted the companies Noddy owed money and paid off his debts before we could concentrate on his funeral.

The funeral was a low-key affair, as Nobby didn't have any friends to speak of, as they were more drinking partners, who would only be around when he was staking them a drink. The few people that did turn up were some of his relatives, who came to pay their respects. Jackie and I had decided not to have a wake.

However, his family had arranged a small gathering, at one of their houses, so we went along in memory of him.

The old year passed by, it was now 2008, and we could continue with our busy lives, and plan our next holiday, with Theresa and Steve. We found a good-looking holiday on the island of Zakynthos in Greece. As we had such amazing times on our previous holidays together, we booked it early and was scheduled for mid-May.

The hotel was a family run business, and the area that we were going, to was Zante. The flight was the smoothest flight that I had ever experienced. When the captain was announcing, I suggested and imagined him, as the well-known children's character Biggles. As we landed at Zante airport, as usual, the cabin crew were near the doors, thanking the passengers while they were disembarking. We were the last remaining passengers and could now see that the pilot had also come out of the cockpit, to thank everyone. It was incredible, as this pilot was a spitting image, of what I'd imagined Biggles would look-like.

He sported a curled handlebar moustache, and was holding a deerstalker pipe, and was very well-spoken. The only thing missing was a long flowing scarf, and I couldn't help myself but laugh, as did Theresa, Jackie and Steve. It was the start of the precedent for the holiday, as like all our holidays, was nothing but all-round laughter and fun.

At our hotel, there was a great practical joker called Jim. He was middle-aged, but we both had the same mentality and was very much on my wavelength. He had bought a water pistol and was generally having fun, so I purchased one as well, and we were like a couple of kids, and keep the hotel guests amused, as we did the hotel staff.

Every day, Jim would buy an even bigger water pistol, and not to be undone, I would follow suit. In the end, I searched long and hard, and found a triple soaking gun, with pump-action, which beat Jim's previous model hands down.

It was fun-packed, with Jim and me, making the entertainment for the hotel guests, around the pool area. Armed with our water pistols, we would spray people, which their kids loved. We also devised water sports and games, and everyone got involved.

Even the hotel manager tried his hand at what we called steppingstones, which were a series of inflatables in the water, where you had to run across these inflatables, and get to the other side, without falling in. Of course, it was an impossible task, but it kept the entire hotel, entertained for hours.

Although we had a great time with these games, there was one thing that I wanted to do, and that was an excursion to see the ancient site of Olympia. I had purchased a ticket, and rose early, as I had to take a short boat trip, from Zakynthos to the mainland.

The boat and coach journey to Olympia was approximately two hours, but it was well worth the journey time. Like all places of interest, there were several different nationalities. The guides could speak the languages, for the small groups, that wanted to pay to hear their commentaries.

Seeing the ancient ruins are a marvel to behold and are a testament to those ancient Greeks. Sadly, some of the temples had either been destroyed by natural phenomenon, or by invading Turks. However, a lot of them remain untouched, and no visit would be complete without seeing the ancient torch, which is still used to light the modern torches, before the start of the modern Olympic Games.

One of the main parts of The Olympic village was the ancient running track. Everyone who goes to visit is encouraged to go through the arched entrance, and take a run on the track, which would have been used by other athletes, thousands of years earlier. Wanting to be a part of history I did just that, and I ran to the other end, although a short distance, it nearly killed me. As I recovered my breath, I only had admiration, for those ancient Greeks, who competed in the sweltering heat, and as Olympia is in a Valley, this feels just like a blast furnace.

After the tour, I also visited the onsite museum, which housed some incredible artefacts, and you could see that these are still in use today in the modern Olympics. Items such as discus, javelin haven't changed for thousands of years, most of the events like swimming, long jump, boxing, and of course running events, are still around today.

If you have never visited Olympia, then I can assure you, if you are into history, you have to go and admire the splendid beautiful Olympic village. All too soon, the day was at an end, and it was time to go back to the hotel, although exhausted and dusty from the day I had a fantastic time, and even more stories and memories to take home with me.

Back at the hotel, I showered and changed, before meeting up with Jackie, Theresa and Steve by the hotel bar. Throughout the evening, I regaled them with my stories of Olympia and must have bored them to death, with the endless photographs. They all said that they had wished they had come along with me, as my partner in crime Jim, had also gone off with his wife for an excursion, and the day wasn't as entertaining, as it had been, with myself and him in attendance. All in all, the entire day and evening, was one to remember.

The next day, it was business as usual for Jim and me. We devised a quiz for the grown up's, with questions based on our previous days acquired knowledge, from my time at Olympia, and Jim, who had been to see the Acropolis in Athens. The hotel manager printed the questions, and we chose the participants of our quiz at random. We also enrolled the kids, who were armed with our water pistols. The rules were quite simple, if a question were answered correctly, they would get a shot of local liqueur, but wrong answers would result in them being soaked with the water pistols.

As you can imagine, at first the adults we're giving the correct answers, however as the quiz progressed, they were getting more and more intoxicated by the liqueurs. They would now start to give the wrong answers, which resulted in them being soaked with great passion from the kids. Although chaotic, it was fantastic, and everyone around the pool work in hysterics. It was another lucky day, in what became known, as camp Steve and Jim!

It was the last full day of our holiday, as usual, Jim and I were up to our usual tricks, but after a while, we had to put away our toys and hand them down to the kids. I gave my super soaker away, to a little lad who was three years old, and the gun was bigger than him. However, he wasn't perturbed by the size, and I showed him how it operated.

At first, he found it difficult but soon mastered it, apart from filling it up, again and using the pump action. Each time it ran out of the water, and enough pressure, instead of asking his dad, he would run up to me, to allow me to do it for him, which was much to his mum's amusement, but I'm not sure that his dad felt the same way.

Nevertheless, it was another fantastic day. In the evening, unbeknown to myself and Jim, the hotel management had arranged gifts for us both, as they decided that we had been one of the most entertaining guests that had stayed at the hotel. Also, the other hotel guests had clubbed together and bought us a bottle of champagne. Both of us were lost for words, at these magnanimous gestures, and were unable to thank them all enough.

As it was our last night, we shared the champagne around, and the evening went off with a bang. The next morning was departure day, which was a solemn affair, as we had a wonderful time. Although sad to be leaving, we had all made some fantastic new friends, and we would remember them, and the great time, we had spent together.

Back onboard the aircraft, our seats we're located right at the back, mine was a window seat, Theresa was next to me, in the middle, Steve was in the aisle seat, and Jackie was next to him, in the aisle seat on the next row.

Our flight was a replica of our holiday, very entertaining. Theresa had bought with her an inflatable exercise cushion which was the size of an inflatable Castle, and it appealed to my sense of humour. So I thought it would be a good idea to try and tap the aircraft passengers, for some money for a minute's use with it, much to the amusement of the passengers, and crew alike. After several minutes of entertaining everyone, I returned to my seat as the air hostess had started serving.

After eating, I heard Theresa laughing, she told me to take a look at Steve, as I did so, I could see Jackie in hysterics, it took me a while to understand what they were laughing about, it was then, that I could see on his cheek, a trickle of cream. That was amusing in itself, but the best was yet to come, as when he turned his face, on the right side, was covered in cream, which had under pressure, exploded as he opened it.

That was all the ammunition that I needed, and I couldn't help myself as I suggested that he looked like he had been on the receiving end of a pornstars ejaculation!

This comment was enough to keep to me, Theresa and Jackie in fits of laughter, which was made worse by Steve, taking out his handkerchief, and wiping it off at his face which was a picture.

Once again, we were back home, and as always, all of us had a wonderful memorable holiday, that we would remember for a long time.

Back at home, we went back to our everyday lives, and Theresa had made her peace with my sister Tina and suggested that we all go out for a family meal.

I was persuaded by Jackie that we should, and although reluctant to do so, I played along. During the meal, we were all cracking jokes about our holiday, and the kids were all interested in our antics.

As I looked around the table, the only face that wasn't smiling was Tina.

She had her arms folded, and a face like thunder, and it appeared she was grinding her teeth. Throughout the evening, she barely said a word, which was a sign that she was going to start an argument at some point. To my surprise, she left without saying a word to me. However, that wouldn't stop her from criticising Theresa the next day.

When I went around to see Theresa, she was distraught, as was Steve. She told me the full conversation that she had with Tina which had been disgusting. It was nothing out of the ordinary and was what I had expected from her, as she is the most vindictive person I have ever known.

Tina had alleged that Steve had sexually assaulted her and that she hated me, and Jackie, as we had put a wedge between her and Theresa. I couldn't believe my ears, and I wanted to rush to her house and give her a piece of my mind, but they all stopped me.

After this latest tirade, over the next few weeks, Theresa and Steve had made up their minds and were planning on buying, a bar/restaurant in Spain. They asked Jackie and me if we wanted to become joint owners. As this was a shock, I asked if we could think about it, but in the end, we decided not to follow them in their venture. Looking back, I wished we had done it. Very quickly, they found a property in Malaga and sold their home before moving out to start a new life in Spain.

After Theresa and Steve left, we cut ties with Tina and concentrated on our lives for the only family that was still in the vicinity, our niece Lisa, her partner Dan, and young son Kaden. We also ensured that our nephew Lee was OK. I also concentrated on my business and Jackie. We became closer together, and even though I also had my best friend, Steve. Due to Tina's poisonous nature, life would just never be the same. Again, the remainder of the year passed by, and all too soon another year came around.

Chapter Fourteen

New Country New Start

2009 started slowly, although I was working, the building industry is not a stable one, and you have to take the rough, with the smooth. As business was slow, I had to let my employees go, not before ensuring they were financially looked after, they were good boys and deserved it. But they understood that I had to make cuts, as I had to look after my own and Jackie's interest first, besides, they were well known and managed to secure some projects of their own.

After we had parted company, I continued the business by myself, and had to put the hours in, and often worked up to sixteen hours during the day, and another two hours after I returned home. Before leaving for my work, I would ensure that

Jackie had everything she needed, as she had been feeling under the weather for a couple of months because of MS.

She still insisted, in carrying on with her voluntary work, at the Bedford MS centre. I believed Jackie was overdoing it, but she was somewhat stubborn, and wouldn't accept, or take my advice. Once again, she had to put others first, without thinking of her own.

I hadn't been at work for very long when I got a phone call from the hospital that Jackie had been admitted suffering from a severe MS attack. I arrived at the hospital and found Jackie at a ward hooked up to a steroid drip. I'd witnessed her attacks before, but never like this, she looked gaunt and ill.

As I was comforting her, she was very tearful, and kept on apologising, for putting me through all the heartache because of her illness. Upon hearing these words, my heart broke, as I have never thought, that she had ever put me in the position, of being a burden to me.

It was the first time that I have witnessed Jackie with her guards down. Even with all her attacks over the years, she had always remained focused, never seemingly let it get her down. I held on to her hands tightly and assured her, I would do everything in my power, to make sure, that she would receive the best treatment, and I'd be there, whatever the situation. Seeing her like this, was somewhat upsetting, and I would have swap places gladly with her if I could. Jackie was my hero, and would always put myself and others, above her own needs.

Jackie treated with steroids for three days, and when I picked her up from the hospital after her discharge, she was a different person. She once again apologised, only this time, Jackie put it down to having merely a lousy week. I mentioned what she had said in the hospital, and she again emphasised, that she wasn't feeling herself at that time, and Jackie promised to cut down her hours at the Bedford MS society.

Rather than push her for a different answer, I left it at that and trusted her that she would keep her promise of reducing her hours. True to her word, Jackie cut down her voluntary hours and concentrated with her hobbies, which made her a few pounds of pocket money. After a few weeks, we both noticed the difference, and she was getting stronger by the minute. Unfortunately, multiple sclerosis has a habit of dissipating, and then coming back again with a vengeance, at any time.

It was now March, Jackie had recovered, and I was still working hard, and our lives had improved significantly. One evening, I came home, and Jackie was in a fantastic upbeat mood. I was suspicious, and I asked her what was going on. Her first words to me were that she had been 'thinking'.

Being my typical self, I naturally and wrongly assumed that she wanted me to do more work on the house. However, my assumptions were wrong, as she explained, that as we had collateral in our house, why don't we consider moving. I thought that, as ideas go, this sounded like an excellent opportunity.

I asked where she had been thinking of moving to, and she replied Crete! I was dumbfounded at her answer, as I felt that she meant that we move somewhere different, in our own country. I needed to know and questioned the reasoning behind her decision.

Jackie explained that she always felt much better being in the sunshine and that it helped her condition. I thought about it for a moment, and I could see that she had a valid point of view, but didn't think that the idea of moving abroad, was necessarily a good one. I explained to her my reasons, the main one being that it would be stressful enough, moving within our own country, let alone moving abroad.

Each time I come up with a different argument, Jackie had a viable answer, she had even spoken to her GP, who had explained, that the temperate climate and sunshine, although wouldn't cure her, it would help her condition. I told Jackie to let me think about it, and we left the discussion alone for a while. Several weeks later, I was dead set against the idea of moving to Crete, but I felt that moving away from Luton was a good idea.

I'd been working long hours and was now doing a bathroom conversion for my friend Steve and Diane. As I was working at their home, I felt a lump in my right knee, and it was more like ball-shaped. Although it wasn't a concern, I thought I had better get it checked out by my GP. He explained that it was a sack of fluid, which had calcified due to some previous trauma on the knee. I couldn't think of any recent injury, as I would always take care and wear protective knee pads. It was only then that I remembered, I was wounded in action while serving in Iraq.

However, surely it couldn't be from that time, as it had been operated on successfully. I was sent for an X-Ray, and was somewhat shocked, with what doctors found. They explained that tiny metal fragments which were foreign bodies embedded in my knee, the only way that the knee could protect itself, was to encase them, and form, what could only be described as a type of Pearl.

Over the years, this protection had grown larger and was the size of the kneecap itself. The only option would be for a surgical procedure to remove it. The surgeon explained that under normal circumstances, the operation would be a simple one as they would perform it under local anaesthetic, and the wound would be opened up widthways. But like mine, was one of the worst that he could see and feel, it would have to be performed under general anaesthetic and would be opened up lengthways which would mean a more extended recovery period.

Although I had been made aware of the risks, I couldn't put it off any longer, as it was affecting my ability to work. As I had health insurance, I was able to have the operation paid for privately, and therefore jumped the queue.

The operation was planned two weeks after the initial consultation from the surgeon. It was a day surgery case, and I was the first on the list, Jackie came with me, as the operation, was only expected to last for an hour and a half. It meant, she would stay at the hospital while I had the procedure carried out, and we would return home together, as I wouldn't be fit and able to do so.

After the operation, the surgeon told me that due to the way they had to cut open my knee to remove the foreign body, I wouldn't be able to walk, as there was more risk of the wound opening up, and infection to take hold.

When we got home, Jackie insisted that I rested with my knee up. At first, it was a novelty; however, watching her run around and do everything for me, wasn't what I had expected. I could see that it was taking its toll on her, and after a day of resting, I couldn't resist the temptation and started to get up and walk.

I tried not to bend my right knee, as Jackie wasn't happy with me getting around, but I think this was because I was myself in her way, and annoying her. With the amount of moving that I was doing, the advice from the hospital had come true, although I didn't know it at the time, the stitches opened up, and infection started to build up slowly. Four days after I had the operation,

I had a check-up with my GP's surgery nurse, who had removed my bandage and saw the infection. It was an indescribable smell, and I felt sick to my stomach and somewhat lightheaded. The nurse suggested that I lay on the bed so that she could clean the wound and redo the stitches.

As I got to my feet, I momentarily passed out and collapsed, and had to be helped to the couch. Jackie witnessed it and was worried sick, and as any loving partner would do for their spouse, started to nag, as I had gone and against the hospital's advice, in the first place.

The wound was re-stitched and redressed, and the doctor prescribed a high dose of antibiotics. With the nurse's advice still ringing in my ears, Jackie took me home, and like an invalid, I had to rest and accept it. Being the person that I am, I hated being waited on hand and foot, I felt powerless, but I was unable to do anything, and the worst of all, was that the little work that I had promised my clients, I had to farm out to my once employees. Although we weren't short of money, I just felt terrible that I had let everyone down.

I was laid up for two weeks and was getting impatient in obtaining any fresh clients. Jackie took full advantage of this and emphasised her earlier proposal, of moving to the sun In Crete. I listened to her points of view carefully and how the weather helped her condition whenever we have been abroad.

With the amount of information she had bombarded me with, I relented and suggested that we first go over for a three-week holiday, to see how the land laid, before making the most crucial decision. Before we booked up a flight, we spoke to my mum and explained what we had planned to do. Mum was ecstatic that we were considering coming over and live near her.

On our behalf, for potential rental properties, should we decide, and make the move permanent. Arriving at the airport, mum and Robin greeted us and drove back to their apartment, which would be our base while we were on a fact-finding mission. We would also be looking at the rental properties that mum had inquired. After we had settled in at mum's, we were eager to go and look at the apartment she mentioned during our discussions.

We'd assumed that she had a number of them lined up for viewing, but to our disappointment, there was only one apartment we could check, and it was only a 5-minute journey and was in the same village as she was.

The person we were meeting was a lady called Maria, who spoke excellent English compared to our Greek. She was there with her husband, Lefteris, and they both owned the property.

After exchanging pleasantries, we went to look at the flat. It was a large building which housed another Greek couple on the ground floor. The apartment right next to ours on the first floor belonged to her mum and dad.

As we walked inside, we were greeted by the builder's rubble as they had just finished some refurbishments and remodelling of the place.

Lefteris was an architect by trade, and could only speak a few words of English, so Maria was acting as interpreter.

Walking through the front door, we entered a large dining room, with an attached open kitchen area, with marble tiled floor. To the right was the living room, which was closed off by two sliding glass doors. Leading from the kitchen, was a short hallway, to the right, just past the living room, was the bathroom, which had been re-tiled, and a new bathroom suite fitted.

Further down the hallway to the right, the master bedroom was a guest bedroom. Out the back door, was a shared garden with Maria's parents with a separate area of the garden for our use. From the front of the apartment was our balcony, where we had some fantastic views, which overlooked the mountains and the sea.

In front of the shared garden and communal area was the main road through Istron, which stood several other buildings, one on the ground floor was a tourist supermarket, and above that, a bar named Pinocchio's. After viewing the apartment, Jackie and I had a private conversation, and it was evident that she had fallen in love with the place, and I have to admit that I had a good feeling about it myself. Speaking to Maria, we asked about the rent per month. She told us that they wanted 420 euros per month excluding bills.

I wasn't happy with that as it was overpriced, even our mortgage payment on our home was only £240 per month excluding bills. I took over negotiations with Lefteris and Maria, but he was adamant that the price was very reasonable. I then told them that we were not interested and ready to walk away as we had worked out that we would be paying 120 euros over the top of other properties in the area that had three bedrooms.

Maria, realising that they may not be able to rent to anybody else, spoke to Lefteris before they both agreed to 300 Euros per month excluding bills. Before finalising the deal, we also reached an agreement that we would take the apartment, and pay a deposit, as long as we had everything in writing with a tenancy agreement. Again, after a short discussion, they agreed. We were asked to come the next day to sign the deal and pay the deposit. We did so with independent witnesses because we were still reluctant and unsure of the Greeks.

After signing the tenancy agreement, we were now committed to moving to Crete. We have a lot to do when we returned home, as we still had to put our home on the market, finalise, and to tie up any loose ends. We also had to arrange for our furniture to be moved from England to Crete and needed to find a suitable removal company to do so.

While in Crete, we decided to buy some pieces of furniture and electrical goods, so that we could move in as soon as we finalised everything without any discomfort. The 3-week holiday was a constant daily challenge of shopping and making deals with the furniture and electrical stores.

The Greeks were very accommodating when we went to discuss buying the items that we wanted. We worked out that we saved nearly £3000, compared to what we would pay back home. We also had spoken to another ex-pat couple, who had used an international moving company under the trading name of Nomads. With everything now in place, we returned home and put our house on the market.

The estate agent valued the property at £166,000 and assured us that we would have no problems due to the location and extensive refurbishment I did on the property, which also included all the safety certificates required. The day our agents advertised our property, within two hours, we had a call from the estate agent to attend the first viewing.

The person who came around to look at the property was very picky, and didn't like our decoration, and dared to ask if we could repaint the house in the colours they wanted and to remove the stair runner carpet which we liked, and replace it with a full carpet. Suffice to say, when the estate agent contacted us, to inform us that the potential buyers had offered only £146,000, we both refused and told them we would not be accepting any of their offers. Our next viewer was a local boy who was born and bred in Luton and wanted to be closer to his family.

He was a manager at a factory that manufactured plastic car components for Vauxhall motors. As he arrived, we welcomed him and had a good feeling about it. We showed him around before we went outside in the garden to allow an interrupted tour by himself.

When he'd finished, he joined us in the garden. The buyer was very impressed, and he promised to think about it and we would hear from him soon. Two hours later, the estate agent called and told us the guy liked the property and was offering £163,000. They recommended that we reject his first offer and see if he could increase it.

Later on, that same afternoon, he improved his offer, which now stood at £165,500, as this was only £500 less than the asking price, we agreed. We sold the house subject to contract, and surveyor report. Although not finalised, we contacted Nomads, to arrange an evaluation of transporting our furniture over to our new home In Crete. The next day, their sales manager arrived and took an inventory of our belongings with a total price of £2500.

Over the next few days, we had a nail-biting moment as everything was going in a rush.

We shouldn't have worried as everything went smoothly, and just two weeks after returning home from Crete, we sold our home. We now have a date to leave the property. We arranged for Nomads to come and collect our furniture before our departure.

The day we finalised our contracts and handed in the keys, Jackie and I took one final wishful look around, our once beautiful home and garden, and all the beautiful memories we had while living there was now history. As we locked the front door for the last time, we did so with a heavy heart, and couldn't help but shed a tear, as it was the last time we would see it and also the last time we would be seeing England.

After handing back the keys to the estate agent, we went to the Travelodge hotel in Luton where we'd booked for two day's stay. As we entered our room, we were both overcome and broke down in each other's arms, as the reality of our situation had struck us. Although we were heading off into an unknown adventure, it was like we were grieving, and therefore were neither happy, nor unhappy with what awaited us, or what we had left behind.

We managed to compose ourselves and settled in to relax before we freshened ourselves. We were meeting Jackie's uncle and aunt at a nearby restaurant for a farewell dinner.

The next day, we met up with our nephew Lee and our niece Lisa to say our goodbyes, and to let them know they would be welcome to visit us at any time. After meeting up with them, we had one final thing we had to do; we reserved our seats for the coach journey to Gatwick the next day.

Our flight was at 09:30, and we had booked the coach to pick us up at 06:30, allowing us plenty of time to relax before departure. It was a chilly morning, and I wasn't feeling well when the coach arrived, I couldn't wait to get into the warm coach. I felt terrible as I sat in my seat and reclined in it.

Jackie was concerned because I was drifting in and out of sleep. She even asked the driver if he could turn the heating up as I felt frozen.

I started to feel warmer and managed to sleep until we got to the airport. As soon as we checked in, we went to have our breakfast. Due to the stress, Jackie was in her wheelchair as her legs weren't working well.

It was like the blind leading the blind, as I was rather ill, and we must have looked like a right pair of idiots to other passengers. After breakfast, I only drank two glasses of orange juice, as all I wanted to do, was to sit as close to the departure gate, as it was going to be a long walk, and I wanted to get on the aircraft as soon as possible.

While waiting for our flight to come up, Jackie took herself off to buy some magazines, and try to find some medication. When she returned, she had some paracetamol which I took, and could not get enough fluid into me. As our flight was called, it was like a race to the death for myself and Jackie as I covered the ground at speed, much to Jackie surprise.

I just needed to get on the aircraft and settle down so that I could sleep once again. Now in our seats, I asked for a pillow and a blanket, as I was feeling terrible. I usually would enjoy take off, as I had always found it exciting. However, in this instance, I couldn't care less, as all I could think about was closing my eyes and sleeping.

Now airborne, Jackie woke me up, as the cabin crew we're handing out the refreshments. All I wanted was some water, as I couldn't face any solid food as the cabin air pressure was making me feel even worse. One of the cabin attendants asked Jackie if I was OK, as I looked very pale, but we both assured them I would be fine. Knocking back the water, I took two more paracetamol, and as I was feeling a little better, I even managed to eat the in-flight meal.

After eating, I once again rested my head and pulled the blanket around me tight and fell into a deep sleep. As we were coming into land, Jackie woke me up again. All I could now think of was getting off the aircraft, as all I could think of, was sleep and a beautiful warm bed. When we had landed, we tried to get through the departures as quickly as possible and to meet up with mum and Robin and go home.

As we were waiting for our luggage, the automatic doors, kept opening and shutting due to a fault, it was there, where I could see mum and Robin. I managed to pick up the bags, and Jackie and I got out of the arrival hall with haste. Mum was horrified when she saw me, as I was looking ghastly, and she was concerned and wanted to get us home urgently.

Robin took our luggage, while mum pushed Jackie in her chair, thankfully their car wasn't far away. Although it was mid-August, I was shivering as if I was in a freezer. The journey seemed to take forever, and I was sleeping in the back, resting my head on the window, while Jackie was holding my hand.

Mum opened the door; I couldn't wait to get in and go to bed. I stripped down to my underwear and got under the bedclothes, and immediately drifted off to deep sleep. Periodically, Jackie would wake me up, to ensure that I was drinking plenty of water, she would also place a cold flannel on my head and stay with me until I fell back to sleep again.

I was in and out of sleep for most of the day. I woke up at around 7 pm, where I put on a T-shirt and shorts to go and sit in the living room with Jackie and mum. They could see that I was looking better but was still not out of the woods just yet. Mum had made some ham baguettes, which at first, I wasn't hungry, but after a short while, I managed to eat two, and drink plenty of fluids. I don't remember much after that, apart from occasionally waking up, and going to the toilet, after I had been drinking copious amounts of water.

The next morning, I woke up feeling much more refreshed. Jackie had already been up for several hours and was in the kitchen, talking to mum. I could tell by their expressions that I was looking and feeling much better, compared to the previous day. We put it down to the recent stress, and that I hadn't been drinking enough fluid, and become severely dehydrated.

I had some breakfast, then had a shower, dressed in shorts, T-shirt, and trainers, I looked much better. We planned to go and pay off the items from the electrical and furniture stores which we had ordered a few weeks earlier. At the electrical store, we'd purchased a 42-inch flat-screen TV, an oven, electric hob, extractor hood, washing machine, and an American style, double door fridge freezer, with built-in cold water and ice-making facilities.

After paying the balance, the store told us that they would deliver the next morning. At the furniture store, we purchased a dining room table and six chairs, a new double bed, and traditional Greek style ceiling lamps. These items would also be delivered the next working day. We also wanted to paint the apartment in different colours, as we were not keen on the bland white walls and white ceilings, we went to the local hardware store, where they mixed our choices. I wasted no time in painting the apartment by myself while Jackie and my mum stayed out of my way and ventured to the beach and explore other areas. By the time 1 o'clock had arrived, I had finished painting the entire apartment as living in a warm climate the paint dries very quickly, and I was able to do two coats in each area.

After cleaning up, I went out to have my lunch, where I was to meet up with Jackie and my mum. When I arrived at the taverna, I ordered a Greek salad and home-cooked chips, just in time for Jackie and mum to join me. Mum didn't stay long, as she had to go and prepare lunch for her and Robin, as he was still at work.

Jackie and I enjoyed our lunch, and afterwards, we walked to our new apartment so that she could view my handiwork. She was impressed by the colours we had chosen, and we could now both visualise what the apartment would be looking like once we had our furniture installed.

We locked up and went for a long walk around the coastal orchards, which were full of orange and lemon trees; the smell was divine. We spent several hours admiring the scenery in our new adopted country. Shortly before we went back to mum's house, we sat and talked about the future, and what our dreams could become.

As the sun started to die down, we returned to mum's apartment to freshen up before going out for a drink at the friend's bar. We were greeted like old long-lost friends, by the owner Manolis, who seemed genuinely pleased that we had decided to come and live in the village.

We felt most at home in the bar. It was as if we were destined to move there after seeing the island for the first time on holiday with mum and Robin. After a few hours, mum and Robin joined us, before we took them out for a meal at the Taverna opposite their apartment, named Maria's. We had a pleasant evening with them, surrounded by amazing Greek locals.

The next morning, I had a phone call informing us that our deliveries from electrical and furniture store would be with us within an hour. Jackie and I made our way to our apartment and ensured that the access area was clear of any rubbish and hazard.

As the deliveries got nearer to Istron village, I had another phone call from the driver, asking if I could stand outside, and wave him down, as he wasn't sure of the address. I stood outside Pinocchio's bar, and flagged him down, before directing him to the apartment. The driver spoke perfect English, as did his mate, and they wasted no time unloading our electrical items.

With the items in situ, they not only plumbed in the American style fridge freezer, but they also fitted the washing machine, dishwasher, and the oven and hob, all free of charge! This excellent service support was better than any, that we had ever had, while we lived in the UK. As they had gone the extra mile, we wouldn't allow them to go away empty-handed and gave them 20-euro tip each. As we stood back and admired our new items, the phone rang again from the furniture store, who was five minutes away, so I went back outside to flagged them down, as soon as they had reached the area.

Like before, two drivers delivered our furniture and built the sectional bed. Again, impressed by this Greek hospitality, we also gave them 20 euro each. After they'd left, we admired our new furniture, and sat down at the dining table, as we did so, there was a knock at the door, there stood Manolis from friends bar, who had bought around two chairs from his bar, as these were the only things missing from our lounge.

We went to give him a tip for such a generous gift, which he refused. Jackie and I were overawed with such generosity, as we had never experienced it back home. With everything in place we required, we decided to go shopping to buy some groceries. We telephoned mum to ask if she wanted to join us. A few moments later, she turned up in the car, and I suggested that I take the wheels as I needed to get some experience on the Greek road network, plus mum's driving was a lot to be desired.

Mum's suggestion was to go to the next town from Istron in Ierapetra. We drove along the beautiful coastal road, with amazing views, wherever you looked. Throughout the journey, mum and Jackie were talking nonstop. I remained silent, as I knew I wouldn't get a word in edgeways.

Finally, we arrived at the supermarket and ventured inside. We were amazed at the freshness of the fruit and veg section, fresh grocery, and meat counters, and overall impressed with the layout of the store.

We picked up our essential store cupboard ingredients before going to the butchers opposite the supermarket, which had been recommended by mum. We were greeted by the butchery staff, where the assistant manager spoke perfect English, who skilfully cut and butchered our meat of choice, which was very fresh.

We had a great conversation with him. I noticed that the manager could speak German, and I engaged him in a conversation, as I had learnt German when I have been with the army. This level of customer service was incredible, as when we went to pay for our items, we were given free of charge, a whole chicken and a jar of Cretan honey.

We couldn't believe how generous the Greek people had been to us, mum explained, that all of them were the same, and we would experience more of it, as it was the Greek way of living.

Back at home, we planned our first meal in our new home, while I was cooking, Jackie was relaxing in the lounge. I decided to prepare some beautiful pork chops, with garlic potatoes and fresh veg.

As we sit down to eat, we heard a noise at the back door. To our surprise, it was our landlady Maria's mother, who had let herself in, with her key!

We were both dumbfounded by this and somewhat annoyed that she had let herself into our flat. Although not rude to her, I rang up and complained to Maria, that although it might be a Greek custom, it wasn't acceptable, as we were paying rent for the property, therefore, we wouldn't be at all happy for her mother, to just come and go as she pleased.

Maria was embarrassed at this, and assured us, that she would let her mother know, if she wanted to come to see us again, she would have to knock on the front door. Although we had assurances, I made doubly sure that she couldn't enter our home with her key, so I changed the locks.

After we'd eaten our evening meal, we relaxed for a short while, before deciding to go and have a drink, at what would now be our local pub Pinocchio's.

As we walked up the stairs to the bar, we heard music blasting out of the building, although it was around 8 pm, and was at the height of the tourist season, we were the only patrons. The owner, also named Manolis greeted us, and like all Greeks, was warm and inviting. Manolis was a middle-aged, balding man, with a friendly personality.

He spoke perfect English, and although we were the only customers, we had a somewhat enjoyable evening. As all the places, he was most generous, and before leaving, he poured us both, a free local liqueur, as a nightcap. Walking over the road to our home, we could now hear the cicadas chirping away. The air was warm and had a fantastic smell from the surrounding orange trees. When we got back home, we were over the moon that we had made the right choice, and our life at that time, couldn't be sweeter, as although we had a reasonably good life in the UK, nothing compared to what we had now had.

He next day, we were awoken early by the chorus of cicada. Also, by the bright, intense sunshine, that was peeking through our shuttered windows. I got up to prepare the breakfast, while Jackie had a shower before myself showering, we sat on the front balcony, and enjoyed our breakfast, in the beautiful atmosphere that we now found ourselves.

After breakfast, I showered, and Jackie and I went for a long pleasant walk admiring our beautiful home surroundings. Everyone we met with greeted us with 'calimera', which meant 'good morning'. It was a welcome change, as whenever we had been in the UK, we never experienced such greetings from our people.

Our walk took us around the coastal areas, and we ended up at the beach.

We sat down for a while to appreciate the stunning scenery. One of the locals who was walking a beautiful old English sheepdog greeted us and moved closer. We spent a pleasant time talking with them before we went our separate ways. We later meet up with mum for a morning coffee at Friend's bar.

Over the next few days, we got to know the village very well and met many new friends and acquaintances. Robin also introduced us to his boss George, who owned the local car rental place. He was selling one of his fleet of cars, a Renault thali.

This type of Renault is not available in the UK but a saloon version of a Clio. George wanted 8000 euros for the car, but I wasn't prepared to pay such an amount for a car that was 9500 euro as a new car. It also had 56,000 kilometres on the clock, and four years old! After negotiating with him, we agreed on a fixed price of 5400 euro.

We had to go with him to re-register the car into my name, and that was the first time we experienced Greek bureaucracy. To be fair, it's like something out of the middle ages, and somewhat antiquated. It took us nearly four hours to complete the paperwork, as it had to be stamped by each department.

This was farcical to say the least, as we had to go from office to office five times, to have one person stamp the documents, before we moved on to the next office, to have it stamped again, and so on and so on. Finally, we would have to go back to the first office to have it stamped one last time!

Looking back, I can now see the reason the Greek economy was in such disarray, as they tend to just give people jobs, with very little work involved. It would have been more cost-effective and beneficial to the Greek government if it was all done in one office. However, although it may seem draconian, it was their way of life, and we soon adapted to it. The Greek philosophy 'zigar, zigar,' or 'slowly slowly' is very apt indeed.

With the car now registered in my name, it meant that Jackie and I could venture out further afield without relying too heavily on mum and Robin. It is not to say, that we wouldn't require their company or advice, but we felt it necessary, for us to learn our way, in our new home, as mum tended to treat us like little kids.

We had now been at our new home for nearly three weeks when we had a phone call from Nomads that our furniture from the UK would be delivered in a few days. We made sure that we were prepared for its arrival, and all hands were on deck to help us as soon as it arrived.

The day of arrival came, as promised, Nomads arrived at our new home on time.

Mum, myself and Jackie were ready to get stuck in to help offload our furniture. However, our apartment has a slight location problem. Nomads' lorry is a small box van and was unable to get through branches which formed an archway to the entrance of our property.

Thankfully, Maria's dad came to the rescue with his flatbed truck. He drove back and forth for several hours until everything had been delivered. Although we offered him money, he refused to take it. However, we did buy some bottles of wine for him and his wife.

We made short work of the packing and making our new home complete. As exhausted as we were, both of us felt the need to celebrate with a housewarming party, and we welcomed everyone, including our new Greek friends, who were in awe of our furniture.

Our new life in the sun was as idyllic as could be expected. However, as magnificent as it was, I felt that there was only a certain amount of times that could be wasted on sunbathing. Although Jackie loved sun-worshipping, for me, I needed something more stimulating and challenging, so I decided to obtain my scuba diver instructor licence.

I'd initially obtained my open water license many years back when I got hooked on the sport while serving in the army in Cyprus. I took myself down do the local scuba diving school based at the Istron Bay hotel. The owner was named Tasso, and we immediately hit it off, as he had served in the Greek military. We agreed on a deal for the costing involved for me to obtain my full instructor licence.

For me to become a full scuba diving instructor, there were specific requirements, and I wasted no time in completing every element. My first requirement was becoming a rescue diver, the second was as a divemaster, culminating in becoming a scuba diving instructor.

I now had something to focus on, rather than just sitting in the sun and topping up my tan. Jackie had also found another interest. She joined a local taekwondo school and was doing very well. The school was improving Jackie's health, and the combination of sun and exercise made her feel as if she hadn't had MS at all. It also meant that we both had something else to talk about, and we loved every minute of it.

Even though we had an idyllic lifestyle, small cracks started to appear in our relationship. Although like most couples, we had our ups and downs in the past, this was different, as Jackie was getting more frustrated with living in the apartment. It turned out that she was missing the UK and her brother Alan.

We had a few choice words as regards of this, as I explained that we had moved at her request, due to her condition, as it was her recommendation and insistence that we had done so. It was about the same time that our friends Steve and Diane came over for their first visit to Crete.

Of course, Steve and I had a great laugh, and the girls would talk regularly, but we would all have an enjoyable time together, either with a home-cooked meal or a meze, at one of the many tavernas in the village. While Steve and Diane were at our place, Jackie had spoken to Diane and explained that she was feeling homesick. At the same time, Steve had asked if I wanted to see Queens Park Rangers in an away game at Blackpool.

It was an excellent opportunity for us to kill two birds with one stone, as we could go back to the UK for a short break, and Jackie could see her brother Alan, and I would be with my friends for a weekend away in Blackpool to see my football team play. That would be a solution to Jackie's homesickness, and we could both get away from Crete for a short time and away from the same old routine that we had got ourselves in. After Steve and

Diane had gone home, we looked at flights back to the UK, and we booked our tickets for a week away, where we would be staying at Steve and Diane's place.

Our flight was a Friday, and Robin dropped us off at the airport. We were somewhat excited to be going back to the UK, as we both missed it and our friends. We arranged to pick up a hire car from the airport, as we wouldn't have to be reliant on Steve or Diane. The first thing we noticed when he landed at Gatwick was how cold it seemed, although it was only the beginning of October. Driving from the airport to Steve and Diane's house felt strange, as I had now been used to driving In Crete, however, I soon got back into the swing of UK time, and couldn't wait to see our friends once more.

Going back to the UK was like a breath of fresh air, we wasted no time in getting the party started at Steve and Diane's. The week had been planned for us, with Diane looking after Jackie, while Steve had organised the tickets, and bed and breakfast bookings to Blackpool the next morning. We woke early, although we were nursing hangovers from the previous night's entertainment, myself and Steve had a hearty full English breakfast, to soak up the booze from the previous night.

We awaited the arrival of Jay, who had hired a six-seater people carrier. There were six of us going, which was me, Steve, Jay, Rob, Scotty, and Jay's cousin also named Rob. After we said our goodbye's to Jackie and Diane, we set off to Blackpool.

The journey was a laugh a minute, all of us laughed and joked at each other's expense, and we were like big kids or a school outing, especially when we stopped off at the service station for refreshments. Steve and I were the main protagonist, and nobody in our group was safe from our practical jokes.

While we were being served, I decided to act like a spoiled brat, I was stamping my feet and screaming. My partner in crime, Steve had to follow suit, and both of us were rolling on the floor, acting like two spoilt brats.

Of course, our antics didn't go unnoticed by the other patrons, much to the embarrassment of our fellow travellers. The only way that they could stop us was to buy us both a cream cake. With our antics over, we all sat down and had a great laugh about it.

Back on the road, we continued taking the mickey out of each other, and we were also pretending to be bored teenagers in the back of the car, asking Jay our driver, 'if we were there yet'. We arrived in Blackpool and turned up at the bed and breakfast accommodation. At first glance, it looked okay. However, we could see why it was so cheap, at £25 per person per night.

To say that the rooms were shabby, would be an understatement as if they were intended for animals, then the RSPCA would have them condemned. Mine and Steve's rooms were next to each other, and Steve's bed had three legs, which was a source of amusement later on when he was sleeping.

As we had five hours to kill before making our way to the football ground, we decided to make our presence felt in Blackpool. The weather was atrocious, with a cold, nasty force ten gales blowing from the North Sea, which took the wind chill factor down to -4. As I had arrived from Greece, I felt it the most, and I decided to purchase a hat.

Being the person, I am, I couldn't resist, and I bought a novelty Rastafarian hat, complete with dreadlocks. The others took my lead and decided to follow suit. After donning our new headgear, we headed off to the nearest café for a much-needed coffee. As we entered, sitting with his partner was a real Rastafarian with dreadlocks, complete with Rastafarian hat.

His face was a picture as there was us, six white men, with the same soppy hats, with dreadlocks. His partner thought it was hilarious, all we could do was go up to him, and each gave him a 'high five'. I must say he took it all in good humour and had a great time sharing jokes.

After coffee, we decided to checkout Blackpool Pleasure Beach, to while away a few hours, which was disappointing, as most of the rides were closed, as it was the end of the season. However, this didn't deter us, as we went to ride the Pepsi Max rollercoaster. Just like our antics at the service station, again we all acted like big kids. After we had our fill at the Pleasure Beach, we made our way to the football ground.

From the outside, Blackpool's ground looks rather lovely. I'm sorry to say, it was only for the home fans, as the away fans, have to make do with no more, the few scrappy wooden benches with one pathetic refreshment stand.

The away stand is open to the elements, and the toilets were just a couple of hastily arranged brick walls with no cover. You can now imagine, 3000 'away fans' clambered into what can only be described as a shithole! As the game kicked off, all of us were half-frozen, but that didn't dampen our spirits in cheering on our beloved team.

The first half was rather non-descript, and neither side looked like scoring. All of us were relieved when the half time whistle blew, so we could at least go and buy some much-needed hot refreshments. Due to the number of away fans, and the pathetic refreshment stand, the choices were limited.

As Steve and I patiently waited in a never-ending queue, I decided to poke fun at the two police officers that were standing nearby. Being a somewhat pedantic person, I tried to goad them into saying something, as they were standing there, somewhat bored themselves.

I mustered a laugh and a smile from both of them when I said, 'is it because I am black officer?' Everybody who was in the vicinity thought this was somewhat amusing. Although I'm sure that had I continued being stupid, it would have resulted in being arrested, but fair play to the police, they just laughed it off.

We got to the front of the queue, and I tried to order some hot tea or coffee, because of the lack of facilities, we had to make do with was a cup of Bovril. Somewhat annoyed by the pathetic ground, we returned to our arse splintering benches, to resume watching the second half which had now started. Although, the second half was just as dull as the first. It was now getting dark, and the rain was starting to kick in. We didn't think it could get any worse, until the last minute of normal time when they scored.

That was the final straw, on top of us being frozen solid, we had to endure walking back through the jubilant Blackpool fans soaking wet, on our way back to bed and breakfast. Back inside the warm, we wasted no time in showering and changing, for a night on the tiles. We assembled in the bar for much-needed drinks. While we were enjoying ourselves, the owner decided to tell us a few stories.

One story, in particular, was that the week before we arrived, they had a pigeon fanciers convention. He was deadly serious, when he explained how brilliant it was, and we would have loved every minute of it talking about racing pigeons.

Steve and I took this as an opportunity to ridicule the owner by asking him if the pigeon fanciers were sexually aroused at watching pigeons strutting their stuff on the catwalk! The owner, not realising we were taking the mickey out of him, turned around and told us,

'Nah you daft monkeys, I mean people who like racing pigeons!'

Of course, we knew what he meant, but we couldn't help ourselves, ridiculing the poor man, afterwards, he suggested that we come back the following weekend to be a part of the whippet racing convention! After we had our fill of making jokes at his expense, we hit the town for a night-long alcohol session.

We started at the local pub at the bottom of the street, where the bed and breakfast hotel was and continued on our pub crawl which culminated in the finale at one of Blackpool's renowned night clubs. By the early hours of the morning, we staggered back to bed and breakfast and could sleep off our drunken stupors.

As I said earlier, Steve had three legs on his bed, and had a somewhat disturbed night sleep, as every time he turned over, it would tip to one side, and he would be thrown out of it. On each occasion it occurred, I heard him swearing and cursing, which caused me to laugh out loud every time.

The next morning, we staggered down to breakfast. All of us were still feeling the effects of our monstrous drinking session the night before. We thought that a good hearty breakfast would make us feel more human. However, the breakfast was somewhat lacking, as all they had on offer was a breakfast cereal, tea and toast. We could now see the reason the rooms and accommodation had been so cheap, as if we wanted a full English breakfast, it would have cost a further £20 each.

After our meagre offerings, we decided to pay up and leave to find a more suitable café, and have something more substantial. We found a nice and cheap greasy spoon, a short distance from the hotel. Ordering the biggest and best-cooked breakfast on offer, we ate like we hadn't eaten in a month. With our bellies now full, it was time to hit the road again and head off home.

As Jay was the designated driver, he wouldn't allow any of us to take the controls of the car, not even to help him out so that he could rest. The journey back home was tranquil as the rest of us fell into a deep sleep.

Back at Steve and Diane's, we talked about our weekend. Jackie had visited her brother Alan with Diane and was pampered at a spa day. All too soon the week ended, and we returned home, we had the holiday blues, but after a short time, we got back into the Cretan way of life, and it soon passed.

The year flew by, and the holiday season was coming to an end, the tourists were few and far between, which meant that the island was somewhat quieter without them. I still hadn't any work, and both of us found it challenging to adapt to a more peaceful way of life.

As the Greek football season was about to start, I was invited by Manolis from Friends bar to join his local football team, which were about to be involved in a beach football competition. I had never played beach football before, which was six a side team, and I thought that it would be easy, which was anything but that.

As although I was a goalkeeper, I was exhausted, as we played at a frantic pace on heavy damp sand.

Our team got through to the final, and although we played well, we lost 2-1 with the final goal scored in the last second. I enjoyed the competition, and they asked me to join the local team, as their full-time goalkeeper, for the upcoming season.

Back at home, I noticed a change in Jackie's persona. She started to become very down and depressed, which was very unlike her, and I put it down to our recent trip home.

No matter how many times I asked her, and looked for tell-tale signs, she just kept repeating, 'I'm okay, or I'm just having a bad day'. I thought long and hard as to her situation but couldn't see why she was in a dark place. Worried as to her health and wellbeing, she admitted that she hadn't been feeling well for some time.

We managed to find an English-speaking doctor, with knowledge of multiple sclerosis symptoms. The doctor was a world authority on the illness. His diagnosis was that Jackie required a stint in the hospital for steroid treatment. He also explained that although the sun and vitamin C helped MS sufferers, the heat and humidity had the opposite effect, and we should have never come to live In Crete.

When I heard these words, my mind went into overload as this was one of the worrying factors I had objected to moving to Crete in the first place. However, for now, I had to bite my lip and keep my thoughts inside my head and concentrate on helping Jackie recover.

After Jackie had her treatment, like always, she would bounce back, and be the same cheerful person, that she had ever been. It was a week after she left the hospital that mum and Robin asked if they could come and meet with us, for a drink at friend's bar. Both of us thinking that this was a nice gesture, agreed to meet them. Jackie and I got to the bar and ordered some drinks for ourselves while waiting for mum and Robin to arrive.

When they did so, we ordered their drinks but could see they appeared somewhat nervous. It was as if neither of them wanted to talk, after much persuasion, I managed to drag it out of them, bearing in mind that I had already gone through enough stress with Jackie while she had been in hospital.

What they told us next, was a complete shock, as mum nervously asked if they could borrow six thousand E12ouros. Although stunned a hearing this, I needed to know and understand, how they had got themselves in the situation, where they needed to borrow money as they had made a good profit when they had sold their bungalow back in the UK.

Coupled with the fact that mum had a good pension and drawing dad's pension, including his army widows' pension.

Also, both her and Robin were working, albeit mum only a few hours in the mornings, but Robin was full time. It transpired that when they had returned to the UK the previous Christmas, mum had drawn out from her UK bank account £25,000 in cash.

They stopped in Italy and stayed at a hotel for the night. On their way back to Crete, they forgot mum's handbag, which contained her jewellery in the car parked in a secure car park. A thief broke into the vehicle and stole her bag.

Suspicions of this, I decided to make further enquiries. It was only after that they admitted that no damage had occurred to the car, although it was being ransacked.

I thought that this was somewhat odd, as no locks or windows had been broken, nor were there any signs of any forced entry. Bearing this in mind, I asked them outright the reason they never mentioned it before, and we had even thought about moving over to be near them. All they could suggest was that they were too embarrassed and ashamed and therefore found it difficult to confide in us.

After much deliberation, we agreed to help them out, as we couldn't bear to think that they were going to struggle. After lending mum and Robin the money, I spoke to Jackie about my suspicions. I couldn't get the thought out of my head, that the car was not damaged in any way. I felt that there was more to it than what they were telling us.

I was pissed off at this time and wanted to dig deeper, but Jackie persuaded me not to, as she didn't want any bad feelings towards either of them. I agreed, but I made it known in no uncertain terms that I was far from happy with the situation, and woe betides anyone or anything, that would upset me, as I was like a powder keg, ready to go off!

It was only two weeks after I had made my promise to Jackie when mum tearfully told us that her landlord Yiannis had wanted her and Robin to move out of their apartment, which they had paid thousands of pounds for, as he tried to let it out to new rent-paying tenants! I hit the roof with this news, and had a go at both mum and Robin, for allowing this 'shit' as I saw it to happen.

I told them that I'd be going with them to see Yiannis and his thieving family. Mum, Robin and Jackie were concerned, as they knew I would hold nothing back, and could easily injure anybody who got in my way.

However, nothing was going to stop me, not even the entire Greek armed forces, police or Greek population. It took a while, for them to calm me down sufficiently so that I could act responsibly and rationally.

After calming down, I researched on the internet the legal aspects to help them in their case.

I found that European legislation, was on their side, as regards their rights as tenants, and printed off this information, not only in English but in Greek. At first, Robin and mum wanted to go by themselves for fear of what I would do if I accompanied them. I pointed out that there was no way, they or anyone, was going to stop me from coming along. Plus, the fact that myself and Jackie had given them 6000 euro to help them out. Eventually, we compromised, with Jackie also agreeing to come along to ensure that I remained calm.

We arrived at the Taverna at 8 pm, although it was coming to the end of the season, there were still a few patrons there. As usual, Yiannis and his family greeted us warmly, but I was in no mood for pleasantries, I refused to shake hands with any of them

We sat around the table, with me, Jackie, mum and Robin on one side, on the other, was Yannis and his entire family. Mum tried in vain to explain hers and Robin's situation, as she was getting somewhat teary and upset. Robin being the wimp that he was, just sat there like some sort of dickhead.

Yiannis and his family were unmoved, and we're trying to justify what they were about to do, to mum and Robin. As they were disrespectful, I let nothing hold me back, and gave it to them with both barrels, explaining they were disgusting, thieving, little Greek bastards. Mum tried to defuse the situation, and so did Jackie, but by now, I wasn't letting them get to me, or listen to what they had to say.

I made it clear in front of the holidaymakers that Yiannis and his family were thieves. Also, to make sure that they were getting the message, I told the people eating, that the health inspector had warned them, as they had poor hygiene in their Taverna. This comment made Yiannis and his family sit up and listen, as they could not afford, to lose any customers!

Handing them all a copy of the European directive, I could see them squirming at the possible legal implications that they could face, which would include a hefty fine and a term of imprisonment!

After they had read the documents, they started to discuss the options in Greek. However, I was very adept at learning languages, and knew what they were discussing amongst themselves, and wouldn't allow them any breathing space should they try to wriggle out, of their responsibilities.

I made sure that in me, they had met their nemesis. Several moments elapsed, and they agreed to my terms. They would reimburse mum and Robin a sum of 15,000 euros, and also agreed to pay any other expenses involved in moving to a new apartment, just as soon as one became available, which mum and Robin would love.

I made it clear that the money would be paid in cash the following day, or I would be back again, to ensure that their business would suffer.

With limited options open to them, they agreed to the terms and signed the contract, which I had written up by one of my Greek friends, who happened to be a lawyer and who specialised in Greek, and European directive law.

The next day, I went back with mum and Robin, although I was prepared for a fight, Yiannis handed over 15,000 euro's in cash, and assured us they would be true to their word, and pay the removal costs which they had agreed to. With the money in their hands, mum and Robin could breathe easier. All they needed to do now was to find an alternative apartment.

They didn't have long to wait, as another local bar owner Kristos, had an apartment complex, in the final throes of construction, and would be ready after Christmas, which was only two months away. Both of them viewed the unfinished apartment, and Jackie and I went with them, as they wished to have our moral support.

The new apartment was behind Friend's bar and was also a closer walk for Robin, who was working for George, and his car rental business, which was right next door to Friends. Even though the apartment was still unfinished, it was beautiful, and had a covered balcony, with amazing views of the ocean, and the mountains. It had a separate living room, dining room, fitted modern kitchen, three large size bedrooms, and two bathrooms, with a walk around balcony to the side and rear, which included separate covered storage.

Kristos had spared no expense on the construction materials, and we all thought that it was a better apartment from their former home. It also boasted central heating, rarely heard of in Crete.

Below this apartment was another one, which was also in the final construction phase. Being a builder myself, I had to go and take a look, out of sheer curiosity and found that it was equally as lovely, if not better than mums. This apartment also, had three large size bedrooms, two bathrooms, a large through lounge dining room, and fitted kitchen.

To the rear, was a fair size patio with two giant planters, it also boasted central heating. At the front was the drive, which could, when finished, would be used to park at least five cars comfortably. With the viewing over, mum and Robin, loved the first apartment so much, that they agreed on terms with Kristos, and would be moving into it, in the new year.

Now at home, Jackie wanted to discuss mum's and Robin's new apartment. She wanted to go back to take another look and speak to Kristos regarding the condo below theirs. I was somewhat confused about why she wanted to move below mum and Robin, as our apartment that we had was adequate for our needs. Also, mum could be somewhat pedantic at times.

Even Jackie would admit, that occasionally, she had a love-hate relationship with her. After a short discussion, I'd looked at both sides of the argument, and agreed, that there would be no harm in taking a second look, as deep down, I had fallen in love with the new apartment myself.

The next day, we took a leisure stroll through the village, and onto Kristos' bar. We ordered some coffee and sat down with Kristos to discuss the possibility of renting the downstairs apartment. He inquired as to why we wanted to leave our present apartment. We gave him a straight answer, the new apartment was more modern and would be more suitable for our needs.

Kristos informed us that the rent would be 20 euro more than what we were paying now, and would have to pay electric separately and share the cost of heating oil required for the central heating system with mum and Robin. He also explained that he was planning to put in a roadway for us to gain access with our cars.

After we had spoken with him, we agreed with terms and would be moving at the same time as mum and Robin. When we had finished, we went around to see mum, to tell her the good news. Upon hearing this, mum was ecstatic, and couldn't wait to move in. The only thing that we had to do was to speak to Maria and her husband and give them notice that we intended to move out.

Maria was most understanding and accepted our notice of termination, which was a relief, to both of us. Now we had the unenviable task of packing and preparing for Christmas. Over the next few weeks, we continued with our lives, and we're looking forward to moving in the new year.

It was now two weeks before Christmas, everything was in place, for the move.

One early morning, we were awoken by some hysterical screaming, emanating from Maria's parent's house next door. I threw on some clothes, and rushed out of the back door, to see what was going on. Maria's mother ran up to me and was crying her eyes out, asking me to help.

She almost dragged me off my feet and into her home. I could now see what she was so upset about, as her husband, was lying on the bed, not breathing. I quickly rushed to the side of the bed and administered CPR. The neighbours from downstairs alerted by the screams and tears had also come in to assist.

I tried in vain, but it was too late, as Maria's dad had already passed away. The downstairs neighbours called the paramedics, who attended the scene and praised me in my CPR techniques. The house was now filled with people while Maria's family thanked me for my efforts.

I was numb and shocked at what had happened and returned home, where Jackie comforted me. Throughout the day, well-wishers from the Greek community, turned up to pay their final respects, which is a tradition in Greece. One older woman also smashed a plate, which we later found out, signified that it would scare away any evil spirits.

The funeral director turned up to remove the body which had now been prepared for burial, which included two coins, placed over the eyes, to pay the ferryman. As Maria's father had died in the early hours of the morning, as is the Greek Orthodox religion, he was buried later in the afternoon, as is the custom. Maria's family invited Jackie and me to the wake held at the local Taverna, where we were the honoured guests, which we found most humbling.

The next few days after the funeral was somewhat sad as neither me nor Jackie, could forget the last few days. However, we still tried to remain focused on finishing the packing and preparing for the upcoming Christmas. Manolis, from friend's bar, rang me up to inform me that the football team were having a game, against the second-placed team, and asked if I wanted to play as their first-choice goalkeeper had sustained an injury, and they needed a replacement.

Speaking with Jackie, we both agreed that due to recent events, maybe I should go, and she would come along for support, which would take our minds of it. Although I had played for them in the beach football, I hadn't been part of the regular team, but I relished the challenge. I was a little nervous, as wasn't fluent in the Greek language. However, the team told me a few words, that would be in support of the group whilst I was playing.

The day of the match arrived, and I was very nervous, but I was made most welcome, by the rest of my teammates, and looked forward to playing, my first full-time football match for the team. At the start of the game, I started to shout out the words of encouragement that the team had told me, which were, 'Ella malaka, scarcie mama'! As I was shouting out, the ref blew the whistle and came to talk to me. At first, he spoke to me in Greek but soon realised that I was English.

He asked, if I understood, what I was shouting to my teammates. I explained that I was calling words of encouragement, however, to my shock and horror, what I had been yelling, were the words, 'hello wanker, go fuck your mother'! Upon hearing this, I humbly apologised and could now see my teammates, laughing and joking at my expense.

I continued with the game without any further outbursts, and we all had a good laugh after we had finished. We celebrated with a barbecue and beer after we had won 2-0.

The game was just what I needed to take my mind off the previous day's sad events even Jackie, who had come to watch, thoroughly enjoyed herself, and we were both welcomed into the Greek community.

Christmas Day arrived, as it was our first Christmas away from the UK, and mum's last Christmas at her old apartment, it was decided that we would have a joint effort, and share the costs of the food, where I agreed to do the cooking at mum's house.

It felt strange celebrating Christmas in Crete, as although the various bars and restaurants all have Christmas trees, the Greek religion being Orthodox, they don't celebrate Christmas like the British as their official Christmas is in January.

Also coming from the UK, we are used to the cold and damp weather conditions, compared to our first Christmas in Crete. The daytime temperature was eighteen plus degrees and full sunshine, although due to the snow on the mountain tops, there was a slight cooling breeze.

Mum had invited several of her ex-pat friends along for Christmas dinner, and we had a marvellous time meeting them. Although hard work, it was well worth the effort, as we made some new friends, amongst the ex-pat community, as by large, Jackie and I had kept ourselves to ourselves.

Christmas came and went, as quickly is it arrived, it was soon approaching the new year, and we were looking forward, to starting afresh in our new apartment. We'd arranged for our furniture to be delivered by one of the locals recommended to us by our new landlord Kristos. The total cost for him, to move both mum and ours was 500 euro. True to his word, mum's old landlord Yiannis footed the bill, and the move into both apartments went without incident.

Our new apartment was a dream, and we both had a good feeling about being there. We spent our time in arranging our furniture, adding a few new items we had purchased; a surround sound system, and Nintendo Wi gaming consul. Along with some new beautiful artwork, and pride of place was our tropical fish aquarium!

It took us several days to unpack, but it was well worth the effort of moving, into such a well-constructed and clean apartment. It was only mid-January, the weather was gorgeous, and the temperature was starting to climb. As we were admiring our new surroundings by having breakfast outside in the patio area, the weather changed from bright sunshine and started to snow which was unheard of in the village.

We assumed that it wouldn't settle, or last very long. However, to our surprise, the snowstorm lasted for a good half hour, which made the whole area, very picturesque. We went to the village and were surprised that the Greeks, were out playing like children in the snow, as it was such a rare occurrence. To see them enjoying themselves, made us feel happy and contented before we joined them in a snowball fight.

As we were frolicking the sun reappeared, which melted the snow as quickly as it had settled. Although it had been short-lived, it was a marvellous morning for all concerned, which was a great discussion topic amongst the Greeks for a few days.

Now settled in our new apartment, my focus was to now find work. I had paid to become a scuba diving instructor but hadn't been successful in finding any job, not even with the diving school where I trained. I started to frequent with some of the ex-pat builders, after meeting with them, I found that they were somewhat reluctant to offer any kind of work.

In my opinion, this was due to them not being qualified builders but had made money doing so by bull shitting about their abilities to unsuspecting clients. Desperate for a start, I went and asked one of the Greek business owners named Lefteris, who owned a hardware store. I found Lefteris to be a genuine person and very helpful. He put me in contact with some German clients who required some building work at their home.

The name of these clients was Manfred, and his wife, Mariella. I went around to meet them, and we hit it off immediately. I was somewhat fortunate that both of them could speak perfect

English. As I could speak German, we had a lot more in common than others around the area, who were not bilingual. The job entailed repairing the roof of the gazebo. After fixing a price, we set a date, and I was now on the road to obtaining my first job in the building trade.

The day arrived for the start of the work. Manfred and Mariela met me in their front garden. Before setting to work, they offered me to have breakfast with them, and we had a great conversation before we start working together on the roof. As the pavilion over hanged the building, Manfred had devised an ingenious safety harness system.

Like all Germans, he was very particular and precise. It was a bright sunny day, as it was early morning the temperature was nice and cool. However, it wouldn't take long for the weather to rise. After removing the old tiles, it was deemed too hot to continue. Both of us went downstairs, where Mariella have made some delicious food, and we spent a few hours talking. Their Dutch friend named Frits soon joined us. I had several hours with them all before returning home and sleeping off their generous hospitality.

When I woke up, After I had awoken, Jackie and I spent the afternoon relaxing in our garden, where we discussed the morning that I had spent with Manfred, Mariella and Frits. I suggested that she came with me the next day to get her out of the house and meet some new friends, rather than her just socialising with mum, and she agreed.

The next morning, we woke up early and went around to meet Manfred and Mariela. As usual, they were sitting in the garden, enjoying the early morning sunshine eating their breakfast. As before, they offered the same hospitality, as I had received the previous day.

While Manfred and I went to continue with the work on the roof, Jackie stayed with Mariella, and she had a marvellous time making new friends. She helped Mariella in preparing lunch for all of us, while Manfred and I continued with the repairs. After a few hours, we completed the job. We cleaned up the tools before going back downstairs, where our lunch was waiting for us. Before we sat down to eat, they paid me for the work, and they would recommend my services to other friends of theirs.

Jackie and I had made two new friends and would go on to make more from our encounters with Manfred and Mariella who were some of the nicest people one could ever meet. As our apartment was in the middle of the village, we frequented and socialised a lot more, made a lot of new friends from the ex-pat community.

The prominent meeting place where we socialised was Commotions bar, a short distance from where we were staying. It was here I met with Brian, we had a brief encounter several months earlier at Pinocchio's bar. Brian was larger than life character with a shaved head and a goatee beard. I instantly liked him, as he was somewhat down to earth, as was his wife Bernie, and her mum and dad Jim and Irene.

Brian was a talented musician and was also involved in the building trade, where he was working for another ex-pat named Mike Kilner. Brian offered to put me in contact with Mike, as he had a lot of work, and was always on the lookout for new people to join the team. I gave him my mobile number, to await the call from Mike, in the hope that I would get more work, and build up my reputation.

A few days later Mike called me, he was interested at that time but didn't have enough work. He promised that as soon as work improved, he would contact me again. Although I was a little disappointed, I needn't had worried, as Lefteris had recommended me to the new owners of the Elpida hotel we had all stayed at on our first holiday to Crete previous the year.

I met with the owners who were Greek Cypriot, and very different from the local Greeks, as they had a more modern way of thinking. I later became their main repairman. The job would involve various building repairs to the hotel complex, which the previous owners had let its fall into disrepair by not spending any money on maintaining the building itself, which is the trait of most Greeks.

We agreed on terms and hours of work. I would be paid1800 euro's a month directly into my bank account, which also meant, that I would be subject to the Greek income for tax, and social security payments. I asked the owners if I could pay dual tax, to both the Greek and British governments, just in case, I ever had to return to the UK again. They agreed and gave me a start date.

The first day in my new role, I met up with the senior repairman whose name was George. He was also Greek Cypriot, and the owners brought him in, he showed me what was required, and he would help out for a few months to get the hotel up and running before the holiday season, which was three weeks away.

George and I worked well together. I had a wealth of experience in the building trade. I'd never been involved in the hotel trade and learned a lot from him. Being Greek Cypriot, he explained that the local Greeks were at least 30 years behind the rest of the world. He also told me that when the owners purchased the hotel, the previous owner hadn't only let the hotel go to rack and ruin, he'd also failed to pay any tax to the Greek government, for the last ten years!

I wasn't surprised about this, as a lot of the older generation Greeks had the attitude of not paying any tax as they felt that it was unnecessary to do so, which was one of the direct results Greece was in financial difficulty. The government paid people for unnecessary jobs. The retirement age was fifty for women, and fifty-five for men and they would be drawing state pension for the rest of their lives, and the average life expectancy was eighty-five.

Over the next few weeks, George and I worked our socks off. We had replaced new light fittings, new air conditioning unit with remote access, which would go off as soon as the occupants had left the room. We installed new kitchen appliances, storage cupboards, refrigeration units, food preparation areas, ovens, main fuse box, new doors, locks, updated plumbing in most of the antiquated rooms.

After that, a team of decorators painted every room and communal areas to freshen up the hotel before accepting guests. We also fitted a new reception desk, new bar area, and rectified every antiquated and unrepaired location of the hotel. Although it was a mammoth task, we both came through, as we had worked like a well-oiled machine.

The only drawback was the hotel manager, who was the nephew of the previous owner and had been allowed to keep his job by the new owners. He thought that he was in a position to treat me disrespectfully, expecting me to replace any broken TVs in the guests' rooms, which was a big mistake.

It wasn't part of my duties, and he didn't like that and tried to stamp his authority when George and the new owners returned to Cyprus.

However, I pointed out to him that I wasn't a skivvy, or a regular Greek that he could push around, which he didn't like, and he tried to continue to order me around. I ignored him and told him to 'fuck off and stay out of my way.'

I continued to work ignoring his advice, which only aggravated the situation, between him and myself, until one day, the owners returned from Cyprus to try and diffuse the situation.

I reminded them that we'd a signed legally binding contract regarding my duties, and they agreed, but asked if I could help out by doing the tasks the manager wanted me to do.

As the season had well and truly started, I declined and stood my ground, as regards of the contract, where I put them in a position, that I would leave, unless they honour the contract. After a short discussion, the owners decided to agree, as they had no other choice, but to do so or they wouldn't have anyone to carry out the hotel repairs.

The owners told the manager that if any guests required a TV, then it would be up to him, or another member of staff to put one in the room. The decision didn't go down too well with the manager, but he agreed with them, and we left it at that.

After our meeting, the owners returned to Cyprus. However, a short while later, the manager started again, insisting that I would do what he would tell me to do. I ignored him, as I wasn't going to be pushed around by anybody. With him trying to be disrespectful, it left me no choice but to contact the owners myself and resigned my position.

The next day after hearing from me, they flew back to Crete, to try and persuade me to remain. It was too late, as I had already made up my mind. They paid my last wage, and we parted company. I heard later on that they dismissed the manager due to his attitude of dealing with staff.

Now out of work, I concentrated my efforts by spending more time with Jackie because when I was at the hotel, I had been working long hours, and spent very little time with her. I hadn't noticed the change in her, due working such long hours, and felt that I'd to make amends by taking her around the island, getting to know more of the ex-pats in the area, especially Brian, whom I had become good friends.

Jackie and I met up with Brian and his wife, Bernie, for a coffee at Friend's bar. Seizing the moment, he asked if we wanted a puppy, which had been found abandoned near where he had been working. At first, I wasn't keen on the idea, and neither was Jackie, as we weren't sure if our landlord would allow pets.

It was when I was in the centre of town where I received a phone call from Jackie, to ask if I could buy a dog collar and a sleeping basket. Also, could I contact Brian, as she had spoken to the landlord, who agreed to allow us to keep pets.

I was first of all shocked at Jackie's turn around, but deep down, I was pleased, as we had both seen the photograph of the puppy and had fallen in love with it. Without hesitation, I contacted Brian and told him I would meet up at Friend's bar when I returned from town.

Furthermore, I went to the local pet store, to purchase a dog harness complete with lead, a comfortable dog bed, food bowls, toys, and also pet food. I returned to Istron, where I met Brian and the beautiful puppy. I couldn't wait to get her home, and was like a proud father with a new-born baby, cradling her in one arm, whilst carrying everything that I'd purchased from the pet shop. As I walked through the front door, Jackie rushed up and took her from my arms. I could see the undying love that she had for what would become our baby.

We were going to name her Meli, which is the Greek word for honey, as her fur resembled the colour of honey. However, we noticed that she had white paws, so we decided to call her Socks.

We were falling in love with Socks, as she was the closest thing to us, in having our own child, which we had never had. Of course, like all puppies, she was a handful, having said that, she was a bundle of joy, and we were like two proud parents, and she made our family complete. After a few days, we had her checked out by a local vet, who microchipped her and gave her deworming medication.

We have also been given a pet passport and a clean bill of health. He also explained that she was no more than around six months old. Jackie had a keen interest in a television pro-gramme, called the dog whisperer, she also bought for one of his books so that we could train her properly.

Being young, Socks was into everything, and had to explore every centimetre of the apartment, and also enjoyed chewing on the wooden furniture. We used various techniques we had picked up from the dog whisperer and implemented them daily. Although not all of them were successful, so we had to improvise and obtain help from one of mum's friends, who had been a dog trainer, back in the UK. With her guidance, Socks settled down and was now part of the family, and wild horses wouldn't tear her away from us.

One morning, I was walking socks around the village, and down the beach road, when two German tourists asked for my help. I could see the female tourist, holding a towel close to her body, they unwrapped the towel, and inside was a tiny puppy, of around four months old. They found it discarded in the bin.

I would like to point out that this is a daily occurrence in Greece, as the Greek people are not as pet or animal orientated like the rest of civilised societies around the world. I told them, I'd take care of him, and they handed him over, where I put him under my tee-shirt to keep him warm so that I could take him home.

As I walked through the door, I told Jackie that I had an-other surprise for her. I asked her to close her eyes and hold out her hands. I gently placed the new puppy in her hands, and she adored him. I prepared some breakfast for Socks, as she was eat-ing, the new puppy barged her out of the way and started to eat.

It was quite cute, watching Socks looking perturbed at him cheekily eating her breakfast, there was only one name we could call him, which was Rascal. With our ready-made family, we were ecstatic.

The dogs were like the children we were never blessed with and spent most of our waking hours with them.

I would go on long walks with them both, but for Jackie, due to her MS, was limited to only short walks. As the tourist season has not yet really started, I would take Socks and Rascal along the deserted beaches, where we would play games.

Socks loved to play with stones, and I would throw one into the sea, where she would dive in, and fish it out. I also threw them as high as I could, onto the surrounding mountainside, where she would scamper up, a high speed, and try and retrieve it before it rolled down the ground level.

Rascal, on the other hand, preferred just to run up and down, exploring the surrounding areas, but would always come back when I whistled for him. It was a joy to behold, to see him running towards me, and giving me a lot of affection.

On these walks, I'd talk to them, as if they were human. Often, we would sit on one of the many benches, at the top of the mountain pass and overlook the ocean. By the time we arrived home, we were all exhausted, but I can say that it was all worthwhile.

After watching them playing together, and observing their movements, I decided to write a children's book, about the adventures together, aptly named, 'Puppy dog tails, the adventures of Socks and Rascal'. Although I had a friend to illustrate and edit them, no publishers would take it serious enough to have it published.

With the amount of time that I was spending with the dogs, I hadn't noticed that Jackie wasn't her usual self. I inquired as to her wellbeing, to which her answer was, that she wasn't feeling 100%, and was feeling very tired. Concerned about her health, I suggested that we go back to the specialist, to see if it was her condition acting up. We arranged a consultation, where he confirmed that her MS had gone into the next phase. I felt somewhat guilty, that I hadn't noticed, and kept apologising, but Jackie being the fantastic person that she is, refused to allow me to take the blame.

The only course of treatment that was available was for steroids to be administered, and she would remain in the hospital for one week. I would visit her every day and ensured that she was well looked after and spent the entire day with her while she was recovering.

In the meantime, our landlord had failed to secure the plot of land next to our apartment from the landowner, which meant that the only access would be through Robin's boss George's car rental property. In itself, this would cause problems, as there would be no access with a car to the apartments. I tried in vain to speak to the landowner to allow us to use the land, as Jackie would be unable to walk the steep road up to the apartment.

He was the most arrogant and unsympathetic person I've ever met. And to add insult to injury, a fence was put up, he stopped any access from the road across the short piece of land he owned made it easier for Jackie when she returned from the hospital. I was livid at this, and we had an argument, where he told me that the English have no rights in Greece.

I pointed out that as European citizens, we were subject to all rights under European law, to live and work in any country in Europe. Unperturbed by this news, he stood his ground and ignored anything that I said, which would, later on, come back and haunt him, as the Greeks in effect, disowned him and his wife, of whom was a lovely woman but had to suffer, due to his indignant attitude.

With Jackie still in the hospital, and the idiot next door putting up the fence boundary, myself, mum and Robin were effectively cut off.

The only way we could get out of our homes was to climb over an adjacent wall down a ladder. Due to the inconvenience, our landlord Kristos had to act fast, and build the roadway between George's car rental place and the apartments.

He hired a team of builders, who had to hand dig the slope going down to what would be the exit. Next, they laid reinforced mesh and hired a concrete mixer, and elephant pump to lay the concrete which took one day to complete. However, it was somewhat inconvenient for mum who was struggling to climb over the ladder.

It was also a problem for myself, as I was unable to walk the dogs, and they had to exercise in the back garden. Due to the heat, the concrete soon dried, and we were able to at least walk down the slope. It was going to be somewhat tricky for Jackie when they discharged her from the hospital, only two days after the slope had been finished.

The only solution to my problem was to get Jackie an electric disability scooter. One of our Greek neighbours told me there was a disabled shop in the town named Euromed. Without hesitation, I went down to speak to the owners and explain the situation that had occurred. They were very helpful, and Jackie was entitled under Greek and European law, for a part-funded mobility scooter. I had taken mum along, as although she was non-disabled, I needed someone who could test out the machine.

As mum had a bad hip, she was the only alternative. I settled on a four-wheel scooter, which had easy controls for someone who had MS. It also had lights, which would come in handy, as the new slope, at that time was unlit. The average cost would have been 6500 euro, but due to the part funding, I only had to pay 1500 euro. The company also delivered the scooter the day before Jackie was discharged from the hospital. I have to admit, the company and the people who worked for them were terrific, and I couldn't thank them enough.

It was the day that Jackie was coming home, I'd explained what had gone on, but that she had a mobility scooter, so, she shouldn't have any problems with getting to and from street level to our apartment. It was great to have her back again, as I had missed her, and so had the dogs who made a fuss over her, and wouldn't leave her side. I believe that animals have a sixth sense, and tend to know when their human owners are not feeling well.

As she settled in, I took the dogs out for a walk to allow her some quiet time so that she could rest. At the same time, mum had picked up Kristos daughter Mariella, whom she looked after three days a week, and took her to see Jackie.

I was coming back, and I heard shouting from the bottom of the slope. Concerned as to what was going on, I sprinted up the hill with the dogs, where I could now see Jackie giving mum a whole load of abuse. Jackie had knocked over one of the potted plants and was trying to clear it up, which mum thought was a stupid idea as Jackie had just come home from the hospital.

Jackie was in a terrible state, now with my breath back, I intervened to find out what had happened when they explained, I took Jackie's side, and told mum not to interfere, as Jackie was quite capable of sweeping up a small potted plant. Mum tried to explain that she was only concerned for Jackie's wellbeing, which I understood. But I told her, steroid treatment was such, that MS sufferers felt invigorated after treatment, and need to carry on as normal. With the argument now diffused, mum took Mariella upstairs, while Jackie and I went indoors. Back inside, we discussed what had happened. I was in support of Jackie, and I would back her up in everything that she decided to do.

Over the next few days, the argument was well and truly forgotten. With Jackie's new scooter, she was able to have a lot more freedom and was able to come on walks with the dogs and me. Our lifestyle was perfect, although due to Jackie's condition, it was about to change. Our friends, Steve and Diane, wanted to come over for a two-week stay, along with another friend of theirs named Rob. We had no hesitation in allowing them to come over and couldn't wait to see them again.

We'd briefly met Rob when we were over their house, we didn't know all of his traits, even though Steve and Diane, had tried to explain them to us. We were meeting them at Friend's bar, as they had decided to take a taxi from the airport instead of allowing me to pick them up as they pulled up outside the bar, we went to greet them.

Steve told us while Rob went to the toilet that they felt they had made a mistake inviting him, as, during the flight, he had eaten some cheesy snacks, which covered his fingers with residue. Still, instead of going to the bathroom, he sat there, with his fingers in the air not moving, which infuriated them both. I took this is an opportunity to turn it into a fun holiday for them, by highlighting, and taking the piss, at Rob's expense.

As soon as Rob returned from the toilet, I saw how easy it would be to wind him up, especially when he told us about his choice of clothes. We couldn't believe our ears when all he had brought with him apart from the clothes on him were one pair of shorts and four T-shirts for the entire two weeks. It was an opportunity to tease him. I knew that Steve would be a willing participant, and my partner in crime, as we would become the deadly duo and tag team in making fun at Rob's expense.

Back inside the apartment, we showed them their rooms. Steve and Diane had a spare room with a second double bed, while Rob had to sleep on an inflatable mattress in the next room. That evening, I had decided to cook a curry for all of us, as I was doing so, I realised I needed some tinned tomatoes, and asked if one of them could go down to the shop to pick up a can. Rob volunteered, and without further ado, he went down the slope to pick up the tomatoes.

As I was cooking, he stood in the kitchen with the can and asked where I'd like him to put it. It was my first opportunity to wind him up. I told him to stand in the middle of the dining area and hold it until I was ready. To my surprise, even though I had gone to sit down and talk, he stood there for at least ten minutes without saying a word! The rest of us just ignored him and continued with our conversation.

After he'd been standing for some time, I told him to put the can on the work surface and join in our conversation. I couldn't believe my ears when he turned around and asked,

'What part of the worktop shall I put it on'. That was another opportunity to rile him, and my partner in crime, Steve suggested that he put it on top of the wall units.

Again, we were gobsmacked when he asked if we possessed a step ladder so he could do it. And that was our cue to start laughing at his expense. After a while, we composed ourselves, and with tears in my eyes, I got up and took the can from him to stop any further embarrassment. The first night was a booze-filled laugh from start to finish, even being the butt of our jokes, Rob even managed to see the funny side of his actions.

The next morning, I went to walk the dogs as usual, with Steve tagging along. Rob stayed back with the girls, which was a relief for us, as we didn't have to listen to them blithering about what the state of play was, and how they were going to be entertained for the day. As we walked back home, I badly twisted my ankle, and although I managed to limp back home, I was in agony.

As I struggled to the top of the driveway, mum was outside talking to the girls and Rob. They must have realised that I was in pain, so they filled a bucket of water with ice to reduce the swelling. After a considerable amount of time, my foot was frozen, and I couldn't stand to keep it in the bucket any longer. Mum applied a bandage, and I took some anti-inflammatory painkillers. I suggested that we spend a day at the golden beach, a short distance from where we were living.

For me to get around, I had to use one of Jackie's walking sticks. As I was unable to apply much pressure on the foot, I allowed Steve to drive to the beach. However, I had forgotten that the golden beach had a long steep stepped footpath to the beach area itself. I allowed the others to go before me and hobbled my way down slowly, which took at least ten minutes.

I finally reached the sand and struggled to where the wooden walkway was, and I joined them.

After what seemed an eternity, I made it to where everyone had settled. I eased myself on the sun lounger, and I let out a deep sigh of relief.

I laid back and watched the world go, and as the temperatures soared, I decided to go for a swim in the cooling water. Fortunately, our sunbeds were quite close to the water, so I didn't have to go far.

Now immersed, I went for a long swim, and my foot felt much better. After a while, I returned to the sun lounger to dry off and reapply the sun cream. Jackie and Diane had gone for a long walk along the beach edge towards the cliffs. I was now left alone with Steve and Rob, and we got into a discussion about football. It was now fast approaching lunchtime, and when the girls returned and suggested that we go upstairs to the beach cantina for lunch, I was hesitant.

Although my foot was feeling better, the mere thought of climbing the steep steps was a daunting prospect, so I decided to stay with the sun loungers, and Jackie and the rest could bring some food for me after their lunch. When they returned, they'd got a gyro, which is a Greek kebab, and it included chips, salad, and slow-cooked pork. After eating, I spoke to Rob and asked him how he was enjoying his first holiday abroad. Instead of giving a short answer, he seemed to go on for ages, much to Steve's annoyance, who got up and went for a swim with the girls.

I noticed that Rob was going very red and I suggested that he apply more sun cream. I couldn't believe it when he explained that he had bought a sun factor 40 cream, and he added that he could stay in the sun for a more extended period, with only one application. I told him although it was a high sun protection factor, applying it once would not protect him from sunburn because Rob had such fair skin. I recommended that he reapplied it again, and stay entirely in the shade as he wasn't used to the sun.

When Steve and the girls returned, I suggested we should head back as it was late afternoon, and the dogs needed walking and feeding. As my foot was starting to ache, Steve volunteered to take Socks and Rascal out for a walk himself. The rest of us stayed behind and enjoyed a quiet afternoon sitting around the garden bench with the parasol up as the temperature was extreme.

As we did so, mum came out onto her balcony and saw us enjoying ourselves, and came downstairs to join us. She noticed Rob's sunburnt skin, so she went back home and returned a short while later with a pot of natural Greek yoghurt. She asked Rob to remove his shirt. Reluctant at first, Rob did what mum asked, and she liberally slathered over yoghurt onto his skin.

Rob's face was a picture as mum applied the yoghurt, she explained that it would cool down his skin and take away the burning sensation. Now covered in yoghurt, Rob sat there all confused much to our amusement. After a short while, Steve returned with the dogs. At the same time, I went to prepare their food, I could hear the explanation, as to why Rob was sitting there, covered in yoghurt, I heard Steve laughing at Rob's misfortune, although Rob didn't see the funny side of it, and went off to take a shower, and change his clothes.

That evening, we decided to take in one of the local tavernas and enjoy a traditional Greek evening. However, as my foot was still swollen and painful, the only way I could get to the taverna was for someone to push me in Jackie's manual wheelchair.

Steve agreed to do it, which meant Rob would to push me back home later in the evening. We decided to venture to the Istron taverna, which had a local Greek band as entertainment. As the others had never really experienced this type of music before, it was a must. As their custom in Greece, everyone was invited to join in the festivities, and of course, the evening wouldn't be complete without the famous Zorba The Greek tune, played on the bouzouki. As the evening drew to a close, we left to go home, and Rob pushed me in the wheelchair.

I'm not sure if it was because he had overeaten, or I gained a colossal amount of weight in the short time we were out, but Rob was struggling. When we got to the top of our driveway, I realised I had forgotten to remove the brake but didn't tell him until we were indoors. Everyone, except Rob, thought it was hilarious.

Over the next week and a half, Rob was the butt of our jokes on many occasions. However, even Rob thought that our practical jokes were a source of amusement and joined in for the most part. It was only the night before they were due to fly back home that we saw a different side of him when he snapped at one of our practical jokes, which backfired on both myself and Steve. I have to say that I did feel guilty, and Steve and I apologised.

The next day we drove them to the airport, and I learned from Steve that Rob suffered from Asperger's syndrome. Had I known this before they arrived, my views would have been different.

Several weeks had passed since Steve, Diane and Rob went home. Jackie seemed to be in a very melancholy mood, and nothing I did change it. Finally, the truth came out that she not only missed our friends, but her brother Alan. I suggested that she book a flight home to the UK to visit them for a week or two.

At first, Jackie was reluctant to do so, as she felt guilty, I was unable to come with her because I had to remain behind to look after the dogs. I told her that her happiness was of paramount importance, and although I would miss her, I was thinking of her needs above mine. Upon hearing this, we booked a flight, and she left and would be back within ten days.

With Jackie now in the UK, and missing her, I concentrated my efforts with our dogs, Socks and Rascal. I found new areas to walk them, predominantly up in the mountain areas. On our walks, I would talk to them as if they were my flesh and blood. I even thought about how nice it would be if they could talk back.

We were inseparable, and I loved them, and I knew they loved me too. We also had another thing in common, we all missed Jackie, and would assure the, that we would be back home in time, to talk to her over Skype. Whenever she was on, I would have both Socks and Rascal sitting next to me so that they could hear Jackie's voice.

The ten days ended, and I couldn't wait to go and pick Jackie up from the airport, and welcomed her home as if I hadn't seen her in years. As soon as she came in through the front door, the dogs bounded over to greet her, almost knocking Jackie off her feet.

It was an amazing sight to behold, and it made it all worthwhile in what I saw, as a happy family. Although Jackie had been away, it seemed that she was somewhat distant in being back. No matter how hard I tried, she would never let on her true feelings. It was only after a month of her being around that Jackie explained she was unhappy at the apartment, that mum was always interfering, and she insisted that we moved.

A few days after she told me this, we spoke to one of the expats, Julie in the village who was moving back to the UK, and her apartment in Vathi Bay would be available. She promised and to speak to her landlord in transferring the rental agreement over to us. Although this offer sounded good, we could only make a final decision after we had viewed the property. The next day, we went around to the property located on the other side of Istron, overlooking the Bay.

The apartment wasn't as big as our current home, but it had stunning views, overlooking all of the beaches, mountain areas and beautiful green slopes. We could also see villages of Kala Chorio and Istron. The owners also landscaped the communal areas outside. To the left of our apartment, was four other separate apartments, whereas ours was in a group of six. The buildings and the land were owned by two brothers, who also owned a taverna in Aghios Nicolas. After viewing the apartment, we fell in love with it, and the surrounding areas. It was far away from mum and Robin, but still close enough to go and see them.

The next morning, we arranged to meet Julie at the brother's taverna to exchange details and to sign a new contract. We would move to the apartment, as soon as Julie had moved out. After we've finalised everything, we went back and told mum and Robin our news.

We broke the news to them gently and explained the reasons we would be moving. Naturally, they were slightly disappointed but wished us luck. I also arranged with Brian if he could help us move to the apartment, as his boss

Mike had a pickup truck and would allow him to use it to help us.

Moving from our apartment was somewhat tricky, as we had to transport everything down the steep slope to the bottom. After several hours and a lot of help, we managed to move without too much drama. Jackie had spent the day, with our German friends Mariella and Manfred, where she had also taken the dogs so they won't get in the way. After Brian and the boys had emptied our old apartment, I picked Jackie up and noticed that she was a lot worse for wear, as she had enjoyed the hospitality of Mariella and Manfred too much. I got her home, and settled her down on the balcony, with an iced coffee, while I went to buy some food.

When I returned, as I went to hand over the food, she started to get angry and called me all the names under the sun. Her behaviour was strange, and I put down to alcohol she drank on an empty stomach. Rather than react and cause an argument, I just sat there and took it, trying to ignore what she was saying.

My inaction aggravated the situation more, and she told me to 'fuck off' before storming off to bed. As the food had been un-eaten, I placed it in the fridge and sat down on the sofa to watch a film. I was concerned about Jackie and ensured that she was safely in bed, and was lying on her side, where I placed a bucket in case she started to vomit.

I decided to sleep on the sofa, just in case anything hap-pened. The next morning, Jackie woke me up with a cup of tea and was very apologetic from her previous night's rantings. Be-ing myself, I told her not to worry, as I was prepared to put it all behind us.

As time went by, we settled into the new apartment. Things seemed to be going well because I'd managed to obtain some work from Brian's boss Mike Kilner. It was now the end of July 2009. Our lifestyle was idyllic, we had terrific views and a lovely quiet apartment, where many times, we would sit and watch the sunset, moonrise, and watch the sunrise.

Surrounded by mostly English ex-pats and two Greek fam-ilies, we all got on well in the small community. Jackie had also got involved with Joan, the Co-owner with a husband George of the bar Commotions, and who had started a charity for stray dogs.

Joan had asked Jackie if we could look after a puppy for a few days before sending it to Holland to its new owners. Sitting on the balcony with the puppy, and when the weather was getting extreme, Jackie suggested that she wanted to go home when Steve and Diane revisit us. I was confused until she explained it would be the hottest times of the year, which was the end of July and August.

I realised Jackie had a point, as I didn't want the temperature to bring on another MS attack, and I hated to see her suffer. Reluctantly, I agreed. A few days later, Joan picked came for the puppy, and we prepared to welcome our friends Steve and Diane again. Their visit coincided with a small housewarming and barbecue we arranged.

Our invitees had a marvellous time, even contributing to bringing food of their own. Jackie seemed very quiet and hardly spoke all evening. The next morning, still tired from the previous night's entertainment and the barbecue, Steve and I walked the dogs.

As we were taking in the beautiful morning, and the fantastic smells of wild herbs, liquorice, which were abundant in the area, Steve asked,

'What would you do if Jackie didn't come back?'

Shocked at the blunt question, I told Steve that she was only going for a short time and that if he knew something, now would be the time to say. Steve realised that he had made a mistake, tried to cover up for his question, and told me it was just a hunch.

On the way back home, he tried to make small talk, but I was still thinking about what he said. When we got inside, I asked to speak to Jackie alone on the balcony, and I asked what Steve said. At first, Jackie was reluctant, and with tears in her eyes, she confessed.

It was like having my heart ripped out. Jackie told me she didn't love me anymore would not be returning when she went back to the UK with Steve and Diane. Upon hearing these words, I was numb, in shock, and needed to get away for a time to think.

I made my excuses and got into my car for a drive. I had no real plans on what to do, and stopped near the tobacconist kiosk, and bought a packet of cigarettes although had not smoked for over five years. As soon as the smoke hit my lungs, I felt a dizzy feeling coming over me.

Unperturbed at the effect of smoking for the first time after such a long period, I drove off along the coast road and stopped off in the layby. I sat on a bench I had enjoyed several visits while I had been out walking the dogs. Sitting there, I was an emotional wreck, and I couldn't believe that it was happening, and tried to rationalise what I had heard.

My head was a screwed-up mixture of emotions, and as hard as I tried, I was unable to comprehend, what was going on. I hadn't noticed that I have been chain-smoking and tried to choke back the tears, but it was all in vain. My phone kept on ringing, it was Steve trying to get through to me, but each time, I just disregarded the call. I managed to compose myself and returned home to face the music, and get answers that I so desperately wanted.

Arriving home, with a heavy heart, I opened the door. As usual, the dogs were going crazy as they greeted me, but I just brushed past them. I made my way to the balcony, where I could be alone with my thoughts. Steve came to join me in a vain attempt to put things right. Without thinking, I told him to 'fuck off, and take Diane with him,' which was out of character. They took themselves out for a walk and left Jackie and me alone. All I wanted to do was scream and shout at her, but I couldn't think of what to say.

She tried to sit down and talk to me, but it just came out as garbled, as I wasn't listening to what she was trying to say. Jackie took hold of my hand in a vain attempt to get me to look at her, but I just kept my head bowed, as I didn't want her to see me crying. Her words were making an impact, and I now felt able to look at her and listen. She too was crying her eyes out, although she kept repeating that it wasn't working for her anymore, and she needed to go back to the UK.

Deep down, I knew this wasn't Jackie. To me, she was my hero, my rock and my inspiration. Regardless of what I said to her, it seemed to make no difference, as she had made up her mind, and would be leaving the same day with Steve and Diane. Over the next few days, we tried to resolve our differences, but it was all in vain. I made a promise to Jackie that I wouldn't inform mum or Robin about her decision because she didn't have the physical or emotional strength to deal with mum who would make her feel even worse.

I tried to put it out of my mind when I was working, but I had to explain the reasons why I was down. Brian, Mike and Chris understood and were supportive of me.

As the week drew to a close, Jackie and I talked about her health because I was still concerned was for her. Even though I suggested that I return with her, Jackie wouldn't have any of it, and she said we would remain friends.

The night before they were going to be flying home, we went out for dinner, the whole process tinged with sadness. After our meal, we were going to have a few farewell drinks at commotions bar.

We made sure that none of the ex-pats who were our friends knew what was going on.

As it was karaoke evening, I wanted to sing, and the only song with lyrics 'The wind beneath my wings' aptly described my feelings for Jackie. You see, throughout our life together, there was only ever one real person whom I could rely on, and that was Jackie. She was not only my wife, but she was my very best friend, and my hero in my eyes, I wanted her to know that through the song.

The next morning was a sad affair, Jackie had written a letter to my mum, and she asked me to hand it to her after they must have gone. We made the most of the few hours that remained, but as the taxi arrived to take them all to the airport, we couldn't contain our emotions any longer. Both of us held each other and cried in each other's arms before our final farewells. As the taxi pulled away, we waved to each other, never knowing if we would see each other again.

It was then that it hit me, and I collapsed in an emotional mess and was comforted by Socks and Rascal. The date was 23rd August 2009, which was two days before our 15th wedding anniversary. Some considerable time later, I managed to compose myself. I decided to go to mum's house, and take the letter that Jackie had written for her. Before leaving, I read the message, and the content broke my heart.

Jackie explained that she had to leave due to her MS, as the condition had worsened since we left the UK, and even though she had tried to make the best of it, she was unable to continue to do so and had to look after her best interests. She also made it clear, that I wasn't to blame, and although her love for me had changed, I would always be in her heart, and asked mum to ensure that I was okay and to look after me.

Jackie further wrote that she was sorry because she didn't have the strength, either emotionally or physically, to speak to mum directly. After reading, although challenging, I understood her reasoning. I placed the letter back into the envelope, before leaving, I said goodbye to the dogs and told them I would be back home soon.

The journey to mum's, although only five minutes away by car, seemed to be an eternity, as I just didn't know how I was going to break the sad news to her. After parking, I made my way up the long steep driveway, which felt like a condemned man on his way to the gallows. I knocked on the door and entered where mum asked if Jackie had got her flight.

With tears in my eyes, I handed her the note and sat down. As mum was reading the letter, she was also trying to comfort me, as at that time, I was inconsolable. I knew that Jackie would have been feeling the same as myself. Mum and I spoke about the situation, as we did so, Robin came in from his work, where I told him.

Looking back, neither myself nor Jackie would have wanted to have been in the position that led us to split up, as we were both deeply in love. Although, like most relationships, we had our up's and downs. Regardless, we would always be there for one another. I know it was the cruel fate of Jackie's multiple sclerosis, and its devastating effects, which caused us so much heartbreak and resulted in our eventual demise.

Chapter Fifteen

From the Depths of Despair

As Jackie was now out of my life, I hit rock bottom. We had been together for twenty-four years, and she was the love of my life. I knew that she felt the same, but each time we tried to speak to each other over the phone, neither of us, could say more than a few words before our voices cracked, and we'd both break down in tears.

I tried desperately in vain, to get her to change her mind, and allow me to come back to the UK to be with her again. Each time, she would knock me back, saying that she needed to be by herself. We both knew that her MS condition had taken its toll on her health, while we were in Crete, and she had stayed because she found it difficult to tell me her true feelings, and that added to my guilt. I felt that I had somehow let her down.

As the weeks passed, the pain we felt was just as intense as any physical pain that either of us had ever encountered. I missed her terribly, and I know she felt the same way, but neither of us could tell the other. It was like we were grieving over the death of a loved one, and we both shared the same grieving process, with all its mixture of emotions.

Try as I may, nothing I had suggested seemed to work, so instead of pushing it, I decided to take a step back, and take stock of what I would do next.

I was finding it hard to cope with living alone, although I had the dogs for company, everything reminded me of Jackie, which included her Disney toys I bought over the years for her. Also, as she had left some of her clothes, the smell reminded me of her. I saw her face everywhere as I had several pictures of us together in happier times.

Mum was, of course, worried, as I had started to drink excessively. It became a daily occurrence after work. Although I had Socks and Rascal, it was if, I was alone with no one. At my lowest ebb, one evening after a heavy drinking session, I sat on the balcony overlooking the Bay. It was a beautiful moonlit evening, and I had bought a large bottle of my favourite drink Metaxa.

Without using glass, I would swig out of the bottle itself. The more I drank, the more I became melancholy. It also didn't help that I was playing songs that remind of me of Jackie. As usual, Socks and Rascal were by my side, although they were keeping me company, at that point, it didn't matter, as I had come to a decision.

In my drunken stupor, I tied a length of rope to the balcony and placed the noose around my neck. Sitting there, with tears rolling down my cheeks, I decided the time to end my life. I also felt I needed more courage, so I continued to drink with the noose around my neck.

I was inconsolable and felt that nothing else mattered. Crying my eyes out, and incoherent, I went to stand up to throw myself off. As I did so, I slipped and came crashing down to the floor. Now lying on my back, I kept muttering Jackie's name and was crying uncontrollably.

While I was lying there in my drunken state, I felt the cold noses of my beautiful dogs against my face, and their warm tongues licking away my tears. It was only then that somehow I snapped back into reality. I realised that I had two beautiful dogs who were reliant on me, just as much as I was reliant on them. Socks and Rascal were my two babies, and I needed their comfort.

Now sitting upright, I realised what I was about to do, but with their love and support, I removed the noose from my neck, and embraced them both as tightly as I could, and knew that no matter what, I could rely on them, for all the love and support that I craved. Without them being there, my life would now be at an end!

After what seemed to be an eternity, with the love and support of the dogs, managed to compose myself, took a shower, before taking them out for a long walk along the moonlit road that leads up to the apartment. Breathing in the crisp night air, I sobered up and felt more human again.

Returning home, I prepared their dinner, ate supper on my own, before sitting down with them on the balcony to take stock of my new life. After eating, I untied the rope and threw it away along with the now empty bottle of Metaxa. I contemplated long and hard about my actions, and felt at peace, as I cuddled Socks and Rascal. After a while, I retired to bed, accompanied by my best friends.

The next morning, I awoke with the sound of the sea crashing against the beach. As usual, it was a beautiful sunny morning, although nursing a momentous hangover, I felt more invigorated, which was something, I hadn't felt for in a long time. The first thing I did was to take some painkillers for my banging headache, along with a quenching cup of tea. As I sat there looking at the fantastic view from my balcony, the dogs joined me, where I felt more at ease in their presence. While I was drinking my tea, and admiring the view, I'd talk to them regularly. Both of them would look at me, and I thought to myself that they understood me more than I could ever imagine.

From now on, I would consider them not only my best friends but my saviours. Going for a shower, not only woke me up but made me feel alive. Attaching the dogs' leads, we ventured outside, where we shared an amazing walk through the beautiful aromatic Crete countryside. Out walking, I started to sing, which uplifted my spirit—thinking of all the fantastic times I'd spent with Jackie. I'm not going to lie, and it brought a tear to my eye, but it also made me smile.

Looking around the unique landscape, I know I was lucky to be in such beautiful surroundings with my two best friends. The further we walked, I started to make plans, and think about what the future would hold. The only course of action I could take would be to take each day at a time, and never give up hope on seeing Jackie again. But for now, I'd enjoy the moment, and how lucky I was to be alive after my selfish act night before.

After a long and brisk walk, we returned home for a welcome breakfast. I thought my dogs deserved meals fit for Kings after bringing me back from the brink. I took out some defrosted chicken breasts before poaching them in chicken stock, allowing them to cool, ready to give my two heroes a breakfast they deserved.

Preparing myself a hearty breakfast, we sat on the balcony and enjoyed our meals. Breakfast now over, it was time to play some uplifting music. Looking through my collection, I picked out my favourite CD, which was Queen's greatest hits. With music now filling the air, I danced along while cleaning the apartment. Periodically, I'd stop and take turns to dance with Socks and Rascal.

For someone looking in, you could forgive them in thinking that there was a deranged bald man, talking and dancing with two dogs! However, I didn't have a care in the world.

As time went by, I was getting stronger by the minute, but would never forget Jackie in all of this. Both of us were a little bit more able to talk to each other, and I was pleased for her, as she was getting healthier away from Crete. I'd arranged after she left to transfer 35,000 euros from the 40,000 euros we had from our

Greek bank account over to her UK account, and everything she'd requested. Neither of us had envisaged that we would end up in this way. Although we were both still hurting, it was deemed the right decision at the time. We would contact each other, as often as we were able to, it was beautiful to talk to her, and see her face once more via Skype call.

The year was now flying past, and it was fast approaching Christmas again. I remembered all of the previous beautiful Christmases we had together. Now alone, I felt that I wouldn't be able to endure it alone in Crete. After a long thought, I decided to take myself away from Crete and spend Christmas somewhere different.

Being a creature of habit, I couldn't make my mind up where to go. I decided that the only option I could think of was to close my eyes, and using a pin, go wherever it landed. As I opened my eyes, I could see that I had stuck the pin, in Kiev the capital of Ukraine. Thinking long and hard, I concluded it was a no brainer.

Immediately, I booked the flight and accommodation for three weeks via the internet. As soon as I'd booked the holiday, I spoke to mum and Robin, who agreed along with my neighbour Dawn that they would look after the dogs between them. In my absence, mum was happy to help, but was her usual concerned self, as she was worried that her 'baby boy' was going to a communist country!

Preparing for the holiday, I thoroughly pampered the dogs every day, showering them with love, affection and of course their favourite snacks! I would miss them, as they were my lifeline, and had kept me sane. But I just had to get away from all the painful memories. I knew mum would make a fuss over them and Dawn, my neighbour, so that was one less worry.

I'd also made a new acquaintance, whom I had spoken to several times over the internet and Skype. She hailed from the Czech Republic, and her name is Anja. Informing her, I was off to Kiev for the Christmas and New Year holidays. Anja suggested that I come over to her for the New Year. Although we had never met personally, I felt assured in my heart that it would be fine. So booked a flight from Kiev to the Czech Republic. The only problem I faced was I'd have to fly back to Kiev, return to Crete, as that time of year, there were no direct flights from the Czech Republic to Greece.

On the 19th of December 2009, the start of the holiday arrived. Robin had agreed to take me to the airport, everything was in place, and I had packed and ready. I got up early to get prepared, and more importantly, make more fuss with Socks and Rascal. A few hours later, Robin arrived, and I made bade farewells to the dogs, but I assured them I would be back soon, and I loved them with all my heart. I had planned my itinerary to the minute detail, I had left no stone unturned, so it all went smoothly. I would be leaving Crete at 4 pm for Athens, for a two-hour layover, before catching my flight to Borispol airport Kiev at six, where I would be arriving at 8.30 pm.

The temperature when I left Athens was plus 18 degrees. I knew there would be a complete weather difference in Ukraine, and I had underestimated the temperature drop. As soon as we had landed, it was apparent that my naivety had blinded me from what awaited me, as it was a complete white-out, with heavy snowfall! I had at least planned my wardrobe, with suitable cold-weather clothing, including a full-length coat, which Robin lent me, and my God, I sure needed.

When the aircraft doors opened, the immediate rush of minus 10-degree air engulfed the cabin, and took the breath from my lungs!

While waiting to disembark, I hastily took out the coat, along with thick woollen Arran pullover, hat, scarf, and thermal gloves. The snow was heavy and ankle-deep, and that was before I climbed down the steps to the ground! As I walked to the bus terminal, my first thought was, 'what the hell have I let myself in for'?

Arriving at the terminal was like heaven, as it was nice and warm, and thanked my lucky stars. Trying to get through customs was a nightmare, as I'd made a slight error, and hadn't filled in the entry visa, as it was all in Ukrainian. I found an English-speaking customs officer who helped me. Picking up my luggage, and made my way through to the arrivals, where I was to meet a holiday company rep.

To my horror, my guide was not around. I tried to avoid the numerous attempts by cajoling taxi drivers plying for trade. Thankfully, my rep arrived and motioned me to his waiting car. He spoke perfect English and apologised for his delay, which was due to the extreme weather, and it was to be expected for the time of year.

Driving through the city was a fantastic experience, and we soon arrived at my rented apartment, a short distance away from

Kiev the city centre. After being shown the apartment, the rep gave me the key, and I paid the balance in cash—he told me what to do and what to avoid. If I needed transport, I would have to contact them directly, as the taxi drivers were not to be trusted. They could overcharge, or in some extreme cases, tourists had been driven to remote areas and either robbed or on occasions murdered! I had not envisaged that but it was sound advice.

With the rep now gone, I scrutinised the apartment. It had been refurbished with a modern look. I was pleasantly surprised. There was a 76-inch flat-screen DVD playing TV, a brand-new halogen hob, gas cooker, fridge and freezer, a spa bath, and the décor had been finished to a high-quality standard, with modern up to date heating.

I was impressed because I was expecting the remnant of the old Soviet Union. All I needed now was to purchase a few essential supplies. Looking out of the window, I noticed a small grocery store opposite. Wrapping up warm, I braced the cold Ukrainian night. Walking around the store, I picked coffee, milk, butter, bread, jam, fruit juice and what I assumed to be sugar.

Going back into the apartment block, I could tell the building was built initially when the country was still part of the old Soviet Union. However, it was immaculate in the communal areas. Back inside the apartment, I made a sandwich and a coffee. Now relaxing on the King-size bed, I turned on the television and played my preferred DVD.

As the movie started, I took a swig of my coffee. I could have died, as the sugar I bought turned out to be salt. Pausing the film, I spat it out down the kitchen sink and discarded the rest. The salty taste had given me a raging thirst, and I grabbed the large carton of juice in one go. Lying back on the bed, I settled down to watch the film, and enjoy my sandwich, laughing to myself for making such a schoolboy error.

After a relaxing sleep, I woke up refreshed and invigorated. My first port of call was the bathroom and a nice welcoming shower. I got dressed, made coffee and a round of toast and jam. I opened the balcony doors, to allow some of the crisps clean air to enter the room. There had been heavy snowfall, and there were no cars on the road. It was a peaceful morning; I marvelled and watched the Kiev citizens going about their daily business regardless of extreme weather conditions. After breakfast, I wrapped up warm before leaving to explore the city.

Although cold at minus sixteen degrees, I felt warm and was in awe of my surroundings.

The beautiful city was nothing like I had imagined it. I thought it would be something leftover from the cold war era of the ex-Soviet Union. Boasting unique ornate architecture, a mixture of East meets West, with many modern brand name shops, bars and restaurant.

As I walked further into the city centre, I was following the herd and headed for the underpass, which was not only a tributary to various parts of the city, it was also a vast underground market. Coming out at the North end, it opened up into an annexe with more specialist market stalls, selling a fast variety of foodstuffs, associated with the rich and famous. One particular stall specialised in tins of beluga caviar. I was expecting to see a King's ransom in price. However, although an authentic product, a 500-gram container it was the equivalent of two British pounds.

I thought for a while and couldn't understand the reasons fancy restaurants and hotels in the West would charge such an extraordinary price for something as cheap as chips. It just goes to prove that these prices back in these fancy places are incredibly exaggerated and inflated.

Had I'd been so inclined, I could have packed a suitcase full of the authentic delicacy, and gone back to the UK making a small fortune in the process. I would reasonably live comfortably in Crete for such minuscule initial outlay. As tempting as this was, my dream was cut short when I got back into the open air where the actual reality of the city became apparent.

As in many cities across the world, there are homelessness and poverty. However, none that I'd seen could compare to that in Kiev. I'd come out next to a prestige car showroom, inside it housed several expensive supercars including Lamborghini, Ferrari, to name but a few. Looking around, a large black Hummer vehicle, with tinted windows, pulled up in front of the showroom.

Several well-dressed henchmen, flanked what I assumed a wealthy businessman, or important VIP, as the bodyguards were heavily armed. Trying to look inconspicuous, they walked past an old lady in worn-out rags begging for a few coins, and into the showroom without batting an eyelid, she might as well have been like a speck of dust underneath their shoes.

I realised Kiev and Ukraine in general, were either extremely wealthy or in abject poverty. I couldn't very well ignore this and handed her some small change, which some may argue, would be a foolish thing to do. How would I know that it was genuine? Well, my answer to that, is I'd been around the block a few times, and seen many walks of life, and know the difference, between genuine homeless people, and those unwashed dregs of society, of whom are quite happy to sit back, and take, without giving anything in return.

I continued my journey through the city, taking in the fantastic sights. Being December, many areas were decorated with Christmas trees and nativity like scenes.

Although like the Greeks, the Ukrainians mostly practices the Russian Orthodox religion, similar to the Greek Orthodox who celebrate Christmas in January. However, I believe most of these scenes are there primarily for the tourist.

Stopping off at a tobacconist kiosk, I purchased two packets of Marlboro cigarettes. I thought it would be pricier because it was imported; however, the two packs were only one pound.

I walked around and stopped in front of the memorial of the former Russian leader Lenin.

I lit a cigarette, and an older man in his early eighties approached, dressed in an old Russian army uniform with his chest adorned with various medals, I noticed he had been marching the length and breadth of the memorial.

As the old chap stood in front of me, he looked very frail. He was speaking but unable to understand him, the man finally gestured with his hands for a cigarette. Without hesitation, I opened the pack, and he took one gratefully with a smile, and I helped him light it.

The old soldier was very grateful and shook my hand vigorously. His fingers were frozen to the bone, and his lined face told a tale of a proud soldier. Being an ex-serviceman myself, I couldn't allow a comrade in arms, albeit different generations apart to go without money, so I gave him a few quid and a packet of the Marlboro cigarettes. What happened next, I would never forget, his face lit up with a beaming smile. Not only that, but the man also kissed me cheek to cheek, and couldn't stop shaking my hand. It was a beautiful gesture, and although we couldn't speak the same language, it made my day. After bidding him farewell, we parted company, and I continued on my sightseeing adventure.

As I was walking around the city, I started to get hungry and looked for a suitable eating establishment. I was surprised at the number of westernised food outlets, ranging from McDonald's to Burger King, Pizza Hut, Starbucks, and one of my most favourite TGI Friday's.

I thought I could do with a filling lunch, so I entered TGI's. Sitting down at an empty table, I waited for a server to bring me a menu. A very beautiful looking young lady greeted me and handed me a menu. She asked if I wanted a drink in Ukrainian.

Of course, I did not know the language and proceeded to inquire if she spoke English. Her command of the English language was better than mine, as she was fluent, which was impressive. She handed me an English language menu, where it had all of the usual favourites associated with the chain. I opted for beautiful rib-eye steak, and while it was being prepared, my server came over to speak with me.

She introduced herself as Svetlana and asked why I had come to Kiev. We had a wonderful conversation, and she offered her services after her shift to show me around the famous sites. While we were talking, I decided to keep out the cold and treat myself with a glass of Hennessy champagne cognac. As I sat at the bar, the waiter, a nice-looking man named Peter, could also speak perfect English. He took a beautiful balloon cognac glass, warmed it for me before pouring a perfect measure, which went down a treat along with a beautifully cooked steak meal that I'd ordered. After I'd eaten, I spent a pleasant afternoon talking to him; he was a very knowledgeable person and very friendly.

To show my gratitude for his warm service, I left a £10 tip for him and the serving staff. True to Svetlana's word, after her shift, she after took me around Kiev, explaining the history of the city as we strolled through the town.

It was now getting dark as the temperature dropped to minus eighteen degrees. I felt warm inside due to my hot meal and several large cognacs.

I was concerned that Svetlana was taking up her valuable time with me, instead of being home with her family. Svetlana explained that she lived outside the city and was staying nearby with her good friend. I thought it would be a nice gesture if I could offer her a coffee or a drink, and I suggested that she ring up her friend and we could have a lovely evening together.

We walked into a local Starbucks, where we sat down and ordered some coffee. While we were waiting, she rang up her friend who came to join us and introduced herself as Sofia. We spent several hours having an excellent time and fantastic conversation. Although Sofia could speak some English, it was left to Svetlana to translate the rest.

The time was now approaching 10 pm, and my hosts, who both worked at TGI's, explained that they were starting early the next morning for their shift. Before they left, we arranged to meet up the next day and visit the cinema, which was showing the blockbuster Avatar!

As I walked back to my apartment, the temperature had dropped again and was now at minus twenty. On my way back, I stopped off at a German-run supermarket named Billa for some more essential supplies, including some much-needed sugar. As I walked with my groceries, I had a massive grin across my face, thinking of my amazing day in Kiev, and the new friends that I'd made. Now back inside the warmth and comfort of the apartment, I made myself a coffee and a banana sandwich, before settling back to watch the TV.

As I flicked through the hundreds of channels, I came across an old black and white film, starring Sean Connery titled, 'The Hill'. Set in the middle of a desert, it was a Second World War British army prison. The prisoners undergo a brutal punishment regime by the prison officials. In the central area of the complex, there was a man-made stone and sandhill. Prisoners are always forced to go up and down the man-made structure. The film was an ideal end to a perfect day.

I woke up refreshed, and couldn't wait to get back outside, to explore the areas of the city, which I hadn't seen the day before, and to visit, various museums and galleries that were abundant. I made breakfast, and while I was sitting there eating, the weather report, which was in English, explained that the temperature, had now dropped to minus twenty-four degrees, with a further icy wind chill factor, would stand at minus thirty-two.

I took a long hot shower, and dressed warmly before going out into extreme freezing conditions, which I had never experienced before, or since. As soon as I hit the outside air, my breath vapour had frozen in mid-air. I wrapped my scarf around my mouth and nose, to try and warm up my breathing, and that only resulted in ice crystals forming when I breathed.

Taking the usual path I did the previous day, I reached the underpass, which would take me under the city to my destination. Before going through the doors, I stood on the steps leading down to have a cigarette. There was a group of young men drinking Russian vodka at 8:30 am.

One of the men came over to talk to me and offer me a drink. I politely refused due to the time of the morning, and somewhat reluctant to get into a conversation. The man realised I wasn't Ukrainian and spoke in broken English. He also acted as a translator to his other friends, and all appeared to be very friendly.

From what I understood, they worked in the market and were on their version of a tea break. Although the men offered a drink to me several times, I couldn't accept it, as it was far too early for myself, and the fact that I'm not a lover of vodka. After our conversation, I said my goodbyes and went on my way.

As I got to my destination on the other side of the subway, I walked to the cathedral, which had the crowning glory of the onion style globe spires. Although not religious, I ventured inside and was amazed at the ornate architecture, and frescoes that adorned the walls.

Kiev has terrific museums, as a history buff, I enjoy learning about different traditions and cultures from other countries. I spent several hours admiring the city and its grandeur. Spotting an Internet café, and entered so I could Skype call Jackie, to see how she was doing, and what her plans were, for the Christmas Holidays.

As I entered, there were at least eighty computers. I went to the bar, ordering coffee and paid for an hour on the Internet. As I got through to Jackie, she looked terrible and had contracted flu. I felt so sorry for her as she sounded rough, what made it worse was when I asked her plans were for Christmas Jackie said she would be spending it alone. My heart sank, as I felt so guilty, as to what had gone on between us. I must've apologised one thousand times, and Jackie being the person she is, kept on repeating it was okay, and I should not apologise.

I didn't want her to be tired by talking, so I promised to contact her every day, even on Christmas Day. After the hour had finished, I tried and found a florist to get some flowers delivered and a gift for Jackie, I arranged it to be delivered on Christmas Eve. After placing my order, I made my way to TGI Friday, where I would be meeting Svetlana and Sofia.

I walked to the bar and ordered a large cognac and waited for the girls' arrival. I hadn't waited long when they both appeared looking stunning. I ordered more drinks, and we sat down to enjoy lunch together. Over lunch, they told me more about their lives, the most poignant part of it, was that they were six years old when they had to be evacuated from their home city of Pripyat which was near ground zero, at the time of the Chernobyl nuclear disaster.

I was listening intently at their devastating story, how they both lost their parents at an early age from radiation sickness, and that they both required hysterectomies, which was a direct result of being affected by the radiation disaster.

I couldn't believe that these two amazing women would never be able to have children caused by something they had no control over. What made it worse was they were very young.

Hearing their words made my problems pale in comparison, but I was amazed at how positive they both were, and like everyone who had a dream, theirs were to become translators. Inspired by the story, it was then a light bulb moment struck me, and I was determined to change my life for the better, regardless of what the future had in store.

After eating, they insisted on paying for the meal, and the cinema tickets. I protested at this until Svetlana explained they had invited me as their guest, and that it would be deemed rude and non-customary.

The cinema was an amazing experience, a modern Multiplex venue with comfortable seating, unlike the ones that I'd been in the UK.

I assumed that the film would be in the Ukrainian language with English subtitles, but how wrong I was as it was all in English. Seeing Avatar on the big screen was spectacular, and the sound was incredible, coupled with the fact that either side of me were two beautiful young ladies, highly educated and knowledgeable.

After the film had ended, I wanted to somehow pay them back for the immense generosity. As both girls were off the next day, I inquired if there was a nightclub where we could all go and enjoy, have a few drinks, and a meal. The venue was heaving with people of all nationalities, we all had an amazing time.

While we were in there, Svetlana and Sofia asked if it would be okay for them to come back to my apartment, as they had now missed the last bus home. Of course, I would be foolish not to, let's just say it was the most incredible night of my life.

The next morning, I treated them to breakfast at a local café before they both returned home, not before we arranged another date for the next day. When the day arrived, it was to be a historical tour. They took me to places, explaining the history of how Ukraine had once been part of the Soviet Union, and how they became independent.

The Soviets tried to take back Ukraine as part of the USSR, but they hadn't reckoned on the might of the Ukrainian armed forces and were beaten back to Russia. The girls showed me were several tanks owned Russians, and captured by Ukrainian armed forces. They were now used as monuments. It showed how Ukraine won the war.

Being with Svetlana and Sofia was a great experience, and one I will never forget. Sadly, I forgot to take their details when I returned home to Crete, which I regretted.

25th of December 2009. It was now Christmas Day. Or at least it was for me, although there were many Christmas trees, and references to Santa Claus around the city, as I'd already explained, being Russian Orthodox Christians, the Ukrainians celebrate their Christmas in January as the Greeks do.

I'd spent several days with the two girls, and I wanted to be alone, as it was my first Christmas without Jackie. My first port of call was at the Internet café, to Skype call her. Still full of the flu, Jackie was feeling a little better and was very cheerful and happy after receiving the bouquet and gifts that I had sent her.

She'd also been invited to her friend's house for Christmas dinner. It was nice talking to Jackie, and seeing that she was happy, or at least was putting on a brave face. Wishing her a Merry Christmas and hoped that she had a wonderful day with her friends and would contact her again on Boxing Day.

Not knowing what I would do for the day, I ventured out once more to the city, and still bitterly cold, the temperature had risen to a respectable minus sixteen degrees, which was a considerable increase, from the last few days, which had been minus thirty-two degrees. I pondered what I could do for Christmas dinner, I'd tried many of the fast food and restaurants that the city had to offer, which included Ukrainian cuisine, which was very nice, but I wanted something basic and boring. It was a toss-up between McDonald's and Burger King, after a brief thought, I chose McDonald's, only as it was the closest to my apartment.

My Christmas dinner consisted of Big Mac, large fries, an apple pie and hot chocolate. It was a far cry from the Christmas meals that I had previously, but as I sat down and tucked into the food, I realised that you don't need fancy expensive food to have an excellent time in the festive period. I felt most at ease, and somewhat upbeat, to see my fellow diners enjoying themselves, and I couldn't be happier even though I was alone, I had unforgettable memories to keep me going.

With only two more days left in Kiev, I made the most of it by spending some time with Svetlana and Sofia. My day of departure had arrived all too soon. It had been arranged by the agent to pick me up to take me back to Borispol airport for my flight to Prague, and then onto an internal flight to Brno.

Arriving at Prague, I went through to speak to the information desk who explained that there were no internal flights to Brno, as it had been cancelled, due to industrial action at Brno airport. However, a taxi service had been arranged although it would take nearly two hours to drive there.

On route, I rang Anja and explained what the situation was. However, she and her son Thomas were already waiting at the airport when I arrived. Driving through the Czech countryside with Anja and Thomas reminded me of the UK, I had a warm overall feeling about the country itself.

Arriving at Anja's home, her son Thomas bid me farewell, as he had to go off to his workplace. Anja introduced me to her parents, and she acted as interpreter. They had laid on a beautiful spread of traditional Czech buffet-style food, which tasted amazing. I felt thoroughly welcome as if I had known them for a long time.

The house was a three-storey townhouse, and the street is like any other in the UK. There are local pubs and a few small shops nearby. The top floor of the house was more like a separate home with a lounge, kitchen, bathroom and two bedrooms. It's also boasted a large balcony, overlooking the garden and, beautiful Czech countryside.

Hitting it off straight away with Anja and her family, they even suggested that I move from Crete and live with them to become an English teacher. I thought about their offer, as I had just completed a Tesol course, but needed time to think about my plans.

Over the next few days, I had an amazing time revolving around the pub, which is a great way of getting together with new interesting people. Each pub that we went into, the locals would be in fits of laughter while watching the TV.

At first, I didn't understand what they were laughing at, and then I realised they were watching Mr Bean!

I later found out that Mr Bean was somewhat of a cult hero in the Czech Republic.

It was now New Year's Eve 2009. Anja had purchased two tickets for the New Year's Eve celebration in nearby Slovakia. Of course, The Czech Republic and Slovakia were once the same countries in Czechoslovakia. The evening was a fantastic night, with fabulous food, drink, and entertainment. I made the most of it as I would be returning to Greece on the 2nd of January 2009.

The day of my returning home had quickly arrived. I had spent three amazing weeks in two unique countries and met terrific people from ordinary walks of life. I felt somewhat sad when I was driven to the airport, as I was torn between being a part of a family, and my home life back in Crete.

The things that changed my mind was the thought that I was going back to my beautiful dogs, Socks and Rascal whom I had missed. I knew they had been well looked after and spoiled back home when I called home. My journey would take twenty-four hours to complete, as I had to fly back to Borispol airport in Kiev, transferred onto a flight back to Athens, and returning home to Crete.

I was picked up by Robin upon my arrival back home, and somehow, was more uplifted. My depression and melancholy that I had suffered before going to Kiev and the Czech Republic had dissipated. I now felt more at ease with myself, with the fighting spirit and determination to go forward with my head held high, rather than being selfish and feeling sorry for myself.

Arriving home, I placed the key in the lock, and as soon as I opened the door, Socks and Rascal almost dived on top of me, showering me with love and affection which I returned a hundredfold.

I'd bought them both presents which they loved, and while I made myself a cup of tea, I spoke to them and told him all about my amazing adventures, but I'm sure that the goodies that I bought for them were more important than listening to me ranting about my holidays.

Sitting on the balcony, I reminisced and thought long and hard about my plans for the future. After much thought and consideration, I felt that my place was in Crete, and was much more determined to succeed in whatever I had planned to do. I had weighed up the pros and cons. I didn't want to move again, as it would feel like I was about to run away. I would face up to my demons and put them well and truly behind me. But for now, I was content in being back home again, with my beautiful dogs. If not for them, I wouldn't be here now, telling this story.

Chapter Sixteen

Future Plans

Over the next few days, I started to make plans for the future. I'd resigned to the fact that Jackie and I would never be together again, and that I had to respect her wishes. After all, there is a saying 'if you love someone, set them free'. I decided to devote all my energies in work, and looking after dogs, ensuring that they would have a happy and fulfilling life.

My neighbour Dawn, who had her dog Fudgy, ensured that Socks and Rascal were well looked after while I was at work, and would take over the reins until I came back. They would want for nothing, I likened us to the Three Musketeers, as we were all inseparable.

As time went by, Mike had acquired some large contracts with ex-pats, who had purchased old, dilapidated Cretan buildings, to be done up for their retirement. We had a good team which included Mike, Brian, Chris and myself. Although the work was hard, due to the extreme temperatures in dusty conditions, it was somewhat rewarding. Several months had passed after returning from Kiev and the Czech Republic, where I'd changed my life for the better, especially as I was enjoying myself when I was with Socks and Rascal.

It was now May 2010, and the tourist season was in its earliest months. Not only was I working for Mike, but on weekends, I also worked for Tassos, who owned the local scuba diving centre. I had the best of both worlds it seemed.

In the diving school, I was signing up holidaymakers, who would either dive with me for a short hour-long open water dive. And sometimes, more experienced divers would be taken by myself and Tassos on his boat for more technically challenging dive sites, around Crete.

As May rolled into June, I received a Skype call from Jackie, who had some devastating news that she wanted a divorce. Try as I might convince her to change her mind, she didn't.

Upon receiving the paperwork, I noticed the grounds for divorce was unreconcilable differences. At first, I was devastated, but I didn't want any animosity between us, and I signed without question. As the divorce was finalised, I spoke to Jackie, who admitted that she never stopped loving me but didn't want to be a burden on me when her condition worsened. I would have done everything in my power to ensure that she would never suffer alone, and I made it clear to her at the time, as I loved her with my heart, soul and always will!

I put off telling mum and Robin about the divorce, as I didn't want them to feel bad about Jackie. Both of them were very understanding, although mum was disappointed, as she always thought that we would both get back together again, as she always thought highly of Jackie, and told her on numerous occasions that she was more like her daughter than my sisters.

Over several weeks, I continued working as hard as I could, trying to forget what had happened. Apart from mum and Robin, nobody knew what happened between Jackie and me. However, that was about to change, as mum told her best friend, Eleanor. We'd met Eleanor once before moving to Crete. We both thought there was something about her neither of us liked, but we kept quiet about our misgivings to mum.

A few weeks after mum has told Eleanor, I started noticing a change in the community. It transpired she had been going around spreading malicious rumours and gossip about Jackie and me. As soon as I heard this, I was livid, not only with mum but with Eleanor herself. I wanted to nip the rumours in the bud before it got out of hand. I contacted mum, and gave her a piece of my mind, she apologised profusely, defending herself that she had told Eleanor in the strictest confidence and never envisaged that her best friend could stoop so low.

Now on the warpath, I would be going after Eleanor and wouldn't hold back with my wrath. It took two weeks for me to catch up with the nasty piece of work, as she had been lying low after mum had spoken to her on the phone. I noticed that her car was outside Friends Internet café; I was fuming and had to control my temper.

As I walked through the door, I saw Eleanor sitting with her friends, and I gave her a piece of my mind. She went bright red and tried to avert her eyes from my glare, trying her best to stop me from embarrassing her further, which was a total waste of her time. The only thing she could do was leave, and had she not done so, I would have certainly lost my temper.

From that moment on, no one would dare spread any malicious rumours about me. You see up to that point; nobody had known what I had done previously and only knew that I had been in the building industry. They only found out that I had been in the military when I was telling Eleanor off.

Later on, my background became common knowledge and was confirmed after my friend Brian and his father in law, came around to see me after the Eleanor incident, and noticed my campaign medals which were proudly on display over the fireplace.

After the incident, everyone from the ex-pat community wanted to be my friend, and every bar that I had frequented I didn't have to buy a drink, as everyone was queuing up to buy them for me. Although I was flattered, I've never been one for any kind of hero-worship, as I have always felt and maintained, that I was merely doing my job at that time. However, it was nice for them to acknowledge my past endeavours, after all, who could pass up a free drink?

Several months had passed, the episode had been forgotten as the ex-pat community had moved onto something else, and secondly, Eleanor had kept away from the village, and was rarely seen, which suited me. I'd also moved on with my life and was taking each day as it comes. I focused on Socks and Rascal and devoted a lot of time with them.

I was living like a recluse but was persuaded to show my face around the village again eventually, as my friend Brian, had secured a gig with his band 'bad language' at Manolis Friends bar.

It was a big occasion. The band were made up of other expats, and a couple of local Greek boys. Although not keen at first, I put on my best bib and tucker and went.

By the time I got there, the gig had already started. It was a packed crowd of all nationalities. I sat at the far side of the seating area, hoping not to get noticed, or that was my thought!

Sitting there sipping my drink, I noticed over the rim of the glass, a pair of eyes transfixed on me from a beautiful mature woman. At first, I tried to ignore her attempts to gain my attention, but the more I tried, the more she looked over.

The gig was now in full swing, and gaining momentum, and the band were fantastic with the finale. It was a rendition of Gerry Rafferty's Baker Street. Instead of the saxophone solo, Brian had belted it out on his guitar, which brought the house down, so well played Brian! As the gig came to an end, and with her gaze still transfixed, I finished my drink and was about to leave when two of her friends accosted me. I knew them but couldn't remember their names; in the end, they dragged me over to meet this woman.

They introduced me to Cheryl, and I must say she was a lovely woman. With introductions over, we hit it off, as we both had a lot in common. As the night went on, I thought we could take things further if I played my cards right, and besides we were both single, so why not? As Cheryl had drunk a lot more than me, we called it a night, and I offered her a lift home, and she cordially accepted, so my thought would soon be realised.

She lived in the next village down called Kala Chorio, so it wasn't too far from where the gig had been.

As I pulled up outside her home, I helped her out of the car and walked to the door.

I wasted no time in getting to the bedroom; in fact, it was Cheryl who dragged me into it. After spending the night, it was time for me to head off home, as I had left the dogs alone, and they would have been lonely. Before going, I promised to meet Cheryl later in the evening, although she thought that I had my 'fun', and would never see her again, I am an honest man, and I never break my promises.

Arriving home, the dogs went mad when they saw me, and they showered me with love and affection. I made their breakfast, showered while they were eating.

I got changed and took them on a nice long walk. Remembering the events of the previous night, I had a wry smile all through the walk, and couldn't wait to for my 'next date' with Cheryl again.

The date was planned for 6 pm that same day, so I spent the entire day spoiling Socks and Rascal, as I had no idea if I would be staying out overnight again. However, my neighbour Dawn had returned to Crete, after being away for six months working in the UK, and as she had a dog of her own who got on well with mine, she agreed to 'dog sit' for me, so I could enjoy my date without worrying.

I was a bit nervous about the date. As we'd both been the worse for wear the night before, I had no way of knowing if Cheryl had remembered our arrangement.

The time soon arrived, I drove down the winding mounting road to where Cheryl lived. I had butterflies in my stomach because I had not been on a date for a while. As I pulled up, I took a series of deep breaths to compose myself. I didn't want to start talking gibberish in her presence. 'Come on Briggsy, buck your ideas up, man,' I said to myself, as I made my way around the side of her house. I took another deep breath before knocking.

As soon as Cheryl appeared, she gave me a beautiful smile, which dissipated my nervousness.

Opening the door to me, she looked stunning, by this time, my face had lit up, and I was grinning like the Cheshire cat. She stood on tiptoes and placed her arms around my neck and kissed me before beckoning me in for a drink.

As she prepared our drinks, her cats strolled in one by one. As customary, they looked at me, before sniffing my outstretched hand.

I don't know what it is, but somehow animals seem to like me. They strolled in and out, competing with each other vying for my attention. It was the matriarch Mia, who took the lead and jumped onto my lap. I hadn't been unaware that Cheryl had been watching me with her animals until she piped up, 'you are privileged, as they never go to strangers'.

A compliment indeed! We sat there talking for a while, before heading off to a beautiful taverna that was called 'Top of the world.'

It was an apt name as from the vantage point, you had an all-round view because it was perched on top of the mountain. Also, being there took us away from the village, and the pathetic gossips. Also, it was much cooler with breath-taking scenery. Sitting there was not only tranquil but very absorbing, where we talked, ate and drank until sunset.

Sadly, the evening went quickly, and neither of us noticed that it was the early hours until the taverna owner reminded us. I paid the bill, and we drove through the moonlit scenery back to Kala Chorio. I was invited in for a nightcap, where we talked some more, before I said my farewell, and left to go home to my beautiful dogs.

Over the coming weeks, Cheryl and I saw each other daily. Neither of us wanted it to become too heavy, as both of us were still trying to cope with failed marriages. As we were enjoying each other's company, my work with Mike dried up, and I couldn't get work with Tasso the dive school owner, as he had been closed down due to tax evasion.

This pissed me off somewhat, as I almost had my diving gear confiscated by the Greek authorities, and only managed to keep them when I provided proof of purchase. I was now starting to feel the pinch, as I was living on some small savings, which I knew wouldn't last indefinitely.

The only solution was for me to sell some of my possession, which was not only almost new but cost a lot of money at the time of purchase. I advertised the items in commotions bar, and the ex-pat community were fighting each other to try and bag a bargain at my expense! They were offering derisory amounts, which frankly was somewhat of an insult to me. Most of them I told to 'fuck off', and not waste my time. I would rather starve, so my dogs could eat.

Using most of my remaining funds to ensure Socks and Rascal could eat, rather than myself. I could always rely on mum to provide me with a hot meal. This was a suitable arrangement, as I managed to sell the items for a reasonable price by standing my ground.

I knew the funds wouldn't last long, as I had no job offers on the horizon. I had to make cutbacks and limited my expenditure, however, this was still not enough. Soon the time came, where I had to make the heart-breaking decision about Socks and Rascal. I spoke to Joan who was the joint owner of commotions bar in the village, who also operated a dog rescue centre charity, where displaced and abandoned dogs could find a new home in Holland.

After a lot of soul searching, for the benefit of Socks and Rascal to be rehomed. I spoke to mum my sad news, and I asked her to come with me to the airport when the dates were arranged. Mum didn't hesitate as we both knew I would be devastated at losing them, as I'm a real softy at heart!

It had been arranged for Socks to go first, with Rascal a few days later. The sad day arrived, and I was heartbroken, but I wanted to spend some quality time with both of them. I'd spoilt them rotten in the days leading up to it.

Dawn, my neighbour, looked after Rascal, as I took Socks to the airport with mum. On the approach to the airport, stopping in the layby to give her a last walk on Crete soil, I sat down on the grass and couldn't contain myself any longer. Holding her close, I sobbed like a baby, but still tried to reassure her, that she would be Ok. As I looked into her beautiful brown eyes, I was sure that she understood, and pressed her cold nose into my neck, and snuggled into my embrace.

We sat like this for what seemed an eternity, but I knew that I'd to try and compose myself before placing her gently back in the car, to make the final short journey to the Airport animal welfare unit. By this time, I was a gibbering wreck, and my heart was breaking, trying to choke back my tears but to no avail. My last act was to remove her collar before placing her into her transportation cage.

I had a few last moments with Socks and told her I would always love her and wished she had a beautiful life with her new adopted family. I will never forget the look on her face when they were wheeling her out. She was subdued and started to whimper, which tore me apart! And just like that, she was gone! The pain I felt was immeasurable, and I knew she would be feeling the same.

As I walked away, mum placed her arm around me, and we hugged, with me still sobbing! The walk back to the car seemed to be everlasting; each step seemed to go on forever. Mum suggested that she drive, however, as heartbroken as I was, mum was not a good driver at the best of times.

The journey back home was in silence, my mind was all over the place, and I had to wipe the tears away so that I could see. I dropped mum back home, where she hugged me again, reassuring me that Socks would be fine. When I got back to my apartment, I made a point of spoiling Rascal, but he sensed that something was wrong, and meandered from room to room, searching for his friend. It was also heartbreaking, as I felt incredibly guilty that I had let them both down. After all, a few months earlier, both of them had saved me from taking my own life, and in my mind, I owed them everything, and considered them my heroes!

After a while, I rang Cheryl and told her, she suggested that I come over to her house, and to bring Rascal with me. As soon as I arrived, Cheryl fell in love with him and spoiled him rotten. It wasn't the same with the cats, as they spat and hissed at him, all the while we were there. Cheryl and I went for a long walk with Rascal and would stop periodically, as I would start the waterworks again. She was very understanding and would hold me tight reassuring me. As the day progressed, I felt more at ease, but I knew it would be short-lived because, within two days, I would be saying goodbye to Rascal, and relive it all over again!

The dreaded day arrived, and Rascal would be going to Holland and a new home. It was if I had been stabbed in the heart over and over again. What made matters worse was that the foster family in Holland had sent me some photos of Socks and an update.

They explained that Socks was missing me, and would look out of the window to see if I was coming home. To see her sad face again killed me inside. However, the foster family were and still are very loving, and were soon to rehome Socks, with a loving Dutch family. Although sad, I was genuinely pleased for her and prayed that she would enjoy her new home.

S J BRIGGS

Once again, mum came with me to the airport as support. Just as I did a few days previously, I'd thoroughly spoiled Rascal, but had to somehow find the inner strength to let him go. I pulled into the layby approach road and took him out for a walk on the grass verge, just like I had done so with Socks. My pain was unbearable, and my heart was breaking, and like any other physical pain, but 1000 time worse. I sat down, and hugged him, telling him that I loved him, and hoped he would understand.

I started to tell him stories and reminded him of when Jackie was still here, that I had written a book aimed at children, which I titled 'Puppy Dogs Tails, The Adventures of Socks and Rascal,' and I still have a copy of the original manuscript today. Somehow, I found the strength to report to the animal welfare, and relinquish him to their care. Again, they allowed me a few moments to say my last goodbyes.

It was when I saw him disappear through the doors that the floodgates opened again, to such an extent that when I got outside the facility, I screamed in immense pain, before sinking to my knees breaking down. Even mum's attempts to console me were to no avail. Several moments passed before I could prise myself away for the long drive back home. Before leaving, I rang Jackie, to tell her about Socks and Rascal. She felt my pain, and we both wept.

Back home again, I still had to get rid of their toys and bowls, but no matter how hard I tried, I just couldn't bear to part with them. In the end, I asked my neighbour Dawn if she could do it for me, as many memories came flooding back. Bearing in mind, I had bought them both up since they were puppies, and in my

• 428 •

mind, they were like my babies whom I cherished and adored. More importantly, they saved me from suicide and self-destruction.

With both dogs gone, I fell into a depression, as I felt that I'd let them and myself down. However, after a few days of soul searching and feeling sorry for myself, I realised I had done my best and had given them the best start I could, in the couple of years that I had them.

I had beautiful memories and pictures. Being a spiritual person, I believed that they would understand. Besides, the regular updates from the foster family and adopted families were excellent. I could now see how happy they were in their new surroundings, so, all's well that ends well.

As hard as it was losing my two best friends, Cheryl was a rock, and we talked over things with a few drinks until the early hours. With her cats, it was like a therapy, and I was happy that I had someone close to confide in, although I had mum and Robin, their advice never hit home, without niggling me in some way

Cheryl kept three cats, which were neglected by the Greeks, and being an animal lover herself, she took them in and gave them a loving home.

The matriarch was Mia, a beautiful black and white cat, who kept the other two in check.

A few years ago, a man hit Mia with a spade, inflicting life-threatening injuries on the cat.

The other two were called Lily, another tan and fluffy white cat. The other was Sophie, who had a novel way of getting a drink by knocking the tap and would drink from the flowing water, although she still hadn't learned to turn it off.

For a few weeks, at least things were going well. I still hadn't managed to find any work, at least I made some excellent friends in Cheryl and her bundles of joy, who kept both of us amused for hours with some of their crazy antics. The other thing was that she had a fantastic courtyard, which was a riot of colour. Her home was a nice size, with upstairs and amazing views from the walkaround balcony. I had been spending so much time with Cheryl that I had taken my eye off the ball, and I was struggling to pay rent for my place.

However, salvation arrived when another ex-pat needed to move, and inquired if she could take the apartment off my hands and take over the lease. At first, I was reluctant, as I didn't know if it would work out between Cheryl and I. Cheryl's home was a two-bedroom apartment, I suggested that we became flatmates and share the bills.

To my surprise, she agreed and moved in shortly afterwards, so at least part of the pressure eased. Amanda was a great laugh and liked a drink, and many were the night she would burst through the door pissed out of her head, much to my amusement.

After Amanda moved in, Cheryl went for a short break to France. At the same time, I received a phone call for a newspaper called the Chronicles, which was a bilingual rag owned by an American Greek owner. He told me that I had won an award for poetry. At first, I was bemused as I have no recollection of the said poem.

It appeared that I had sent in a poem a couple of months ago and had won first prize. I then realised I had sent in while Jackie was still living in Crete. As Jackie was no longer there, and Cheryl was in France, I asked Amanda and mum, if they would like to come to the presentation ceremony.

The venue was in Elounda, and when we left to drive to the venue, the heavens opened, and it hammered down sheet rain where you couldn't see a hand in front of your face. The wind was blowing a gale, and we never thought we would make it. As soon as we arrived, the storm blew out, as quickly as it started. The event organisers greeted us warmly when we arrived, and we went to sit down at the table. Several other contestants had won smaller prizes and were there with their families.

We had been chosen out of 500 entrants, both Greek and English competitors. My poem was titled, 'A smile for all'. As part of the evening, I stood up and recited it, as did the other contestants with their poems. My prize was a brass mounted plaque, and 200-euro prize money. After we'd been presented with our awards, we sat down to a buffet-style meal and had a good evening. Mum was as pleased as punch that I had won and posed with me for a photograph. At the end of the evening, we returned home, only this time in better weather.

We dropped off mum, and Amanda suggested as a celebration that she would buy me a drink. After several hours, we returned home worse for wear, but I admit it was well worth it.

A few days later, Cheryl returned to Crete, where I wasted no time in contacting her. She sounded somewhat distant; after questioning her, she admitted that she didn't want anything to do with me. Cheryl told me that she was too busy doing up her house, ready to sell on in Kritsa. I thought long and hard about the conversation, and I needed to find out more.

I drove to where she was doing the work, and when she saw me, a huge smile light up her face, but she still turned her back towards me. I was unperturbed because I needed to find out exactly what was going on as it was the least I deserved, and I wondered why she had dramatically changed her mind. Cheryl maintained that she couldn't get involved, but her answers we're not making any sense.

Questioning her further, Cheryl reiterated the fact that she was scared for the future. After listening, I explained that I too was afraid of the future, but sometimes we have to be brave and take a chance. I realised that Cheryl understood and agreed with me that we should take it slow to see how it would end up.

Several weeks had passed since had a heartfelt conversation at her home in Kritsa, and we got along really well. So much so that Cheryl asked if I would like to move in with her. After much thought, I agreed, as not only could we build our relationship, but it also served a purpose because she was also struggling to pay rent by herself.

Even though Amanda and I were sharing the costs of my flat, I found out that she had a friend that needed to move out of her apartment.

So, through mutual agreement, we transferred the rental agreement into Amanda and her friend's name. After we agreed with the terms on my remaining furniture, I left with my few remaining belongings and moved in with Cheryl.

Moving in with Cheryl was amazing, she had explained, that the house was haunted, as we are both spiritualists, I relished the thought of sharing a property with a spirit. Although, it would take a while for me to experience any spirit activity. We had been living together for nearly three months before I finally encountered the spirit that was sharing the home.

We'd just finished our evening meal, and I was about to go upstairs to watch a film, while Cheryl was staying in the kitchen to finish off her online business work. At the foot of the stairs, I heard heavy breathing and footsteps on the stairs. Looking around at Cheryl and we both smiled. She explained that it was only the start of it!

Later on, I would hear and see the spirits that dwelled there. As I went to relax on the sofa to watch the film, I felt a hand stroke the top of my head.

I knew that Cheryl was downstairs in the kitchen, and besides, I would have heard her walking up the stairs. Unperturbed, I continued to watch the film. A few moments later, I could hear a Greek voice.

Also, my computer chair moved several feet by an unseen hand. It was followed by laughter and another Greek voice. I will never forget the words, as the spirit was welcoming me into their home.

I was somewhat intrigued, and had no fear nor was I scared of the spirit, and spoke to them in Greek, thanking them for allowing us to share their home. A few moments later, Cheryl came to join me. As we snuggled together and dimmed the lights, we saw an apparition walking from the balcony, across the lounge floor, disappearing on the other side. Neither of us was worried about this, and a few days later, we held our séance!

Suffice to say that we contacted the spirit that shared our home. His name in life was Georgiou, and from then, he made himself more at home, which never bothered us, whenever he was present, the cats could sense his spirit and would hiss.

Although not a nuisance to us, sometimes when our friends were around, they were always afraid when a chair or ornament moved, which shows that Georgiou was present. Although, we would shrug it off, and tell the spirit to come back later, which he did with a laugh. For us, he was welcome, as it was once his earthly home, besides we got used to it.

Life was on the up for Cheryl and me, I even received a phone call from Mike Kilner, whom I had worked for before. We arranged to meet at a coffee shop in town to discuss the work that he had lined up. Mike had kicked Chris into touch, as he was becoming greedy, and wanted 400 euros a week, as he thought that he was a fantastic builder.

In my opinion, Chris wasn't a builder at all and was much like the rest of the ex-pats, who went to live in Crete, claiming to be something that they weren't. Also, Brian, who had worked for Mike, decided to go and work for another so-called builder, called Steve Bick.

As we sat there over coffee, I explained to Mike that would be happy to work alongside him, on the premise that he allows me to use my experience because Mike had no building knowledge whatsoever. His expertise was and came from a frozen desert background in a factory. Mike agreed, and after agreeing with the personal terms, we shook hands, and we would be starting after the weekend. Overjoyed I'd managed to find work; I went to tell Cheryl.

When I told her it was with Mike, she was taken aback, as it appeared that she and Mike shared some bad blood, but she wouldn't interfere with my working with him. After all, the money would come in handy. Mike had a massive renovation project lined up. I was to be the main builder, and he would employ cheap labour amongst the Asian community who congregated daily in town looking for work.

On the site, we examined the plans and what we need to do. Mike would disappear and do the running around to obtain the materials required for the job. I was okay with that, as I could now show off my building skills, and meant that I could be left alone, with the labourers to get on with it.

Mike would turn up around lunchtime, where he had bought us all sandwiches or gyros.

As the project progressed, Mike continued to stay out of the way and would go off to do deals, on other projects and organise tradespeople for jobs that were too big for me, and the labourers to do.

However, I was overall in charge and used my skills for the outcome of the work required.

As the job was near completion, Mike and I went to look at another renovation project, as he required my input of how we should proceed. It was a massive undertaking and would require several other trades, of which he would contract from the Greek builders in the area. After discussing with the client as to what they needed, Mike made a deal and set a date to start, soon after we completed the previous renovation.

With work going well, Cheryl and I socialised more. Mum invited us over for dinner one evening, not only to check Cheryl out but to tell us about a new job that she had been offered after Manolis from Friends bar put her name forward after he'd let her go as his cleaner to save money.

The job was to clean a house which was just past Istron, in a place called Istron Bay.

It was a three-bedroom home and was owned by Philip, who originally came from Crete, but had moved away in his early twenties to live and make a new life in America.

The day after our meal with mum, she invited me to come and look at the property, as Philip required some maintenance done, and mum had sung my praises to her new employer.

The place was huge with two steel security gate at the entrance from the main road. These led to a long steep driveway opening up at the top, allowing at least eight cars to park in front of the house. Gardens surrounded the house, and at least another acre of a wild garden to the rear.

It boasted a roof terrace with amazing views of the surrounding area, and one could see for miles in all directions. With a vast lounge area and a dining room with a large kitchen, which led onto the three large bedrooms, and a fair-sized bathroom.

The work which Philip required was putting suppressing membrane around the beautiful plants in the garden and then cover them with decorative stones. I told mum that I would be interested in the work.

I met Philip at the property when he arrived for a two-week stay to visit friends and family. He was a very slight man in stature, but a nice person in general. He arranged for the delivery of stone chippings, and we agreed on a price for the work. After he had ordered the stones, we sat in front of the garden overlooking the remarkable views and talked over a nice cold beer. After two hours, I left and would see him the morning around 9 am to get cracking with the work.

When I got home, I spoke to Cheryl about the beautiful property and suggested when she had time, to come and see it for herself. The next day, I arrived on time to start the work, just as the delivery had dropped off the decorative aggregate and the membrane for the work. I had a quick cup of coffee, and a small chat with Philip, before getting on with the job. Philip helped me to lay the membrane before shooting off to visit his family. He gave me free rein of his home to use the facilities and help myself to some food and beer if I wish to.

The work was hard, as I had barrels of aggregate to shift onto the membrane, before levelling it off. The results were fantastic, as it set off the garden area.

By the time Philip returned from visiting his family, I had completed the work and was putting away the tools. He was very impressed with the result and amazed at how quickly I had done it! Phillip paid my money and invited Chery and me out for evening meal at the Istron taverna. We all had a great time, and we exchanged details for further work that he wanted me to do. Little did we know that in a few weeks, he would offer us to live in the property.

A few weeks after Philip had gone home, Cheryl received a phone call from the landlords. They were coming over for a holiday and would discuss the rent on the property. We arranged to meet them at the Commotions bar for a drink. I disliked them, as they were loud, garish Manchurians. Although Cheryl had spent a lot of money on doing up the garden and the house itself, they wanted to increase the rent by 150 euro. The initial contract was for Cheryls and a former partner, and she hasn't informed them about me staying at the property which they thought was in breach of the contract. We somewhat annoyed about this, as I had also done a lot of work on the house decoration wise.

Cheryl explained to them that it would be relatively easy to change the contract, and the 150 euro increase was way over the top for the size of the house. It was also against the law to do so, bearing in mind that the rent was already 380 euro. The landlord was adamant, but I told them that they didn't live there and had no idea what they were talking about, but both of them thought that I had nothing to do with it, and I should butt out of the conversation, as in their own words, 'they wanted to talk to the organ grinder, not the monkey!'

Upon hearing these words, I hit the roof and asked not to disrespect me in a and my new partner public place. I told them in no uncertain terms, 'to go back to Manchester, and crawl under the stone or which they come from.' The woman's husband, a short little bastard, tried to square up to me and insisted that I apologised to his wife, but I was having none of it.

Cheryl was trying to keep the peace, but I was angry, and I knocked him to the ground before Cheryl pulled me away. Of course, this caused problems, as they wanted us out of the house with immediate effect. I told them they could have the place, and we would be leaving in a few days.

After the argument, I spoke to Philip on the phone and explained our situation. It was then that he offered his property up for rent. I took Cheryl up to see the property, and she fell in love with it, after speaking to Phillip over Skype call, we made a deal on the rent of 350 euro per month.

I arranged to borrow Mike's van for the move and got a couple of friends to help me to do so. However, my final act on our old place was this; I changed the locks on the front and back door, including the windows and doors. Instead of giving them the new keys, I handed back the original ones and threw away the new keys. I later heard that cost them a fortune, to have every lock drilled out and replaced!

As soon as we moved into our new home, we took steps to make it our own. Both of us started with painting the walls, and Cheryl added her own unique style of paint effects, which made the rooms glow as if the sun was permanently on display inside. The kitchen, although functional, was a lot to be desired. It was a mish-mash of poorly fitted worktops and ceramic tiles which had seen better days. The units had pretty good doors on them, and we left it. I replaced the hideous worktops, with some gloss black new ones that I bought off Mike for a reasonable price. As we had bought an oven and ceramic hob, I purchased an oven housing and matched the colour to blend in.

I fitted the worktops with invisible joints, as I had several meters left, I decided to make a feature, out of the marble half-circle plinth that was in situ along the sidewall. I took a template of the plinth, and skilfully cut out the worktop with my router, so that it would slide easily over the bevelled edge of the marble, which in effect, incorporated the top and marble surface into one. After all the work surfaces with fitted, the next job was to tile the splash back areas.

We decided on a beige tile, that resembled individual four by four-centimetre squares tiles. Above the cooker, I fitted a decorative tile, which was black, and spelt in Greek the words, M α γ ε ι ρ ε ύ ο .. μ ε , τ ρ ώ μ ε , α π ο λ α μ β ά ν ο .. μ ε (cook, eat, and enjoy.) I also added a few more essential electric sockets over the centrepiece, with matching cupboard unit's underneath. Lastly, I fitted an extractor hood, and with Cheryl's decorative touch, our home was now complete.

After we finished our handy work, we settled in for a lovely cosy evening, with a bottle of wine and a nice home-cooked meal. As we were preparing to sit down at the massive glass dining table, the light started to flicker on and off, but thought nothing of it, as this was something we were used to, as the Cretan electric is something to be desired.

However, this was more than just flickering, as the switches would switch themselves on and off. Knowing that there weren't any electrical faults with the system, we laughed it off, even suggesting that Georgiou our spirit friend from our previous home, had also packed his bags and moved in with us!

But joking apart, as the evening went on, we noticed, what can only be described as a mist, engulfing the outside of the house. We went outside to investigate. Walking through the fog, we realised that it was localised near the house. Everything else appeared normal.

Instinctively, we knew that the area was a haven for spirits because the cats were hissing at the unseen guests. As we sat on the balcony, with the sun going down, and with minimal light pollution, we could now see it in all its glory.

The mist had gaps in-between, and can only be described as upright, and not mist-like as it wasn't swirling, nor did it leave any water droplets on anything it contacted. Cheryl and I were excited that these spirit beings had chosen us to grace themselves. What was more intriguing, was the mist would disappear into the exposed rockface from behind the house, and always in the same area!

After our exciting evening with our spirit friends, we headed off to bed for a much-needed sleep. However, the fun didn't stop there, as we were settling down to sleep, we felt the bed depress in areas as if somebody was sitting on it. We could see through the moonlight entering the shutter doors at the end of the bed, there was an indentation, where you could imagine somebody sitting on the top of the mattress, which returned to normal when the spirit left.

Although it was for a moment, it was an exciting moment all the same.

Over the next few weeks, we settled nicely into our new surroundings. I had a lot of work with Mike, and Cheryl was doing well in her online business and her regular hairdressing clients. In between times, Cheryl would tend to the beautiful garden, and add more interesting plants and old ceramic pot, to add to the ambience of the garden. She would also add more artistic touches to her paint effects and painted poppy flowers in various parts of the home.

One evening after I arrived home, we received a Skype call from Philip, who wanted to find out how we were settling in. We told him about the spiritual things that had been going on in the home. As soon as we had explained what happened, he smiled and confirmed it. His family had also experienced the same phenomenon when they had visited whilst on holiday. He further explained the history of the land on the house.

His father spent several years trying to purchase the land from the Greek government but had come across a lot of red tapes, as the land was once an ancient burial ground. Before he could purchase the land, he had to go through a lot of archaeological inspections and get the all-clear to build the property. It took Phillip fifteen years to get the appropriate paperwork to do so. Upon hearing his explanation, we now understood the reason the spirit had ingratiated our lives.

After being in the house for just over a month, Cheryl heard that her adoptive mother had passed away, and she would be returning to the UK to attend the funeral. Before she left, we had spoken about getting a dog, and she wanted me to look out for one. Her explicit instructions were a medium dog of a retriever type. My first thought was to speak to Joan the co-owner of Commotions bar and who has a dog sanctuary.

Although she didn't have dogs of the description that Cheryl had wanted, she did put me in touch with another helper who had some new dogs she was fostering before they found permanent homes in Holland and Germany. I decided to go and see the available dogs. They were all beautiful animals, but one stood out from the rest. The dog was a female and was tiny in comparison with the rest of them. She almost looked fox-like with beautiful honey-coloured fur and attractive fox-like facial features, complete with a bushy tail.

Best of all, to get noticed more than the others who were towering above her, she would stand on her hind legs, and do what I could only describe as 'look at me' pose.'

I fell in love with the dog, as she had a fighting spirit and a boisterous manner about her. Of course, I had the unenviable task of trying to convince Cheryl, but for me, she was the one.

As soon as I got home, I rang Cheryl to explain that I had found a potential dog. I also explained that although it wasn't her exact requirements, I still felt strongly that she would fall in love as much as I did.

Two days later, Cheryl arrived back home; I went to pick her up from the airport. She was intrigued about the dog and asked when she could come along to look for herself. I contacted Joan on route home if it could be arranged.

Although it was short notice, it was confirmed that we could go and see the dog, as soon as we arrived back in the area.

As she had done so for me, the little dog I had fallen in love with, put on her party piece, which I'm happy to say melted Cheryl's heart, and we both knew that we would be leaving with her.

We named her Meli, which is the Greek word for honey. She had a fantastic character, at first, the cats were wary, she was soon put in her place, and would be at the bottom of the pecking order.

Both of us loved little Meli; she gave us a lot of joy. I spent hours with her, walking her in the same areas I used to do with Socks and Rascal. Due to the amount of time that I spent with her, she was daddy's girl. Being so small as she was, I would cradle her in one of my arms as if she was a baby. After all, she was only six months old at the time, and would fit in just past my wrist, and would fall asleep as soon as I tickled her belly.

With Meli and the cats in our lives, myself and Cheryl we're having a wonderful time. It was fast approaching Christmas 2010, and we invited mum, Robin and my old next-door neighbour Dawn for Christmas dinner. We had bought a full set of highbacked dining table chairs. Although they were made from leather, Cheryl's artistic nature took over, and she made some fine covers for chairs. She excelled in decorating the dining table, which looked terrific and ready for our guests. Cheryl was an excellent cook, but it was down to me to do all the cooking, and I have to say, it couldn't have gone any better.

Christmas morning arrived, and we exchanged presents. Cheryl bought me a beautiful watch from the UK and some nice new clothes. I purchased a lovely necklace with her favourite precious stone of emerald, along with some more artist materials, and 100 euro for her to spend on whatever she wished.

We also made a fuss of the animals, and every one of them had their own Christmas present, which we wrapped. It was amazing, to watch them rip open the paper to get at the treats inside, especially Meli, who as you would expect for her age, was just like a child, having their first Christmas. We had arranged to meet Robin, mum and Dawn for a Christmas celebratory drink at Friends bar, before them coming on to our home for the Christmas meal. It was a beautiful day with fun and frivolity for all.

On Boxing Day, we had also invited some of the ex-pat community to come and view our home, and enjoy some Christmas drinks and food. We were a little bit disappointed, that only four out of the twelve guests invited turned up, which included Cheryl's best friends Dave and Denny. However, just like Christmas Day, we all had a great time, and a lot of drink and food went down a treat with the guests and ourselves.

With Christmas now over, it was fast approaching New Year. Commotions bar where we have the usual New Year's Eve party, and myself, Cheryl, mum and Robin went along for the New Year's celebrations. As the clock struck midnight, we looked forward to the future and reflected on the past year and achievements.

It was now January 2011, and it was surprisingly warm. I had decided to propose to Cheryl at a beach party held in March. I knew her favourite precious stone was emerald. I had seen a beautiful engagement ring in the jeweller's shop in town and arranged for him to change the diamond for an emerald. I'd been working my backside off with Mike, to pay for the ring. I paid it off three days before the gig on the beach.

Brian's band 'bad language' were asked to perform. I had already spoken to him about the engagement, and when they finished the first session, he would announce it. Cheryl's friends and my friends were in attendance, including mum and Robin. I was as nervous as hell; of course, Cheryl had no idea what I was about to do. Before the break, Brian as promised handed over the mic, I took a deep breath and asked Cheryl to join me on stage. Without any hesitation, and in front of at least fifty guests, I went down on one knee and proposed. At first, Cheryl ran to hide, but within seconds she came back and gave me the answer, which was yes. With her answer, the party hit the high notes, and went into full swing, as it had not only turned out to be a beach party, but it was now a celebration!

As the night ended mum and Robin left to go home, the few stragglers around were sitting there quietly enjoying the rest of their drinks. I went to the toilet, and in the short time I had been away, there was an almighty argument between Cheryl and the local thug builder Steve Bick's wife. I wanted to find out what was going on, but there was a lot of commotion going on around me. It was then that I saw Steve, and his cousin Mark, holding a friend of mine covered in blood.

Firstly, I diffused the situation between Cheryl and Steve Bick's wife. While she went to calm down, I walked over to Steve and Mark, to ask what the hell they were doing. It transpired that another thug called Johnny had punched my friend with a knuckle duster. I was incensed, as it not only ruined the beach party, it had also destroyed Cheryl's and my night, which should have been a happy moment. I told Steve and Mark to let go of my friend, at first, they ignored my warning, but I persuaded them, by grabbing them both around the throat, and would have gladly ended that thug's life at that time.

I was now on the warpath, as eighteen years' service in the armed forces, I was afraid of nothing and nobody. The next morning, I took my friend back home and went out to exact revenge on those responsible. It was only the intervention of mum and Cheryl that I didn't go and kill somebody. After a few weeks it had all blown over, we even had an apology from Johnny. We also heard from independent witnesses, the whole reason as to why it had happened, as my so-called friend, whom I had not known very long, had been allegedly touching up one of Steve's daughters.

Although the incident had passed, a new problem arose. Mum had been feeling ill, with pains in her stomach for some time, and kept putting it off seeing the doctor, as she thought it was heartburn. I persuaded her to go to the doctor to get checked out. He referred her to the hospital, where she underwent a series of tests.

I would never forget the day when I heard the test results had come back. I had been doing some private work for Joan from Commotions bar at her dog kennels when mum rang and asked if I could go around to see her. As I was five minutes away from her home, I quickly finished off what I was doing and went around there. Walking through the front door, Robin was sobbing his heart out, and mum was sitting by herself, looking somewhat stressed and anxious. Naturally, I wanted to know what was going on, so I sat on the sofa awaiting the news.

Mum's news devasted me. She told me doctors had diagnosed her with stomach and liver cancer. At first, I thought that I had misheard what she said, and suddenly it hit me, as I realised that she had told me that it was cancer! I was gob-smacked with the news, but mum assured me that she was going to have chemotherapy and was determined to beat it.

I could hardly find the words as to what to say next, and all I could do was get up and give her a loving cuddle. Mum was never one for emotional bonds and insisted that I give Robin the emotional support he needed. After a short while, my thoughts returned to normal, and I could now think clearly. I went to sit on the balcony to have a cigarette, and ring up Cheryl and tell her the news. I stayed at mum's and Robin's for a few hours, talking about how to deal with her devastating prognosis.

She was to have her first treatment of chemotherapy in the next few days after her initial diagnosis. I suggested that I come with her, but she would have none of it, as she didn't want too much of a fuss, and that Robin would go with her.

The day of mum's first chemotherapy treatment; I got there early to see her off, and give her some moral support, although Robin was doing his best to keep mum calm, which wasn't work-ing as she was getting into a state. However, after a long chat with her, we managed to persuade her to keep as calm as possi-ble. At work, Mike was very understanding, as his mother had passed away a few years earlier with the same condition.

Although challenging, I kept a professional head, and con-centrated on the task in hand, with the new renovation we were working on. Throughout the day, my thoughts were with mum and how her treatment was going. Robin had promised that he would keep me posted and rang me as soon as possible. It was late afternoon when Mike and I were packing away, and then

Robin rang to tell me that the first lot of treatment went well, and they were almost home. I arranged to come straight over from work and pop in for a cuppa.

As I got through the door, Robin was making some tea, while mum was tucked up on the sofa watching the TV. I went to sit down and asked how she was feeling, and Robin handed me my drink before setting up a small table next to mum, where he placed some iced water, as that was all she could drink. Although mum was exhausted from the treatment and was feeling nauseous, she explained that she was feeling OK in herself, but deep down, I knew those far from the truth.

She also explained that her second chemo session was going to be two weeks after her first, but was still determined to beat her illness. I could feel her pain and had to choke back my feelings after seeing her so ill. I stayed for a couple of hours before kissing her goodbye and allowing her to rest.

When I arrived home, Meli rushed down the hill and chased my car up to the front of the house. As soon as I opened the car door, she jumped up at me, just like a child missing its father. As usual, she would kiss me all over licking my face. Cheryl was sitting on the balcony soaking up the beautiful sunshine.

I put Meli on the floor and smiled at Cheryl, and then I sat beside her to discuss my day with Meli by my side. We spoke about mum's treatment, and my concerns about how it would affect her, not only physically, but emotionally.

Cheryl was a somewhat calming influence and understood what I was going through and kept me calm. We talked throughout the evening, which helped me immensely, as I could clear my head and get on without too much concern. Well, that was what I thought, as my concerns would only be washed away until the next day, where I would go through the same thoughts, but it was always Cheryl that would bring me back again.

The days leading up to mum's next bout of chemo was tough on all of us. Mum had become somewhat abrupt, which we put down to fear, medication, and chemicals they were fighting her disease. All of us were in the firing line of her tongue lashing, especially poor Robin, who had been in the firing line all day. Whereas Cheryl and I only had to deal with it for a few hours at most. Sometimes, when I would go around, mum would let me have it verbally, for what appeared to be no reason at all. Of course, we had to make allowances, as we knew that she was full of anger and resentment, and always had a fear of dying.

Although she was going through the mill, I couldn't help myself but argue back and tell her straight that we were there to support her, and didn't deserve what we were getting. After a while, she started to understand, and her verbal attacks became less frequent. Finally, the dreaded day arrived, and mum would be going in for her second course of treatment. As before I went around her house to add my moral support. When I arrived, Robin, who had been bearing the brunt of her verbal triad, was getting somewhat annoyed and snapping at her. I remained calm and diffused the situation before it got out of hand. I helped her down the stairs to the ground floor and helped her to operate Jackie's old scooter.

Mum was a nervous wreck, all the while I was calmly telling her that she would be alright, we would work together to get her through the worst times. As we got to their car, mum was panicking and asked Robin if he had remembered to bring some ice cubes with him, as this was the only liquid she could bear to touch her lips. Robin snapped back at her, and that he had bought the 'bloody ice'. Again, I wanted to keep the situation calm, and helped mum into her seat, handing her the ice to calm her down.

I also spoke to Robin, and although he apologised, I could see he was under immense strain. However, things calmed down when Robin drove her to the hospital. Just like her first chemo session, I continued working trying to put it out of my mind. And I would be getting constant updates from Robin. Mum was kept in overnight, as she had a high dose of chemo, and was too poorly to return home. Although Robin stayed for most of the evening, when she was comfortable, he came home for some respite, and we invited him around, so at least he could get something to eat, and recharge his batteries.

The next day he picked mum up from the hospital, and she was still under the influence of the powerful drugs. He called me en route and asked if I could help him when he arrived back home. Unfortunately, neither myself nor Cheryl was available, although I did manage to speak to some of mum's closest friends so that they could at least help with the heavy burden.

After I finished my work, I went around where mum was sleeping soundly and had been like that, since she arrived home that very morning. Mum's friends were still there, and we talked about how we could all chip in to take the pressure off me and of course, Robin, who was near to the end of his tether. We formulated a plan, where we would work a type of rota to be there when mum most needed us.

One evening, I was around their house, and there was no real improvement with mum's condition, as she would spend most of her time asleep. Robin and I couldn't put it off any longer and discussed the worst-case scenario. I felt it was the right time to notify the rest of my family, to arrange for them to come over as soon as possible.

I'd notified my oldest brother Peter when mum first became ill, but due to the history between her and my two sisters, I hadn't informed them straight away, which was partially through mum's wishes, and the fact that I didn't want to cause any alarm, which was something that I did regret at the time

By the time my brother Peter arranged for a flight to come over, mum had been admitted to hospital again. Although she was conscious, we knew that it wouldn't be long because the chemotherapy had been too toxic for her. Peter stayed for two days before going back home, as he had a prior arrangement for a new job, which pissed me off at the time. I felt that family was more important than a bloody job.

The same day that my brother flew home, I had been at the hospital with Robin all day. We had also hired a private nurse who would take over, so Robin and I could at least go home and rest, albeit for a few hours. On my way back home, Cheryl rang to meet up at Friends bar, and she must have felt that I needed some relaxation time. Not only have I been working, but I'd been back and forth to the hospital every day, for several weeks. Although I was reluctant, it was a relief to enjoy a drink with Cheryl.

While we were there, Johnny, who punched my so-called friend in the face with a knuckle duster, and his friend Jordan was playing pool.

When they finished, Cheryl invited them to keep us company. I had forgiven them for what happened, I was a bit reluctant to have them as drinking partners, but Cheryl persuaded me to allow them to come back to our home, as it would be nice to talk to someone different.

As the evening progressed and the drinks flowed, we did have a good time. Johnny fell asleep, while Jordon, unbeknown to myself or Cheryl, had found her hairdressers clippers, and thought it would be a good idea to shave off Johnny's eyebrows. Cheryl and I didn't know because we were in the kitchen at It was when we heard Jordan laugh out loud that we realised what he had done. When we returned, he had not only shaved off Johnny's eyebrows but had shaved part of his head. We were mortified by his behaviour which was due to drinking. We did have a bit of a laugh at poor Johnny's expense.

Through the commotion Johnny woke up, I walked over to where he was sitting to apologise. As I went to explain, he stood up suddenly, without warning and punched me in the face. I stumbled back and managed to stay on my feet. But my mouth filled with blood, Johnny had split open an old wound on my lip, I'd received whilst in Iraq which had detached itself from the other side. Looking at him square in the eyes, I spat out the blood.

Johnny looked shocked because he could not knock me over, and I didn't flinch. He sat down again, where I casually walked up to him, spitting out another load of blood. Although Johnny didn't know it at the time that he had just signed his own death warrant. Now standing over him and never averting my gaze, I told h he had that one for free.

Cheryl was screaming blue murder at both him and Jordan to get out, but remaining calm, I diffused the situation before it got out of hand. Besides, I was already formulating a plan on how to exact revenge at a later date. But for now, I let it rest as I had bigger fish to fry with mum being so poorly.

After it had calmed down, I told Johnny that rather him punching me, he should have laughed it off, and told others who may have laughed it off to cheer up a pal who's mum was laying dying in hospital.

Johnny went to stand up again, I could see in the corner of my eye, that he slipped off his knuckle duster, thinking that I hadn't noticed. He offered his hand to me and apologised, which I accepted.

Before they left, I got Cheryl to shave his head, and make Jordan's attempt to cut his hair, look a bit more respectable. After they left, Cheryl asked me why I didn't kill them there and then. I assured her that by punching me, Johnny had made a mistake, but my mum's health was the priority.

After a sleepless night, my sisters contacted me to let me know when they would be arriving. After their call, I called Robyn to tell him that I was on my way to the hospital, and the girls were coming later on.

As I got to the hospital, he saw the state of my face and ask me what had happened. I took him out onto the balcony and explained what Johnny had done; I didn't want mum to know about it. He shook his head in disbelief before we went back in, so I could say good morning to mum. I sat on the edge of her bed, holding her hand. As soon as mum heard my voice, she opened her eyes, confused, and she looked confused when she saw my face. Mum wanted to know the truth, but I lied.

I told her I had too much to drink and fell over, bashing my face on the pavement. Mum tutted and saying softly,

'Silly boy'.

She asked me to move closer so that she could whisper something to me. I did as asked and she cuddled me, and her words were,

'I love you son, and I don't want any crying or distress.'

Now I ask you how anybody with a heart won't cry hearing their mum saying those words.

Choking back the tears, I reluctantly agreed to mum's message, before kissing her on the cheek, allowing her to go back to sleep again.

Robin and I went back onto the balcony for a smoke, and I left to pick my sisters from the airport.

Robin stayed at the hospital. Mum was drifting in and out of consciousness, and he wanted to stay by her side. When they arrived, I was somewhat shocked to see my cousin Sharon had travelled with them. Although it didn't bother me, they explained that Tina had invited her for moral support. En route back to the hospital, I apologised and explained the reasons I hadn't contacted them earlier about mum which they understood. They asked about my face, and I told them the truth.

When we arrived at the hospital, my sisters were understandably starting to get somewhat emotional. Before they entered mum's ward, I told them what mum said. After a few more tears, they wiped their eyes and took a deep breath before I walked them into mum's bed. I spoke to mum and told her that she had some special visitors who had come to visit her.

By this time, my sisters had stood my mum's bedside holding her hand. Mum opened her eyes, and a beaming smile flashed across her face at seeing her daughters for the first time in about five years. It was as if all the heartache had all were behind them. Sharon, Robin and I left my sister and mum together, and we went downstairs for some fresh air and to stretch our legs.

When we returned upstairs, the hospital had moved another patient in with mum. These were Greek Gypsies, whose family member also had cancer. I tried to speak to them in Greek but found them somewhat unfriendly, and even the nurse thought they were disrespectful for not acknowledging us. My sister sat by mum's bedside, holding her hand as she drifted in and out of consciousness. The other family were getting somewhat rowdy and boisterous, and the doctors warned them of their behaviour because they were disturbing mum and the rest of the hospital staff.

My sister Tina and I went into the corridor to free up some space in the ward. We noticed some of the gipsy's family were talking to one of the doctors who was attending to mum. They were complaining about mum been there. The doctor explained that she had every right to be there, just as they had with their family member. As the doctor was talking to them, he was getting annoyed with their questions. But they were adamant that mum had no right to be there.

All the while, I was translating this to Tina, who was getting somewhat agitated herself. After a time, the doctor came over to talk to both of us about the gipsy family. I told him that I spoke Greek and understood what they were saying. He informed us that they had been warned that if they continued with their protest, they would be moved, or even removed from the hospital. He assured us that mum had more rights to be there than they did.

After he spoke to us, Tina returned to the room, and I walked down the corridor to clear my head. I walked the full length of the balcony towards mums' room. At the far end, and I saw two gipsy men talking outside the room, and my sister Theresa standing nearby. She asked if I was OK, as I was talking to her, one of the men told the other,

'The English bitch shouldn't be here!'

Upon hearing these words, I lost my temper and started to walk towards them, swearing and shouting at them in Greek. I didn't give a care about who I would hurt, as I just wanted to beat the living crap out of them. They started to quiver and told me that they wanted no trouble. Had it not been for my sister Theresa's intervention that stopped me from throwing them both over the balcony.

The doctor who had spoken to them and other members of staff heard the commotion. My sisters were in tears, as the disrespectful gipsy were treating our mother in that way. I was incensed, as were the hospital workers, especially the doctor. My cousin Sharon took me out of the equation, as I was ready to kill somebody. As we were leaving, I heard the doctor tell them, that the police would now be called, and they will be removed from the hospital, and that their relative would be placed in a different ward, and would only be allowed, one visitor.

As Sharon and I were walking down the stairs, the police arrived. Sharon and I went for a long walk, where we talked about anything and everything, including Jackie and my life as it stood, at that time. When we returned, the situation was calmer, and the hospital had transferred the two dear old Greek women into the ward with mum. The Greek nurse explained to them what had been going on with the Gypsies, they were disgusted and were very embarrassed, but I reassured them that they were not to blame, as they couldn't be held responsible for a few un-educated individuals.

The rest of the afternoon was more tranquil, and we became friendly with the two old ladies, who were named Maria and Mary. As time went by, mum was now in a deep coma, and all the hospital could do, was to make her comfortable, and increase her morphine levels. Although it was a sad occasion, I tried to make light of it and turned it from a solemn event into one of joy and laughter.

Looking around at what I could find, I noticed a box of latex gloves in a side room. I took it as an opportunity to raise every-one's spirits, so I stretched one over my head, and walked into the room, flapping my 'wings' and clucking like a chicken! Eve-ryone in the room was in stitches, especially Maria and her friend Mary, who said, 'that is what life should be about, a cele-bration.' Even the hospital staff, thought that my antics were hilarious, including the doctor, who was tending to mum, as did the other patients from the other rooms. As the rest of the even-ing progressed, mums breathing became shallower and more erratic, she was now close to passing.

My sisters and Robin stood close to her, talking and holding her hand. While Robin was gently wiping away the saliva from her mouth, Sharon and I stood at the bottom of the bed, we all knew that her time was near. Sharon placed her arm around me for comfort. My sisters and Robin were in tears.

I tried to keep it together and choked back mine. When mum drew her last breath, she was now at peace. My sisters were in pieces, as was Robin. I walked away to fetch the doctor to con-firm that she had died.

We all left the room while they pulled the curtains around, after a few seconds, the doctor reappeared to confirm that mum had died peacefully.

The date was the 29th of April 2011, which was the same day as the Royal wedding. After a few moments, mortuary attend-ants took mum's body away, and we started to pack her few possessions. One of them was a walking stick, I noticed that Ma-ria had an old tree branch which he had used as a walking aid, so I thought it would be a nice gesture to allow her to keep mum's. Maria was delighted. She hugged me and thanked me for such a wonderful gift. Before we all left, both Maria and Mary thanked us all, and that they would always treasure their memories of us. After a lot of hugging and kissing, we left.

My sisters and Sharon went back to their hotel room, while Robin and I drove home independently. I had no idea how I managed to drive home safely, as I was devastated. When I arrived, Cheryl was in bed, and I sat down on the sofa. As usual, Meli came over to give her dad hugs and kisses. Suddenly, Cheryl appeared from the bedroom and came over, holding me tight in her arms, and I let go of my emotions.

The next morning, not only was the mood sombre, but the weather had taken a turn for the worst. The heavens opened, and we had a heavy downpour. Even though it was raining, I needed it to go and clear my head, so I went to the local shops to buy some bread. In the bakery, one of mum's old friends Joan was standing there buying bread for herself.

She asked how mum was doing, and with tears in my eyes, I told her the sad news. You see in Greece when somebody dies, they are buried on the same day as it is the tradition, but as mum had died at night, it wasn't to be. Also, we still had to wait for the death certificate, which would be translated into English. George, Robin's boss, acted as a mediator with the authorities, and on this sad, dreary day, he was at the hospital with Robin to finalise the paperwork.

After buying the bread I went home, knowing that Joan would spread the news of mum's passing. As I was driving, the sun slowly appeared and would show its face again. Back at home, I sat on the balcony and kept reminiscing about the good old days, and how mum had always been there for me. All Cheryl could do was to talk and comfort me, as every so often I would breakdown.

Also, the animals seemed to know that there was something wrong with my demeanour, and wouldn't leave me alone, Meli, wouldn't leave my side, and jumped up onto my lap trying to lick my tears away. After a while, Robin rang us to tell us that he was back on his way with the death certificate, and would be picking up the girls and that he and George had also arranged the funeral.

Several hours passed when my sisters and Sharon arrived at our home. We decided to go to the village and have a coffee at Friends. Walking in, we were greeted by my friend Manolis, who gave his condolences, as did the rest of the patrons. About an hour had passed, we had been talking about mum, and how she had been when we were younger. Although a sad occasion there was a lot of laughter, mixed with a lot of tears. We were soon joined by Robin, who spoke to me privately, telling me that the entire cost of the funeral would be 24,000 euros.

I thought the price was over the top, so we both went to speak to George, who explained the reason it was expensive. Not that I was entirely happy with his explanation, but it had us over a barrel. Neither Robin nor I had that kind of money, the only thing I could do to raise that sort of cash, was to sell most of my expensive building tools. After we told my sisters, they promised to help out and set up an account in the UK so that we would also contact my eldest brother Peter for help. However, I am sad to say, even though I managed to pay for the entire funeral, I have yet to receive a penny from my siblings.

After we met with George, me, my sisters, and Sharon went for a walk through the village. As mum's death had now been officially announced, the printers had posted on the lamp posts and telegraph poles, her eulogy explaining when the funeral would be taking place. My sisters would be staying until after the funeral, planned on the 1st of May 2011.

It was the day of the funeral and what a glorious day it was. The sun was shining; the temperature was fast approaching twenty-eight degrees. We had arranged for mums wake to be at Friends. Cheryl sent me out shopping to buy some food, so she could make a buffet for all who turned up to pay their last respects. When I was out, I got side-tracked by a couple of ex-pats in the village, Scottish John and his wife, Linda.

The thing that annoyed me about these morons, as the first thing that came out of their mouth was,

'Did you watch the Royal wedding on TV!'

I just looked at them gobsmacked, as they had known that mum had died on the day of the wedding. Disgusted by what they had asked me, I told both of them 'to go and fuck themselves, and to stay out of my way.' It was only then that they realised what they had asked and was shocked that they had done so.

I decided to get back to Cheryl, rather than face further confrontation with those morons. As I was walking around to my car, they called out to apologise, but I never looked back. When I arrived home, Cheryl, who was under immense pressure, started an argument for taking my time, as she had a lot to do.

She was snappy at me, which I could understand, as we were all under a lot of strain. She told me to 'piss off, out of her way,' and get ready, while she finished off the buffet. Putting on my black suit and black tie, I went back into the kitchen, where she hugged me and apologised for her unprecedented outburst.

We gathered up the food and placed into the car, ensuring that the animals were safe, we locked up and drove off to Friends to drop off the food, before heading off to the Cemetery. The sun was getting hotter and was blinding my eyes, so I put on my sunglasses. Cheryl remarked how good I looked, and reminded her of the film Men in Black. That lightened the mood slightly on our way to the Cemetery, however, as I pulled into the car park, there were at least 250 ex-pats, and Greek well wishes packed. The crowd truly brought tears to my eyes, so I kept my sunglasses on to shield my sadness. We were all ushered into the small church on site.

Before the ceremony started, I spoke to George that I want my mum buried with the poetry award I won, and also a copy of her eulogy I'd written. He assured me that he had carried out my instructions George said he had carefully rolled it up into a scroll and placed into her hands, with the award placed on her chest.

The service was held in Greek, and although we were not religious, mum had been bought up in a Catholic home when she was younger. Robin and I thought it would be appropriate to say a few words in Greek. With the service over, and now outside into brilliant sunshine to watch the funeral directors carry mum's coffin to its final resting place. The crowd stood at either side of the pathway, leading down to where mum's grave. As like all Greek funerals, it had been built into a sarcophagus with two bars which mum's casket would be placed. As the priest said a few prayers, mum's casket was lowered into place.

Due to the size, and the combination of mum's weight, the boys struggled to lower her in. One of the bearers remarked how heavy it was, which some may see as being disrespectful, but everyone in my family understood, and we chuckled to ourselves.

Finally, mum was laid to rest, before they replaced the concrete blocks on top, to close off the casket. My sisters, Sharon, Cheryl, and Robin, and I placed roses on top of her coffin. With the last concrete slab placed in position, we all headed off to Friends bar for mum's wake.

Manolis who owned the bar had set aside in memory of mum two hundred euro to pay for the drinks. Well-wishers bar crowded into the bar, and the buffet went down well with everyone. I asked Manolis if I could use his microphone to read out mums' eulogy. I had practised several times, and I want to be composed.

My stomach had butterflies; I felt sick and somewhat shaken, as I wanted to do her proud. I took deep breaths and stood in front of two hundred people and recited what I had written for her. Although it went well, it wasn't all unwavering, and I had to choke back tears several times, but at least, I managed to get through it. Incidentally, I also included a copy of mom's eulogy included at the end of this book. The day went without a hitch, although I drank a lot of alcohol, I never felt under its influence as it just didn't seem to affect me.

As the evening progressed, the wake slowly died down, and everybody left to go home, Cheryl suggested that we continued to honour mum at our home. Before leaving, we all thanked Manolis for his kindness and generosity before returning home to continue in private. We partied on until the early hours. The cats had long since disappeared to separate rooms. However, we showered Meli with affection, and she loved every minute of it. We all had one last drink in memory of mum before retiring.

In the morning, I got up and cooked breakfast. My cousin Sharon had overindulged at the funeral, and she declined to eat anything because she was feeling somewhat poorly.

After breakfast, Robin dropped off my sisters and Sharon back at the hotel before going on to his work with George. Cheryl and I had a quiet day alone.

Cheryl suggested that we should move to France, as it was something that she had always wanted to do. I couldn't give her an answer straight away because there were a few loose ends that needed tidying up, including my revenge date with Johnny. I told her I would think about it and would get back to her as soon as possible.

The next day, we went to a restaurant near where my two sisters and cousin were staying, it was here that I produced a mock-up of mums will. My sisters at first, were concerned, as they thought it was the dreaded letter that mum had always threatened them with. My oldest sister Theresa wanted to read the letter, but I suggested that I read it, that way I could soften the blow.

As I got into reading it, their fears turned into laughter, as it was somewhat mocking and jovial, a fitting tribute to mum.

The evening went well, except when we all parted company. Robin had parked his car in Lidl's car park which shut at 9:00 pm. Dawn, my ex-neighbour was also there to pay tribute to my mum. She looked around for something that we could make into a ramp so that we could get out.

Robin was standing there scratching his head, which didn't help the situation. As time went on, the temperature dropped and started to rain, so we all ended up trying to look for something suitable so we could escape. After a long search, we found some old pallets stacked at the side of the building and some old rusty corrugated iron.

Placing them either the side of the curb, allowing Robin to drive over, and get on to the main road, where we were standing. It was a bit of a cock-up, but all's well that ends well, but it didn't stop us from taking the piss out of him and laughed at his mistake.

The following morning, my sisters and my cousin Sharon were leaving to go back to the UK. I picked them up from their hotel and drove them to the airport. As I did so, my middle sister Tina, thought it would be smart to slag off my ex-wife Jackie.

Her remarks annoyed me, and I stopped the car on the hard shoulder on the motorway, and I dragged her out of the vehicle. I wanted to leave her at the side of the road, as she is a nasty, vindictive woman. If it hadn't been for the intervention of my sister Theresa and my cousin Sharon, I would have most certainly left her there to rot. Although I was saddened to see my eldest sister and Sharon go, I couldn't wait to see the back of Tina.

A few days after the girls had returned to the UK, my eldest brother Peter came over with my sister in law, Lynn, to pay his last respects at mums' graveside. It was a chance for me to ask him if he could help contribute to the costs of mum's funeral. When we got back from the cemetery, we went to have some coffee, and I asked him of helping out with the costs of mum's funeral. However, Peter told me that he wasn't in the position to help, explaining that he'd just started the new job he started before mum's funeral.

I was shocked and disgusted at his reply and told him that our sisters had offered to set up a bank account for the cost of the funeral. I knew that he wasn't short of money, as he had an excellent pension from the fire service, and he was also mortgage-free. Lynn's parents had always helped them out, and they gave them a lump sum of £50,000 when her mum died. Lynn's dad had sold his house for £350,000. Peter was unmoved and was still adamant that he was unable to help.

After hearing this news, I spoke to Robin and Cheryl that Peter was unwilling to help out, which pissed them off just as much as I was. They suggested that all three of us have it out with him. I told them that he wouldn't back down as he has always been a greedy man. Instead, I hatched a plan, to at least claw back some money from him. So we invited them out to dinner at the most expensive restaurant in town, where I would shame him into paying the bill for all of us.

At the restaurant, there was me, Cheryl, Robin, Peter and Lynn, I also invited some of my friends, and make it look like a coincidence. The prices on the menu ranged from Thirty to sixty euros per head excluding drinks. I, Cheryl and Robin, all decided that we would order from the sixty euro menu which included lobster, whereas Peter and Lynn chose the less expensive thirty euro menu. I also introduced them to some of my friends. As the restaurant owner had known mum, he suggested that we have a toast in mum's memory, which I felt that it would be appropriate to order bottles of Moet and Chandon champagne.

I also announced to everyone in the restaurant that my very generous brother, Peter, would be footing the bill! His face was a picture, as I had shamed him into agreeing to pay the entire account, which came out at seven hundred and twenty euros.

Although it wasn't exactly any help financially towards mum's funeral, at least it made me feel better, knowing that I had got one over, my greedy despicable brother. Two days later, Peter and Lynn returned to the UK, and that was the last time I have ever seen him or his family. To be quite frank with you, it was good riddance to bad rubbish, as I believed in karma, which came back and bit him in his greedy backside on that night.

Over the next few weeks, things had calmed down and returned to normal. I was back at work and gave Mike his due because he had been paying me even though I have not been working during mum's funeral. Cheryl once again suggested that we moved to France, and we had discussed it many times, and now that mum had gone, there was nothing to hold us back in Crete.

The only thing that kept us there was that I still had a ten thousand euro debt to pay back, and also my revenge date with Johnny. I was working my backside off and had already sold all my expensive tools. I also was working on my revenge plan.

Over weeks, I would seek out and follow Johnny at every opportunity. I lulled him into a false sense of security and assured him that I had forgiven him for punching me in the face, a few days before mum had passed away. It was all a part of my final plan, as the time had to be right. All I knew was that he would feel my wrath when the time came.

The day in question arrived. I had been working with Mike and a new guy Mike had taken on as a labourer, his name was Jim and lived in Crete for over thirty years. He had married a Greek woman and had two kids with her. I spoke to him about Johnny, explaining what had happened. As he had lived in Crete for all of those years, he knew the laws better than I did. He explained that in his experience, I would have no problem with the law.

Armed with that information, after work, I drove to Commotions bar in Istron.

I parked away from the building so that no one would notice me. I spotted his scooter parked outside. It was late afternoon, and there were only four people inside. One of the customers was an ex-pat named John. He and his partner had asked me if I had watched the Royal wedding, and my mum had died that same day.

Nearest the door were two holidaymakers. To the right, very close to the toilet, John was enjoying a beer with a friend. A bit further around was Johnny sitting by himself, while George, the bar owner, was behind the bar setting up for the evening trade. Johnny was busy playing on his phone, which made it easier for me. It was as if I was invisible because nobody looked up and hadn't noticed me walking in. That was my opportunity, as I walked past, everyone was busy talking.

I called out Johnny's name, as he turned to look at me, I caught him a good right hook straight in his nose, which split open knocking him off his chair. Before anybody realised what was going on, I was on top of him, punching his face with all the rage and resentment I had bottled up inside me. George rushed from the bar and pulled me off, and as he did so, Johnny was still exposed, I was still close enough to put the boot in. Now enraged, the red mist well and indeed came over me wanting to kill him.

George used all of his strength to stop me from causing too much damage to Johnny, whose face was a blood-filled mess. I heard him shouting, and that brought me to my senses once again.

Johnny was now cowering in a crumpled heap on the floor. I looked at George and apologised before walking away. Before leaving, I turned around and could see Johnny getting up on his feet, trying to feel in his pocket for the knuckle duster, in case I came at him again. I barked out a warning to him that, 'you know what you did, and if he ever you tried to hit me, or anybody else with a knuckle duster again, then would swear on my mums grave, I would kill you!' With that warning, I left and went home.

As I pulled up outside of our home, Cheryl was sitting on the balcony. She could see that I was enraged and asked what happened. I gave her all of the gory details. Although she was pleased that I had exacted my revenge, she was somewhat concerned about any retribution and insisted that I lock the gate to the entrance of our driveway.

However, her concerns were misplaced, as a couple of days later, I went into Commotions bar to apologise to George for my actions. George was very understanding, and bore no grudges against me, and could see why I had done it. At that point, Steve Bick entered the bar and came up to me to shake my hand and buy me a beer.

What I hadn't realised was that Johnny fell off his stool after my initial attack, the knuckle duster had dropped out of his shorts. George later found it. It also transpired that Johnny's Aunt, who was married to Jimmy, the lead singer of 'bad language' heard about the fight and that George found the knuckle duster.

Upon hearing this news, Jimmy had rung up Johnny's mum who informed her that Johhny had gone to Crete, as he was on the run from Manchester because he had attacked a woman who landed in the hospital with a broken eye socket and jaw and been in a coma for three weeks. Johhny had punched her several times with the knuckle duster because she had shunned him, and his pathetic attempts to bed her.

The only problem was that the victim was married to a notorious drug dealer and had put a price on Johnny's head. Although I don't agree with drug dealing or condone anything to do with drugs or woman beating, I now realised the reasons Johnny had fled the UK.

Steve bought me a drink, and we talked like civilised adults about the incident. He explained that he had nothing but admiration for me. He produced an envelope containing six thousand euros and explained that it was to help with the costs of mum's funeral. At first, I declined his offer, as there was no way I could pay it back. But to my surprise, Steve had given it as a gift. I must admit that I had Steve all wrong over the years I'd lived there, and I thanked him for his unselfish generosity.

Steve also told me that he had warned Johnny after he attacked me that I was the wrong person to brag about punching. He said he had advised Johnny to get out of Crete, and never return. Unrepentant, Johnny ignored this advice, as he thought that he was untouchable, much to his ignorance.

After the Johnny incident, Cheryl and I were welcomed everywhere. Even though Johnny was still on the island, everyone had shunned him. He was still living at mine and Cheryl's previous apartment in Kala Chorio, but was struggling to make ends meet, and would do anything to try and make a little money, only his days were numbered, and he knew it.

One evening, we went to have a drink at Commotions, we sat at the far side of the bar, enjoying the night's entertainment. Suddenly Johnny arrived, he wasn't welcome, even his best friend Jordan kept him at arm's length. I needed to use the toilet as I did so; Johnny entered the bar area to use the loo himself. When he saw me making my way to the toilet, Johnny rushed in and must have had the quickest piss on record, and soon rushed out again and out of the building.

I chuckled to myself. A few days later, I found out that Johnny had left Crete for good. It seemed that justice had been served by myself. People might think, I'm a punch happy person, it's the opposite, as I deplore violence, and will only use it as a last resort against those who deserve it. I have no time whatsoever, in wife beaters, thugs, and those who think that it is acceptable to go around beating kids or causing havoc attacking older people. Woe betide anybody who strikes me or mine, as they will end up badly hurt!

With the money that Steve had given me, I only had four thousand euros to pay back for mum's costs. I needn't had worried, as I had made a deal with Alan, the local drunk to buy my car for six thousand, five hundred euros, which would go through in a few weeks.

Over the next few weeks, Cheryl and I packed our belongings ready for our move to France. We used Nomads, whom I'd used when I first moved over to Crete with Jackie several years earlier.

It was my task to find a suitable place we could settle in France. Cheryl had specific areas where she would like to live, and I set out to find our animals a new home. I found a lovely Gite owned by a British couple who had their organic vineyard, located between Bergerac and Bordeaux, in the area named St Michel de Montaigne. It was two bedroomed with a lounge kitchen combination, a small office, separate from the downstairs bedroom. Next to that, the bathroom, the second bedroom was upstairs in the converted attic space. Although it was attached to the main building, it had a large gated fenced off garden and boasted a large barn with a separate firewood storage area.

We set a date for our departure to France, and we would be transferring the animals and ourselves in Cheryl's small Fiat, which was fitted with a roof box, and would be driving via Italy and the Mont Blanc tunnel.

Chapter Seventeen

Vive La France

26th of October 2012 was the day we were leaving Crete for the last time. We got up early to start preparing for a long journey. The previous day, our furniture had been picked up by Nomads and was now en-route to France. Any furniture or items we weren't taking, we burnt. We don't need for them anymore. While Cheryl was busy cleaning the home, I took out the things that required burning, in an ideal place away from the house.

As I was sitting there stoking the fire, I took some time out to have a cigarette and reflect on the time that I had spent over there. The memories came flooding back. When Jackie and I first moved to Crete, and the amazing times that we had spent in our first apartment, and how excited we first felt when we had moved there. Then into our second apartment below mum, where we first got our beautiful dogs Socks and Rascal, and how we loved them. Finally, to our third apartment, which although had stunning views, it wasn't to be with Jackie.

It also brought back terrible memories of how I had let myself down and tried to end my own life after Jackie had left. To relinquishing Socks and Rascal, to give them a loving home in Holland so that they could have a better chance with loving families. The sad news about mum, and the problems over the years, and what happened with Johnny, Steve and other things that had not gone entirely to plan.

However, somethings had come good—Meeting Cheryl, who was as likeminded as me and was an amazing person. The love of our beautiful cats, and of course, little Meli, finally winning my poetry award. And now, we were embarking on a new adventure, in a beautiful part of France. Although the tears flowed, it was a combination of sadness, and celebration, that we were going on to pastures new.

As I was tending to the fire, Robin turned up with the cash he got from Alan, minus the four thousand euro used to pay off the final settlement for mum's funeral, leaving two thousand, five hundred euro. It seemed to be a pretty good profit, but one last thing had to be done before leaving Crete. Cheryl had arranged with some of her friends for mum's grave to be taken from the concrete box and finished off with the finest marble. Not long after Robin had arrived with the money, the phone call came through that the grave was now complete.

We drove to the graveyard to meet up with Ella and Kristos, who made a marvellous job of plastering the sides and framing the top with white Italian marble.

The centre was a combination of white marble chippings, with a marble plaque scribed with mum's name, which was a fitting tribute. At the head, was a white marble sliding glass-fronted box, inside was a photograph of mum, with two candelabras with lighted candles either side.

The total cost of this work was one thousand, five hundred euro but was worth every penny. I hoped mum was looking down and was proud of what we had all achieved in her memory. I was left alone for a short moment, where I took a few treasured photos. I promised mum that no matter what, I would return one day, and hoped, that she was now at peace, and enjoying being back with dad. Saying goodbye to mum for the last time was difficult, but we still had a lot to do, as our ferry to mainland Greece was a few hours away. I thanked Ella and Kristos for the work they had done before Cheryl and Robin returned home for the final few hours.

I placed the last items in the fire, and as the flames engulf them, so did the last of our memories. While Cheryl was finishing tidying up, Robin and I went through the route plan, which I printed off a few days earlier. The last thing I had to do was to put the cats in their travelling cases. Before that, Cheryl had administered a low dose of animal tranquillizers. As they drifted into sleep, we placed them into the back of Cheryl's car near the tailgate, placing a duvet on top of their carrying cases, to keep them warm while they slept. The final items, we would be taking with us were placed in the roof box, which was locked and secured.

It was now 7:30 pm, we had one last look at our previous home, before switching off the lights, and locking the door. For the last time, we thanked the house for keeping us secure, allowing us some wonderful but brief memories with it. However, the short walk to the car seemed like a long walk to the gallows. My heart was pounding and was both tearful. I harnessed Meli into the passenger seat behind myself before handed the keys to Robin, hugging him goodbye for the last time, although, we would keep in touch over the phone.

Driving down the hill, never looking back to our old home, I got onto the main carriageway, went through Istron on our way to the ferry port at Heraklion.

The drive would take us about an hour, as the ferry would not be leaving Crete until 9:30 pm. Both of us were somewhat tearful as we drove, but we both knew that we were doing the right thing, as we had gone through some traumatic experiences while living in Crete.

Arriving at the terminal, I took Meli out for a walk, until we were called forward to board the ferry that would take us to Piraeus on the mainland. As soon as we were parked, we lifted the cats in their cases, and they were sound asleep. Cheryl took two, where I carried the third and Meli on her leash, over my shoulder, a small overnight bag. Entering the check-in desk, we were handed our tickets and keys for our cabin. Once inside, we opened the pet carriers, allowing the cats, who now awake, to come out to stretch their legs.

Cheryl went for a shower, ensuring that the cats were fed and rehydrated after their journey. I wanted to be on deck, to take Meli for a walk so she could have a toilet break. After cleaning up, I picked her up, and lit a cigarette, looking over the port, just as the ferry moved away from the quayside. Looking back at Heraklion port, as the ship slowly ventured out of the Harbour, leaving Crete for the last time. My heart sank, but there was no turning back. Besides, I had many beautiful memories, which outweighed the sadder moments. With land out of sight, I returned to the cabin for a long-overdue sleep.

As I lay on my bunk, Sophie lay beside me, and fell asleep into my arm, whereas Meli, slept with Cheryl along with Mia and Lily. What seemed to be hours later, I awoke with a start as Cheryl was panicking. Opening my eyes, I could see she was getting dressed and asked her what the problem was, and she informed me that we were coming into port. I jumped up, got dressed, but thought we needed to investigate as to what was going on. Leaving the animals in the room, we walked down the corridor, which was empty except for a few crew members, as all of the passengers still in bed.

It appeared that Cheryl had dreamt; we were about to enter the harbour and thought we only had a short time to get ready and load up the animals prepared to disembark. As soon as she realised it was a false alarm, we laughed, before returning to the cabin, and went to bed. The next morning, we were awoken by an announcement, informing us that the ship was almost at its destination, and all passengers had forty-five minutes before we were due to dock. Cheryl showered first, followed by me and we prepared the animals breakfasts, before heading off to the restaurant for a coffee and bite to eat.

After breakfast, we returned to our cabin to administer the tranquilliser to the cats, gently placing them into the carriers. We gathered our belongings and Meli, ready to head down to the car deck. Now fully loaded, we waited patiently for the crew to instruct us that we could disembark. Now back on dry land, it was 7:00 am. We had several hours to hang around, before heading off to Patras to catch our second ferry, which would take us on to Italy.

Taking Meli for a deserved walk, we both had a coffee and looked around at our surroundings before I consulted the map and driving instructions on how to get to Patras. However, the instructions weren't as straightforward as I had liked, so I asked a taxi driver if he could give me directions. He suggested that we follow him behind his taxi, and I offered him ten euros for his trouble, which he declined.

Now on the road to Patras, we had at least two hours' drive ahead of us. As we were under no pressure, we could at least stop off, and allow the animals to stretch their legs. We arrived at the ferry terminal, where we still had an hour of which to wait before we could board. We ensured that the animals were fed and watered, before we went to a café ourselves, with Meli in tow. After eating, we returned to the car, pulling into the loading lanes, to await further instructions.

Now boarded, we were shown our cabin, where we could allow the cats to roam free. To spoil them, we had bought cans of tuna, which was their favourite. We also spoiled Meli with a chicken dinner. And they were well hydrated after being stuck in their boxes for hours. I took Meli out on the deck, just as the ship was leaving port, the temperature dropped somewhat as we headed out to sea. I treated myself with a coffee, and make a fuss of Meli, before returning to the cabin.

Cheryl and I settled the animals, before refreshing ourselves with a nice hot shower, then heading off to the restaurant for a meal. We noticed the stormy seas were battering the ship, and the crossing was rough. After eating, we returned to the cabin and tried to get as much sleep as we could. With the stormy sea, we found it difficult, and only managed to sleep for two hours, so we decided on a walk. We ventured on deck to get some fresh air, and walking was somewhat tricky, a lot of the other passengers were somewhat seasick, just as myself and Cheryl were. Due to the rough passage, our journey time was extended by an hour.

After a while, the storm died down, and it became more tranquil. We went back to the cabin to see if we could rest some more. We had hardly closed our eyes when announcements came out that we were nearing port, and making our way down to the car deck ready to disembark. The loading Bay doors opened, where we were called forward to drive down the ramp, onto Italian soil. The road from Italy to France is just one straight road. I was determined to drive through the night and cross over the border by morning.

The road was pitch black, and the fog was coming down thick and fast, and I couldn't see a hand in front of my face, let alone the carriageway. I was slowing down, as I was unsure of the roads and visibility was next to zero. I was worried for the safety of us all; my anxiety levels were through the roof. What made it worse was that after refuelling, with the fog and plummeting temperatures, the car started to bunny hop and splutter. At first, I thought that they had put in the wrong fuel. However, the engine management light came on, I assumed that we were going to breakdown, and be stranded in the middle of nowhere, with three cats a dog and of course Cheryl, relying on me to get them there.

I managed to pull the car to a safe area and switched off the engine. I was reading the manual to see what was going on. After consulting the troubleshooting section, I realised the engine management had never experienced cold weather and was trying to rectify itself, by forcing in more fuel, which was backfiring the car. I opened the bonnet and remembered some advice that I had been given, to disconnect the fuel management system, which would rectify the problem.

After disengaging the fuel management, the car was driving sweetly, and we could be on our way without any further disruptions, except the occasional fuel stop, and bathroom breaks. It was now 6:30 am, we had been travelling for over six hours since arriving on Italian soil. Our final stop before going through the Mont Blanc tunnel was a service station that had everything you could think of. We took the animals out for comfort break, before having a coffee and a short break, before heading off through the tunnel.

The tunnel itself had strict speed limits, which had been implemented after a terrible fire had occurred, caused by a severe accident, a few years earlier. I was exhausted from all the driving, but there was no way that I could stop until I got through the other side. Emerging from the tunnel onto the French side was a relief. I planned to find a service station or area where I could at least relax, and have a short sleep before continuing. It was now almost daybreak when I saw a supermarket car park. After letting the animals out for a short break, I sat back in my chair and reclined it, so I could get some sleep, as did Cheryl.

Although we fell asleep quickly, we were awoken an hour later by the sound of dust carts and dustman, collecting rubbish. It was now time for us to continue our journey. I estimated that I had a further six hours of driving ahead of me, we should arrive at our new home by 2:30 pm. We once again set off, and travelled the French motorway network, heading towards our new home. We had known that France was a great one for toll roads, we had come prepared, and had an abundance of coins at our disposal. We'd been travelling for approximately two hours when we came across our first toll road. As you would expect, the traffic was heavy as it was now the beginning of early morning rush hour.

Paying our dues, we continued on our journey, mile after mile of French countryside rolled by and I was getting tired. We stopped for fuel and a welcome break. Even though I was exhausted, I was determined to get there as our journey had taken almost three days.

Now on our last part of the journey, the time was 1:30 pm, we were nearing our exit, concentrating on the road, my tiredness was affecting my rational thought. I asked Cheryl to check driving instructions for our junction towards Saint Michel De

Montaigne. Cheryl was confused and tried to hand me the paperwork. I shouted at her, which wasn't deliberate; I was just frustrated that she thought I could read while travelling at sixty miles an hour.

Unfortunately, due to our bickering, I hadn't noticed that we had missed our turn off. I saw we were now heading towards Montpellier when we should be heading towards South of France instead of South West. The further I drove, the more agitated myself and Cheryl got with each other. I needed to find somewhere to stop and try and get ourselves back on track. A few miles down the road, we came across a service station and parked up. By this time, Cheryl was ranting at me, and I needed to go out from walk to clear my head.

When I returned, I apologised that I made such an error in judgement. I understood why Cheryl was frustrated, as we had the animals, and was worried about their wellbeing. To diffuse the situation, I ventured inside for two coffees and asked somebody who may be able to help. Ordering coffees was no problem, but with limited French, I couldn't explain clearly, which only added to my frustrations. Returning to the car, I handed Cheryl her coffee, stood outside with the map across the bonnet, trying to orientate myself. As I did so, a man approached and spoke in French. I asked if he could speak English, fortunately for us, he was fluent and helped me to understand where I was going.

Cheryl had got out of the car to ask if he knew a hotel or guest house nearby. She had now calmed down and realised that, even though I had been doing my best, I was dead on my feet. He explained that we were just around the corner from a hotel, drawing a rudimentary map of which to get there so that we wouldn't get lost. Before setting off to the hotel, we finished our coffee and a cigarette for a well-earned breather.

The map, although basic, got us to the hotel without any further incident. Cheryl stayed with the animals, while I went to inquire about a room for the night, and that we had animals. The owner of the hotel was very understanding and welcomed us. I returned to the car to tell Cheryl of the good news. We offloaded the cats and Meli and booked ourselves in for the night.

Our room was a welcome sight with a huge King size bed, en-suite bathroom, TV, tea/coffee making facilities. We were surprised at the price, only eighty euro for the two of us, which included breakfast. In the grounds, was a cafeteria where we could have an evening meal. First ensuring the animals were fed and hydrated, Cheryl and I went to the café, where we had soup, a plate of chips and a nice coffee.

After eating, we returned to our room, and we settled in for long comfortable sleep. Of course, no night would be complete without the animals finding a place on the bed next to us. The following day, we awoke refreshed and ready for our next challenge, the last leg of our mammoth journey. It was a beautiful sunny day, and pleasantly warm for the time of year. The priority was to feed and water the animals, and to allow them to stretch their legs and go to the loo. We returned to the hotel room, where we enjoyed a long hot shower before breakfast.

At breakfast, the hotel owner was extremely helpful. She handed me a hand-drawn map to get back on the right road leading to Saint Michel de Montaigne. We paid our bill, giving her an extra thirty euros for all her help and support. We loaded up the cat's, securing Meli in the seat behind me. Before setting off, I rang up our future landlords to explain that would be arriving later on that day. Our unscheduled detour meant we would be on the road for an extra nine hours. However, after a good night sleep, we were more able to reason to keep us going and ensure we were heading in the right direction.

Now back on the motorway, although the start of morning rush hour, we kept a steady pace. Seeing the sign to Bordeaux, we travelled on for a few hours, before taking a break to refuel, and stretch our legs. Both of us were getting excited, as we knew our epic journey would soon be at an end. The hours flew past, and it was now dusk when we saw the exit for Saint Michel. We were now in the region of Aquitaine and the Dordogne.

Travelling through the French countryside surrounded by vineyards, was a joy to behold. We were now about an hour away. It was now pitch black, and the mist had risen and had turned into a thick fog. We were now on single track country roads, and night had well and truly arrived. I knew we were in the area and pulled into a layby to ring up the landlords. I spoke to Liz and told her that I was at a crossroads, describing what I could see. She explained that we should continue straight down for four hundred metres, where she would be standing there shining a torch. Stopping on the track next to her, she told us to go straight ahead, through a gate, where our new home was.

As we pulled up outside our home, Nick and his two sons, Frank and George, welcomed us. Entering our new home, it was warm and inviting, as they'd lit a wood-burning fire. Shortly afterwards, Liz joined us, and after a brief chat they left us alone, so we could bring the animals in, and allow them to settle.

While Cheryl took Mia, Lily, and Sophie to the upstairs bedroom, I went, to offload some essential supplies from the roof box, to make a well-deserved cuppa, and prepare the animals dinner. Our epic journey had taken three days, where I had driven over two thousand miles across Europe.

Although exhausted, I was pleased that we had all arrived safely, albeit later than scheduled. Before settling in for the night, I took Meli for a walk around the village. The thick fog was a new thing for her, and it was a new area for her and cats to explore.

Walking past, the various houses and barns breathing in the crisp fresh French air, was marvellous. At the end of the lane, I could just make out another winery, and couldn't wait to see what the area looked like the following morning.

Returning home, Cheryl came up to me and gave me a big hug. She apologised for putting me under stress, for causing an argument on our journey. She also thanked me for getting us all there safe and sound. I too apologised to her, for reacting the way that I did while we were on the road.

We settled down, and snuggled up on the sofa, to watch some TV and to ring up Robin, to tell him that we had arrived, better late than never. We decided to open up the bottle of red wine that Nick and Liz had given us, from their vineyard. As we drank, we were in awe of the warmth, that was coming from the fire and felt at peace. After finishing off the bottle, we went to bed and fell into a deep trance-like sleep.

The next morning, we awoke to the sound of birdsong. We could see that it was a lovely bright day, through the gap in the curtains. Typically, we would have been woken up by the animals, but they were still sound asleep upstairs. I got up to make some tea, as I entered our living room, I noticed Meli was lying on her back, fast asleep near the fire, which was still glowing red. Without disturbing her, I opened the door, placed a couple of new logs onto the smouldering embers which soon caught, and breathed life into the fire once more.

While I was waiting for the kettle to boil, I took out the last remaining cans of tuna fish and made the animals breakfast. As soon as I opened the first can, they all bounded downstairs so that they could eat. Meli woke up and came to join them, while they ate their breakfast, I finished making the tea, and went back to the bedroom, placing Cheryl's cup on her bedside locker.

After a few moments, we were joined by our menagerie, and had a few precious moments with them, before taking turns with a nice hot shower and dressing. I opened the curtains, and I noticed the fog was lifting and was making way for the sunshine. I took hold of Meli's leash and took her to explore our new surroundings. Walking up the track to the end of the road, I could now see the winery which I saw the previous night. The air was crisp and clean; several other buildings and surrounded us with rows upon row of grapevines.

Walking along the country road, I came across the crossroads, which I had stopped at to ring up Liz. It was beautiful signage, which had been topped off with an effigy of an Angel. As I was admiring the area, one of the locals came out of his property, and we exchanged pleasantries in French. On our walk, we came across free-range geese, wandering off for their breakfast.

Meli had never seen animals like this before, she was somewhat wary, as they were honking, and being somewhat noisy. We turned around and was walking back home, where we encountered other farmyard ducks and chickens. Although neither of us could see them, there was a sound of cows and sheep, from a nearby farm. Turning back down the lane, I saw Nick and Liz with their two sons heading in the direction of our new home.

They were coming around with the paperwork for us. The boys were in their element, as were the cats and Meli who were lapping up the attention from them both. Me, Cheryl, Nick and Liz could now sit around the dining room table and signed the paperwork without any interruptions. They told us where the nearest supermarket was and the local shops. They also invited us around their home that same evening to enjoy dinner with them as a family.

After they left, we went shopping. Apart from a few items that we had bought with us, the cupboards were bare. Ensuring the animals were safe, we set off to the supermarket. After loading up the car with groceries, we walked around town to visit the other stores. We found a French version of B&Q, except for a few small stores, the city was somewhat uninspiring. Arriving home, Meli was over excited to see us again, the cats had moved from the living room and now cosied up on our bed. We put away the groceries before taking Meli out to view the garden and enjoy the French countryside.

Both of us were in awe at the beauty of the area that we had chosen, and we also looked in on Liz and Nick, who invited us both in for a coffee, to show us around their beautiful 100-year-old, French Chateau style farmhouse. Being interested in art and architecture, we were overwhelmed by the beautiful traditional fixtures and fittings, which had been tastefully incorporated with the modern. They explained that Saint-Michel-de-Montaigne, is a commune in the Dordogne department, of Nouvelle-Aquitaine in southwestern France.

The Château de Montaigne, where philosopher Michel de Montaigne lived in the 16th century, was also situated in the commune. Nick had done most of the work himself, with Liz being the artistic one with the decoration. Before moving to France, and living the dream of becoming winemakers, and owning their vineyard, both of them, they had been in the teaching profession. We found them somewhat interesting and charming people.

I informed them I was a builder by trade and inquired if any building work was available, to let me know. Although I had sold the most expensive tools, I still kept my building tools, my slide chop saw, and carpenter tools. We also enquired, if they could arrange delivery of Oak logs for the fire, as the small pile they had given us, wouldn't last long, so they arranged for a minimum order of one ton. After spending an hour with them, we walked the short distance back home.

Later that evening, we once again found ourselves in Nick and Liz company for dinner, along with the two boys. We had a kind of French fondue, where we had various slices of uncooked meat, with an indoor style barbecue on the table, and dipping sauces, French baguettes, and selection of crudity, and finest French cheeses. Also, the evening wouldn't be complete, without a bottle or two of Liz and Nicks organic red wine. Even Frank and George enjoyed the odd glass. We had an enjoyable evening with them and felt truly welcome on our second night in France. Before leaving, we purchased a case of their wine, as it was finest, we had ever tasted.

Returning home, we continued with the evening's entertainment in our nice and warm, relaxed environment. We snuggled up on the sofa and talked, with a blazing fire, surrounded by our loving animals. The next morning, we awoke to another beautiful sunny day. As I was making the tea and preparing the animals food, the phone rang. It was Nomads, informing us that our furniture from Crete would be arriving the next day.

I explained they wouldn't get close to the building, as it was down a country lane, but instead gave them the coordinates of the nearby open space, next to Liz and Nicks home. After the call, we both got ready and went around to see them and inform them that our stuff was arriving the next day, and asked if would they be able to help us. Liz and Nick agreed without hesitation. Nick even emptied his minibus to act as one of the vehicles to transfer the items. We went home and hastily rearranged the furniture, to incorporate our personal belongings. It took most of the day; in the end, we were exhausted and had an early night.

The next day, we were up early, as Nomads would be arriving at 08.30. We were awaiting the call from the Nomads driver.

After breakfast, the call came, and I rushed around to Nick and Liz that it had arrived, we all set off the short distance where the truck was parked. It was all hands on deck, and even the kids lent a hand. With all of us pitching in, we unloaded in record time, all that was left to do was to find homes for it all. For the moment, the best option was to store it all upstairs and then unpack at our leisure.

It was left to me to unpack under Cheryl's guidance, as she was busy with her online business, and was the only breadwinner, as I had yet to find any work. I felt guilty that I was not contributing financially, as I always had a job in the past. However, Cheryl assured me that it was OK, as she had her money, from the sale of her house in Kritsa. Besides, she had every faith in me in finding work in the new year.

Although I wasn't working, I kept myself busy by keeping the house clean, tending to the animals, and making our meals. You could say that I was a Gopher, you know the ones I mean, go for this, and go for that! When the firewood arrived, the weather had changed for the worst, and it was freezing. There were a few snowflakes in the air. Now a ton of firewood may not seem a tremendous amount, but it took me all day to shift it from the front of the house, staking it neatly in the wood storage barn.

Also, there was an area in the kitchen under the stairs, which was an empty space. Cheryl suggested that we went out to purchase a piece of flat-packed furniture to fit. However, after rummaging in the main barn, I found four old cupboard doors in good condition, also two solid Oak barn doors, which had been discarded. I drew a plan to turn these objects into a contemporary sideboard, I even found an old wooden fence post, which I could cut down to make four feet. Cheryl loved the idea, as she was into reclaiming and making furniture, and other household items out of discarded items.

I put my building experience into practice, measuring the size of the timber required, to turn my plan into action. Removing the old rusted handles and hinges off the old doors, I cut off the badly damaged ends cutting them to shape sanding them, ready for final assembly. I was working in the middle barn, the temperature was freezing, as the snow was starting to fall. That didn't deter me inspired me to work harder to keep warm.

Every so often, I would go into the house to have a welcome cup of tea, and a quick bite of a sandwich, or some toast. I finished the sideboard, and waxed it, to bring out the beautiful colour of the Oak grain. All I changed on the whole piece, was the handles, of which I found in my toolbox, these were four wooden turned doorknobs, of which I waxed them to match. When finished, I took Cheryl outside with her eyes closed. I had been working alone and not allowing her to see it until completed. She was over the moon, and couldn't wait to get it into the house, into position under the stairs. Although heavy, it fitted perfectly and finished off an otherwise dull empty area, under the stairs. Our home was now complete, as we added our personal touches, and were in love with the place.

We wanted to see more of historical France, and took in the sights of Bergerac, named after the famous playwright and novelists, Savinien de Cyrano de Bergerac and reportedly to have a big nose. His effigy being part of the town's makeup, and proud history, which stands on the banks of the Dordogne river, a fantastic place, steeped in history, with amazing architecture cafes, shops, and the people. We also visited Bordeaux, of course, famous for its wine. Again, a beautiful place, with so much to see and do.

Our favourite town we often visited was Saint-Émilion. Its history can be dated back to prehistoric times. The town is now a UNESCO World Heritage Site, with fascinating Romanesque churches, and ruins stretching all along steep and narrow streets. The Romans planted vineyards, in what was to become Saint-Émilion, as early as the 2nd century. It was in the 4th century that the Latin poet Ausonius lauded the fruit of the bountiful vine.

Saint Émilion was originally called Ascumbas and was renamed after the monk Émilion, a travelling confessor, who settled in a hermitage, carved into the rock, back in the 8th century. The monks who followed him, started up the commercial wine production, in the area. Due to its immense history and wine culture, Cheryl and I would regularly visit, as the vintners would hold a regular wine tasting, of some of the Grand Cru wines, which are exquisite, when sampled with the free crudité, and fine French cheeses.

We learned a lot about the commune and history of the winemaking. It had been explained, the Grand cru wine ranking, originates from the wine classification of 1855, by order of Emperor Napoleon III. He believed that wines of recognition and long-standing reputations should undergo a specific classification. The literal term Grand cru (good growth), refers to the classification of a vineyard, which is known for maintaining, a consistent reputation year after year, producing quality wines.

While other "cru" terminology for classification, often refers to specific wines and wine estates. Grand Cru status focuses more on the vineyard and the uniqueness of the terroir. The classification began mainly in Bordeaux. However, Burgundy and Alsace also utilize this status classification.

In some regions, the Grand Cru status can represent the best of an entire region, with Premier Cru status, following second. In some areas, this is not always the case.

Although the terminology of Grand cru started in France, cru status also exists in Germany, often referred to as top grapes which produce quality wines. In certain regions, like that of Alsace in France, as in Germany, there are only specific grapes for wines, which can achieve cru or Grand Cru status. Throughout other parts of the world, Grand cru may be found on a label of wine. There may be no official governing body, that is to say, a specific vineyard, estate or grape, can be given this title. Typically, these are wines from a unique single-vineyard, or a wine (sometimes blend), which is traditionally made, as their signature high-end wine, or a wine which has been made, in an exceptional vintage, or limited quantity.

Armed with this knowledge, we became a novice wine buffs. Nevertheless, whenever we went, we always ended up somewhat tipsy. This was especially so, when I was introduced to a 35-year-old aged Cognac, which I am slightly partial, and drink either Hennessey or Courvoisier. However, this stuff made them seem inferior in comparison. Of course, these amazing wines and

Cognac, come with an amazing price, as the average bottle of wine from Saint-Émilion, was forty to fifty euro, with the Cognac topping a cool eighty-five euros. The price didn't deter us, as we treated ourselves, to enjoy a special celebration.

By December 2012, with Christmas fast approaching, or as we learned, the French word is, Joyeux Noël of which we both preferred, as it sounded more festive. I wasn't as fond of Christmas as I once was a kid, through various situations over the years, Cheryl loved the season, and wanted to make it memorable. Both of us went for a walk with Meli, to find suitable natural items to make traditional decorations for the tree and home. There was no shortage of seasonal foliage, such as holly with berries, pine kernels, mistletoe.

Cheryl had an artistic nature. She made some fantastic decorations and enrolled me in to help. Making our decorations, reminded me of how as a family with my siblings, we would spend hours doing the same, albeit with coloured crepe paper. The crowning glory was Cheryl made 'paper chains' out of holly, mistletoe and some of the pine kernels. Her attention to detail was incredible, and this extended to the tree itself. Also, she made some stained-glass hanging ornaments, which was a hobby of hers, and she encouraged me in making them as well, of which I enjoyed.

As we were putting up the decorations, Nick came around to say hello, and to inform us that he and would be going away for Christmas with his family. They would spend it at his parent's house in the UK. He also wanted to ask if I could help him fit a sliding patio door, as he tried to do it before they went away. I saw this as an opportunity to show him my building skills and agreed. I told him I would come later as we were busy right now. When he left, Cheryl asked the reason I didn't go around straight away, I explained that I wanted to ask her advice on how much I should charge, or would she prefer, If I asked for a discount off rent.

Cheryl left it up to me if I wanted to take the money or the discount. If cash, I suggested If I should charge him a minimum of eighty euro. As soon as we had discussed it, I left her to the decorations and went around to see Nick. As I had no money, I wanted to buy Cheryl a Christmas present, so I put it to him that I would help at the cost of eighty euro. Nick nodded his head in agreement, and I will be there the next day at 9:00 am to do the job.

The next morning, I arrived at 8:30 am to start work with Nick fitting the patio doors. Nick planned to offer up the patio doors, where they were to be fitted. The doors had been delivered with a glass, and I suggested it would be easier to remove the glass, as it would be a lot lighter to the position. I also recommended that we removed the old window, take a look at the brickwork to get an understanding of how easy the job would be. All due respect to Nick, I don't know how he'd managed to refurbish any of the buildings, as he had no idea of construction, or building industry protocol.

I showed him how to remove the glass from the frame before putting the doors to one side. Next, we pulled out the old window, which I took the lead, as Nick wanted just to rip it out without protecting the surrounding area. With the window now removed, we offered up the patio doors, while ensuring it was square, Liz had marked around the area of the wall, to be removed. Nick's tools were a lot to be desired, which consisted of a lump hammer, bolster chisel, a saw, and expanding foam. I told him that it would take hours to do it the way he'd planned, so I went back to pick up mine, including a diamond cutting angle grinder for the brickwork, SDS drill for drilling through the frame and brickwork, ready for the fixing bolts to secure the door correctly.

While I was cutting out the brickwork, Nick headed off to the hardware store, to pick up the fixings which I advised him on. By the time he returned, the front brickwork had been removed and was taking apart the wall, on the inside. In effect, I was a professional, and Nick was my apprentice. With the internal wall now gone, we cleared up the area, before offering up the patio door. With the door in position, we ensured it was square and level, before drilling it in.

Cheryl came around as she was walking Meli to see our progress. At this point, Liz had brought out some coffee and sandwiches for us to take a welcome break. While Nick and I had our breakfast, the girls were having a chat before venturing inside, leaving us to carry on with the work. Drilling out the holes in the frame, inserting the bolts either side to secure it, all the while making sure the door was square and level. With the structure connected, we refitted the glass. The last job was fitting the decorative bead with exterior silicon to make it watertight.

Nick and Liz were impressed with how it looked, especially as I had also plastered up the internal reveals. Nick took me to another building on his land, to inquire how much it would cost to finish off the renovations so that they could rent the property, in the new year. I knew this was an opportunity for me to make some money, and to get back to full time working again. After looking at what was required, I told Nick that I would go back home to work out a price for him.

I spoke to Cheryl and told her about the job, asking her advice on whether I should price it up. The options were, get paid cash, or cut a deal, where we didn't pay rent. Weighing it up, we agreed for cash payment, that way, I would have money myself, and the remainder would be put towards the housekeeping. I was working out the cost to be six thousand euro, which would include the entire refurbishment, plastering, carpentry, tiling, fitting a new bathroom, and a modern kitchen.

The electrical work already had the first fix done, that was one job, I wouldn't have to do, as Nick's friend was an electrician. We went around to see Nick and Liz offer them the price. At first, I was concerned they would think the quotation was too high. My fears were unfounded, as they thought the price was reasonable and agreed for the work to be carried out. After shaking hands on the deal, Nick opened a few bottles of wine to toast the occasion.

We had only been in France a short while, not expecting to have any work, until at least March or April the following year. However, I'd secured a contract for the refurbishment of their second home. Cheryl had made some important contacts on her online business, and hairdressing. We could breathe a sigh of relief and look forward to the future in our new home.

The next day, I went with Nick to place an order for materials at the builder's yard. While we were there, we picked up some essential materials and got the project underway before the rest of the items were delivered. Nick would be my labourer and would be working together for the next ten days.

Working together, we became good friends and laughed while carrying on with the work. I taught Nick some plastering skills, and I must say, for a 1st timer, he picked it up, like a duck to water.

While I was working, Cheryl would often go, and enjoy some quality time with Liz, who introduced her to some new clients, who wanted hairdressing to be done. All of us became close friends and were regulars around each other's houses, including the two boys.

In the evenings, to relax, I went back to writing, as I'd been inspired to do so. I had already written a couple of novels while we were living in Crete. Initially, I had been published through an American publisher, neither of them done very well, as the publisher wasn't as renowned, as he liked to make out. I wasn't getting paid any royalties, although I knew that some copies of the titles had been sold. I took back the copyright, and at a later stage, I would republish them myself. But for now, I concentrated on a new title.

I kept getting the word Juden in my head, the German word for Jews. As I sat in front of my computer and wrote the title, the words flowed, and found it difficult to stop, and take a breather. Researching the Holocaust, and the concentration camps, from that period. I renamed the book Juden Arbeit Macht Frei, after the name used above main gates at Auschwitz concentration camp.

Within a month, I had completed the title and sent it off to many potential publishers and literary agents. I had a lot of interest, offering to publish the title, in the guise of vanity publishing where I would have to pay for the publishing. Even some agents, who were willing to take me as a client, wanted me to pay them upfront, to obtain a publishing contract. There was no way I could afford their ridiculous fees, so I pushed ahead, and found a free publishing platform through Amazon, where I self-published the title, without incurring any costs.

23rd of December 2012. It was the day that Nick and Liz we're going back to the UK for Christmas. Over the past few weeks, Nick and I had made significant progress on the renovations. All the materials were now on-site, and I would continue working in their absence over the Christmas period. Before leaving, they handed us the key to their home, and also an extra one thousand euro for any sundries that I may require to continue with the work.

After they left, Cheryl and I went to our Christmas shopping. We noticed the French were out in force and were buying up crates of fresh oysters, to be consumed on Christmas Eve as their tradition. Since our arrival in France, we had noticed that the French people were very family orientated and would spend quality time with their family and friends, unlike the UK.

Christmas is a big issue in France, and on Christmas Eve they will gather together to enjoy a Christmas Eve feast. Also, their lunch breaks were a big affair which could last for around two hours with at least five different courses from the menu. It was a magical time for Cheryl and me, and it reminded us of days gone by in the UK when we were kids during Christmas.

The shops were heaving with Christmas shoppers and the tills were buzzing, and we were in awe of the spectacle I felt the Christmas spirit in the air. Although we would be alone at Christmas, it was a magical day as we celebrated with our own unique family which meant the animals at home all had their own presents.

I had taken two days over the Christmas period to relax with Cheryl, and enjoy the festivities.

Now back at work, I made the house watertight. All I needed to do was fit the kitchen, bathroom and till the areas Nick and Liz had wanted.

Nick's friend Bob turned up to complete the second fix electrics, while he was busy doing his tasks, I had fitted the bathroom and finished the tiling. The week between Christmas and New year went quickly.

By the 31st of December, I finished fitting the kitchen and would return on the 2nd of January 2013 to tile around the splashback, and that would be the last job before Nick and Liz returned on the 4th of January. Cheryl and I had a quiet Christmas together with the animals, and our French neighbours invited us to celebrate the New year with them.

Although not fluent in French, we had acquired enough of the language to join in and celebrate French style. The French know how to throw a party, there was no shortage of food, wine, and of course, no New Year's Eve would be complete without obligatory fireworks heralding the New Year. The celebrations were the icing on the cake for Cheryl and me.

We'd only been in our new home for a couple of months and met some fantastic people, making some good friends in Nick and Liz and their two boys, also now amongst the French community. It was a far cry from when we were living in Crete, where we had few friends, we also had a lot of enemies, and bad memories from Crete, but France was turning out to be an idealistic haven.

4th of January 2013. It was the day that Nick, Liz and the family returned home from the UK. Both of us were busy tidying up the renovations as I had only finished the tiling and grouting the day before. As we were doing so, Nick, Liz and the two boys turned up, and were amazed, at what I had done. After a brief conversation, we were invited around for dinner later on in the evening.

As evening arrived, we went around Nick and Liz, and was welcome into the kitchen dining room area, joined by the two boys at the dining table, the waft of cooking filled the air, and we sat down. As we were waiting, Nick opened a couple of bottles of wine and had a small celebration to usher in the New Year.

When dinner arrived, it was terrific, a traditional roast chicken, all the trimmings. Nick told me he would recommend my services for any future building work, before handing me my final payment. They also inquired if we would join them, and help with the bottling up of their wine, when it was ready, in a few months. We jumped at the chance, as neither of us knew anything about it, and felt it would be of interest. We were in the heart of wine country, as the saying goes, 'when in Rome, do as the Romans do!' For the first time in a long time, Cheryl and I felt more at home in France, than we ever did in Crete. It seemed to be an idyllic lifestyle.

The months flew by, we were both happy in our environment, as were the animals. I hadn't been able to find any other work since I completed the renovation for Nick and Liz. Therefore, I had to contend with ensuring the house was immaculate, carrying out the cooking, shopping, and looking after the animals, while Cheryl was concentrating on her online business. Part of me felt useless, as I wasn't contributing to the household. Cheryl never judged me, as she had faith that I would soon find work.

It was now the beginning of March. I was outside tending the vegetable garden when Nick came around to talk to me. He had put my name forward, to a partial friend of his, named Jerry. Nick warned me that Jerry was a pompous, arrogant arsehole, also the biggest bullshitter in the area. I told Nick that I would be interested but would need to speak to Jerry myself. With that in mind, Nick went back home to arrange a meeting with Jerry, where I could talk to him face to face.

An hour later, Nick came around, with Jerry in tow. He was a short, stumpy, fat, bespectacled man, and I could now see what Nick meant about his personality. I took a dislike to Jerry, but I could ill afford, to turn down the chance of some work. He had brought the architectural plans where I studied them. It was a large project, landscaping and installing a swimming pool, for his client.

After studying the plans, I suggested to Jerry that I should have a look at the project to get a scale and work involved so that I could work out the best price possible. He agreed to take me there, as it was only a twenty-minute drive from where we were.

On route, Jerry was making small talk, questioning my background. I explained that most of my life had been in the building industry, as a self-employed builder, and had eighteen years of military service under my belt. Jerry piped up that he too had been in the military.

I asked him the branch of the service he was, and Jerry told me was a gunner, in the Honourable Artillery company. Trying to impress me with his stories, of how he enjoyed being part of a crew, that was used mostly in ceremonial purposes. I asked if he 'd seen any action with the regiment, which he hadn't.

Even though I had nothing against the regiment when I asked him basic questions, he couldn't answer them. I asked him about his service number. He paused for a moment to try and think; it was then I knew he was talking bullshit! I kept pressing him on his service number, as it is the one thing, that determines your role in the armed forces, and ingrained in your brain. Each time I tried to press him for an answer, he would try and change the subject.

For the rest of the journey, I ignored him, as I felt he was making a mockery of the service. We arrived on site, I went around the back of the property to view the area which required landscaping. As I was standing there, surveying the area, Jerry introduced me to his partner in crime, named Derek, or Del as he preferred to be known.

He was a scruffy looking individual, with unkempt hair, and scraggly beard, with what looked like most his breakfast sticking in it. His hands and fingernails were grubby, and I ignored his gesture of a handshake. I thought Jerry was a big bullshitter, but compared with Derek, he was a mere novice. Both of them tried to teach me how to suck eggs, but neither of them had any building experience at all, and couldn't read the plans were trying to make it up as they went on.

I was having none of it, as they wouldn't be able to pull the wool over my eyes. I spent an hour on the site and got a measure of the area that needed landscaping. I called Jerry to take me back home and told him that I would work out the price, which included travelling to and from the site, with paid lunch breaks.

When he disappeared, I went to speak to Nick, who gave me a heads up. He'd made enquiries whilst I had been with Jerry, and found out, that due to Jerry's obnoxiousness and ignorance, all the builders French or English, refused to work on the project. As a result, he was at risk of defaulting on the contract.

This information meant I could negotiate a better deal, and in effect, run the project professionally, keeping Jerry and Derek out of the picture as much as possible. Their only input would be to purchase the materials required. I contacted Jerry and told him that I wanted one hundred and sixty euro as a day rate. After a brief pause, he had no choice but to agree to my terms. He came around later that evening, and we finalised the deal in front of witnesses, which included Nick, Liz and Cheryl. I also agreed on a start date.

I knew I'd him gripped firmly by the balls, as he had no other choice, solely down to his bloody-mindedness and arrogance, towards building community in the area. That meant that he would have lost the entire contract, and what little reputation he had left with any clients.

The following Monday, I made my way to the site. When I arrived, Jerry and Derek were sitting in the dining room, having breakfast, I opened the patio doors, and walked in ready to start the job. I was surprised that at 8:00 am, alongside the croissants and coffee, both of them had glasses of beer. I noticed, when we were in conversation, that their speech appeared somewhat slurry as if they had been drinking for some considerable time, which made me slightly apprehensive on their ability to carry out any work.

The morning had a chill in the air, and the ground was partially frozen. But the sun was appearing through the clouds, and the area was starting to warm up. After coffee and a cigarette, we made a plan of action to remove the old paving slabs and dismantle the old, dilapidated swimming pool. I went outside to start lifting the slabs, leaving the two of them in the dining room, assuming that they were right behind me ready to start work.

Half an hour passed, and they still hadn't come outside to help. That pissed me off, as I wasn't going to be taken for a ride by two incompetent jokers. I walked back to the house, slid open the patio doors, giving them a piece of my mind. Neither of them recognised what the fuss was about, but I made it abundantly clear that they, as well as myself, were being paid to do a job. Both of them raised their eyebrows and tutted in a way that annoyed me even more, as they were acting like two petulant brats.

They knocked back the contents before casually walking outside. I decided there and then, to keep my eye on them, telling them exactly what was required so that we could make progress. To my surprise, after their earlier indiscretion, they both knuckled down and started working. After a few hours, we had cleared the slabs and begun dismantling of the pool. It was now noon, and we broke off for a well-deserved break. The cold morning made way into a beautiful bright sunny day, and we decided to sit outside for al fresco lunch.

We were making small talk through lunch, which was much to my amusement, as I now had, two of the biggest bullshitter's in stereo, talking codswallop as regards of their past conquests. I thought Jerry's story of his military service was hard to match, but Derek trumped him on that card. He told me he was in the Falklands during the hostilities, and after his service in the army; he joined the Navy, and worked his way up the ranks. He added that within a short space of time, he became a Royal Navy Captain.

I couldn't help but laugh at this, as he was three years younger than me as I was fifteen during the Falklands War, and that would have made him twelve years. Even Jerry was taken aback, all I could do, was take the piss out of both of them. After lunch, we continued dismantling the pool, and by late afternoon, we had cleared the area and marked out the place the building work would start. We went back into the dining room to look at the plans. I pointed the architect had referred to a one-metre in-depth foundation. Both of them assumed it meant surface-mounted foundation and were planning to shutter off the central area of support in timber.

I couldn't believe, they were that stupid and hadn't understood the plans when it was quite clear from the drawing, the foundations had to be dugout, with reinforced concrete poured in the area. After a while, and much explanation, it sunk into their tiny minds, and either hire a mini digger or get somebody else to dig the area for us. Neither of them had a clue of who or where to lease equipment. Both of them were clueless, and I told them I would make inquiries of my own later that evening.

Now back at home, I met up with Nick and told him about how the day went, with Jerry and Derek. We both had a good laugh at their expense before I asked if he knew anybody near the area that either hired plant machinery, or subcontractor. He put me in touch with a father and son team, and I rang to enquire about their services. I spoke with the dad called Bob, and explained the situation, and what the job entailed. I arranged to meet him on site the next day at 8:00 am.

I arrived at the site at ten minutes to eight to await the arrival of Bob and his son. As I walked through the patio door, Jerry and Derek were sitting at the dining table drinking beer. I was unimpressed with this; I made it clear to both of them that it wasn't wise to mix drinking with construction work. They argued that it was only one before work.

As I finished the lecture of the two morons, there was a knock at the front door, and it was Bob and his son whom he introduced as Damian. Bob came from my neck of the Woods, from West London, and he grew up in Shepherds Bush and supported Queens Park Rangers. I felt this was a good omen, instantly liking him and Damien.

I took him outside, showed him the plans, and what we required, and then agreed on the terms. In the meantime, Jerry and Derek were standing at the patio doors talking.

Bob disliked them but was more than happy dealing with me. I asked when they would start the foundations and the new pool area. To my surprise, he had bought a small JCB to start work and would leave Damien to begin digging out the foundation, while he returned home to pick up his dumper truck.

Now ready to crack on with the work, I gave instructions to Jerry and Derek to pick up reinforcement bars, and arrange for the delivery of aggregate, sand, cement and hire a concrete mixer.

This way, it would get them out of my way, for at least an hour, which suited me to the ground. By the time Jerry and Derek had got their act together, Bob had arrived with his dumper truck just as they were leaving.

With his dad back on site, Damian started to fill up the truck with the soil, that he had excavated from the foundations. I could now mark out the areas the architect had drawn up plans for the pump house, outside bathing huts, convex retaining wall, and the swimming pool. By the time I had finished, Bob and Damian had moved the earth, and started digging out the pool area.

As they were doing so, they hit bedrock, which meant that they required their biggest JCB with a hydraulic pick attached.

It was now midday before they set off to pick up more massive plant machinery, we broke for lunch. While enjoying lunch, Jerry and Derek returned. They too had been enjoying a lunch break, and it was a liquid lunch because they stunk to high heaven from booze. I wasn't impressed again because I was concerned over site safety, and wouldn't be able to help in the afternoon, and we exchanged a few words. Bob put his opinion across about the two of them, which didn't go down too well. However, before it got out of hand, the materials arrived and were unloaded by Jerry and Derek.

While the materials were being unloaded, Bob and Damian returned home to collect the bigger JCB to crack up the bedrock. As soon as they brought the materials, I set up the concrete mixer and got Derek to start mixing. While he was doing so, I explained to Jerry that we had to construct a reinforced structure to place in the dugout trench retaining wall foundations. Of course, this was somewhat difficult as we had to bend the bars into a convex shape. As we were cracking on with the foundations, Bob and Damien arrived with the JCB, which they put to good use in the swimming pool area, and the father and son team were like a well-oiled machine. By the end of the day, all five of us had made good progress, which would leave us in good stead for the next day, where construction could at least start.

The next day I arrived on site, surprisingly Jerry and Derek were setting up to start work. It was good to see. However, it was only a short while later that I realised the reason. The client had come over on a surprise visit, and they were running around like blue arse flies. I fired up the concrete mixer, as I did so, the client came out of the house and introduced himself as Paul. We shook hands, at that point, Bob and Damian arrived on-site to continue excavation of the pool area. Before starting work, Paul wanted to have a chat with us. We sat around the dining table, and it was apparent he wasn't in the best of moods. He wanted to know why the project had not progressed far as Jerry and Derek had described.

I assumed he knew the project had only started a few days earlier. However, unbeknown to myself, Bob and Damian, Jerry and Derek had informed him that the work had indeed begun several weeks before. I was shocked to hear this and told him that I met up with Jerry the previous to discuss the possibility of carrying out the work. I also explained that daily on-site, Jerry and Derek had been drinking before they start any work. Bob and Damian backed me up, and we Paul that Jerry and Derek were the liabilities.

Paul turned his attention to both of them, and they denied everything. Paul was an astute person and saw through their pathetic attempts to pass the blame on me, Bob and Damian. Things started to get heated between Jerry and Bob to such a point, that Jerry tried to grab Bob by the throat but Bob being a large man, defended himself and headbutted him. I managed to get in between them before further violence.

After a while, things calmed down, and Paul warned Jerry and Derek to work harder, or he would cancel the contract and hand it over to Bob and I. Jerry, now nursing a broken nose, wasn't too impressed, and insisted that they were more than capable of running the project. Paul demanded that I would now be the site manager, while Jerry and Derek, would organise deliveries of materials to the site when I needed them. After a short while, both Jerry and Derek thought about his proposition and agreed. With everything now sorted, we reluctantly shook hands and got on with the job.

Back at home, I noticed that Cheryl wasn't her usual self. She seemed distant, no matter what I asked her, she would snap my head off.

I stayed out of her way, and retired to the attic room, to do some writing. As soon as I started, she called me downstairs. She was sitting there drinking gin and tonic and looked like she had more than one. I asked her what was going on, and she explained that for a few weeks, she had been looking into moving to another part of France, where she had seen a rental property with an attached small business.

I questioned why she had kept it from me because I had always known that she wanted a small shop to sell her artwork d'art, which she made out of stain glass and scrap pieces of wood. I breathed a sigh of relief, as I had thought that I had upset her. But now, she had come clean, and we could now talk like adults.

She showed me the potential new home and business opportunity, which was in a place named, Saint Junien Les Combe, situated in the Limousin region of France, part of the borough of Bellac. From what I could see, and from the pictures and the area, it was an idyllic position. I suggested that we at least go and view it, as I hated to see her unhappy. Cheryl explained that she had held off telling me because of my work, and didn't want to put a stop to it.

Nevertheless, we arranged to go and view the property and business opportunity at the weekend before discussing our options. Back at work, I just concentrated on the job in hand and kept quiet about our plans. Quite frankly, it had nothing to do with them, and they didn't need to know. Secretly, I was somewhat excited about the prospect, as it meant that if we took up the opportunity, we could work together.

The weekend arrived at last, and we headed off with Meli to view the property and attached business. We were greeted outside the very picturesque commune by the hosts David, and his wife, Vicky. They were charming, and there was a difference in their ages, as David was fifteen years older than his wife. They showed us around our potential new home and business with a dining room, separate living and kitchen areas, three upstairs bedrooms and a large bathroom.

It also had an enclosed separate garden, with a beautiful veranda which overlooked a large paddock. At the bottom of the paddock, was a natural stream, being fed at the left-hand side by a weir. There was an old railway sleeper bridge, crossing the stream, which led up to a wooded area, part of a beautiful hillside. Next to the home, was David and Vicky's, renovated old stone French farmhouse and annexe, with several guest apartments for rent.

To the rear of their property, which blended in with the open paddock, was a guest swimming pool, to the far side was a woodland area, which separated them from the nearby farms. The commune had various other homes, which led up from the main road. Attached to the house, was a storage barn, which in turn, had the small shop, as part of its fabrication. Next was another barn, and right at the end, was a separate closed off area, which housed a chicken coop.

The left-hand side of the buildings was an open turning area for vehicles, and this joined onto a single dirt track, surrounded by wooded areas, and another farm. I had to admit, I was taken by the place myself, and could see the potential of moving from where we were, building a business, which we could both enjoy. After viewing, they invited us in for a coffee with David and Vicky.

They had two beautiful dogs, one older female called Katie, and the younger female, who had been blind from birth, named Poppy. She was very playful, and although she couldn't see, Vicky would look after her. Of course, Meli wanted a piece of the action, so we let her off her lead, all three dogs were playing in the kitchen area, while we sat down and discuss our options. Although we already lived in a beautiful part of France, this was an opportunity we could not miss. After a while, we agreed on terms to take over the tenancy of both the new home and business.

We told them we had to give a month's notice, and they agreed to keep the property open for that time. After we'd struck the deal, we took a nice leisurely drive back home, and we planned on how to tell Nick and Liz. We didn't want to upset them, as they had been exceptionally good to us. Also, a month's notice would give me just enough time to carry out and finish of most of the building work, and make enough money to help out with the costs of moving, and pay for our first month's rent. Although nervous in telling Nick and Liz, after explaining to them, they were very understanding. It would be a sad time for all of us, as we'd become excellent friends.

I cracked on with the job in hand and worked all the daylight hours. I was pleased with the progress. The only thing left was the exterior rendering, which I had entrusted to a couple of Damian's French friends. While I was working, Cheryl has been busy packing up our belongings and arranged for someone to deliver our stuff to our new home. The day arrived, once again, we were on the move. We had loaded up the removal truck in the early hours of the morning, while he was on route, Cheryl and I gave a fond farewell to Nick, Liz and their two boys. We were somewhat tearful about leaving, but we thought of the opportunities that awaited us, which outweighed any doubts that we may have, and it would be another adventure.

When we arrived, David, Vicky and the driver of the removal had almost emptied the van and placed into the storage barn. Our new place was fully furnished, and that meant that most of our items would be kept in storage until we found a place for them to go. Cheryl took the cats into the home to look after them, especially Sophie, who got distressed throughout the journey. A short while later, I had finished offloading the van and joined her in our new home. David and Vicky joined us; I made coffee before we all sat down to recover.

It was then that they told us, the tenant of the shop had decided, rather than close the shop, they wanted to keep it open for themselves. Cheryl and I were somewhat perturbed by this news, as we moved across the country, on the strength, the shop was part and parcel of our new arrangement.

It appeared that the shop was being rented out, by one of their closest friends, who had decided to give up the lease, before we signed the contract, and moved.

At the last hour, they had decided to keep the lease, which put us in an awkward position. We now had no way of making a living, and I had given up the renovation job, which would have bought money in, for at least another month. Cheryl started to get agitated, I was annoyed myself, and intervened before it got out of hand.

I suggested that we share the shop, at least we could make some money. Also, due to the fact, we felt we had been duped into moving, we get a discount on the rent. David and Vicky felt guilty we were in this position, they had no choice, but to accept our conditions, they agreed to reduce the rent by eighty euro a month, and share the shop with their friend, and would be speaking to her, as she put them in an awkward position themselves.

After they had left, we talked about the situation, although we were still fuming, decided to give it a go, and see what the future held for us. For the rest of the day, we relaxed and unwound from the move. Later in the evening, there was a knock on the door, and it was David, Vicky, who was flanked, by their friend Sharon, who had the lease on the shop.

Neither of us was in the mood to be civil, but we decided to listen to her side of the story. David had bought around a bottle of wine, and Sharon had bought some flowers for Cheryl, which was their way of trying to justify the predicament, they landed us in.

We sat around the dining table. Sharon's explanation was, she had been back to the UK for a few weeks and was her intention to give up the shop, as she wasn't sure she was going to return. Neither of us was impressed with her story and gave it to her straight that we had moved from our previous place, on the understanding the shop, was part and parcel of the contract. She informed us that David and Vicky had made her aware of our dilemma and was more than happy to share the shop. She also added, she would be willing, to pay our costs of moving, and reimburse us for the first month's rent.

Cheryl and I went into the other room to discuss the options, upon our return, we agreed as long as it was put in writing by Sharon and signed by David and Vicky.

They all agreed and would return later on in the evening, with a new contract which we would all sign. True to their word, they returned at around 8:00 pm with a few more bottles of wine, some cheese and the new contract, which we read carefully, before putting pen to paper. With that out of the way, we had an enjoyable evening. Any previous misdemeanours had been put to bed.

The next morning it was bright but crisp, the animals were nervous at first, but after a while, they settled down. Cheryl was eager to unpack her artist materials and stained glass to make more stock for the shop. On the other hand, I wanted to explore the beautiful countryside that surrounded us, but no walk would be complete without Meli in tow. We walked through the back door, down a stone staircase, across the paddock, to the other side of the bridge, into the wooded, hilly area.

As we reached the brow of the hill, I noticed there was a football pitch, with two local teams playing and a local gathering of supporters. I stood there momentarily to watch the game and have a cigarette, before continuing the walk in this incredible landscape. We came across a beautiful village about ten minutes from where our new home was. It was a typical French village, and everybody was enjoying the morning, and each one of them responded, with a cheerful 'Bonjour.'

We continued to walk through the countryside, along the road, which flanked either side with farmland, and beautiful wooded areas. Stopping for a rest with Meli, we found a beautiful spot near a ditch, perching on some fallen trees, to admire the area. After our break, we continued with the walk, coming across the dirt track near our home, and took the short cut back. Halfway down the path, we ventured into an open area, surrounded by trees.

The ground was covered in fallen cobnuts, and chestnuts, and started to gather up as many as I could carry. By the time I'd finished, my pockets and jumper were crammed packed, which made me look like I had put on weight. Returning home, I unloaded my bounty onto the kitchen table, much to Cheryl's surprise, who had just set up making stain glass ornaments. As we settled in for the day, Cheryl took a phone call from her son Scott, who wanted to visit for the weekend.

I had never met Scott, but Cheryl had told me all about him, and he was just like his father into bodybuilding, smoking dope, and other drugs. I wasn't happy to have anybody in the house who do drugs. But he was Cheryl's son, and I could hardly refuse.

As the day progressed, the weather changed for the worst, and it began to snow. At first, it was just a few flurries, then blizzard conditions which blanketed the areas.

It was amazing to see the whole area covered, which made it look like Winter Wonderland. The cats weren't keen, but Meli was intrigued, so I took her out with Cheryl, which she enjoyed. By this time, snow was still falling, at least two foot in places. Meli loved it and was jumping into snowdrifts, covered in small snowballs attached to her fur. She thought it was a game, a beautiful sight to behold, much to our amusement. After the walk, we returned home, to a nice roaring fire, and the welcoming hot bowl of homemade soup.

While we had been out, I explained to Cheryl about Scott's impending arrival that I wasn't keen on him doing drugs. Cheryl assured me that she had told him not to bring any over, and if he did, then he could go straight back home again. After our chat, I felt more at ease, and we returned to make some more arty things for the shop.

The snow continued falling for the next few days, and the roads were now impassable. Cheryl was worried, as Scott would be arriving the following day, and would be driving. I understood that she would be concerned about her son, so I suggested that we go to see David and Vicky for a drink. We walked the short distance to their home, as we arrived, they were already entertaining some new guests, who rented out the annexe next door, and they invited us to join them.

The guests introduced themselves as Peter and his wife, Pat. An interesting couple, who were staying short term, as they were in the process of looking at purchasing property nearby. They were planning to retire in a few months. Vicky brought several bottles of wine and fine old cognac. She had made a few canapes, and we sat around the vast dining table and had an exciting evening. Cheryl was still worried about Scott, she calmed down after several drinks, and became more upbeat.

The next morning, we were up early, as she wanted to get the house clean for the arrival of Scott and his friend. The snow had continued to fall throughout the night, and still coming down quite heavily. Due to the weather, the road leading up to the houses had several feet of snow on it.

David told us the main routes were covered in snow. Partly due to the wind that was drifting the snow from the fields around us. Upon hearing this news, Cheryl started to panic about Scott again. She became somewhat snappy and irritable with me, and unlike her, was annoyed with the animals. As a result, they kept a low profile.

After sorting out the house, we sat around the dining table, where Cheryl continued with her online work, and I researched material for my new book.

Sometime later, I suggested continuing making goods for the shop, and even this didn't go down too well. After a while, Cheryl received had a call from Scott, who told her that he and his friend would be with us an hour. Cheryl seemed happier that he was OK; her persona changed and became more friendly. She apologised for her behaviour. I assured her, she had no reason to apologise as it was most understandable to worry about her only child.

An hour later, we heard a car coming up the road. Venturing outside, it was Scott and his friend, who made it safely. Cheryl was delighted and introduced him and his friend to me before we went inside coffee. Over the day and evening, we all got to know each other pretty well. It seemed, my concerns about Scott being involved in drugs were unfounded. They both stayed for two nights before returning home.

After Scott's flying visit, things went back to normal. The snow had started to thaw out and was now getting warmer. Cheryl had made a fantastic display in the shop. Since I had no work, I resumed taking care of the animals and the home. I had felt ashamed of not having any work myself, except for helping out at the shop with Cheryl, by fetching and carrying new stock. I felt like I had gone back to the days of being a gopher, although Cheryl assured me that it was alright.

She suggested that I have a day to myself, and suggested that I pursue my passion for history by visiting the martyred village at Oradour, near Limoges. Taking her up on the idea, I took myself off to this historical site, where 642 men, women, and children were massacred, by the Nazi's in June 1944. As I arrived, there was a T.V crew filming an interview, with the only survivor, Robert Hebras.

Keeping my distance, I waited until they'd gone, before casually walking over to this great man, for his autograph. As we were speaking, I told him about my passion for writing, and inquired, if he would allow me to immortalise his life in a book. Without hesitation, he agreed and told me his version of events, which I finally wrote down titled 'Oradour Villages Des Martyrs'.

Over the coming weeks, things at home remained the same. Still, with no work, I concentrated on keeping house, and being my usual menial self in a guise of a gopher for Cheryl, who was still adamant, that all was well, and to keep doing what I had been doing. However, soon, her attitude towards me changed.

I remembered the day that it all started to fall apart. One Friday morning, Cheryl and I were sitting at the dining table on our laptops, where I was reading a news article from a Labour MP, named Tom Watson. He'd raised questions, at Prime Minister's Question Time in Parliament about the Righton diaries. It coincided with an earlier conversation presented about the notorious paedophile Jimmy Savile, who died in 2011. Jimmy was disgraced after his death for his paedophile tendencies.

Reading through the article, it sent a shiver down my spine, bringing back memories of Righton, all the way back to the 1970s. The author of the report encouraged people who knew Righton, or his associates to contact the author through their website. Reading the article, over and over, at first, I was reluctant to leave my details, as I wanted my past buried. After a lot of soul searching, decided I would put my details on the site, as I thought, living in France no one would bother to contact me.

Furthermore, even if they had done so, I had no faith in the British justice system, and nothing would ever come from it. However, an hour after I had placed my details on the site, my phone rang. To my surprise, it was Tom Watson himself, who was looking into the link between Savile and Righton, and their involvement in the paedophile movement. As I was speaking, Chery looked up from her work and was listening intently.

I agreed for Tom to pass on my details to the Metropolitan police, who were carrying out the investigation. After the call, Cheryl asked why I had decided to give them my details. I explained that I'd already told her what happened, and wanted justice, not only for myself but for any other victims that may come forward. I will never forget what she next said to me.

In her own words, 'that was disgusting.' At first, I thought what she meant was that what happened to me was disgusting, but I was wrong, as she went on to say,

'You allowed it to happen, and you should be disgusted with yourself for letting it happen!'

I was gobsmacked with the answer, as I had never envisaged, Cheryl would ever say those words. I told her I was a kid when the abuse happened, but she was unperturbed.

Choking back the tears, seeing her face with a disgusted look on it, made me realise, that any future that we may have had just been blown out of the water.

After hearing her words, I couldn't contain myself, and the tears started to flow. I asked her why she would believe that I was responsible, as I was a child at the time. She seemed unmoved and reiterated what she had said earlier.

As I sobbed, my phone rang again. It was the Metropolitan police. I composed myself before speaking. I was talking to a sergeant who received my details from Tom Watson—introducing himself as Andy, and he was part of 'The paedophile and Sexual Crimes Unit'. As we were talking, I was still trying to compose myself so that I could answer his questions. All the while, I felt Cheryl's eyes, burning a hole in me. But at that time, I couldn't care, there would be no turning back now, as the truth was long overdue.

While speaking to Andy, I heard a female voice in the background; it was one of Andy's colleagues named Rebecca. I made it clear to both of them that I had no faith in the British justice system nor the police, and both of them understood but assured me that they would leave no stone unturned, to bring the men to justice. Initially, they suggested that they would come to France, and take a statement from Cheryl and I., But Cheryl made it clear that she wanted no part of it. After a while, I agreed that I returned to the UK, at their expense, to give my statement. When the call was over, Cheryl tried to justify her actions, and she said I was crazy to talk to the police. However, I told her I had to do it, even if nothing came of it, as I had carried the guilt with me for all these years.

After a few days, the Metropolitan police sent tickets to return to the UK. Days earlier, Cheryl didn't talk to me. She claimed she loved me, but I knew that it wasn't to be and thought long and hard about what I was going to do when I returned from the UK.

The day arrived for my flight back to the UK. Andy and Rebecca picked me up from Stansted Airport and took me to the hotel. En route, we spoke in-depth, to how the investigation would proceed. They would pick me up at the hotel the following morning and take me to the police station, where I would give video evidence.

The next morning, right on time at 9:00 am I went to the police station with Andy and Rebecca. I felt at ease in their presence, and for once, believed they would do everything in their power to bring those responsible to justice. They ushered me into the room where Rebecca would be conducting the interview, while Andy would be next door, listening and recording it for the video evidence. I went into great detail about what happened to me all those years ago. I recalled everything that had occurred, provided names, dates, times, in as much detail as I possibly could.

Recalling my memory from all those years ago was a daunting an emotional affair. I would often break down in tears, but rather than have a break; I wanted to get it all out in the open. After I gave my evidence, Rebecca questioned each part of my story, as I had not drawn breath when speaking, and she needed to break it down into pieces to make sense of the whole situation. After several hours, the interview was over, they both shook my hand, and thanked me, for being brave enough to come forward, especially, as I was the first person to do so.

They took me back to the hotel, and later I Skype called Cheryl and told her that the interview went well, and would be returning home the following day. She appeared unhappy, but I had no other choice, and I felt good in myself for coming forward. The next morning, Andy and Rebecca picked me up, to take me back to the Stansted airport and catch my flight back home. They would be in touch and keep me informed of the investigation. I thanked them both for their dedication to duty as police officers. I had a lot of respect for them.

I was picked up at the airport by David, who drove me home. Part of me felt sick to my stomach because deep down, I just couldn't face seeing Cheryl again. When I arrived through the door, she was busy cleaning the living room and hadn't noticed me, as she had been using the vacuum cleaner. I tapped her on the shoulder, which made her jump, I apologised for scaring her, handing over a bunch of flowers, which I had picked up from the airport. It was nice to see a smile on her face, as I had dreaded coming back. I explained what happened, and I felt the tension in the air. I thought I'd make the best of a bad thing and keep things bottled up.

Throughout the day, Cheryl was drinking large gin and tonics, I kept out of her way, by either taking Meli out for long walks or doing some writing on my computer. In the evening, I was relaxing in the lounge when Cheryl came in to join me. I could see that she was drunk, but I remained silent.

That seemed to antagonise her, and she started an argument. After several hours, I left her to it and went to bed. Next day, early in the morning I heard loud banging and crashing in the bedroom. As I was starting to come out of my slumber, I heard Cheryl telling me to get up.

As she left the bedroom and stormed downstairs, I looked at my watch it was 3:00 am. I got up, had a shower and got changed before walking downstairs. I asked her what was going on. She had a face like thunder, and told me to 'fuck off,' as I no longer live there anymore!

I looked at her puzzled, and she started to push me out of the back door, all the while telling me too 'fuck off.' She pushed me so hard that I fell out of the door and stumbled over my belongings.

Getting back onto my feet again, I went to walk around into the house again. However, she slammed the back door, which caught me on my arm, and locked it. Now in pain, I realised that she had kicked me out. I tried knocking on the back door, but kept hearing her tell me to, 'fuck off.' I knew then there was no going back, although shocked at her actions, deep down I was relieved. Gathering up my belongings, I started to walk down the road, not knowing where I would end up, or where I was going.

The nearest town was Bellac, and I had to walk there. David and Vicky's friend Sharon lived in town, and I've been there a few times to help David pick up some items. It was pitch black, and I knew I had a long walk ahead of me. As I was walking, a motorcyclist stopped and asked where I was going. I explained that I spoke a little French, but I think he realised that I had been kicked out. He offered me a lift of which I declined, as I had far too much for him to carry on his motorcycle. He embraced me and wished me luck before driving off.

The walk took nearly two and a half hours to complete. It was still only 5:30 am, nowhere was open, and I would have to wait a further three hours before I could Sharon ask for her help. Using my case as a seat outside her home, wondering what I would do. However, I felt upset about Cheryl's response after contacting Tom Watson. I don't deserve to be chased out of our home. I had a mixture of emotions and felt aggrieved about what happened, but a part of me knew that it was for the best.

At 8:30 am, Sharon came out of her front door, and I asked her for help. Without hesitation, she took me inside her home and made me a coffee. Explaining the situation to her, Sharon contacted David. She asked him if he could drop me off at Limoges airport. About an hour later David arrived, he'd bought some other items which belonged to me, before driving me to the airport. Helping me out with my belongings, we shook hands and bid me farewell. There was one flight back to the UK, which would arrive at Stansted Airport at 3:50 pm.

Chapter Eighteen

The Streets of London

By the time I got through customs baggage reclaim it was 4.10 pm. My first port of call was to change up my remaining euro, which came to a princely sum of thirty-five pounds. Once outside, I had no clue about what to do. I knew the closest town from the airport was Bishops Stortford in Hertfordshire, some seven miles away. Making my way to the taxi rank, I asked how much it would cost to go to Hertfordshire. The driver informed me that it would be fifteen pounds. I thought for a second, that if I were to be able to find a room for a night, I would need all my money, and took the option of walking instead.

Carrying all my belongings, and dragging my case added to the stress of walking, although a fast walker, it slowed me down somewhat. The entire journey took nearly four hours with the extra burden, and I had to make frequent stops to catch my breath. It was now 8:00 pm; I still had to find a guest house or bed and breakfast to book a room. I came across a guest house, and spoke to the reception manager, about getting a place with breakfast. Things are more expensive in the UK, and in a way, the reality has not dawned on me yet.

Although the guest house had a room, it was way beyond my price range, and it was £65. It dawned on me that I would have to sleep rough, for what I thought was going to be for one night only. Not familiar with the town, I needed somewhere secure, dark, and away from prying eyes. Coming across a public footpath next to a church, I noticed a suitable area, with heavy foliage surrounded by trees, even though the pathway was lit, the place was ideal for my needs.

Ensuring that no one was following me, I made my way over into the thick canopy and foliage. It was a perfect spot, as it wasn't visible from the footpath, and the light was barely noticeable. It was well shielded from the elements, with leafy canopy and dense bushes. I used my case as a makeshift mattress to keep me coming into contact with the cold ground. Unfolding it, arranging my clothes in such a way, that was reasonably comfortable. I also made a pillow out of some of my clothes, pulling my zip on my snorkel coat, ensuring the drawstrings were pulled tight. My legs and feet were wrapped in my sweaters to keep as warm as possible. I laid down, for some much-needed rest. Before sleeping, I looked up into the Night Sky, and I noticed the North star, which I felt was a good omen, and was there to protect me.

Overcome by exhaustion, I fell asleep, and I would wake up periodically due in part to strange noises, cold and vivid dreams.

I awoke somewhat disorientated, the time was 6:30 am. There was a light breeze in the air, gently rustling the leaves on the trees and bushes. It was almost dawn, and I could now see where I had stayed the night. I had set up camp on top of someone's grave! Looking around, I realised it was part of the church's graveyard. I apologised to the occupants, but also thanked them, for keeping me safe and allowing me to stay.

Hearing some noises, not knowing what they were, I remained silent. It was only when the noises came closer that I could see there was a couple of early morning joggers. I saw them, but they were oblivious as to my existence. I removed some layers, to pack them away, and took the opportunity of trying to have some kind of a wash to keep some of my dignity. I also went for a pee in the bushes, making sure I was well out of sight.

Now feeling a little more refreshed and awake decided to venture into town to find some sort of café or coffee shop to warm up. Walking through the door, I immediately felt the effect of the warmth. The other customers didn't look up and were busy on their phones or reading newspapers. Ordering a coffee and went to find a table. I re-evaluated my options while sipping at my coffee, and I thought my best chance of obtaining help was head into central London.

I only had just over thirty pounds in my pocket, which wasn't going to last long. I returned to where I spent the night to work out how I could make some more money. I was determined, not to let my situation get to me, and was confident when I got into London, I would obtain the help I needed.

Now back in the graveyard, and the safety of the bushes; I rummaged through my stuff to see if I had any valuables to sell. The only thing valuable was my laptop, a gold necklace, which my mum and dad had given me for my twenty-first birthday. And lastly, my treasured medals. It dawned on me that I wouldn't get any money for the laptop, as I hadn't picked up the charger, and therefore, would be useless trying to get any kind of price for it. I didn't even have my mobile phone, as Cheryl locked me out before I could get it. Sitting there, contemplating my future, and a lot of soul searching, I decided to sell the necklace and the medals.

For some considerable time, I sat there looking at my medals and necklace, realising these were a link to my past and were irreplaceable. I had no choice and desperately needed money to survive. I walked through the town and found a pawnbroker. I stared at them for the last time before taking some deep breaths and going in. The pawnbroker checked out the necklace and the medals, and they offered me £165 for the two items.

I knew it was well below market value, but my survival instinct kicked in, and was a case of, 'beggars can't be choosers.' Now with just under two hundred pounds in my pocket, I purchased a ticket and made my way to Victoria, an area I knew well, and thought it would make a suitable base for me to start getting back on my feet again.

Now in the centre of Victoria, I familiarised myself with the area. My first plan was to seek out a suitable place to sleep, should I not be able to find and obtain any help. The most apparent area was next to McDonald's in the heart of Victoria. My second thought was to find the nearest employment service so that I could at least sign-on. By the time that I had found it, they were closing, but I would be nearby the following morning.

It was relatively mild as it was the beginning of May. I thought it would be ideal if I could find a shop where I could buy a sleeping bag. I was confident in my abilities to obtain help; I was also realistic. I had no idea, of how long the process would take, as I had never been in the situation, where I had to rely on government assistance before. After many hours, I found a shop that sold camping equipment and bought the cheapest sleeping bag they had on offer for eighty pounds. It was a large chunk from my money, but I was soon to discover that it was money well spent.

I headed off to where I had planned to stay the night, next to McDonald's. Before settling down, I purchased a Big Mac meal and a hot chocolate, before making myself comfortable next to their premises. It was now getting dark, but the streets were just as busy and noisy. I tried to keep myself as inconspicuous as possible. I found a quiet corner, which was quite dark before climbing into my sleeping bag, and settling down with my meal.

My thoughts were racing throughout, and I wondered how my life turned out the way it did. A few days ago, I had been living in France, surrounded by beautiful animals and beautiful countryside. Now on the streets, and all because I'd decided to give a statement to the police! Part of me was angry to have been placed in a position like this. The other part deep down was re-lieved, but I felt that Cheryl had betrayed me if she thought I was the disgusting one.

I tried to take my mind off things, as I cradled my hot choc-olate, and calming thoughts entered my head, taking me back to my childhood and happier times. As a special treat, we would be allowed a cup of hot chocolate, made with full-fat milk. It may sound daft for some to comprehend these days, but back in the day, it was a big thing for us.

These thoughts bought a smile to my face, although slightly tinged with sadness, as I wondered if I would ever see the likes of these again. Feeling tired, I set up my case, just as I had done so the previous evening, only this time, inside my sleeping bag, which also had a hood, and therefore, I could wear less clothing and feel much warmer. I had made myself as comfortable as pos-sible and drifted off to sleep.

Around 7:00 am, I awoke with a start, and had to acquaint myself to my surroundings, after a few moments. I sat up and allowed myself time to adjust before packing up, and heading into McDonald's for breakfast, and use their facilities. Ordering breakfast, I found a quiet area of the restaurant to sit down, to work out what I was going to say, to the unemployment office.

I had at least an hour to kill, taking my time over breakfast before heading off to sign on. Although it was only a short walk, by the time I had arrived, quite a few people were queuing up. I kept away from them and waited for the doors to open. I took my time and waited for the crowd to die down before entering the building myself. I had never been unemployed and didn't know what to expect. I took a ticket waiting for my turn.

After what seemed an age, my number was called, I walked up, and sat in front of the advisor.

Explaining my situation, they advised me to fill out the forms and hand them back in. As I had never been in this position before, I didn't know what the protocol was, so I did what was asked of me, as I thought, I was supposed to go back, in a day or two for an answer, but how wrong I was.

Day after day, I would return and get no answers from the staff. Because I lived on the streets, my money was dwindling. No matter how many doors I opened for myself, I would get the same answer which was, 'you will be notified in due course'!

As I had no definitive answers, my mind and thoughts were irrational, and I started to let myself go, as my only thoughts were where I would be sleeping, or where my next meal would be coming from. I tried to remain focused and positive but no matter how hard I tried, I couldn't think.

I was like a wild animal, roaming from place to place, it was as if I had never existed at all, and treated as if I was transparent. The days turned into weeks, and I was like the rest of the homeless people living on the streets, my clothes were dishevelled, although I tried to keep myself clean, it was almost impossible, as I had to try different places around London so that they wouldn't recognise me. As my money was fast disappearing, I rationed my eating, and would go days without food, and would fill up an old plastic bottle with tap water, from the bathroom in McDonald's.

I had now been on the streets for the best part of a month. No matter what I tried to do to get a leg up, each door that I opened would be slammed back in my face. I learned to find food, as I now run out of money.

I scavenged through bins at the back of Tesco metros and other stores, trying to find any out of date sandwiches. Sometimes I was successful, and occasionally other homeless people had beaten me to it.

I couldn't even get any help from a Salvation Army and was at desperation point. Occasionally, if I were lucky and got there on time, I would get a hot meal at the homeless day centre. However, most of the time, I would be too late and turned away. I was disgusted with myself, as I thought, it would be easy to get help from the authorities, especially as I was an ex-serviceman.

Also, I had paid tax all my life to the UK government, even when I lived abroad.

Day after day was relentless, I was a mere statistic, and nobody took any notice. With the amount of walking, and lack of food, my body fat was eaten away, and I lost several stones. Some people may argue that losing weight is a good thing, which is if you are trying to diet, but in my case, it wasn't through choice. I tried to keep a positive thought, but it was nigh on impossible. My mind was playing over and over in my head, the song, 'Streets of London' by Ralph McTell. Was this the way it was going to be from now on? I couldn't believe that my life had come to this, a bloody song lyric! I had to do something and quick, if I was to survive, and get myself the help I needed. Nobody else could do it for me and had to dig deep, to do it for myself.

Standing on London Bridge, looking down into the dark, murky water of the Thames. My mind was racing, as my thoughts were all over the place. As I looked around busy streets, and the hustle and bustle of the crowds going about their busy lives, I could only think of one thing, albeit for a split second.

I had had enough, and dark thoughts entered my head, depression had got the better of me. For the second time in my life, I had sunk to a new low and thought about suicide. As I contemplated the consequences that my actions would have, should I be brave enough to do it? No matter how hard I tried to find something good about my life at that time, I couldn't think of anything, apart from jumping off. It was starting to get dark, as London illuminated, a light breeze came across me, and seem to snap me into reality.

My self-harm thoughts gave way to anger. Something inside me stirred up every emotion, where I thought long and hard, and concluded that I wasn't going to let the bastards get to me. I was entitled to get help, and wasn't going to let them deter me in any way any longer. I was going to be heard, even if it meant getting arrested, I was going to be bloody well heard.

A least, if I got arrested for making a nuisance of myself, there would be a bed for me in a police cell, which would include at least one hot meal. With those thoughts now entering my head, I decided to head off the bridge and find a dark corner to recharge my batteries, ready to fight back the next morning.

As my mind was determined to come up with a solution, I could only manage short bursts of sleep. As the hours ticked by, I was getting more and more, pumped up by the second, it was as if my fighting spirit had well and truly entered my body again. After all, I was a fighter. I had spent a third of my life, as a professional soldier, and had seen combat. I wasn't going down without a fight. Over the last few weeks, I had lost many battles with the authorities, but this time, I was going to win the war!

It was now 7.00 am I had a couple of hours to kill. As soon as McDonald's opened, I went in to use their facilities while it was quiet. I stripped down to the waist, for a good wash, I even managed to shave, and put on the cleanest clothes that I possessed, and felt more human again!

I went back into the restaurant, checking my pockets, I just had enough money, to buy myself welcoming coffee. As I sat there drinking, the manager came over to speak to me, and my first thoughts were that he was going to ask me to leave, to my surprise, he handed me over a breakfast muffin and another coffee. I could hardly contain my emotions, with tears in my eyes, I thanked him for his kind generosity.

After eating, I prepared myself mentally to go and do battle, with the social security office.

I walked out of McDonald's, I was a man on a mission, striding as I walked with my head held high. As with previous visits, I took the number and waited my turn to be called. When my number came up, I confidently walked over to the desk and sat down in front of an Asian young lady. I stared at the advisor straight in the eyes, and I told her that I had already made a claim, and wouldn't be going anywhere until I got the help that I needed. Looking at her unsympathetic face, made me feel even more determined, to get what I was entitled to, but even though,

I had prepared my answers, I wasn't prepared, for what she told me next.

She told me three things that I would never forget as long as I live.

The first was, 'all the money that I had paid in tax, had gone.'

'I had now lost my British citizenship.' And the one that made me laugh more than the others was, 'I would now be classed, as an immigrant asylum seeker!' Hearing these words pissed me off somewhat, and I smirked at her reply. Nobody was going to stop me, and my response to her was also three-fold.

I looked her squarely in the eyes, I responded by asking her, 'who's spent all the money I paid in tax, and had they enjoyed, a good Jolly up on my money?' Secondly, 'that I couldn't lose my British citizenship, unless I decided to renounce it, and even then, it will be difficult!' My third and final answer, 'to give me the forms, so that I can claim for everything that the immigrants are being handed over, and allowed to claim!'

The advisor wasn't impressed with what I had said, after my last sentence, held up her right hand and told me, 'it was the rules, and I would have to leave.' However, I wasn't going anywhere, and I would make myself obnoxious, as I possibly could. Smiling right back at her, I told her, I wouldn't be leaving until I got help. With that, she raised her right hand again and beckoned over one of the security guards. I noticed he originated from Poland, although I have no problems with any race, at that time I was severely pissed off and had resentments.

I told him, I wouldn't be going anywhere and he would be wasting his time, trying to convince me otherwise. He beckoned over another two security guards, and again these were of Polish descent. I stood up, to be at the same level as the three of them. Even in my weakened state, I was prepared for a fight, therefore stood my ground.

Looking around each one, in turn, I smiled and told them,

'Listen here, boys. There are three of you and only one of me. We are all adults here, and there is no need for any violence, so suggest that you all fuck off, and get some more blokes, then it would be a fair fight!' With that, I sat down and folded my arms.

Not knowing what else to do, they told me they would call the police, and have me arrested. I simply said to the security guys.

'Go ahead'. I wasn't going anywhere.

The advisor asked if I could move to a different chair, which I ignored. Finally, she vacated her position, and I was left by myself, which suited me to the ground. After about half an hour, the police arrived and were discussing my case with the management and security guards.

As I looked over to where the police were standing, one of the faces seemed familiar. There were two officers, one male, and the other female, as they started to walk towards me, I realised where I had seen the male's face before.

Standing in front of me, I could see that it was a friend of mine, we served together in the army. He also recognised who I was, but didn't let on to his female colleague. Being professional, he asked if I could leave the premises, or face being arrested. Not wanting to cause a scene, I went with them flanking either side. Once outside the building, we walked to the awaiting police car, so that we could talk. Now safely inside the vehicle, he explained to his colleague who I was.

I told him, I was in desperate need of help, taking out his wallet, he handed me a £20 note and told me, he would ring ahead to the Veterans Association in Buckingham Palace Road, where I would receive the help that I needed. He also asked why I haven't gone to them in the first place. I explained that it merely didn't enter my head, as living on the streets has a detrimental effect on your mental ability. With that, we shook hands, and they left.

I went back to McDonald's to pay for my earlier breakfast. However, the manager wouldn't accept my money, so changed it up, and I left five pounds in the charity box, thanking him again, before making my way over to the Veterans Association.

By the time I arrived, now exhausted, it was if all the stress, had taken its toll on me. I opened the door, and the stairs seemed like the North face of Mount Everest. I had no energy and struggled with my belongings. As I got a few steps in, I was greeted by a member of staff who carried my belongings, while I took one step at a time. Stepping into the reception, and almost collapsed in the chair. I was a mess and needed some time to compose myself, as I couldn't contain my emotions any longer.

After about five minutes, I'd calmed down sufficiently, to tell my story and give my details, including my previous service. When they did all the paperwork, they offered me tea and a sandwich, which I ate within a few mouthfuls. By the time I had finished, the office manager had given me a hotel voucher for three days, sixty pounds in cash for food and sundries, and an

Oyster card, with ten pounds on it. He also handed me a map and address.

He explained that after three days, I should have to to obtain another voucher and some more cash, as it would take some time, to find suitable permanent accommodation. I was helped downstairs with my belongings and thanked them for their help before setting off. The hotel was in Paddington. When I arrived, the staff already had my details and were expecting me. After signing in, they showed me my room, and it included breakfast. Now left alone, I rested and recover. The room was basic, with a single bed, side table with lamp, dressing table, with a TV placed on it, and a mirror. The window was small, with a safety opening, there was also a tiny hand washbasin

Although small, compared to what I had been used too, it was a palace. Down the hallway, was a shower and a small bathroom, which I couldn't wait to use. As soon as I had settled in, I made tea. I also washed my clothes in the sink and hung them to dry in front of the window. After my tea, I gathered up my washbag, and one of the hotel's towels and headed off to the shower. Feeling the hot water cascade over my aching body, reinvigorated my senses, which made me break down again, as I hadn't had a shower or proper wash in six weeks.

After showering, I returned to my room. It was then that I noticed what living on the street had done to my body. I knew I had lost weight but hadn't envisaged on how much. Hardly able to recognise myself, my ribcage was obvious, arms were thin, and my facial features were gaunt, eyes sunken with dark circles. Throughout my body, were various pressure sores, and covered in bruises, across my back, legs, and torso was a direct result, in sleeping on hard ground.

Although I had suffered, I reminded myself that I was now safe and secure, and things could only get better from now on. I dressed and went out to check the area, to find a shop where I could buy a charger for my laptop. I didn't have too far to go, when I saw a computer and phone supplies shop, I had my computer with me, and they managed to match a charger. As it wasn't a generic charger, it was only twenty-five pounds, and I was suspicious that it may not work.

Returning to the hotel, I wasted no time in plugging the charger into my laptop and was half expecting to hear some kind of bang or short out, but my fears were unfounded, as it worked a treat. While waiting for it to charge up, I put on the TV and laid down to relax. Now settled down, then I fell into a deep and exhausted sleep. I awoke after five hours of a deep sleep, with the TV still playing which I had been oblivious too. I had to orientate myself to my surroundings, as for a few minutes.

I wasn't sure where I was until it dawned on me, that I was in my hotel room, which was something I had to get used to and I got up and splashed water on my face, putting on the kettle to make a drink. As it was boiling, I picked up my laptop and switched it on, the charger had done its job, and it was fully charged.

I searched through my emails. There were several from Rebecca, the Met police, who were dealing with my case. I replied, explaining my situation, I'd been in over the past six weeks, at least I had some form of contact with them. I also responded to an email from a solicitor named Tracy, whom I had contacted, prior to being kicked out by Cheryl. I wanted to find out if I would have a compensation case for being sexually abused as a child. Tracy contacted me to arrange for a face to face meeting. As I was in London, she suggested that we meet up at the barrister's office, in 'The Middle Temple', part of the 'Four Inns of Court', located near the Royal Courts of Justice.

I also heard from Rebecca, who explained, they had tried to contact me in France when Cheryl told them that she kicked me out several weeks ago. She also explained that the investigation was ongoing, and they had made preliminary arrests of Richard Alston, and Charles Napier who had been questioned by them under caution.

Napier had denied all knowledge of meeting me but admitted to several other offences regarding sexual contact with other young boys from his past. Alston admitted that he knew me as he was one of my previous teachers at Cavendish, which was a good start in their investigation. Sadly, they told me that Peter Righton had died back in the mid-1990s. However, they were confident that they could build a case against Napier and Alston, and both of them were on police bail pending further investigation.

Now able to breathe a sigh of relief for the immediate term, my life was slowly going to get back on track. I made arrangements to meet with Rebecca and the investigation team, as they required more information to assist their ongoing case. They were dedicated to bringing these vile men to justice.   After emailing, I focused on contacting those who knew me from social media sites. I had good feedback, and some even offered to transfer money to me, which I declined, but their kind gestures and moral support uplifted my spirits.

I felt on top of the world with their encouragement, but part of me felt ashamed for not going directly to the armed forces charities when I first arrived in the UK. I may not have been homeless.

On the other hand, I thought that maybe, this was a lesson that needed I needed to learn. Besides, the streets seem to have a detrimental effect on one's persona, as each day arrives, one can become transfixed on where the next meal was coming from, or where one would be sleeping that night!

Also, I thought that it was a good thing in the long term, as deep down, Cheryl's reaction to my abuse was on omen, and being kicked out was the best thing that could have happened, although, at the time, I thought it was harsh.

Maybe, I was naïve not to have noticed what she felt about me. My thoughts about Cheryl were well-founded when a short time later, she sent me a personal message on Facebook, calling me all the names under the sun. The final straw was when she signed off, hoping that 'I die painfully!' Disgusted by her comments, I blocked her from contacting me again, as she had proved, underneath her mask, was a nasty piece of work, and was glad that she had kicked me out.

After her written outburst, I need to go out and get some air and clear my head. It was a lovely warm evening, and I walked around, taking in the sights and sounds. Only this time, I could appreciate it, with the bonus of knowing I had a bed to sleep later. Finding a small urban public garden, fenced in by ornate spiked railings.

As I entered, it was like being in a piece of paradise and shut out the street noises. I sat down on a bench and gathered my thoughts.

First of all, I thanked the spirits of mum and dad, as I felt they had been with me all the time, and eventually guided me onto the right path where I could look forward to a rosier future. The very thought brought a smile to my face, as well as memories of happier times.

I could now see the distant spark of light at the end of a very long tunnel, and was excited at the thought, of where it would lead to! After making my peace with myself, I returned to the hotel, to enjoy a good and relaxing evening, watching the TV.

After a peaceful night's sleep, I showered and went to join my fellow guests, in the dining room for breakfast. I had assumed there would be a variation and include English breakfast. However, it was like a continental affair, although that didn't concern me, as I loaded up my plate, and sat down, for the first real meal I had in a long time. Going back to my room, I checked my emails before setting off for my meeting with Tracy, my lawyer. It was a nice sunny day, and I felt like a new man, with a wonderful new life ahead of me.

Here I was, only twenty-four hours later, it was if, the last six weeks had never happened. I knew I had a long way to go to get back to where I was, but I had a feeling in the pit of my stomach, that from now on, things were on the up for me. Arriving at the inner temple, I waited patiently to meet with Tracy. I didn't stay very long when I was greeted by a well-dressed, good-looking woman who introduced herself as Tracy, before shaking my hand.

Showing me into a side room, we sat down around a large table, where she explained that I would meet with a specialist barrister whom she had worked with in historical child abuse cases. She had been successful in prosecuting many cases with the barrister and felt confident that they could do the same for me. As we were talking, the secretary arrived with some coffee, and news that the barrister was unable to make the meeting, as he was tied up in court.

Unperturbed, Tracey explained the situation, asking me some questions about my case. While recounting my horrendous past, I started to become physically upset, but she reassured me in her calming manner.

Tracy felt I had a strong case. However, she hinted that it hinged on the successful conviction of my abusers. She explained that it might be difficult even with a guilty verdict. It wouldn't be impossible to make a case against the local education authority at the time because they employed Alston when the abuse took place.

I asked about my legal fees, but Tracy assured me that any legal costs on my part, if successful, would be taken out of the final settlement, at no more than ten per cent of the overall award. It would be offset by an insurance policy, which would reduce the percentage down to six per cent. In other words, it was based on a no-win-no-fee basis. How could I refuse such an offer? To me, it was a win, win situation and one that didn't need much thought. Ok, it was based on securing a conviction, in a case that was in the early stages of the investigation, and there was no guarantee that it would go in my favour even if the case came to court.

However, I had one thing in my arsenal, that kept me going, and that was confidence! Confidence in the investigating team, unearthing enough corroborating evidence to secure a conviction. Furthermore, I was confident in Tracy's ability in obtaining a favourable settlement, even though we had only met, she had an air of confidence about her, and I felt at ease that she would do everything in her power, to do so. I was still technically homeless, which Tracy had taken into account, as she brought the preliminary documents for my appraisal and signature.

I thought about the ethical side for a moment, and how it may affect the police investigation, as any defence, may look at it, and assumed that I had fabricated the entire story, just to make money! But this was far from the truth, as coming forward was to obtain justice for the suffering I endured, at the hands of vile, despicable creatures. I voiced my concerns to Tracy, who suggested I come clean and inform the police which I had intended too, but she had made me feel justified in what I was doing.

Putting pen to paper, I duly signed, this was the second step, into securing a better future for myself. And then the courage to come forward to speak with the police in the first place. After signing, I thanked Tracy for meeting with me, and we parted company, but she promised to keep me informed at regular intervals.

Back in the beautiful sunshine, I felt much lighter, as if all the weight of the world had lifted off my shoulders. In no hurry to return to the hotel, I took a stroll along the Embankment, enjoying the moment. I had pounded these same streets every day, for the last six weeks, only this time; it was a joy, not a burden. Buying a tea and sandwich, I sat down overlooking the Thames to take in the scenery, which I could now admire, rather than despise! Now, a smile lightened my face, which turned into laughter. My mind went through the scrapes, I used to get into when I was a kid, and even as an adult.

It must have appeared odd to a passer-by witnessing it, and God knows, what they must have been thinking. But It had been long overdue, although, I had no idea why. Besides, I deserved a brief moment of madness, and treated it as my steam release, either that or bursting into tears. But I have always been in the mindset that laughter is the best medicine! Feeling upbeat, I returned to the hotel for a much-deserved rest and fell asleep.

Over the next three weeks, I lived a nomadic lifestyle, moving around London, and staying at different hotels. I had purchased a cheap prepaid mobile and was in constant contact with the investigation team, and Tracy, who told me that things were moving in the right direction. My health had improved, and I had even gained weight. I had been from Paddington, Marble Arch, East Ham, Shepherds Bush, Notting Hill, back to Paddington, with no news of a permanent place for me to call my home.

As the third week was drawing to a close, the Association manager called me to inform me that they were unable to find anywhere down South, and would I consider Rosendael house

Veteran's home in Broughty Ferry? As I had never heard of it, I inquired where it was. I was gobsmacked when I found out that it was in Dundee Scotland! Of course, I had to think it over, and they gave me forty-eight hours to make a decision. I was given another hotel voucher for a more upmarket four-star hotel in Cockfosters. At the hotel, I checked Rosendael's website, which was terrific. After seeing the site, I made my mind up and took them up on their offer. I phoned the Association and informed them of my decision, I was to return on Sunday morning, so they could finalise the details, and purchase the coach tickets!

I also informed Rebecca who suggested that we meet up near Victoria coach station, as one of her colleagues wanted to liaise with me, for an update and required further statements. Sunday arrived in an instant it seemed, making my way back to the Veteran's Association, which was to be my final time. George, the manager, was waiting, and wasted no time, accompanying me to the ticket office for my one-way ticket to Dundee. I would be travelling via National Express from Victoria coach station and would be leaving at midnight. He also handed me a further cash float of sixty pounds. We shook hands, and I thanked him for his hard work and dedication to duty for getting me off the streets.

With several hours to kill, made my way from Buckingham Palace Road to Victoria by tube, to meet up with Rebecca. I had butterflies in my stomach since I had awoken at the hotel, with mixed feelings about moving to Scotland. I met up with Rebecca and another colleague named Paul, who was now part of the investigation team.

They bought me lunch, and while eating, Tracy explained that since my initial evidence, further victims had decided to come forward. The investigation had been split into two other separate operations involving politicians, and other prominent celebrities. In contrast, mine was solely to do with everyday persons, with Andy had the task of the lead investigator.

All of them had one thing in common; they all had links, with the underground paedophile group, PIE. An anagram of the Paedophile Information Exchange. Peter Righton was a founding member in the 1970s. They explained further that both Napier and Alston were also past members. Although not surprised at this news, it made me feel sick to my stomach, but again I was immensely proud for coming forward and hoped that all of us, would one day, see our abusers face the justice, they so richly deserved.

I also heard that Righton had also been the subject of a BBC documentary, 'Inside Story' back in 1992, titled 'The Secret Life of a Paedophile'. Rebecca and Paul brought a copy of my new statement, which had been amended because I had to take out a claim, with my lawyer Tracy. And it had to be clarified and passed on to the CPS.

They also wanted to see for themselves, where the crimes took place, and drove me to the flat, in Barbican Close in Greenford West London, where Alston and Righton once shared. I sketched the layout of the flat, and they took notes. With everything now in order, they drove me back to Victoria. Before they headed off, they wished me luck for my journey and would contact me in a few days, for further updates. Now alone, I tried to take my mind off my case, and my final destination. I found a coffee shop, and I decided to relax and unwind before my departure. The hours seem to drag on, which only intensified my anxiety before I boarded the coach for a nine-hour drive to my eventual new home!

Chapter Nineteen

Discovery

Settling back in my seat, I removed my laptop to watch pirated copies of Steptoe and Son. I was getting uncomfortable when the fattest bloke I had ever seen decided to sit next to me. He was almost shoehorning, his bulky frame into the seat, which was a source of amusement as rolls of blubbery fat crept over the centre armrest. I rested my arm on it, of which he didn't notice. I tried to stifle my sniggering, and to my defence, I put it down, to the on-screen antics, of Albert and Harold, well that's my version, and I'm sticking to it.

After a while, it eventually grated on my nerves, and I couldn't wait to get away from him. Thankfully after a pitstop, he missed the coach, as they were unable to find him when it was time to go, so I had the two seats to myself, and could fully relax. As night made way for the day, we came to the Scottish border and its iconic welcome to Scotland sign. Just as soon as we crossed into Scotland, I had an overwhelming feeling rush over me, and I cried.

I knew I had some Scottish in me from dad's mum, I had some of her blood, coursing through my veins, and the feeling that I had returned to my ancestral home. There were still hours to go before we got to Dundee, but the miles of the amazing Scottish countryside, more than made up for it. Soon enough, we arrived at our first scheduled drop-in Glasgow, I was getting closer by the minute, our next stop was Edinburgh, and then Dundee.

Arriving, just as they had demolished an old council office, which had opened up the city, I could now see it for the first time. As we pulled into the coach station in Seagate, I felt relieved but exhausted. I had no idea how far Rosendael was, or even how to get there. Asking at the information desk, I crossed the road, to board the bus to Broughty Ferry. I explained to the clippie where I was going and sat down. An older man sparked up a conversation, as he had overheard me talking about Rosendael and seemed highly informative, welcoming me to Scotland, which was a nice touch.

Pulling at the stop, I was shown the direction to the home. Crossing the road, I came to the gated entrance. I walked up the inclined path towards the house. It opened up, into some amazing well-maintained private gardens, leading up to the enormous stately home, which I had understood, was once a privately-owned property, and been donated by the previous owner in the memory of a much-loved brother, killed in action in WW1.

Walking up the few steps leading to the front door, I pushed the intercom and waited for my contact Maggie to appear. The door buzzed, where I ventured into, a fantastic period wood-panelled entrance hall. To the right, was a vast sweeping stair-case, which was illuminated by an amazing stain glass window. I was in awe of the place that I would call my home.

Maggie appeared, and officially welcomed me in, before proceeding to introduce me, to the other members of staff.

I was introduced to the manager named Max, who seemed pleasant enough at first, but would soon show his colours later on. I was ushered into one of the various suites to carry out the paperwork, before being taken to the dining room, where I had my first ever, traditional Scottish breakfast, and my first taste of tattie scones!

After breakfast, I was shown to my room and was left alone to relax. The room was a fair size, with a single bed, sideboard, wardrobe, and en-suite. It was pleasant enough and was comfortable for my needs, and I likened it, to the various hotel rooms back in London.

I unpacked my few belongings, before taking a refreshing shower, and much-needed sleep. Waking up sometime later, I felt at home, and it was so quiet and serene, I got up to explore this fascinating building, and hopefully, meet up with some of the residents.

I walked through the winding maze of corridors, occasionally stopping to admire the various displays of donated medals, adorning the walls. I entered the grand entrance hall. I picked one of the many doors to find a row of static computers and combined TV room. There was also, a partially glassed dividing wall, where I could see a full-length snooker table, and went to look.

This room joined onto a fantastic conservatory, with stunning views of the garden, where I went for a walk around the grounds. At the front, what I thought was a well-manicured lawn, when I first came up the drive, turned out to be a bowling green around the side was a car park, and to the other, was another hidden garden and greenhouse. I sat down in front of the planted areas, near the conservatory. As I did so, my phone rang. It was Rebecca, who wanted to find out how everything was. She informed me, she had interviewed my ex-wife Jackie on how I coped and if I Had spoken to her at any stage of our marriage, concerning the abuse.

She had also spoken to my two sisters. My middle Sister Tina wanted nothing to do with me, and even told Rebecca that she didn't care if I lived or died! That is what I had expected from the nasty woman, which suited me to the ground. On the other hand, my eldest sister Theresa had felt guilty and asked if they would supply her with my number, which I had no problems with doing so. After our conversation, I rolled a cigarette when my phone rang again. It was Theresa, and we had a lovely but emotional conversation.

After speaking, I went back in for lunch, where I met up with the other residents, waiting outside the dining room. I hadn't envisaged, we would have to queue up like squaddies outside the cookhouse. What made it worse, there was hardly any conversation, and those who did would stifle their words, almost to a whisper! I later found out that it was the manager Max, rules of no talking in the corridor! I had only been there a few hours, and already felt perturbed that we were being treated like naughty schoolkids, waiting to see the headmaster!

It wasn't my style at all, I wasn't the kind of person to keep my mouth shut, and I struck up a conversation with one of the older residents, named Alec, who had the same outlook as myself, and defied the rules. The doors to the dining room opened, and we shuffled in like cattle which was an absolute joke, as we were all grown adults!

I did notice the older residents spoke their minds, and it was only the younger ones that seemed scared of Max, it wouldn't be long before we crossed paths.

The tables were set out, just like a quaint, old-fashioned tea-room, and most people had their favourite sitting space. I chose to sit with Alec, from the first impression, he seemed to have a set of balls, and we would forge a good friendship.

After lunch, we ventured outside for a smoke. Alec gave me a few pointers about the place that Max tried to rule it with a rod of iron, much to the annoyance of the older residents.

He explained that Max had been a sergeant major in the medical corps, with a bad attitude towards staff, and residents alike.

As I had just arrived, I wanted to see for myself, as I didn't want to take one person's opinion on Max, until I had ascertained all the facts. I didn't have long to wait because when we ventured back inside, one of the residents was being chastised like a naughty boy, in the entrance hall by Max.

It was just the beginning. Soon after, Max began to do the same to one of the members of staff.

I could now see what Alec had been trying to warn me about, and I made a decision there and then, that I wouldn't put up with it, should he try it on me.

Before I could return to my room, I was stopped by Max's secretary Yvonne, to go through the final paperwork to apply for housing benefits, which would be used for my rent, and personal benefits.

There would be an additional extra charge, to cover the full rent of four hundred pounds a month, which I thought was exorbitant for just a room and meals, as it was a registered charity.

Unfortunately, I had no choice at that time. After filling in the paperwork, I went back to my room and watched my downloaded movies.

Almost as soon as I started to watch, I'd fallen asleep and woke up several hours later.

After sleeping, I had another shower, before taking myself and laptop down to the computer room, to update my CV. Alec came in to join me. Intrigued in what I was doing, he suggested I become involved in volunteer work, and that I team up with him, as he had started up his armed service charity, named the Scottish Veterans Society, or SVS which he preferred.

That was no brainer, as it would get me out of the rut. Also, this would prove useful at my Social meeting scheduled for the next morning, which Alec furnished me with a headed letter, stipulating I was helping him as a volunteer. It would prove valuable in securing the benefits. I felt a bit guilty by using it to obtain benefits, but I needed a helping hand and would take full advantage of the situation.

The next morning, Alec drove me into town, dropping me outside the 'brew' as he called it, heading off to a pre-arranged meeting himself. It was the first time I had been in town, since my arrival a few days earlier. Before going in, I lit a cigarette— someone who also wanted to sign on approached me for a light.

At first, I couldn't understand what he was saying and had to listen carefully before replying. I was thrown when he asked me if, 'ye ken.' Naturally, I assumed, he was speaking about a person named Ken, and said, 'no, I'm Steve.' He laughed at this, realising I wasn't a local, explaining it was Dundonian and that I would get used to it in time. Even so, I felt a bit like a plonker but had a giggle all the same.

Walking in was like being interrogated by the inquisition from the security guards. I wasn't prepared to discuss my situation with them and made it clear that I would only speak, with someone from the brew, as they had no authority. I was shown where I had to be and waited to be called. After a short while, I was called over by my advisor, who bought up my case on his screen. He noticed my original claim from London was still live and questioned the reasons they hadn't helped me. I told him I had no idea why, and that he should know because he was part of the same government department.

He calmly explained although they were different laws in Scotland, I should have never been in the position I was. He also took note of the letter they gave me from Rosendael, which explained that my placement was temporary, and would only cover me for one month! After reviewing my case, he informed me, I would get my Jobseekers allowance payments backdated, and would they would pay me in a few days into my bank account, which was a weight off my mind.

Handing me reams of paperwork, a job search book before explaining I would have to go to the Lily Walker Centre, who would help me with finding a permanent place to live.

As I had never heard of it, he gave me their details. I was now in the system, and things were looking up for me at last. Thanking him for his time, I left. Once outside, I rang up the Lily Walker centre, to make an appointment, which they arranged for the following Monday.

Now with time on my hands, I decided to explore the city. I found out as much as I could about its history.

Finding the library, I enrolled so I could use their computers to search the history. I spent several hours where I learnt a lot about how the city was the industrial centre for Jute cloth and was once famous for being the site of Timex. Also, I had no idea at that time that the Beano and Dandy comics originated from the city. I was surprised when I found out that the famous ship Discovery, that carried Earnest Shackleton, and Robert Falcon Scott to the Antarctic, was housed in the dock on the banks of the Tay.

As a history buff, I was engrossed and wanted to find out more, so I went to the McManus museum and was in awe of the exhibits it contained. Not only that, but I also found the architecture of the city was unique. Spending several hours out and about, I returned to Rosendael exhausted but educated. By the time I arrived, they were already serving lunch. I found a seat next to a resident called Lorne and struck up a conversation.

We talked about our service, of which he had been a corporal, in the Black Watch regiment, and served twelve years, before being invalided out, as he suffered a stroke. I took a shine to him, and we continued our conversation, after lunch in the garden. Originally, Lorne hailed from Arbroath but hadn't seen his hometown for five years since he became a resident.

I inquired as to why he hadn't been back and was saddened to hear Rosendael wouldn't spare anyone to assist him, as the stroke had affected him in such a way that he could only walk short distances, and he had never left the confines of Rosendael. In effect, he was a prisoner, which I thought wasn't on, and came up with a plan of taking him out myself because there were several wheelchairs gathering dust.

Going back inside, I spoke to the office manager Neil, who informed me that he would have to run it past Max.

A few moments later, he returned with an answer, which wasn't what I had expected. He explained the home's policy was that residents had to have insurance, and undergo a training course to use the wheelchairs, and Max wouldn't allow it. I just looked at him and laughed. I ignored his advice and went to fetch one of the wheelchairs.

As I did so, Max came out of his office and tried to talk down to me in the entrance hall within earshot of other residents. I wasn't having any of that and gave him a piece of my mind. I got the impression that he wasn't used to being spoken to in that manner, making him look stupid in front of the crowd that had gathered. I refused to be treated like shit, or a naughty school-boy.

Red-faced, he stormed off into the direction of his office. As I helped Lorne into the chair, Max reappeared with a hastily written note he wanted me to sign. It stated that I take full responsibility if anything happened. I laughed and humoured him and signed it, but not before adding the words, 'Malaka Max', which is Greek for 'Wanker Max.' Of course, he had no idea what it meant, and I was past caring.

Lorne and I headed off to Broughty Ferry for our first trip out. Although tough going, the scenery more than made up for it. I had never been there before, and due to his condition, neither had he. We stopped off at a coffee shop, and sat outside, where we had an interesting conversation. Lorne kept thanking me for getting him away from Rosendael. I told him it wasn't necessary, as I would do the same for anyone in his position.

We discussed going to Arbroath for the coming weekend as Max didn't work at weekends. However, I don't care if he did, as nobody was going to stop me from helping my new friend. We spent several hours enjoying Broughty Ferry before heading back to the home. By the time we arrived, Max had gone home for the day.

One of the wardens, Brian, approached me. He had just started his shift. Brian took me to one side and shook my hand, saying Max had met his match and didn't like what I told him. He also handed me a letter from Max 'summoning me,' to his office the following morning before breakfast, which amused me.

I thanked Brian and told him to pass on a message to Max.

'I wouldn't be joining you, Max, because I had a previous engagement!'

Brian laughed at my reply before going about his duties. After tea, I met up with Alec, who invited me up to his room for a drink, which I duly agreed, after all, it would be rude not too! I was expecting him to hand out the Scotch, but admitted that he couldn't stand the stuff, handed me a cognac.

He wanted to show me old copies of the courier concerning several incidents at the home before my arrival, which were a direct result of Max's involvement. I found out that the room they allocated to me once belonged to a previous tenant who committed suicide due to various, hushed up accounts of bullying, from Max and some of his minions amongst the younger residents. The poor boy had overdosed and had died alone in the room. According to Alec, no member of staff, including Max, had bothered to check when the boy did not show up.

Of course, an investigation by the police and care commission was undertaken, but Max and his cronies got off scot-free, for 'lack,' of evidence. However, the commission's report was damming about the standards at Rosendael, and changes were implemented. Alec told me, Max earned the nickname of 'Teflon,' as it seemed that nothing stuck. Alec added that previous members of staff who witnessed these incidents of bullying were dismissed for whistleblowing, and yet the little turd Max remained. I took it upon myself to bring in change!

The next day, I met up with Alec at breakfast, first choosing to ignore Max's summons, which Alec loved, as he had no respect for the man, and asked for my help as a volunteer for his charity.

Without hesitation, I jumped at the chance. After breakfast, we were walking through the entrance hall when we heard Max calling my name—turning around, and I saw Max walking at speed, towards us. He asked if he could have a private word with me, in his office.

Looking down at him, I politely declined because anything he wanted to say, could be discussed in front of Alec. Furthermore, as he had a trait of speaking to some residents and staff alike in the hall, it seemed an appropriate venue. We could see from his face, he was incensed by this and had a face like thunder; it was all red and flustered. He tried to talk down to me and asked why I hadn't gone to see him as he'd requested before breakfast.

Unperturbed, I simply told him that I wasn't a lapdog, nor was I a naughty schoolboy, and the fact that the social was paying for my upkeep, I was technically a paying guest, and wouldn't stand back to be treated like shit! Alec laughed at this, backing me up on this point. Max did try and say that he had the power to cancel my contract as an undesirable! Again, a pointless exercise, as I had read every square inch of the document, where the terms and conditions clearly stated that to secure an eviction, they would have to apply to the court. I also added that unless, he'd say anything of interest to say, to go about his business, as he was holding us both up.

Unable to argue his case, Max turned heels and went back to his office. Feeling pleased with myself, we headed off, as a more deserving veteran, was requiring our help. After an eventful day, returning to Rosendale, which was buzzing, with gossip about this new boy, taking on Max and not giving a fuck! As although, I had only been there a few short days, I noticed an air of intimidation, and grown ex-servicemen and women, as well as staff, mostly the younger generation, seemed shit scared, of this 5 foot 4 weasel of a man. In my opinion, he was a nobody, and myself, and the older veterans, weren't prepared to put up with any of his nonsense. I gathered, with all new tenants, he would try and test the waters and see if he could cast over, his intimidating spell, and bow down to him. He failed with me and would soon regret pissing me off in the first place.

For the next few days, I continued to work with Alec, and had very little dealings with Max, as he had kept a low profile. I even kept my promise to Lorne and took him to Arbroath on the train. I'd even managed to persuade Neil, to arrange a packed lunch as it was Saturday, and Max wouldn't be in the know. I had never been to Arbroath but had an expert guide, and we had a great time. Lorne insisted that he paid, as he was grateful for my help, and wouldn't have it any other way. He wouldn't even allow me to buy him a coffee, and I felt humbled at his generosity, after all, I would have settled for nothing more, than seeing him happy.

Now Monday, Alec dropped me off for my appointment at the Lily Walker centre. I explained my situation but was stopped in mid-sentence by the advisor, who informed me that, 'I was the wrong nationality!' It seemed like I was back to the days, of trying to get help from the social back in London. Gobsmacked, at what I thought was a racial response, I inquired was it to do with being English? The advisor shook her head, and said, 'no Mr

Briggs, you don't understand, my meaning. You are the wrong nationality.' It was then the penny dropped, and she was referring to foreign immigrants!

I couldn't believe what I was hearing, were they for real? All they could offer to do for me was to put me in touch, with a private landlord or letting agency, as the council wouldn't even entertain it. Even though they had the letter from Rosendael, stating that was there as a temporary measure. Shaking my head, I agreed, and they made an appointment, for that same morning.

Disappointed, with their advice I left, and Alec dropped me off, outside the rental agency, above Cash Converters in Whitehall Crescent, while he went off to Perth. Still raging, I took a deep breath, before venturing inside, thinking this would also be a waste of my time.

However, my disappointment was short-lived as they explained, they specialised, in helping tenants without deposits, and DHSS. The news lightened my mood. After taking my details, they had an ideal one-bedroom property based in Douglas. The only drawback was it only had electric heating. At that point, I didn't give a damn if it had no heating, as I needed a permanent base to operate from, and I asked for a viewing. After speaking with the landlord, they arranged a viewing for the next morning.

After the meeting, I felt more at ease. Regardless of what the flat looked like, even with the electric heating, I was determined to have it. Spending most of the day in town, I returned to Rosendael later in the evening. Brian, the warden, called me over for a chat and told me that I had some mail, but I wouldn't like what I saw. He wouldn't go into detail, but I instinctively knew there was a problem.

Going to my room, I found my post strewn across the floor. It wasn't the letters that I had a problem with, it was the fact, they were opened, and my items, especially my passport, I had sent off to the social for my claim was on the floor. I hit the roof, and someone was going to pay. I stormed downstairs and confronted Brian, who explained that he had been handed them by Max, and had been opened by him.

He felt guilty that he had been told to post them, and had shown his disgust, to Max. I couldn't blame Brian, it was Max, who would exact my wrath.

I immediately put in a written complaint; Brian ensured me he'd log it onto the system.

As I was leaving to go back to my room, Alec walked through the front door and I explained to him what Max had done. He was also incensed and asked if I wanted him to be there when I confronted Max.

I refused his offer, as the way I was feeling, things might get messy.

After a restless night brewing over it, I stormed downstairs to confront Max. As I walked through the door with the evidence, I was stopped by his secretary, who incensed me further by asking why I was making a complaint. I was angry and told her to leave me alone. Then I added, 'how dare you open my letters!'

I headed towards Max office, and she told me he was in a meeting with Neil and couldn't be disturbed. I ignored her advice and told her to 'fuck off' again!

Bursting the door open to Neil's office, Max stood there, as if butter wouldn't melt in his mouth. He even had the cheek to ask,

'What's wrong pal!' I flew at the bastard and told him.

'I'm not your pal or your mate. Explain this shit!' He casually walked out and towards his own office.

By that time, a group had gathered including Alec and were cheering me on. Opening his office, his secretary asked,

'Do you want me to come in, Max?' As the door closed, I was angry and asked the reason they were opening my mail, which was a crime, and that I would be reporting it to the police. He tried to deny it and blamed his staff, but what he didn't know was that I had proof that he'd done it. I looked him square in the eye, and told him, 'to get lost!' Barging past him, making sure, I made contact with his shoulder, as I did so.

Returning to my room, Alec came with me when I rang the police. Half an hour later, they arrived and took details. They told me Max and his secretary had owned up that they had opened my mail, and would investigate further. By the time they disappeared, I was late in getting to the viewing. Alec dropped me off and came with me, as I was still fuming. I met up with the agent and landlord named Steve.

I apologised for my delay and explained the reason I was late. Looking around the flat, I instantly took a shine to it and said I would take it, as I needed to get out of Rosendale before I did something I would later regret. Steve was happy for me to take over the lease, as I didn't have a bond, I was glad to pay an extra ten pounds on top of the three hundred and thirty monthly rent. All that needed was to sign the dotted line, there and then, they handed the keys to me.

As soon as we returned to Rosendale, I penned a letter, giving them a week's notice to leave, handing it to Max. As he read it, I was visibly relieved that I was going, as he wanted to be rid of me; I had become a thorn in his side. However, he did shake my hand and wished me luck.

Moving day arrived, the past week, hadn't come soon enough, for my liking, as Max, had pissed me off several times, which he would soon regret, as I would be leaving him a parting gift. I had arranged to meet up with one of Alec's friends, who was a reporter for one of the local newspapers the Courier, who had reported damming stories about Max and Rosendael before I came on the scene.

I'd already read these stories and had the first-hand experience about his nasty ways. Alec had already informed me that one of the residents had taken his own life, through bullying from Max, and his younger minions. The poor boy's body was discovered four days later alone in his room. This disgusting little man was also the instigator, in hounding out one of the therapists who had been employed to help residents by using gardening as therapy. She'd kept a diary into her experiences, but was too scared to take it further, due to intimidation! I was now in possession of this diary, which was grim reading.

Although these incidents were reported to the authorities, Max always seemed to get away with it, but not this time! Before heading to my new home, Alec and I picked up a donated cream leather sofa, and a wardrobe. As the flat was unfurnished, Alec suggested that I keep it as I was helping him in his charity. As a veteran myself, my needs were just as crucial like others that we had helped. I was overjoyed in his suggestion; at least I would have a makeshift bed instead of a cold floor.

Although donated, these few items were like a godsend. I felt like all my birthdays and Christmases had come at once! We also stopped off, at a local charity, that had some essential household items, such as plates, cutlery, pots, cups, duvet, kettle, and a few basic groceries.

Back at home, after unloading, while I made some tea, Alec contacted Dundee house, to apply for a start-up grant, for a bed, fridge freezer, and a cooker. The flat had a separate fridge, freezer and washing machine. The idea was to sell some of the items, as all I was entitled too was a single bed, which wasn't appropriate for my needs, any cash left over, would be used for groceries, and electric. OK, this was a bit of a cheat, but needs must. He also managed to get a friend of his to lend a small DVD TV!

My first night in the flat was bliss, I didn't have a cooker, and relished my first meal of sausage supper, from the local chippie! The next morning, Alec came to pick me up, as we had arranged to meet up, with the reporter from the Courier, to tell my story about Max and my experience at Rosendael. I wasn't holding anything back, as his comeuppance was long overdue!

Also, the information I'd been supplied from the member of staff proved valuable. A damming article was written, which included my photo. As a result, the Care commission reopened a case into Rosendael, which lead to an inquiry. Max was hauled over the coals by his superiors, but they fell short in sacking him. However, changes were implemented, which benefitted the residents, so all is well that ends well.

The flat proved to be a godsend, and a few days after I moved in, my cooker had arrived, along with the upright fridge freezer, which I sold for eighty pounds, and that allowed me to get the double bed. I had been allowed a cash allowance for a single bed.

With everything in place, I could now concentrate my efforts in finding employment. I was still helping Alec as a volunteer but needed to earn my own money. My advisor was unable to find me any work in the building industry but suggested I go into the care system. I'd never thought about becoming a care worker before, but the thought appealed to me, and I enrolled in a care course.

It was now the end of November the course was interesting; I passed the first time. During the course, they put us on placements. I opted for care in the community and was placed with Gowrie. I enjoyed learning about the kind of care they offered and hoped I would be offered a chance for an interview at least. The organisers of the course had secured two interviews, one with Gowrie, while the other at Linlathen neurological centre. Doing well in both interviews, it was now just a waiting game of who would offer me employment.

December arrived and I had been patiently waiting for some news of a job. As I hadn't heard anything, I assumed that I was not successful with either company. When I had almost given up hope, a week before Christmas 2013, I received two letters, one each from both companies. As I read intently, I was ecstatic that I had been offered both positions.

However, I was disappointed as the job that I was most interested in at Gowrie, was only offering me fourteen hours a week part-time. I needed full-time hours. I turned down the offer and explained my reasons and opted for Linlathen. They gave me a start date of 6th January 2014.

My first Scottish Christmas was bleak. I had informed the social, I'd been offered a job, and the start date, which of course meant that I would lose my benefits. My rent had been paid to cover me until I got paid from work. However, my benefit was only half of what I had been expecting. It was a freezing time of year, and not coming from Scotland, I felt it more than most. I had no money to buy any food or fill up the electric.

A few days before Christmas, I went down to see an advisor of ASAP, which is the 'armed service advice project', a kind of citizens advice for ex-service veterans based in the Arndale centre. Through them, they arranged with SSAFA, another military charity for a top-up for the electric. Also, they arranged for the local food bank for some groceries not festive, but welcomed all the same.

The top-up was twenty pounds, which I thought was a bit of a joke, and it meant that I wouldn't be able to heat the flat, for any length of time, as it was an expensive, antiquated electric storage system. Still, being in the position I was, it was better than nothing, spending most of my time wrapped in a duvet! Even, at least I could look forward to a bright New Year, with my new job. Christmas flew past, it was now New Year's Eve. Alone,

I resigned to the fact that I would see in the New Year by myself. However, to my surprise,   one of the neighbours invited me to join them for the Hogmanay celebration.

I explained I hadn't anything to bring, as regards alcohol, but this didn't faze them and insisted that I come along. I was so glad I did, as I was given a warm welcome, and have to say I enjoyed my first traditional Scottish celebration, and one I would always remember it with great fondness. The best thing was, I hadn't far to go when I felt a bit worse for wear.

6th January 2014. It was the first day, at my new job. I was nervous as hell, while I walked to work, but elated I was now back in employment. Walking through the door, I pressed the buzzer and waited for a member of staff to come along. I had arrived half an hour early for my shift, as I didn't want to give a wrong impression on my first day. After a few moments, I was greeted by the head of the department, who showed me to the nurse's room, where they allowed me, to get acquainted with the clients care notes.

The department I had been placed in, was home to clients who have Huntington's disease. I'd never heard of this condition, which is an incurable hereditary neurological illness, which over time, robs patients of their life, culminating in them reverting to being babies, and unable to look after themselves.

It was heart-breaking to see these clients, all who had lived normal lives, even having families of their own, robbed of their identity. I was given a mentor who would train me in the care of the clients, based on their care plans. Seeing their photos, and reminders of home life were upsetting, and I wondered if I could cope with the job. Throughout the day, I picked up the duties quickly, and the twelve-hour shift passed by in an instant.

Now back at home, I was exhausted, but elated that I had completed my first shift. I cooked tea, and thought long and hard about the job, and if I could do it to the best of my ability. After a while, my instincts kicked in and told me, I had been through worse, and had got to the other side. As the days passed, I got more and more used to working with the clients, and quickly grew a thick skin, so that it wouldn't get to me. I got on well with my colleagues, was well-liked, and felt more at ease the longer worked there.

It was now payday, being handed my first payslip for a long time, bought a smile to my face. I ensured my rent was covered, before budgeting for my expenditure. The feeling I got, going shopping for groceries, made me feel important, and proud I had earned money, rather than relying on the government to bail me out. In other words, for the first time in a long time, I felt I belonged and was paying my way again!

The days rolled into weeks, the weeks into months, I was now attuned with the job, as if I had been doing it for years. I was also now back in the black and could afford to buy new clothes, and other items for my flat, making it more like home. It was now April, and I received a letter from Gowrie, who now offered me another position, with twenty-eight hours part-time. I contacted them and explained. I required full-time hours and wasn't prepared to leave Linlathen, for anything less than thirty-eight hours a week. I didn't expect to hear from them again, as I had made my position clear.

However, a few days later, I received another letter from them, this time from one of the area managers, asking me to call at my earliest convenience. Without hesitation, I rang and spoke with Ann, who inquired if I would be interested in a full-time position at one of her projects in Birkdale. I told her, I had only been offered part-time hours, and that was the reason I turned them down previously. She understood at my frustration, and pulled some string with the senior management to give me the thirty-eight hours that I longed for, and arranged a meeting the next day, as I would be off.

The informal meeting was at one of her projects at Birkdale Place. At first, I had trouble finding the place, as I had assumed it was a care home like Linlathen and had to ring up, to ask directions. As I was speaking, Ann came out of the front door of a bungalow, which I was standing directly outside. Ushering me in, I sat down, while she made me a tea and we chatted about the job. She explained the project was home to six adult men, all who had varying learning difficulties, and we were sitting in the project office.

As we were talking, another member of staff appeared. Ann asked if she could take me around to introduce me to some of the clients. It was much different to what I was used to, as this was care in the community, with each individual, having their own home. The project was a series of five bungalows, three in Birkdale Place, and two in Hoylake Crescent.

It was more relaxing than Linlathen, and not hospital-like, the more I saw and heard, the more I was impressed with the setup.

Returning to the office, I took Ann up on her offer, which I would put in writing, before returning home, and penning a resignation letter, which I handed in on my next shift. After working my notice, I had a week, before starting my new position at Birkdale.

They gave me a warm welcome, from the project manager and the staff, which were much more formal than what I had been used to. My morning was taken up with acquainting myself with the clients' care plans.

Being the new boy, I was questioned, by the other members of staff, where I came from, what I had been doing, as most of them were women, they even asked if I was single! In the afternoon, they introduced me to my mentor, who showed me the ropes with one of the clients.

Returning home after my shift, I was happy I'd been given the opportunity, to work in the type of care, that had originally wanted to practice. Although grateful to Linlathen, at Gowrie, I felt I had more options for career advancement. Not only that, but it was also more pay, still shift work, it was only eight hours, compared to twelve.

Just as at Linlathen, I settled in well with the duties, and staff alike. As part of the responsibilities, I had to administer controlled medication and sat a written evaluation which I passed. Whereas Linlathen employed overpaid nurses, who in my opinion at that time, were somewhat arrogant, and thought, they were above helping out, apart from administering medication, which didn't go down well, with the support staff including myself, as we were rushed off our feet most of the time.

However, there was none of that at Birkdale. We all supported each other, in carrying out our duties effectively, which was, more of a benefit to the clients, as it meant, we could offer a more effective care system, and encouraged the clients, to live a more normal life. Most of the clients had been residents at Straithmartine hospital, which I later found out, had employed, a somewhat antiquated regime, which affected the client's mental health. By working at Birkdale, my confidence grew. I was optimistic about my future.

Also, Rebecca and her crew had ramped up their investigations into Alston and were building a watertight case. They would frequently travel up from London, where I would be shown, literally thousands of photos, which they had required, after a search of Alston's home.

It was upsetting at the time, but it was necessary if the case was to stand a chance in court. She also informed me, they had contacted all the other names I had supplied them with, and as a result, the investigation had grown. The operation was codenamed 'operation Fairbank'. They were confident that a conviction could be secured, and assured me that no stone would be left unturned, in their quest for the truth.

September 2014, Rebecca contacted me, to announce that the CPS had given them the go-ahead, to charge Alston with six counts of child abuse. At long last, I was going to have my day in court, which was scheduled for 17th of August 2015. Overjoyed by this news, I knew that my future was going to be brighter, I still had a long way to go. But for now, I was happy and proud of myself, as I had come so far in the short time that I had been in Scotland.

December 2014. Christmas had arrived again, and the year had flown by, I was now an established member of the Birkdale team. I had been scheduled to work on Christmas day, which I didn't mind at all. The previous Christmas had been dire, but I was determined to enjoy this one, as people would surround me. Some of the clients had gone to enjoy the festivities with their families. Those who remained would enjoy their time, as all of us who were working made it special for them all. We made the project office kitchen, into a place where we could hold a party for all of them.

Cooking the Christmas dinner was fun-filled, all the clients enjoyed the atmosphere that we had provided. One of the members of staff brought his client, who was music-ma a new music centre, and some opera, of which he enjoyed listening too. To watch him being emotional, upon hearing the arias, bought tears to all our eyes, this made the day even more special. It seemed all our problems, paled into insignificance, compared to what the clients had to deal with, daily. It would be a Christmas I will always remember, which made my own Christmas more bearable, I was thankful for the opportunity. I couldn't wait for the Hogmanay celebration, as I would be off, having worked over the festive period. As I now earned my own money, it meant I could venture out into town, and enjoy myself, seeing the New Year in all its glory, amongst the fine Scottish revellers!

Chapter Twenty

Regina Vs Alston

5th January 2015. A year had passed since I started working again. I had plans to get myself a car, yet I knew I had a poor credit score due to varying reasons. After discussing it with a work colleague, they provided me with a company who specialised in car credit for people with poor credit history. After applying, they offered me a loan, albeit at a higher interest rate of 31% APR. Although more expensive, the payments were affordable, and I had set my heart on treating myself and signed up immediately.

With the money now transferred in my bank, I searched around for different car dealers in the area, opting for a metallic blue 4-year-old Peugeot 308. My new wheels meant that I could now explore Scotland on a larger scale, instead of being confined to the local areas. I would venture out more on most of my days off to admire the beautiful countryside and amazing towns that my new home had to offer.

It was like I had been given a new start in life, and was a great way of escaping the reality of everyday life. I'll recharge my batteries, and enhance my knowledge of this beautiful country, and its amazing people. With work and personal life sorted, I could now concentrate on my next hurdle, my pending upcoming court case! Over the next few months, Rebecca and members of the team visited me several times. We trawled through the gathered evidence and updates. I'd already informed my immediate manager and Ann about taking a holiday to cover my court appearance, which no other members of staff knew.

A week before the trial, Rebecca and another member of the team made arrangements to visit me and go over the finer points of my case. When they arrived, they brought with them, a DVD player, which had my original, and subsequent interview recordings. Hearing them again, brought back so many memories, and I shed a tear or two.

They asked probing questions, which were designed to test me and my reactions in the courtroom, and were based on questions that a defence Barrister may ask.

Satisfied that I was ready for court, Rebecca gave me my train tickets, and accommodation details, explaining they would meet me at Southwark Crown Court.

She and her team were confident they had secured enough evidence to ensure Alston would be convicted. Although I still had reservations myself on how the jury would vote.

Throughout their investigation, I had built up a rapport with the investigation team and had confidence in their abilities. It would now be down to me to convince the jury, that this vile bastard would be locked away, preferably for a very long, long time, and rightly so.

Sunday, 16th August 2015. After a long arse numbing journey, I arrived in London. I'd been booked into The Tower Hotel right next to Tower Bridge on the bank of the Thames. After booking in, I was shown into a plush room, I wasn't expecting such an expensive hotel. I assumed it would be a cheaper, as the British taxpayers were footing the bill. However, it was most relaxing and allowed me to remain calm for my court appearance the next day.

After refreshing myself from the journey, I went out for some fresh air and take in the sights, which may seem to be weird to some, as I'd pounded the streets when I was homeless almost two years earlier. It was a bright sunny day, and it was buzzing with tourists, and Londoners alike, out to enjoy the beautiful sunshine and frequent the bars and restaurants, around the area.

I walked up the stairs to the bridge pavement. Now walking along this impressive bridge for the first time, taken aback at the fantastic views from this engineering marvel. I stopped at one of the towers to admire the view. It was a far cry from when I last looked over the Thames, when on the streets from London Bridge.

I felt at ease, and hadn't a care in the world, even though, in less than 24 hours, I would be facing my abuser in court, for the first time in over 40 years. Walking across the other side, I'd now stepped foot in Southwark, walking along the bank of the Thames, with its flourishing businesses, and beautiful skyline, both modern and traditional.

Turning down the side street, where the courthouse was located, I was surprised to see it was surrounded with great places to eat, including Jamie Oliver's Italian, and other interesting landmarks. Standing in front of the court and staring at the famous façade, I took a deep breath and thought about the trial scheduled for the next day.

Then I took a stroll back to the hotel, bought a cup of coffee and sat down, looking at the river Thames. Now relaxed, a large cruise ship was being towed, and the famous bridge opened to allow it to pass, it was a spectacle I'd never witnessed before as I stared in awe as the bridge was drawn upright, to allow a colossal vessel to pass.

My only regret was I did not have a camera to record the amazing event. Returning to my room, I settled down on the bed and fell asleep.

Awaking several hours later, it was now early evening and I went down for dinner. After eating, I went for a walk around the inland waterway near the hotel. I sat down for a smoke and relaxed, breathing in the warm night air. Thinking about the trial, I rang Jackie to tell her I was in London for my court date, and to catch up with her news. I always felt relaxed after talking to her as she put my mind at ease. I also spoke to my mate Steve and had a great laugh as usual. Both of them wished me luck and I felt at peace after talking.

17th August 2015. The morning of the trial, I awoke fresh and ready for anything. Slightly nervous about the proceedings, I felt the only way to settle the butterflies was to eat a hearty breakfast to set up the day. It was another sunny morning, and I felt happy that no matter the outcome, today was going to be the day that I got to tell my story.

The time was 08.30, I wasn't due to appear in court until 09.30, but I took a slow walk across the bridge, to settle any last-minute nerves. Striding out across the bridge, just as I did the day before, only this time, I was a man on a mission. The nearer I got to the court, the more nervous I became. It was a feeling of nervousness, brought on by knowing that through my testimony, I was bringing a paedophile to justice, and felt I should have done it several years ago. Had I done so, I may have saved many victims from Alston evil clutches. In a word, it was more of a guilty feeling, which bought a tear to my eye.

Now in front of the court. I settled my nerves by lighting up a cigarette, sitting on a wall outside the building. As I did so, I noticed Alston arriving in court my eyes keeping track of his every step. At that point, I felt nothing but hatred for that despicable dirty nonce and envisaged breaking his neck, which bought a smile to my face—extinguishing my smoke. I waited until he disappeared before entering myself.

Going through security, I met Rebecca and some of the team at the security gates. Only in front of us, Alston had been whisked away by his legal team, where I was escorted toward the witness room. I sat down, before being joined by a court liaison officer brought in to keep me company until I was called to give evidence. Rebecca briefed me for a few moments, before leaving to fetch the prosecuting barrister. Shaking my hand, he briefed me in the type of questions the defence team would ask. He was confident that a conviction could be brought. But my scepticism couldn't share his enthusiasm.

I made it clear to him that I had no faith in the British Justice system, making my views known. I thought the defence barrister was a disgusting arsehole, wanting to defend a nonce! Unfazed, he reiterated that he had known the defence barrister for many years, and whatever his personal views on Alston, he still had a job to do in defending him. Now I'm not sure, if he was aware of what he would say, or if it was planned, but what assured me of his intentions, when he told me that the defence will be asking questions, but not as in-depth, as they would otherwise do if it were a different type of defendant.

Not only that, but his body language and facial expression appeared to suggest, the defence barrister wasn't keen on defending a paedophile, it was merely part of his job! Either that, or he was trying to ensure that I remained calm. I felt more at ease after speaking with him. After his talk, he returned to court, leaving me alone with the liaising officer.

As time ticked by, I noticed I still hadn't been called. It was now 10.30 am, an hour after I should have been giving my evidence. Now anxious, as I had a feeling, that this bastard was going to get away with it and walk free. A short time later. Rebecca and a member of her team joined me. She explained that they were still going through some legal arguments, and other evidence, so there was a delay in calling me but was confident I would soon be.

I had nothing but respect for Rebecca and the team. I had built up a rapport over the two years I had been involved with them, and their tireless in-depth investigations, and I felt more at ease after her explanation. As we were talking, I heard my name, standing up, I took a deep breath and followed the clerk of court with Rebecca and the team close behind.

Walking through the door of the court, I noticed to the right of me, Alston sitting in the glass-fronted dock, his brother was sitting behind it. To the left was the public gallery, which was full, and included press reporters. Further along the left, was the court reporter and court clerks.

I was shown to the witness stand, which was a table and chair, and nothing like I had imagined.

My heart was pounding and had a nervous knot in the pit of my stomach. As I sat down, to my left, was the presiding Judge, in his red gown and traditional wig. To the right, was the prosecuting barrister, and to his left was the defence, behind them, were the legal teams. Directly opposite was the jury, who I was directed to give my answers too. I was sworn in, and the court was now in session.

My barrister asked me my details before asking me his prepared questions. I answered them truthfully, and always directed y answers at the jury. Although nervous, as each question was being asked, I felt less so, as I was determined to tell my story. I turned my head, to look at that bastard Alston, each time, he would bow his head, and couldn't look at me. To me, this was an admission of his guilt, he knew what he had done, and I was going to make him pay!

As the trial went on, the questions became more in-depth, which would reduce me to tears, as I had to relive the horrors that the scumbag had inflicted on me. Occasionally, the proceedings had to be halted, to allow me to compose myself., with the clerk of court, handing me a glass of water and tissues. The judge asked if I wanted a break, or even a curtain, to shield myself from Alston. I refused his offer, as I wanted to ensure that Alston, knew what he had done, and besides, I wasn't scared of him and felt he was a pathetic, pitiful little man, a disgraceful short nonce, who had it coming!

As lunchtime approached, my barrister asked the last of his questions. Although I had broken down on numerous occasions, I'd managed to give my answers clearly to the court. The Judge recessed so that we could break for lunch, and I was escorted out, still tearful, but proud. As I was walking through the court, Alston shrouded his face and could see various members of the public, openly distressed at what they had heard. Now back into the public area, Rebecca and members of the team greeted me. Shaking my hand, they told me I'd done well, and believed the case was going in my favour.

Needing a cigarette, as I was shaking, and still tearful. A sergeant escorted me out of the building. I hadn't met him before but was part of the team behind the scenes. Like me he was a true cockney, and blow me down with a feather, he also supported QPR. He handed me one of his cigarettes, as my hands were shaking so much and I couldn't roll one myself. We had a good talk, he thought I'd been brave in reliving the horror of my past, but thanked me in helping them in their investigation. That gave me confidence, and I thanked him before heading off for a much-needed break, and even more needed coffee!

I didn't venture far from the court, deciding to find a coffee shop on the banks of the Thames. Stopping off at the first one I came to, I bought a coffee and sat outside on a set of steps to enjoy my coffee, and soak up the sunshine. As I reflected my morning so far, my phone rang. It was my lawyer Tracey, who explained that one of her members of staff, had been in court in the public gallery, and would it be possible for her to call me?

Of course, I agreed, and after hanging up, I received another call from the staff member who introduced herself as Dawn. She told me that the case was going well, and in her professional opinion, had confidence that my testimony would result in a conviction. Her words grew my confidence, and I was more encouraged to face the second half against the defence.

After our brief conversation, I walked the short journey back to the court. I was greeted by Rebecca, who introduced me to her boss, the Chief Inspector. After exchanging a few words, we ventured back inside the court building, where I was escorted back toward the witness room by another member of the investigation team. As we approached the room, we had to pass Alston who shielded his face moving out of our way. The officer told me that Alston had aged significantly since his first arrest, and looked nothing like he did when he was first questioned over two years earlier. Even so, I couldn't give a shit about this arsehole, and hoped that he would be found guilty!

After a short while, they called me back into the courtroom. More confident in my abilities after the morning session. With my head held high, and shoulders back, striding in as if I were a soldier again. Sitting back down, the Judge reminded me I was still under oath, and the session was brought to order. The defence barrister stood up and started his questioning. Trying to hang In a few curved balls, to trip me up along the way, which I wasn't falling for.

Again, through his questioning, I broke down several times. As before, the judge halted proceedings, to allow me to compose myself. After what appeared to be a lifetime, the defence barrister asked his final questions. I answered to the best of my ability.

I'd braved the storm, and told my story, regardless of what the rest of the evidence had come up with, and it was in the hands of the jury. The Judge turned to me, and thanked me for my testimony, before dismissing me as a witness. Relieved, I was escorted out of the courtroom and free to leave and return to my hotel. I'd been advised by my barrister in the morning, that I could return the next day and stay the public gallery, I should go home, as the Judge might still call me back.

Outside the court building, Rebecca and the team thanked me, and they all shook my hand. As the trial was still going on, Rebecca told me she would keep me informed of the deliberation. With an overwhelming feeling of exhaustion, I thanked every one of the team, before returning to the hotel for a much-needed rest.

Back in my room, I went for a relaxing shower, as I did so, I couldn't help but allow tears of joy flow. I was euphoric; at long last, someone had listened to my case. The investigating team had pulled out all the stops and brought a strong case, even though there was still a long wait to secure a conviction, but deep down, I was quietly confident! Making myself a cuppa, I lay on the bed to relax before falling asleep, after such a rewarding but emotional day.

Several hours later, I awoke refreshed and starving. I hadn't eaten since breakfast and thought as it was my last night, I would enjoy the best meal the hotel had to offer.

I dressed and went down for my evening meal. The menu looked amazing and I opted for beef wellington, with seasonal veg. After dinner, I went for a long walk, stopping off for a coffee, relaxing on the banks of the Thames, enjoying the London ambience. I returned to my room before settling down to sleep. I set the alarm for 07.00, wasting no time in showering, before going down for breakfast.

After eating, I returned to my room to pack, before signing out, to catch my train back home.

Back at home, I had an anxious few days wait, to hear if Alston had been convicted. I kept myself busy, taking my mind off the proceedings. Rebecca kept me informed daily about the progress of the trial.

Friday 21st August 2015, Rebecca rang me at 10.00 am, to inform me the Jury had retired, deliberating on all the evidence. The rest of the trial had gone well and they expected a quick verdict. I was a nervous wreck and couldn't concentrate speaking with her. It felt like torture because each second seemed to last hours.

I kept pacing up and down my flat and chain-smoking. At 2 pm, the phone rang, which made me jump out of my skin, my heart was pounding. As I answered, it was Rebecca. It seemed that the jury was still out and that a verdict, might not be reached until the following Monday, as the court closed at 3.30 pm. My heart sank, as I thought the bastard Alston was going to get away scot-free, as his brother had once been in the diplomatic corps, and no doubt pulled a few strings!

Now helpless, all I could do was hope for the best. As 3.00 pm came and went, I thought that this was it, and would have a long agonising wait over the weekend. I resigned myself to the fact there was nothing more I could have done, and worrying wouldn't make it any easier.

As I hadn't been out all day, I started to make a grocery list. Perhaps some shopping would take my mind off it, I thought. As I was listing what I required, the phone rang, I noticed the time was 4.30 pm. To my surprise, it was Rebecca, asking if I was sitting down, as she had some news from the court.

I thought that it was to tell me, he'd been acquitted, but my anxiety turned to triumph, as she announced that a guilty verdict had been reached for two of the five counts. Disappointed at first, until she explained the two he'd been found guilty on, were the more severe indictments, the other three would be kept on file. I was in shock, not able to speak, at long last.

Composing myself, I thanked Rebecca, who would keep me informed of the sentence, which the hearing would be held the following week. I decided the shopping could wait, this was a cause to celebrate, and why not, it was long overdue! Monday arrived, now back at work. I had a wonderful holiday, and even better weekend, safe in the knowledge that Alston was about to be put behind bars.

I threw myself into my work, to take my mind off, waiting for his sentencing later that week. The call I had been waiting for, came through from Rebecca, with the good news.

For the first count, he was sentenced to twelve months, with the second it was nine months, both sentences to run concurrently, and would have to sign, the sex offenders register for the next ten years!

To some, twenty-one months may seem a reasonable sentence. However, everyone who was involved in the trial, in one capacity or another, thought it to be an unduly lenient sentence. And we complained to the CPS.

As a result, I received a letter from the CPS, stating they were reviewing the case, and looking into the three indictments where Alston was not found guilty to see if it would be in the public interest to take him back to court for these charges and try him again with a new jury!

It all depended on the gathered evidence, and the Judges summing up of the original trial before any determination could be agreed on.

The only good thing was that I was informed that if the counts were upheld, his sentence would be increased to five years. Buoyed by this news, it allowed me to swallow the bitter pill a little easier. Also, Rebecca contacted me to explain that the CPS had ordered them to notify Alston that he might spend up to five years in prison if convicted of the counts.

This news was the best yet, and I couldn't help but quip to Rebecca if it would be possible to give Alston'soap on a rope.' Present. Rebecca laughed at my suggestion, but in all seriousness, told me that being the person he was, and the crime of which he had been convicted, it meant that he would be living in fear. Again, I relished the thought of him sitting in his cell, shitting himself with every little noise, having to look behind him everywhere he went.

After several weeks of waiting for the CPS to make a decision, after serious consideration, they agreed it wouldn't go any further. However, the counts would remain on file and would remain so after he was released. That means, if he committed any other crimes, parole violations, or even failure to appear to sign the sex offenders register, they would bring him back into court, and have his sentence increased! At least that made me feel much better, knowing that he would live in fear, for the rest of his miserable life.

With the trial now over, I could concentrate on my work to become a better carer and climb the ladder. I'd been put forward for an SVQ in the care industry. Being the type of person I am, I spent hours studying in my spare time. Also, my lawyer Tracey had built up a strong case for compensation against Ealing council who employed Alston at the height of the abuse.

Working alongside the specialist, historic child abuse barrister, they were confident that they could secure a substantial claim against the council. They had uncovered Alston in January 1979 in Aberdeen. They had admonished him, and it was the equivalent of a Police caution, and under English law, after admitting one count of lewd, indecent, libidinous practices with a boy. Although this was never used in court, part of me wished it had been, as maybe the dirty nonce would receive a heftier sentence.

Having said that, life for me couldn't have been sweeter, with a rosier future it seemed. The year had flown past, it was now November, and was well on my way of passing my SVQ. I was happy but had some sad news to contend with, and I heard one of my good friends I'd served with lost his battle with prostate cancer.

I took a day off work to attend the funeral in England to pay my last respects. The next day, I was back at work, and kept quiet, concentrating on assisting one of the volatile clients. As I was writing his care notes, I was joined by Ann, who shared her condolences which was gratefully received.

However, that was short-lived, as she dropped a bombshell by telling me that I have to attend a disciplinary hearing. There were alleged accusations brought against me from the other members of staff, who claimed I had been disrespectful against them. The worse thing was that I had alleged to have been sexually abusive toward some of the female staff members!

Upon hearing these allegations, I was gobsmacked, as I had kept myself out of their way at work, and only spoke to the female carers on a professional capacity. Although I respected them as persons, I never once thought about them sexually, nor would I ever dream about being disrespectful against them.

There was no way, I was going to be the scapegoat for something I hadn't done, and refuted the claims. After Ann left, I continued working with my client, trying to be professional at all times but felt sick to my stomach.

As soon as Ann disappeared, I went back to the main staff office at Birkdale, where I spoke to my immediate boss Carol. She couldn't talk about the disciplinary but thought it was disgusting, I had been accused, and even said, 'there was some nasty bitches in the project!'

She explained that while the investigation was going on, I would have to be escorted at all times, which she thought was wrong, but had to follow company protocol. She also would forgive me if I went off 'sick' throughout the investigation.

Upon hearing this, there was no way I was going to allow them to scare me off from a job I loved and would carry out my duties to the best of my abilities. Over weeks, I lost weight due to stress, and Carol and some of the other members of staff were worried.

I wasn't eating, and I was chain-smoking, living on cups of tea. My sleep patterns were seriously affected, but I dug deep to stay at my post. I had been called in to give my side to the investigation team and denied every accusation. It would be several weeks before I would be called in for the disciplinary itself.

While waiting, I had a week's holiday, which was a welcome break, as I was well away from prying eyes, and gossip. The only downside was I had been notified through a hand-delivered letter, the disciplinary was to be held during my break the coming Friday.

I contacted Carol, who asked if I wanted a witness to come with me, which I declined. Also, while I was off, I received another letter from a previous job I had applied for before I had known about the disciplinary I had forgotten about. The job itself was working in a special school in Perth which specialised with helping kids that had been abused either physically or sexually.

As I'd been through abuse myself, I thought I would be best placed to understand the trauma they were going through. The letter also stated if I could contact them to arrange for an interview, at a time and date that would be suitable for me. Not knowing the outcome of the upcoming disciplinary, I thought it best to wait.

Friday arrived all too soon. I wasn't to appear for my disciplinary, until 2.30 pm at the head office. The good thing was that there wouldn't be too many prying eyes, as the office staff would have finished for the weekend, and it would be limited to myself, the investigating team, one of the other area managers, and the HR manager.

Although nervous, as I'd never been involved in anything like this before, and I decided if I were going down on trumped-up accusations, then I would go down fighting. When I arrived, I found the door locked and waited for someone to appear. I was greeted by the area manager, who showed me to the room, where the hearing was to take place.

Sitting down, I was informed of how the proceeding would take place. Then the evidence was put to me, which I refuted all allegations. During the proceedings, the same three names were banded around the room, which was three of the female members of staff who had brought the accusations against me.

These three ladies had made serious claims, about what I had so-called done, and were the same members of staff I had made a complaint to my immediate boss because of their laziness.

It seemed to me that this was their way of exacting revenge. What I hadn't envisaged, was that my immediate manager Carol, had furnished the investigating team with evidence that exonerated me from all these malicious claims, like the dates when I had been alleged to have said, or done, I hadn't been on duty!

Even the area manager couldn't believe the reasons I had been hauled in and dismissed the claims. Although this was a relief, I was still up on a charge for taking two of the clients out by myself, which was a result of being on a sleepover duty at the time with the clients that lived in the same home!

Again I argued my case, as I had no choice, as firstly, the duty had always been a ratio of one to two, which came from the project manager. I was unable to obtain any help from other members of staff at the time because there was a shortage of staff on the day in question, which meant I had no choice!

They took this into account, and the company rules were strictly one to one ratio. It seemed I was to be made a scapegoat, and was given a final warning, which disgusted me, as I'd not missed a shift, and was always ready to step in, to cover shifts from others who had gone sick or had turned up late!

After leaving, I rang my immediate manager Carol and told her the outcome. She kindly changed my duties so that I would be on nightshift the following week that way I wouldn't have to get involved, with the bastards of whom had brought the now unfounded allegations against me. On my way home, I was more determined to leave and contacted the company I had already applied.

I was now on nightshift; I arranged an interview for the following Friday after my shift.

It was Friday at last. I couldn't wait to finish the handover to the day staff, to get away to Perth for my interview. The night before, I practised what I was going to say, in the explanation about my recent disciplinary. I had a copy of the findings, which stated that I'd been found guilty of a minor misdemeanour, against company rules, but didn't warrant informing the Care Inspectorate.

As welcome as it was, it could still scupper my chances, but I felt confident, as Carol had assured me she would give me a glowing reference.

I arrived at the school and the nerves set in. It was a combination of tiredness, and concern brought on by the disciplinary. However, I was determined to give a good account of myself. Furthermore, I wanted to be honest and open with them regarding the disciplinary, even if it meant a failure in obtaining the job. I was greeted by the general manager, who I'd met several weeks earlier, in an informal interview before knowing about the disciplinary. Offering me a drink, which I accepted, and served in the communal room, just like that rest of this impressive stately home. The oak-panelled door with original artisan period, architectural features, appealed to my historical side. He explained that the interview was scenario-based and would include meeting some of the pupils, finally culminating in the formal interview with himself, and the school coordinator.

As I went from room to room, I grew in confidence, meeting several pupils, and having a written test, gaining a score of 98% out of 100. Not bad for someone who had been on duty for ten hours. Next to the interview itself, initially nervous, I was made to feel at home, and answered each question precisely, and with conviction. The hardest part was explaining the disciplinary. Nervous as hell, I showed them the copy of the outcome, noticing they didn't seem perturbed by it, which boosted my confidence a thousand-fold.

They asked probing questions on the subject. I answered them honestly. I explained that I was ashamed of myself but felt that I still had something to offer, should they give me a chance to prove myself. However, I would fully understand, if I wasn't successful, and thanked them wholeheartedly, for at least giving me the opportunity.

The interview was now over. I felt proud of myself and been honest with them. Throughout the process, they seemed impressed and hadn't given any indication that they were perturbed by my disciplinary. Shaking their hands, I was told, I would hear later on that day if I had been successful or not. Outside, I breathed a sigh of relief, and headed home, for some much-needed sleep.

After a good uninterrupted sleep, I was ravenous, as I hadn't been eating properly. I got ready to go shopping and treated myself with a greasy fry up with all the works. I kept myself busy, trying not to think about my earlier interview. Although confident, I had a nagging doubt as regards of telling them everything but felt relieved that I had done so, as it wasn't my style to mislead anyone, and had always felt honesty was the best policy. As I settled down, I received a call from the General manager. Upon hearing his voice, I felt sick to my stomach, but my nervousness was soon forgotten, when he announced, I'd been successful, were offering me the position.

I was temporarily lost for words and stuttered, trying to speak, taking a deep breath to compose myself, I inquired as to why! He explained, not only had I scored highly in the written test but had been approved by the pupils of which I'd be helping, and they'd been impressed with my honest and open approach at the interview. I was overjoyed by his news and thanked him most sincerely. He suggested, I didn't resign my position, until I received, the official written confirmation, through the post.

Not only that, but the new position also came with an extra thousand pay increase, a considerable amount, compared to what I was paid at Gowrie. So, all-round a good result, and one I wasn't expecting at all! As it was the weekend, I decided to celebrate and got suited and booted for a night out in the town, where I put the past month's stress, well behind me.

As Monday arrived, I was on a middle shift and would be starting at 11 am. As I was getting ready for my shift, the postie arrived, and with it, the letter of confirmation, from my new position. I was over the moon and penned a resignation letter, which I handed to Carol when I got into work. She was extremely happy for me, as she'd been disgusted by the way I'd been treated, and would give me a more than favourable reference, and would be sad to see me go. To my surprise, she gave me a reassuring hug, which was most unexpected, but heartfelt.

My official finish date was 22nd December 2015. I kept my head down at work, the staff knew I was leaving, but I kept tight-lipped. I had lost respect for most of them, apart from a sprinkling of good people. I'd been assigned from Carol to work alongside my favourite client, who was terminally ill with stomach cancer, and now a patient at Ninewells. I relished this, as most of the time I wouldn't have to put up with any of the bullshit from the other staff at work.

There was also changes afoot at the project, as my actual evidence at the time of the disciplinary and failings within the project were being investigated. My only regret, I wouldn't be there to witness it.

It was my last day, and I was working at the project with another client, keeping a low profile, only associating with the staff when I had no choice. As I was on a morning shift, finishing at 4 pm. Preparing to leave for the last time, the team presented me with some parting gifts. Back at home, hastily opening the letter, I'd been expecting from the new job. Excited to be getting a start date, my excitement didn't last long, as the contents shocked me, the job offer had been withdrawn. I rang up the school and made inquiries and it turned out that the reference had been somewhat unfavourable and they weren't prepared to go into further details.

Not only shocked by this. I was now unemployed, and bloody angry. How could I get such a bad reference, when Carol promised she would provide a good one?

As I had Carol's home number, I rang telling her what happened. She was devastated and assured me that she sent a good one, sending an emailed copy of the original. A short time later, Carol called, as she'd made inquiries as to what had happened. It transpired that the area manager Ann had intercepted Carol's reference, and superseded it with one of her own! I was livid and had to get to the bottom of it.

The head office was now closed, and I had a long night stewing and getting angrier. The next morning, I drove down to the head office to speak to the HR department, and obtain a copy of the reference. As I read it, I was disgusted, the woman had written such a bad reference, and I understood the reason the school withdrew the offer. I was helpless, it was too close to Christmas to do anything about it, and would have to wait until the New year!

Christmas 2015 was bleak and seemed to drag on for ages. I couldn't wait for the New year, at least I could get the ball rolling, and obtain some advice on what to do. Like most people, I thought it was illegal to give an employee a bad reference. I sought professional help from an employment lawyer based in Meadowside,

4th January 2016. Armed with the references, and confident I had a case, against Ann and the head office. I explained my situation, showing the documents, and expecting some good news. I was unprepared for what he told me. Although on my side, and sympathetic to my case due to a change in employment law, as I hadn't been working there for two years, he wouldn't be able to argue my case in court, and the Sherriff wouldn't entertain it.

He'd explained that it was wrong and unethical, it wasn't illegal, for someone to give a bad reference, and could even refuse to provide a reference. Not only disgusted but livid, as the woman could get away with it knowingly. And it would affect any chances for future employment. However, he suggested I write to the HR department, and a plea to their better nature, highlighting my cause and further suggesting sending a copy to the Managing Director who may be able to overrule any detrimental references. Disappointed with his advice, I thanked him and left.

The only good news was that he didn't charge me for his time. Even though I hadn't got the advice I hoped for, I had to remain focused, heading off to the Library to write my letters, and apply online for jobseeker's allowance. I intended to hand them in to the head office personally but thought better of it.

They had already stitched me up, and I didn't trust them an inch in passing on the copy to the Managing Director, so opted to post them instead. Back at home, I contemplated my options, which were limited. Contacting my landlord, and explained my situation, followed by car finance. I kept positive and wasn't going to let it affect me, and would do anything to remain so.

Forty-eight hours later, I received two hand-delivered letters, from head office. One from the Managing Director, which I never envisaged, would reply to me. Reading his reply, was an eye-opener, he was very apologetic about my circumstances, and ordered the HR department to send another reference, as regards of my entire record of employment, and not one written as a personal attack on my credibility. From what I understand, he was far from happy with one of his managers, giving such a bad reference to an employee, which would affect their chances of future employment.

Enclosed in the other letter, was the reference, which was a true reflection, and surprisingly good. It did not refer the misdemeanour or the disciplinary. I breathed a sigh of relief, and I could now apply for work with confidence.

Finding a job was proving to be a nightmare, as the days and weeks passed, I was struggling. Not only was I out of work, but I was also, not in receipt of jobseeker's allowance or housing benefit. It was due to leaving my job voluntarily, even though I had proved I had done so, believing I was to start a new job.

I had no money or means of supporting myself. Now in debt with my landlord for non-payment of rent. He understood my predicament and cutting me some slack. Not only that, but I was also in debt with the car credit company, who were chasing me for payment.

I was at my wit's end and falling into a deep depression. I had to do something before my life spiralled out of control. My only hope was to speak with ASAP, the armed service advice project, who got me help with food banks, contacting various armed service charities to help with other essential needs.

After eight weeks, of banging my head against the wall with the Social, they relented and awarded my benefits. By this time, I was in severe debt. However, I received a lifeline as Tracey my lawyer had contacted me, stating the education authority, which employed my abuser Alston, had admitted liability. She and the specialist barrister had put in an initial claim of £50,000, which would be batted back and forth until a final figure would be agreed. At last, some good news it seemed, it would be several more weeks, or even months, for it to be finalised.

May 2016, I was still unemployed and had taken steps to have the car returned, which stopped the hounding calls but even meant, I would be liable for the arrears, They'd frozen the interest, which I negotiated on my behalf via a debt specialist. Now at my lowest ebb, I was affected, and couldn't see any light, at the end of the tunnel. Trying desperately to find suitable employment, I sank into despair and couldn't motivate myself. Sitting there feeling sorry for myself, my landlord rang to inquire if I was at home, and my heart sank. I believed he wanted to come around to speak about the rent arrears, and I would be made homeless again.

As the buzzer sounded, I felt sick and had resigned to my fate. Opening the door, Steve was standing there, with what I thought was his groceries. Walking in, handing me the bags, and said he had bought them for me. He knew I was in severe debt with rent but had no intention of kicking me out. I could feel the tears forming and tried to remain focused. However, I couldn't stop them from flowing when he handed me a twenty-pound note and a weekly bus ticket.

I couldn't thank him enough, he owed me nothing, but his kindness was more than I expected. He also suggested that I apply for a job as a bus driver, at the garage he worked at and put his name to the application.

When he left, I cried like a baby. I stared at the food he kindly bought, what made it even worse was I had been living on basic groceries from the food bank. Although I was grateful that they did. After composing myself, I vowed to forever be in his debt, and pass on his kindness to others, including himself, when my claim was settled.

Some months passed, I'd found some temporary work with an agency, working in care homes. It was a start, and couldn't be happier, earning money again. At the same time, my compensation claim had been settled at £35,000. My cut after fees was £24,000, and I wasted no time in paying off my debts, especially Steve, giving him £100 as a gift to thank him for his help. I had enough left over to buy a car outright. Life was moving up, and I was feeling upbeat for the future. Steve came around as he would be fitting central heating.

As I'd a building background, the preparation and remodelling work after fitting would be done by myself. The cherry on top of the cake with Steve's help was that I'd been given an interview at the garage, and I passed with flying colours. All that stood in my way was passing a medical, theory, and hazard perception, before being offered a position as a bus driver—passing both tests, having to wait until December for my medical. As it was now close to Christmas, I would have to wait until New Year for the results.

January 2017, I still hadn't received my medical test result's and called the garage, to find out. I was told the doctor I saw at Michelin had put down that I suffered from depression, and would be contacting my GP for further information before proceeding with my application. A few days later my doctor called me to explain he'd sorted it out, and was somewhat dismayed the company's chosen specialist had made such a mistake. After his intervention, I was contacted by the Garage to arrange a start date. As I was still working, a date was set for 26th March 2017, so I could tie up any loose ends. At last, I was going places. I had a great training team at the garage, passing my test the first time. It would only be a few weeks later it would be out in service.

Chapter Twenty-one

Walking Tall

So, what for me now? As this chapter's title name suggests, I'm walking tall. Although I've always walked tall, I didn't recognise it until now.

I now work in the transport industry where I've forged friendships with some amazing people. As a man of my word, so they all have 15 minutes of fame, I'll introduce you, to my closest friends.

Alec Law. Been in the industry for donkey's years. Deeply knowledgeable, quick-witted, and such a laugh. Calls me his sweetness, never have a dull moment, when he's around. Alan Donnelly. Brilliant bloke. Been out with Alan many times, such a nice person. Incidentally before driving a bus, he was in the film industry, rubbing shoulders with the stars most nights! As glamourous as it seems, he was a projectionist. I have the utmost respect for him.

Davy Kerr. Another likeable character, whom I have a great laugh with, especially when out with Alan, and other drivers on a night out. Originally from Dunblane, if it hadn't been for him nursing a hangover, he may not be here today, as he was at home, when the maniac went on the rampage, killing innocent victims. Eden Whitcombe. An amazing person loves a 'swally' as he puts it, we've been out on numerous occasions, having a good blether, laugh, and more than a few jars! Derek Mawhinney loves a flutter on the footy. Both of us drive the same route, keeps himself to himself mostly, but still a great all-round fella.

Mark Selerowicz. Or shaky as we all call him, on the account, due to a heredity condition, his hands shake. Loves a laugh, and can handle a joke, giving as good as he gets, from us taking the piss! Vito Giannico, of Scottish and Italian descent, relatively new to the industry, I hit it off with him straight away. Many a time, we've had a good blether and laugh within our clique. Would do anything for anyone.

Malcolm E Creegan (Malky). In a word amazing! When he heard I was writing my autobiography, inquired if he, could be one of the first to read it, as a freebie! After trading a jovial insult, going one better, allowed him to read a few chapters of the manuscript. Bowled over, when I asked him, for an honest critique. I'm glad I did, as a few days later, caught up with me, and loved what he had read so far, and couldn't wait for the finished copy.

He explained, he cried his eyes out, not only through sadness but through laughter, which is a complete honour for me.

John Dunbar. A biker, nice fella. Stupidly, we had a bit of a fallout, over a trivial matter. Glad to say, it's all ironed out, and we're good friends again. Gary Cassidy. Love the bloke, calls me the 'Guvnor!' Had more than a few laugh with him, as well as a few bevvies.

Willie Faulds. Another great bloke, always laughing and joking, always got time for you. Helped me out more than I can remember. Always there to lend a hand, a larger than life character.

Last but not least, the ladies that I work with. Mary Hepburn. A great woman loves a laugh with us, whenever she gets a chance, and a good listener. Yvonne Wilson. Left the garage to pursue other interests. A kind of a Bet Lynch character, off Coronation Street. Bold as brass, and with an infectious dirty laugh, certainly don't take no shit from nobody. Sometimes, I haven't got a clue what she's saying, as she is a broad Dundonian!

Yvonne Leslie. Nice all-round person, likes a blether, has given me good advice, when asked for it. Wendy Cooper. Always got a smile on her face, easy-going type person. Karen Higgins. Not only a genuine lady but good looking as well. She can have her blond moments.

These ladies, I lovingly refer as The Witches of Eastwick. I'm sure they'll give me a thick ear for saying so, but I love them all. In fact, all of those mentioned, and many more besides, I would gladly help in any way that I can, monetary, a place to stay, or some food, they only have to ask, if ever they found themselves in trouble. I would even go as far to say, even help my middle sister, if she fell on hard times, and show more compassion, than she ever showed me!

For those who are curious, Jackie and I are still firm friends and keep in regular contact. Now lives in Bedford, a stone's throw from the Multiple Sclerosis Society, where she still keeps regular hours, as a volunteer! Her own MS has again taken its toll, and sadly Jackie lost the sight in one eye. I will never allow her to suffer, and many times paid off debts and ensuring she has regular grocery deliveries. It's the least I can do, she will always have a special place in my heart and will be there for her, as long as I live.

What about Cheryl? I vowed never to contact her again after she'd unceremoniously booted me out, and for her vile outburst on social media.

However, a month after starting my first job, I received an unexpected Skype call from her. Firstly, to inquire If I'd like to take Meli, who was missing me. Secondly, she was in desperate need financially, pleading with me to help. Being the person, I am, agreed to both requests.

Devastatingly, two days before I was due to pick up Meli from France, she contacted me in floods of tears, stating Meli, had been killed by a farmer who mistakenly took her as a fox!

It appeared Meli tried to find me, digging under the garden fence, to try and find me after hearing my voice on skype! I was distraught, as I'd let her down, and should have been there. Regardless, I continued to help financially for six months, until she threw it all back in my face again. Since then, I've cut all ties.

Socks was adopted by a loving Dutch family, who live, just outside of Rotterdam. Over the years, they've provided me with photos, updates. Seeing her happy brings tears of joy, I'm glad I made the heartbreaking decision to give her up for adoption, to give her the best life possible, and glad I'd had her in my life, for a brief, but happy period.

Who could forget my lovely little boy Rascal? The original fostering family, who first had him and Socks, when they first arrived in Holland, kept him for themselves, as like me, they fell in love with his cheeky persona! Sadly, they informed me, in March 2019, he suffered a severe stroke and never recovered. Upon hearing this news, I cried like a baby in my bathroom. Since his death, the family planted a memorial garden, sending me photos of him, and the beautiful tribute of his final resting place.

As for my comrades in arms? I keep in regular contact with them via social media. Over the years, I've had to say goodbye for the last parade, for some of them, who have passed away. On these sad occasions, those of us still around, reminisce the comradery we all have for one another, which is still as strong today, as its always been. I salute every one of them, whom I regard as my extended family.

I still keep in contact with Steve and meet up occasionally at his home in West Yorkshire. We'll never change, and still like a couple of big kids, when we're together. Though these days, our mind is willing, and the flesh is weak.

Finally, Isaac. We lost touch for many years, until after the trial against Alston. He'd been questioned by the Police when they were investigating the case. At the time, he made it clear, that I wasn't to blame for the unfortunate events, and inquired if he could have my details, as soon as the trial had been concluded. We regularly ring each other and have a good chat. Although we've led different lives, we are amazing friends. Being a small world, we both work in the same industry! As for the rest of my friends mentioned, we keep in touch via social media and are planning to meet up, in the not too distant future.

As for me? I still suffer from combat stress, although, never easy to talk about mental illness, I regularly have group therapy sessions, which help me, and my fellow veterans. Through them, my flashbacks, are easier to control, and less frequent, but is something, I'll have to live with, for the remainder of my life.

I want to point out, combat stress or PTSD is not depression. It's having to cope with, what I'd endured, when in combat, which affects veterans like myself, in various ways. For me, its vivid nightmares, and is something, civilians will never fully understand.

What of my family? I still keep in contact with Theresa, and my nephew Lee, as well as my niece Lisa. As regards Peter and Tina, I have nothing further to do with them, as they are, the most selfish people I'm ashamed to have as family members. Finally David. We lost contact with him, many years ago, as hard as we tried, we're unable to trace his whereabouts.

The older I get, the more nostalgic I become. Recently I've been reminiscing my past, which has been highlighted since I've been writing this book. Although we are a dysfunctional family now, it wasn't always like that. Remembering the times, we used to share as kids, unlike today, where it's all technology-based, we made our own entertainment. I don't want to make this a political point, for me technology has ruined family values, as well as producing the snowflake generation.

You see, my generation was the ultimate recyclers. We had no single-use plastic bottles or many plastic bags. If we went on a picnic, we'd bring home our rubbish. Any food waste, which wasn't often, would go on the compost heap. Even our clothes were recycled, repaired of hand me downs. If things were broken, they were repaired. I remember when our TV went wrong, it would be repaired in our house, or if too technical, would be returned to the shop for repairs, where they would lend, another revamped TV, while ours went in for repair.

I agree the planet is being destroyed, by corporate greed in most parts, but object to being blamed for the throwaway society, it **has** become today. After all, we never had mummy or daddy drive us to school, we walked! Anyway, enough of that, this is a celebration of ordinary life.

Coming far since that timid kid, who fought to get noticed, in a big family. I've had some amazing times, and many more adventures than most, and for that I'm grateful. I don't look at life as a hardship, it's not what happens to you in life, it's how you deal with it.

Now most of us have asked what is the meaning to life? I can't answer that question for you, but in my instance, I believe that helping others is on the agenda. Some might think, making money is the most important thing, not in my case. Others have differing views, but for me, going through some of the things

I've had to endure, has made me stronger, it opened my eyes to what is important.

Many time, I've had people bitch and moan about life, and don't see what they have. Some blame their parents, for the way their lives have turned out, and how life is shit, because of their upbringing! Well I say to them, the greatest gift, you've been given, is life itself, it's up to you, to change it.

I've been asked many times, why I've written my own story, my answer is 'why not?' Or is it solely, a privileged for the rich and famous? As I believe all of us, have just as interesting lives, but may not, have the voice or the inclination, of which to tell anyone, let alone write about it. Yet one of the best books I've read, when I first came to Scotland, and that book being? 'The Nipper', written by a Dundonian named Charlie Mitchell.

For those who haven't read it, I implore you to do so. I've also been asked; would I live my life again? In a word, absolutely! Of course, I'd change some things, but without a doubt, I would do it all again in an instant, especially the military.

For the most part, my life has been a great laugh. I've been to some amazing places and met some amazing people. My last adventure, I was fortunate to visit Dubai, in August 2019, in a beautiful all-inclusive five-star hotel, I even managed to be offered a business class seat, of which I didn't hesitate to snap up. While I was there, I met some brilliant German's, who forged a friendship, and still keep in touch today, and shall be visiting soon.

Ok so life isn't always plain sailing, but so what! There are many less fortunate souls in the world and thank my lucky stars,

I'm still living and breathing. Yes sometimes, I get fed up like everyone, but most of the time, I have a great laugh with my workmates, either at work or socialising with them. Of course, I'm not perfect, I consider myself, as a moaning old bastard, and go off on one of my many rants. This sometimes gets me into trouble, as some people may get offended, but I will not apologise for the way I am. I respect everyone's opinion as they are entitled to it, just as I expect them to respect mine.

I'm a passionate person, especially when It comes to miscarriages of justice. I'm not referring to miscarriages, for those wrongly accused, of committing a crime, there aren't guilty for, although that itself is wrong, and don't condone it at all. I'm talking about those injustices, that governments impose on the people, of whom, it's supposed to be working for!

These so-called politicians only see what they can scam off the people, and don't give a damn of the consequences, or how it affects those by their actions.

All through writing this, I've never really, thanked mum and dad, for what they did for me. If it wasn't for their guidance, I wouldn't be the man I am today. There is never a day goes by, I don't think of them, and how much, they sacrificed themselves for us and would give up everything I own, just to have one last day with them. So, thank you, mum and dad, I love you both. You are and have always been my inspiration in life. It's the same for those friends, of which I served with. I may be living as a civilian, I don't see myself as one, not in the strictest sense of the word.

I often wonder about the future, and what it will bring. Not one for normally making plans, more like a spur of the moment person myself, I like to think, there are many more adventures to come. Saying that I do have a kind of 'bucket list,' of which, I've been fortunate to have achieved. The world is a big place, and it's my intention, to visit as many countries, the more remote the better, and meet many diverse cultures. I'm also geared up, to continue to help those less fortunate than myself.

I've always maintained, should I be fortunate enough, to either win the lottery or another means, I would ensure I have a house with a garden. That's all I would like, and the rest, would be shared amongst those, I hold most dear. After all, what's the point in having money or wealth, when you can't share it? Besides, who wants to be the richest person in the cemetery? If I've got it, I'm going to share it, as my mindset is such, I get a buzz, from seeing those less fortunate, being able to have a life.

Throughout my life, I've helped people, and I've no intentions, to give up now. Bearing in mind, although it didn't seem like it on occasions, I've been helped, when help was most needed. Like the Rolling Stones classic 'You can't always get what you want, but you find sometimes, you get what you need!'

Since being in Scotland, I've received more help, than I ever did when I was in England. I have joked many times, I've come up here, to educate the Scots. But the truth is, Scotland and its amazing people, have educated me. I've got some amazing mates and would do anything for, and likewise, they would do, the same for me. The way I see it, enjoy yourself, laugh, with no regrets. I know we're all different, that's what makes us all unique, let's face it, if we were all the same, it would be boring. But my advice? Try and be the best person you can be. In my case, the best person I can be? Is simply.......Me!

MUM

You were there for all my life
Through all the good times
And through all the strife

You picked me up when I was sad
And took my side, when I was bad
Your youngest son, your little lad!

You were there when I was in need
and gave advice of which to heed!
Now you're not here, and you have gone
You are the best my number one

So, hear these words
I love you Mum
Goodbye, God bless, Your loving son!

DAD

WE OFTEN THINK OF YOU OUR DAD
WE'VE CRIED A LOT WHEN WE ARE SAD
WHY DID YOU GO I OFTEN PRAY!
IT WAS HIS TIME I HEAR THEM SAY!

WHEN WE WERE YOUNG
WE HAD SUCH FUN
PLAYING WITH YOU
IN THE NOONDAY SUN!

WITH NEXT DOORS KIDS AND WHATISNAMES
WE PLAYED OUR GAMES AGAIN AND AGAIN!

SO NEXT TIME WHEN WE FEEL SO SAD
WE'LL THINK OF ALL THE FUN WE HAD
WITH YOU OUR VERY KIND OLD DAD!

My Family Album

Circa 1969

Left to right front row: Peter, Tina Me at 3 years old, David, Theresa. Back row: Mum and Dad

Top left: My brother David, and I posing with monkeys, Kingston Upon Hull, 1970 Top right: My brother David with his hand up second from left Christmas 1971. Bottom left: centre Me pestering mum, Kingston Upon Hull 1970. Bottom right back row: Eldest brother Peter (left) middle brother David (Right) Bottom row left to right: Me, eldest sister Theresa, middle sister Tina 1972.

Gibraltar Barracks Circa 1982: I'm in the third row from the front 4th from the right.

Mum and I posing in ceremonial uniform complete with officers' sword. Below: Displaying my

poetry award at Crete!

Socks and Rascal

Meli and I in Elounda Crete.

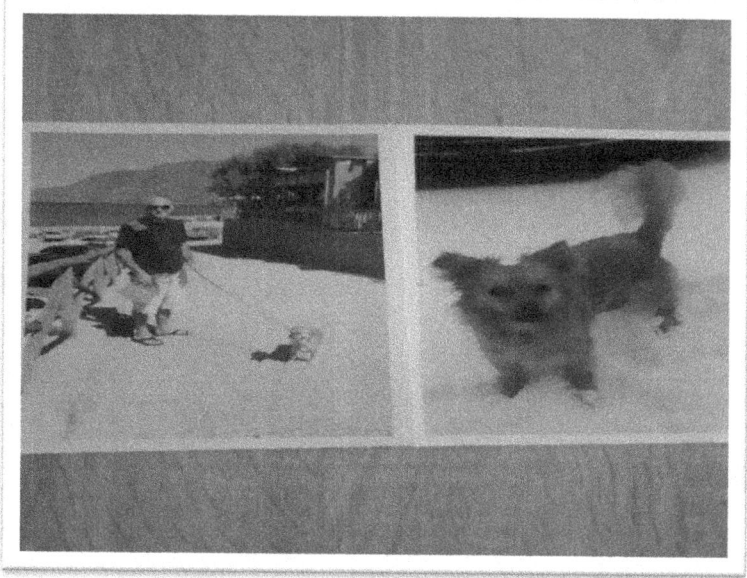

Meli enjoying the snow, St Junien Les Combes, France.

Another view from the balcony Istron Bay.

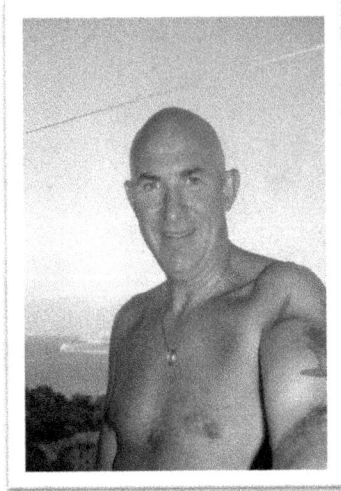

On the balcony of my home in Vathi Bay Crete.

I'm in Scuba gear, displaying QPR team flag, Crete 2009

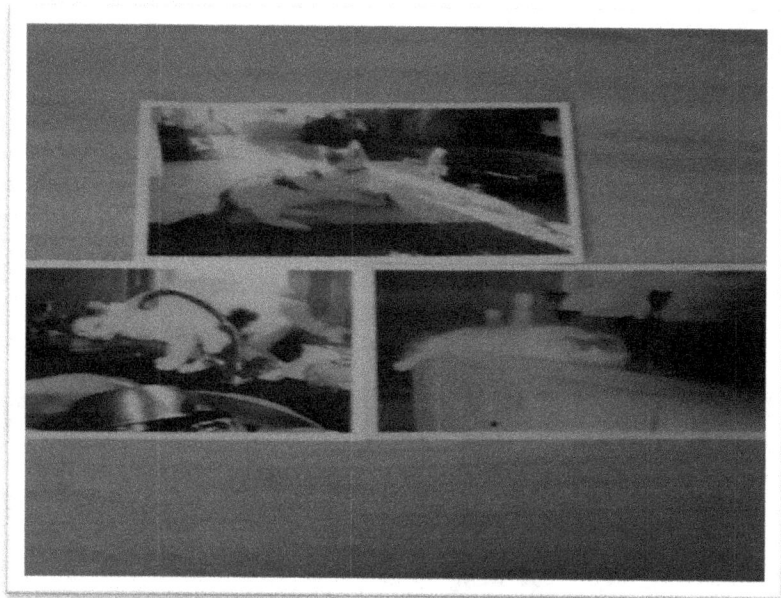

My beautiful girls: (top) Mia, Sofia, bottom left, Lily, bottom right.

Finally, Mum's sad farewell!

www.ingramcontent.com/pod-product-compliance
Lightning Source LLC
Chambersburg PA
CBHW071727270326
41928CB00013B/2583